VM Applications Handbook

Dr. Gary R. McClain, Editor

Intertext Publications
McGraw-Hill Book Company

New York St. Louis San Francisco Auckland Bogotá
Hamburg London Madrid Mexico Milan Montreal
New Delhi Panama Paris São Paulo
Singapore Sidney Tokyo Toronto

Library of Congress Catalog Card Number 88-83964

ISBN 0-07-044948-1

10 9 8 7 6 5 4 3 2

Intertext Publications/Multiscience Press, Inc.
One Lincoln Plaza
New York, NY 10023

McGraw-Hill Book Company
1221 Avenue of the Americas
New York, NY 10020

Composition by Context, Inc.

Contents

Preface

IBM's VM operating system is a multi-faceted and flexible operating system. It has the ability to support multiple online users, run other operating systems as guests, serve as an ideal environment for development—the potential applications are almost infinite. The topics included in *VM Applications Handbook* were chosen to increase the reader's understanding of VM's uniqueness and potential, as well as to provide practical guidelines that can be applied in his or her own organization. Contributors are leading practitioners in the VM community, with specific expertise in the topics about which they are writing.

The technical audience for *VM Applications Handbook* is really threefold: those who are relatively inexperienced in any operating system, those who have worked with other operating systems but are new to VM, and those who are experienced in VM but need more information about a specific topic. Managers and users with technical orientation will also find the information useful in furthering their understanding about VM.

To facilitate the use of the book, by the reader, the chapters are arranged in four sections. The first section, "A Closer Look at VM," includes a more in-depth look at the VM operating system itself and serves as a foundation for the rest of the book. The second section, "Optimal VM Performance," focuses on topics of concern to those involved in keeping the VM operating system "up and running" at its peak. The third section, "VM in the User Environment," explores issues that arise with multiple users taking advantage of VM's interactivity and ease-of-use to perform daily computing functions. The last section, "VM and Development Considerations," looks at the role of VM from the development perspective. Each chapter in the book includes not only a discussion of the issue but practical solutions.

IBM has made it very clear that VM will play a strategic role in the future of corporate computing. The recent addition of complete Extended Architecture capabilities is further evidence of IBM's VM commitment. VM will not only serve as the cornerstone of the total computing environment in many organizations, but it can also coexist with other operating system and hardware platforms, to add its unique capabilities as a complement to other more batch-oriented operating systems.

Acknowledgments

I owe much to the individuals who wrote the chapters in *VM Applications Handbook*, contributing generously of both their time and expertise. It is my intention, as well as theirs, that this book will in turn be a useful tool for those working in the VM environment. Each of the contributors is an active and recognized member of the VM community, and their enthusiasm is reflected throughout the book.

I owe a special word of appreciation to Gabe Goldberg of VM Systems Group for his assistance in identifying potential contributors as well as his efforts in spreading the word that the book was in progress.

Many of the contributors provided terms and definitions for the Glossary. However, a substantial portion of it was contributed by Ron Kral, Chief Technical Officer at Systems Center, Inc., from whom I have learned much about the structure and uses of VM. Tom Foth of Relay Computing also added much to the Glossary.

I am also grateful for the guidance and support that I have received from Alan Rose at Multiscience Press and Bruce Sherwin, who coordinated the voluminous task of turning stacks of paper and diskettes into a real book.

A Closer Look at VM

VM is a complex, multi-faceted operating system, and IBM is rapidly enhancing it to meet the demands of dynamic organizations. In Part A, key capabilities of VM are highlighted, and current developments examined.

Extended Architecture (XA) support is an exciting new function that IBM recently provided for VM/CMS users. Tom Foth, in "VM/XA SP and Bimodal CMS" (Chapter 1), has provided an in-depth look at what XA support means for CMS users, from a technical standpoint, with extensive guidelines for taking advantage of XA capabilities.

Communications between users, on multiple machines at remote sites, has become a critical consideration as more and more organizations have moved toward a distributed approach to information management. Ed Sterling's "VM Data Communications" (Chapter 2) begins with a historical look at communications in the VM environment; using early developments in VM as a basis for discussing strategic directions and suggestions for implementation.

"Service Virtual Machines" (Chapter 3), by Gabe Goldberg, provides diverse functions that greatly enhance the flexibility of the VM operating system and further distinguishes VM from other mainframe operating systems. Goldberg describes the design of service virtual machines, examples of how they may be used, and guidelines for both implementation and maintenance.

Part

A

A Closer Look at VM

1

VM/XA SP and Bimodal CMS

by Thomas J. Foth

Introduction

Both hardware and software have changed dramatically since VM's inception. Hardware continues on its cost/performance curve: It becomes faster and cheaper. As hardware becomes faster and cheaper, programmers leverage it to build more complicated applications.

More than anything, applications programmers have always clamored for more memory. Providing applications programmers the memory they need allows them to concentrate on the application, rather than having to code around the limitations of the hardware and generally "making do." Some applications, such as relational databases, scientific and engineering "number crunching," and artificial intelligence require access to vast amounts of high-speed memory. Forcing these applications to use even the fastest disk drives in place of main memory would seriously impair their performance and make most of them unusable.

Fortunately, slow core memory used in computer systems supporting VM in the 1970s has been replaced with fast and inexpensive semiconductor memory. But large amounts of memory are only as good as the processor and operating systems' ability to support it. IBM's 370-Extended Architecture (370-XA or just XA) family of processors, first announced in 1981, and the VM/XA-SP operating system family, first made available in early 1988, reconciles the availability of memory with the ability of the processor and the operating system to provide it to VM applications.

What Is XA?

370-XA is a somewhat compatible extension to the tried and true 370 architecture. It was designed to deal with addressability constraints faced by users of IBM's MVS operating system. The chief components of XA are:

- 31 bit addressing providing direct addressability to 2 gigabytes of real and virtual main memory. The 370 architecture provided for 24 bits (16 megabytes) of addressability.
- Improved I/O operations that offload more processing to the I/O subsystem (and requires the use of new I/O instructions).
- High-level microcode instructions such as Start Interpretive Execution (SIE) which provides for much of the virtualization of the architecture (including I/O remapping) at the hardware level.
- Miscellaneous nonprivileged instructions made necessary by changes in the processor status word (PSW) to accommodate 31 bits of addressability.

The 370-XA architecture was principally developed for two reasons: to relieve 370 users of addressing storage constraints and to provide for a more responsive I/O subsystem. Other features, such as SIE, provide for better utilization of processor resources by relegating the virtualization of the architecture to microcode where it can be done more efficiently than at the operating system level.

In early 1988 IBM announced a follow-on architecture to 370-XA: the Enterprise Systems Architecture (ESA). ESA's purpose is to remove virtual storage constraints now being faced by IBM's MVS/XA large system customers. It does this by giving applications access to multiple sets of address spaces. Since this is in some ways akin to the way VM manages a system, its applicability to the VM environment is not clear. It is important to note that the new ESA architecture includes 370-XA capabilities. Thus, any processor that is labelled as "ESA capable" is also 370-XA capable.

370-XA mode is only available on certain models of the 4381, all 308x, all 3090, and all 90xx. Reportedly, the 9370 family hardware is capable of addressing 31 bits of memory and may be fully XA capable. IBM has announced its plans to make the 9370 ESA capable:

This would bring 370-XA to the 9370. In addition, an IBM research project that resulted in a prototype 370 on a single integrated circuit was capable of 32 bit addressability and provided many features and instructions present in 370-XA (see *Microprocessor Logic Design*; Tredennick, Nick; Digital Press: 1987). Thus, while IBM has only provided large system implementations of 370-XA to date, clearly small system implementations are possible.

A Bit of VM's Past

VM consists of two parts: the Control Program (CP) and the Conversational Monitor System (CMS). CP is responsible for creating the virtual machine illusion (that is the illusion that each user has a complete 370 processing environment) and managing the real hardware that VM is running on. On top of this environment operating systems such as MVS and VSE run. Any operating system running under CP is considered a *guest*.

CMS is also a guest operating system. Unlike MVS or VSE, CMS is a single user system that relies on CP for support and cannot run standalone on real hardware. CMS's sole function is to provide interactive services exclusively for VM.

VM was first made available in the early 1970s going through six releases as VM/370. Program products Basic System Extension Program Product (BSEPP) and System Extension Program Product (SEPP) removed critical limitations in VM/370. BSEPP, SEPP, and VM/370 Release 6 were the basis for VM/SP Release 1 announced in 1981 (at the same time 370-XA was announced). This was followed by the High Performance Option (HPO), an enhancement to VM/SP that allowed the CP to make better use of the new hardware made available on IBM's XA class processors. In particular, when combined with MVS/SP, HPO allowed one MVS guest operating system to run at nearly the same speed it would run if it were running directly on the system without virtualization by VM.

Along with the announcement of 370-XA and VM/SP, IBM announced MVS/XA and the VM Migration Aid (VM MA). MVS/XA was a version of the MVS operating system that was capable of allowing applications to take advantage of 370-XA hardware.

VM MA was a version of VM that supported virtual machines that emulated the 370-XA processors. Using the SIE facility of 370-XA, it could provide a very efficient virtual machine environment. Using VM MA, MVS customers could run their production MVS operating system in one virtual machine and run a test MVS/XA operating system in another virtual machine, concurrently. This alleviated the need for customers to have to alternate between running MVS and MVS/XA on one processor or buying a second processor for testing.

Unfortunately the CP portion of VM MA was based on VM/370 Release 3. VM MA's CMS was based on VM/SP. This CMS was not XA capable (i.e., it could not address more than 16 megabytes of memory, nor could it use the XA I/O instructions). VM MA forced CMS users to each run a private copy of CMS in their virtual machines because saved system support (the ability of VM to share code and data in memory among users) was not available. This resulted in poor system utilization for large numbers of CMS users. In addition, due to missing functions and incompatibilities in VM MA's CP (see below), many applications (including some that came with a stock CMS) would not run.

Because VM MA was based on an antiquated release of VM and because of the minimal CMS support, IBM made it clear that VM MA was for migration purposes only. It was not to be considered as a long-term production environment, especially when large number of CMS users were involved.

Users had become accustomed to running multiple operating systems on a single CPU in the course of normal production. They found the migration restrictions that IBM placed on VM MA unacceptable. IBM acquiesced and renamed VM MA VM/SystemsFacility (VM/SF). In renaming VM MA to VM/SF, IBM approved of the idea of using VM/SF to support multiple operating systems on one CPU in a production setting.

But other than a change of name, some cosmetic changes, and promises of better support, IBM did little to VM MA when they rechristened it VM/SF. It was still VM/370 Release 3 heavily modified to run XA virtual machines. And, since many of the problems with CMS had not been solved, IBM continued to state that the CMS provided with VM/SF was for systems programming maintenance activities only. Users who wanted to run CMS under VM/SF were advised to run VM/SP or HPO as guests of VM/SF and then run CMS users under one of these guests.

The VM Environment Matures

As VM has become IBM's delivery vehicle for interactive systems, the need for CMS to support increased addressability and more efficient I/O has become more apparent. IBM has pushed VM in scientific compute intensive applications especially in conjunction with their vector processing hardware. These users classically have large amounts of data that must be addressable. IBM offered an interim solution to VM/SF users, called the extended data array facility. It allowed scientific users of FORTRAN and C applications to address memory beyond 16 megabytes. Unfortunately, this was not a general purpose solution.

IBM has also tagged VM to provide the base for high end multi-user interactive systems. It is not unusual for these VM users to run IBM's GDDM graphics package while running SQL/DS relational database system all under PROFS office system. With all of this software resident and the associated data requirements of each, it is easy to see how a user could run out of addressability.

For these users, and the future of VM in general, it was necessary for IBM to provide a CMS environment that could carry users into the 1990s. IBM's answer was VM/XA SP, announced in 1987.

Enter VM/XA SP

Rather than a revolutionary new VM system, VM/XA SP is an evolutionary growth of VM MA and VM/SF. With that heritage, it starts with all of the liabilities of being based on VM/370 Release 3. However, with VM/XA SP IBM has committed to three goals: providing efficient first level CMS support for a large number of users (that is, providing full CMS support without the need for a guest VM), providing a CP and CMS that has all of the functionality of and compatibility with current versions of VM/SP and HPO, and providing a CMS that would allow users to develop applications that could make use of the 370-XA architectural improvements.

Much has been added to VM/SP since VM/370Release3. To see what IBM is up against in making good on these promises, consider some of the features in VM/SP not present in VM/SF:

Inter-User Communications Facility (IUCV) — IUCV allows user programs on a local VM system to communicate among themselves and is the basis for many database systems on VM/SP.

Logical Device Support — Logical device support allows programs to programmatically emulate CRTs. Logical device support makes programs such as IBM's Passthru (which allows 3270 users on one VM system to communicate with other VM systems) and protocol conversion programs possible.

Console Communications Service (CCS) — CCS is an alternative to logical device support and is the basis for VM SNA support.

Transparent Service Access Facility and Application Program-to-Program Communications/VM (TSAF and APPC/VM) — Added to VM/SP Release 5, these facilities allow VM systems to network together and provide program-to-program communications to any application in the network.

National Language Support — National language support provides a single repository for nearly all CP messages and another for CMS messages. By using the SET LANGUAGE command to choose a specific message repository, users can receive messages in their native language.

DASD Block I/O — This is a high-performance service for reading and writing data to DASD. It is used by database packages such as SQL/DS.

CMS File Sharing — Recently announced for VM/SP Release 6, this allows CMS users to share files. It requires APPC/VM.

In addition to lacking these features, some VM/SF services with functionality similar to VM/SP had been enhanced in incompatible ways. This includes some command formats as well as the text of messages.

Note that with all of the incompatibility, only the end usability of users running directly under VM/SF is affected. The ability to provide virtualization of the 370 and XA environment is not impacted. After all, there was a strict standard for that: the Principles of Operation manuals for each of the architectures. Any virtualization of an architecture had to provide compatibility to the specifications found in those documents.

What EXACTLY Is VM/XA SP?

VM/XA SP is:

- A VM system capable of providing large numbers of users access to virtual machines that emulate 370 or 370-XA environments,
- A VM that provides many of the facilities of VM/SP and HPO up through VM/SP and HPO Release 5,
- A VM with a new bimodal CMS that is capable of supporting both old 370 based CMS applications as well as new 370-XA applications.

In addition to these chief enhancements that specifically address the end user, the following features are present in support of the system in general:

- A dynamic channel subsystem for I/O that supports up to 128 channels,
- Real storage addressability of 256 megabytes (as opposed to HPO's limit of 64 megabytes and VM/SP's limit of 16),
- Three-, four-, or six-way processor support (as opposed to VM/SP and HPO's limit of two),
- Vector processing available to all guest operating systems, not just CMS users,
- Support for up to four high-performance guests being assisted by the SIE instruction,
- Support for performance monitoring,
- Support for the RACF security facility.

What VM/XA SP Isn't

As you can see, there is a lot to be excited about with a VM/XA SP. However, there is still a lot missing from VM/XASPRelease1:

- Support for asynchronous ASCII terminals (these terminals can still be supported via hardware protocol converters or some software protocol conversion packages),
- Support for networking via TSAF and APPC/VM,
- Support for SNA (though a guest operating system can run VTAM to provide SNA support for that guest),
- Support for file sharing (because file sharing requires TSAF),
- Support for a full 2 gigabytes of virtual storage (VM/XASP supports virtual machines that can address up to 999 megabytes).

Basically, the CP portion of VM/XA SP adds an almost complete implementation of the functionality of VM/SP and HPO Release 4 to the VM/SF base. New additions to the CP portion of VM/SP and HPO made available in Release 5 (such as TSAF and APPC/VM) are not present in VM/XA SP.

Since the announcement of VM/XA SP, IBM has announced another release of VM/SP: Release 6. This new release of VM/SP borrows the bimodal CMS from VM/XA SP and adds file sharing to it.

It is important to note that while VM/SP Release 6 borrows much of its CMS from VM/XA SP, applications running under VM/SP Release 6 are still only capable of addressing 16 megabytes. This is due to the fact that the CP portion of VM/SP Release 6 does not provide 370-XA virtualization. Still, applications developed under VM/SP Release 6 can take advantage of the applications programming interface (API) from the new bimodal CMS and should easily port to VM/XA SP.

At the time IBM announced VM/XA SP Release 1, it also announced VM/XA SP Release 2. The chief enhancement to VM/XA SP Release 2 will be direct support for VTAM by VM/XA SP (that is, without the need for a host). SNA support will also add support for asynchronous terminals by way of SNA's Network Terminal Option (NTO) when used in conjunction with VTAM. Support for TSAF, APPC/VM, file sharing, larger virtual address spaces, or ESA is not scheduled, though IBM claims they are under consideration.

Bimodal CMS

The leading feature of VM/XA SP is clearly the new bimodal CMS. Bimodal CMS is not simply the old CMS made XA capable; it is a dramatically modified and restructured CMS which maintains much compatibility with previous CMS offerings.

IBM is referring to this CMS as VM/XA CMS 5.5. That is a clear indication of its heritage—it is built on VM/SP Release 5 CMS features. The CMS announced for VM/SP Release 6 is also a bimodal CMS. It builds upon the CMS developed for VM/XA SP (chiefly in the area of file sharing) and is backward compatible to that CMS. Not only can it be used to develop and run applications that run in 370 mode, but it can also be used to develop *but not run* applications that are intended for VM/XA SP.

The major features of VM/XACMS5.5 are:

- A new architecturally independent CMS applications programming interface (API) called the *Preferred Interface* which is consistent with Systems Application Architecture (SAA),
- Addressability for a user space of up to 999 megabytes,
- Restructuring of the memory management system,
- Support for the development and testing of MVS/XA applications,
- Compatibility with VM/SP and HPO Release 5 CMS,
- New program linkage mechanism,
- Support for key IBM program products (such as PROFS and SQL/DS).

The Three Faces of VM/XA CMS Applications

Unlike previous 370 based releases of CMS, VM/XA CMS provides two modes for program execution: 370 and 370-XA (hence the name: bimodal CMS). Because of fundamental differences in I/O and addressing, applications may need to be sensitive to the environment and enhanced to execute in the better performing and less constrained 370-XA environment.

Bimodal CMS applications can be grouped into one of three classes:

370 Mode   This mode is available to applications that run in a virtual machine simulating the 370 architecture. The new features of bimodal CMS pertaining to interfacing, storage, and program management are all available, but the application is limited to 16 megabytes of virtual storage addressability and does not receive the I/O performance improvements possible with 370-XA. Most existing CMS applications will run in this mode. Some applications will need changes to cope with differences between VM/XA SP and VM/SP CP interfaces. Other applications, especially those that are "aware" of CMS's storage management system and interact with it or those that make use of "internal" or previously undocumented interfaces, may also need changes.

Note that the execution of 370 mode applications excludes the execution of XA mode applications in the same virtual machine. To run XA mode applications the virtual machine must be run in XA mode. Switching the mode of a virtual machine requires an IPL of the virtual machine which restarts CMS. Restarting CMS is disruptive to the work flow of a CMS user. As more XA applications for CMS 5.5 appear, the remaining 370 mode applications will be a nuisance to run.

XA Toleration Mode   This is the first of the two XA modes which require the virtual machine to run in XA mode. This mode precludes the use of 370 mode applications.

XA toleration mode allows applications to achieve XA compatibility with the minimal migration effort. In addition to the minor changes outlined above for 370 mode applications, the application must convert 370 specific instructions (specifically those dealing with the PSW or I/O) to XA compatible instructions. Fortunately, few CMS applications directly interface with the PSW or I/O instructions and the new preferred interface might ease the migration for those applications that require a level of intimacy with the virtual processor. This interface provides for some of the missing functionality in previous versions of CMS that forced programmers to directly manipulate the virtual machine environment.

Applications in toleration mode benefit from I/O improvements made possible when the virtual machine is running in XA mode. XA

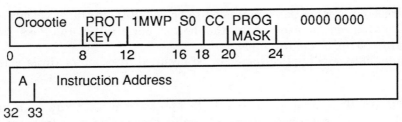

370-XA Processor Status Word (PSW)

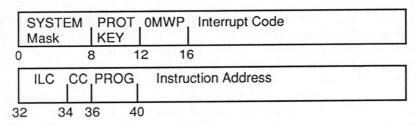

370 Basic Control (BC) Mode PSW

Figure 1-1 PSW differences.

toleration mode applications can coexist with XA exploitation mode applications.

CMS services (such as EXEC, EXEC2, REXX, and XEDIT) all run only in toleration mode. This means that XEDIT has a file size limit of 16 megabytes.

XA Exploitation Mode An XA exploitation mode application enjoys the benefits of increased memory addressability along with the performance benefits realized by XA toleration mode applications.

Two issues keep CMS applications that run in XA toleration mode from immediately becoming XA exploitation mode applications: memory referencing and parameter passing.

Many CMS applications are hardwired to the way 370 instructions function. Probably the best example of this is the Branch and Link and Branch and Link Register (BAL and BALR) instructions. When these instructions are executed in 370 virtual machines, certain as-

I/O Instruction Differences

System/370

Clear Channel (CLRCH)
Clear I/O (CLRIO)
Halt Device (HDV)
Halt I/O (HIO)
Resume I/O (RIO)
Start I/O (SIO)
Start I/O Fast Release (SIOF)
Store Channel ID (STIDC)
Test Channel (TCH)
Test I/O (TIO)

These 370 I/O instructions have no 370-XA equivalent:

Connect Channel Set (CONCS)
Disconnect Channel Set (DISCS)
Read Direct (RDD)
Write Direct (WD)

370-XA

Clear Subchannel (CSCH)
Halt Subchannel (HSCH)
Modify Subchannel (MSCH)
Reset Channel Path (RCHP)
Resume Subchannel (RSCH)
Set Address Limit (SAL)
Set Channel Monitor (SCHM)
Start Subchannel (SSCH)
Store Channel Path Status (STCPS)
Store Channel Report Word (STCRW)
Store Subchannel (STSCH)
Test Pending Interruption (TPI)
Test Subchannel (TSCH)

Figure 1-2 Differences in I/O opcodes.

pects of the processor state are recorded in the high order byte of the return register (effectively limiting the return address to 24 bits). Called routines often use this byte to restore the processor state when returning to the caller. Current CMS applications are littered with BAL and BALR instructions, many of which are used to capture the processor state and restore it as described.

The Load Address (LA) instruction is used to add together the addresses stored in (optionally) two registers with a 12 bit (optional) displacement in the instruction. In 370, the resulting sum is truncated to 24 bits and placed in a target register. The use of the LA instruction to clear the high order byte of a register is such a popular practice it has a name: It is known as *purifying* an address. Unfortunately, this purification also truncates the address to 24 bits.

Other changes to the instruction set provide some problems to utilizing 31 bit addresses. 370 instructions ignored the high order byte of addresses generated. Programmers used this to their advantage to save storage. Addresses were often stored in the lower three bytes of

Non-I/O Instruction Differences

Non-privileged Instructions :

The following instructions that in 370 mode modify the high order byte of their target register have been changed to support 31 bit addresses in 370-XA mode, thus utilizing the high order byte:

Branch and Save (BAS)
Branch and Save Register (BASR)
Load Address (LA)
Branch and Link (BAL)
Branch and Link Register (BALR)
Load Real Address (LA)

The following instructions have been modified to honor 31 bit addresses and return 31 bit addresses in 370-XA mode:

Compare Logical Long (CLCL)
Move Character Long (MVCL)
Translate and Test (TRT)
Edit and Mark (EDMK)

The following instuctions are new to 370-XA mode (and do not operate in 370 mode):

Branch and Set Mode (BSM)
Branch and Save and Set Mode (BASSM)
Insert Program Mask (IPM)

Privileged Instructions :

The following privileged instructions do not work in 370-XA mode and have no counterparts:

Insert Storage Key (ISK)
Reset Reference Bit (RRB)
Set Storage Key (SSK)

The following privileged instruction has been added to 370-XA and is not available in 370 mode:

Trace (TRACE)

Figure 1-3 370 only instructions.

a word and the high byte was used to store flag bits. Programmers would often code programs to simply load a register with all four bytes of the word (including the extraneous flag) assuming that the processor would ignore the high order byte when the contents of the register were used to address memory. This practice also effectively limits the usefulness of these addresses to 24 bits.

To counter problems such as these with programs that relied on these architectural aspects of the 370 family, the concept of *addressing mode* was introduced in 370-XA. The addressing mode of an application can change at any time by simply updating a flag in the PSW. This flag is called the *A-flag*. If it is off, only the three low order bytes of instructions will be treated as addresses, just as in normal 370. Further, BAL and BALR will continue to save the processor status in the high order byte of the return register.

If the A-flag is on, then the processor considers the lower 31 bits as a data address. BAL and BALR stop storing the processor status in the high order byte of the return address (applications in this mode can make use of the new Insert Processor Mask [IPM] instruction). One aspect of exploitation mode applications is to be able to run with the A-flag on (which then gives the application access to 31 bit addressability at the cost of having to make certain the application doesn't make use of instructions in such a way as to assume 24 bit addressing).

To understand the problem of parameter passing, it is necessary to review how CMS passes arguments to CMS applications. Since CMS's earliest days, applications have passed parameters to CMS and other applications by way of a parameter list, or *plist*. General purpose register 1 points to a list of doublewords (eight byte entries) called *tokens*. A plist is terminated by a doubleword that has all the bits set to one (for a hexadecimal value of FFFFFFFF). This terminating doubleword is called the *fence*.

Tokens are generated by the CMS command parser which scans command lines for spaces or parentheses. Every unit of text delimited by spaces or parentheses is tokenized: It is truncated to eight bytes if necessary or padded on the right with spaces. The resulting eight byte field is placed sequentially into the plist.

To accommodate the passing of parameters that have units of text greater than eight bytes, VM/SP introduced the extended parameter list (*eplist*). The eplist is an auxiliary list of addresses pointing to the untokenized command line. The presence of an eplist is noted by a flag stored in the high order byte of register 1. This flag also indicated to CMS how the function was to be found (i.e., should only CMS resident functions be searched, should nucleus extensions be considered, should a list of subcommand processors be considered, etc.).

Therein lies the problem. There is simply no way for CMS or other applications to pass the address of a plist that exceeds 24 bits and indicate the presence of an eplist if the entire high order byte of register 1 is to be used for a flag.

Bimodal CMS introduces two concepts which set XA exploitation mode applications apart from XA toleration mode applications: AMODE and RMODE.

The AMODE of a program refers to its ability to manage 24 and 31 bit addresses. An AMODE of 24 indicates that the application only supports 24 bit addressing and can access only the first 16 megabytes of storage in the virtual machine. AMODE 24 applications run with the A-flag in the PSW off. CMS will pass parameters to this application, as in the past. Further, requests for memory allocation will be granted from virtual storage that has an address of less than 16 megabytes. CMS loads the executable code for AMODE24 applications in the first 16 megabytes of memory. An AMODE setting of 24 can best be thought of as the toleration AMODE: The addresses and functioning of instructions remain as they did in 370 mode.

An AMODE of 31 indicates that the application can accept 31 addresses. The application executes with the processor A-flag turned on, giving them access to 31 bit addressability. These applications detect the presence of parameter lists via a field in the user save area which is a data structure bimodal CMS passes to applications. In response to memory allocations requests, CMS will return addresses anywhere in the virtual machine's memory space.

An AMODE of ANY means that the application will respect the AMODE of the caller. If the caller is an AMODE 24 application, the called application with an AMODE of ANY will run as an AMODE 24 application. The same applies to being called by an AMODE 31 application and executing as an AMODE 31 application.

The RMODE value refers to where CMS will load the executable code for an application. An RMODE of 24 indicates that this application must be loaded and executed in the first 16 megabytes of memory. An RMODE of ANY indicates the program can be loaded and executed at any valid address in the virtual machine.

The AMODE and the RMODE of an application can be set several ways. Assembler H (an extended version of the system assembler) provides new pseudo opcodes to set the AMODE. The CMS LOAD command supports AMODE and RMODE as new options that override any setting by assembler pseudo opcodes. Finally, the CMS

GENMOD command also provides AMODE and RMODE options to override previous settings.

Options of the NUCEXT and SUBCOM macros (which describe nucleus extensions and subcommands, respectively, to CMS) allow the programmer to define the AMODE. Since the code must already be resident to be defined to CMS by NUCEXT or SUBCOM, setting of the RMODE would be meaningless and so it is not present.

In the case of OS formatted modules in load libraries, the OS linkage editor LKED parallels the CMS LOAD command and provides for setting of the AMODE and RMODE.

In all cases, if no operation specifically sets the AMODE or RMODE, both default to 24 at the time of execution.

During program execution the AMODE can be changed dynamically by the AMODESW macro. Further, the AMODESW can be used to call subroutines in a different AMODE from the AMODE currently in effect.

Other CMS Improvements

Memory Management As already mentioned, in addition to supporting 370-XA operation, several other improvements were made to bimodal CMS. As one might imagine, when one adds the ability to address up to 999 megabytes of storage to a system that was designed to handle only 16 megabytes, changes to the memory management system follow.

Previous versions of CMS had two memory management schemes. OS applications (such as compilers, most programs generated by compilers, and some applications ported to CMS from MVS) as well as some CMS applications made use of blocks of storage that started from near the bottom of the virtual machine ascending to higher storage locations.

CMS specific applications and CMS itself used blocks of storage from the highest addresses in the virtual machine descending downward. When these two allocation schemes met somewhere in the middle of a virtual machine's storage, no more memory was available for CMS or CMS applications.

With this type of storage scheme, if "n" blocks of CMS storage were allocated and then all but the last (most recent) freed, OS storage would be constrained by the lowest address of CMS storage. Obviously the same works in reverse for OS storage allocation upwards constraining CMS's downward allocation.

AMODESW Macro

Call a subroutine :

> [label]   AMODESW CALL, [, AMODE={24 I 31 I (reg)}]
>   [, ADDRESS={addr I (reg)}]
>   [, REGS=([ret_reg], [link_reg])]

label	optional assembly language label
AMODE	specifies the AMODE of called routine. AMODE=(reg) uses the high order bit of the specified register to determine the AMODE (1 = AMODE 31, 0 = AMODE 24)
ADDRESS	specifies address of called routine. If not specified, the value in link_reg is assumed.
REGS	specifies registers to be used in call. ret_reg defaults to 14, link_reg defaults to 15

Return from a subroutine :

> [label]   AMODESW RETURN, [, AMODE={24 I 31 I (reg)}]
>   [, REG=([ret_reg])]

label	see above.
AMODE	AMODE to return to the caller in. See above.
REG	Register containing return address. This defaults to 14.

Determine the current AMODE :

> [label]   AMODESW QRY

label	optional assembly language label

This call returns the current AMODE in register 1. If on completion register 1 contains all zeros, the AMODE is 24; otherwise register 1 will have a value of x'80000000' indicating AMODE 31.

Figure 1-4 The AMODESW macro.

AMODESW Macro (continued)

Set the current AMODE :

[label]   AMODESW SET, AMODE={24 I 31 I (reg)}
                                   [,SAVE=(reg)]

    label   optional assembly language label

    AMODE   Specifies the AMODE to be set. See AMODE CALL, above.

    SAVE   Specifies a register to receive the current AMODE setting. The high order bit of this register will be set to one if AMODE is 31; otherwise it is set to zero.

Figure 1-4 (continued) The AMODESW macro.

Bimodal CMS has one storage system for which all calls for storage are made. Subpool management similar to that found in MVS allows for the logical separation of storage by usage.

Previous versions of CMS used the DMSFREE and DMSFRET macros to manage the allocation and deallocation of CMS storage. DMSFREE allowed the programmer to allocate storage from one of four pseudo subpools. These pseudo subpools were based on the use of the memory and which addresses were to be used. *User storage* had a storage protection key of x'0E' and was deallocated by CMS at the time of an abend. *Nucleus storage*, which had a storage protection key of x'00', and survived abends.

Each of these types of storage was further distinguished by its location in memory: *low storage*, which resided below address x'20000', and *high storage*, which resided above address x'20000'. DMSFRET returned either type of allocated storage to one of the four pools of unallocated storage (low user storage, low nucleus storage, high user storage, and high nucleus storage).

Bimodal CMS provides the CMSSTOR and SUBPOOL macros as an alternative to DMSFREE and DMSFRET. CMSSTOR manages the allocation and deallocation of storage, while the SUBPOOL macro (or equivalent implicit actions by the CMSSTOR macro) manages the scope and use of the storage being allocated or deallocated.

```
                 VMSIZE
  System
  Loader
  Tables

  DMSFREE
  High Storage
  (User and
  Nucleus)
                 FREELOWE
  Unallocated
  Storage

                 MAINHIGH
  OS GETMAIN
  Storage
                 MAINSTRT
  User
  Program
                 x'20000'
  Low
  Nucleus
                 x'10000'
  Transient
  Area
                 x'E000'
  Low
  User
                 ANUCEND
  NUCON
                 x'0'
```

NUCON Vaiables

VMSIZE:	Number of bytes in virtual machine.
FREELOWE:	Free storage low extent. First address of allocated high storage.
MAINHIGH:	Highest address of memory allocated in user area.
ANUCEND:	Last address of NUCON control block.
MAINSTRT:	Beginning of allocated OS GETMAIN storage.

Note: *To simplify this illustration, this memory map assumes the CMS saved segment starts at an address greater than VMSIZE (as is typically the case).*

Figure 1-5 VM/SP Release 5 CMS Memory Map.

Bimodal CMS has no equivalents to the older storage location areas of low and high. The equivalent to type classifications is done by subpools. The two default subpools maintained by CMS are USER and NUCLEUS which correspond to their same named TYPE option counterparts in DMSFREE allocation. The USER subpool has a storage protection key of X'0E' and the NUCLEUS subpool has a storage key of zero. While applications can make use of these subpools, most

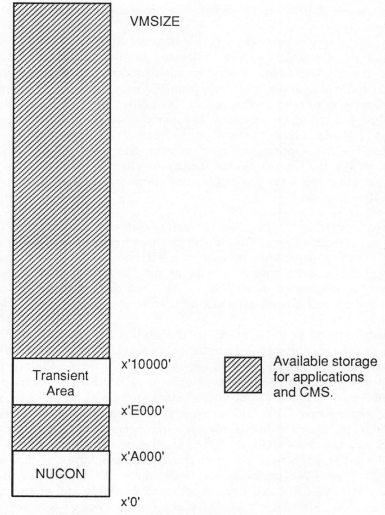

Figure 1-6 VM/SP Release 5.5 CMS Memory Map.

applications will create their only uniquely named subpools (subpools can have names up to eight bytes in length).

This new means for managing memory is a great step forward in the management of complex environments where applications call applications. In the past it has always been difficult for a calling application to deallocate memory for a called application if the called application failed to deallocate memory it allocated. Subpools now allow clearly defined boundaries for determining which application is using storage.

By defining *private* subpools, an invoked function or application indicates to CMS that memory allocated by it should be deallocated when the function or application terminates. *Shared* subpools allow a called routine to allocate storage from the same subpool as its caller for passing data back to the caller. Thus, when the caller deallocates a subpool of storage it allocated, the storage used by a called application to pass data back to the caller is freed at the same time. *Global* subpools allow applications that enhance the functionality of CMS through the nucleus extension facility to allocate memory that will remain allocated after the application stops running or an application abends.

Shared Segments CP provides a facility for sharing program code and data among users. This is called shared segments. Shared segments can appear anywhere in the virtual machine addressable image. Thus, even though a virtual machine may have only requested 2 megabytes of virtual storage from CP, it can still access data stored in a shared segment with addresses starting at 4 megabytes.

Past versions of CMS relied on the ability for applications to be able to reference shared segment storage outside the scope of defined virtual storage to keep shared segment storage from colliding with CMS storage. CMS required segments to be used by applications to be addressed outside of the virtual storage defined for the machine. This was because CMS had no method to block out the use of these sections of storage from its memory management scheme. Bimodal CMS now provides facilities to handle the problem of a shared segment that is addressed inside of the virtual machine's virtual storage. The new CMS preferred interface macro SEGMENT provides a means to have CP make a saved segment available and at the same time causes CMS to set aside the storage used by the saved segment so that it will not be used by other programs requesting storage.

Program Management Previous versions of CMS had little support for the dynamic relocation of programs at execution time. This meant that for applications to coexist, considerations had to be made for the execution addresses of each of the co-applications. Applications generated with the CMS GENMOD command had fixed execution addresses. Typically these applications ran in either the *transient area*, an 8 kilobyte area starting at address X'E000', or the *user area*, which started at address X'20000' and was as large as the lowest allocated memory in one of the two high memory subpools. Applications that made use of OS simulation also typically loaded code into memory starting at location X'20000'. This made it all but impossible for an OS simulation application to call CMS support commands such as COPYFILE which, until recent releases of CMS, ran in the user area. Bimodal CMS's providing for dynamic relocation of modules at execution time prevents this overloading of the user area. Provisions are made by bimodal CMS for applications that have mandatory memory load addresses due to their containing static memory references known as ACONS. The majority of existing applications fall into this category.

In addition to dynamic relocation of code at execution time, a new program invocation macro, CMSCALL, is present in the preferred interface. Because the previous method of passing parameters on the invocation of a program restricted the address of those parameters to something less than 16 megabytes, a new mechanism had to be created to pass parameters that resided at any address in the virtual machine. CMSCALL manages a control block known as USERSAVE to pass information to the called program. In addition, if an AMODE 31 application calls an AMODE 24 application, and the address of the parameters to be passed exceeds 16 megabytes, CMSCALL will optionally move a copy of the parameters to memory below 16 megabytes.

MVS/XA Application Development Support Past versions of CMS only supported limited emulation of the OS environment, specifically enough to allow the compilers to execute. This environment was frozen at MVT 21.8, an operating system that predates the availability of MVS, much less MVS/SP and MVS/XA.

Bimodal CMS provides most of the necessary MVS/XA functionality; lacking is emulation of multi-tasking and 31 bit VSAM support.

Formalization of the CMS API CMS has always been environment where CMS application developers work closely with the CMS source code. Applications developers study the source code, find internal services appropriate for their needs, and then utilize these services. Developers have been forced into this due to the lack of documentation and the availability of a full range of support services that are found in other operating system environments. For example, CMS does not provide the application of a service to use wildcard lookups to search for files on disks. This is a standard offering in even small computer operating systems such as MS-DOS. CMS does have an internal service that it uses internally for exactly this purpose.

CMSCALL Macro

```
[label]  CMSCALL  [PLIST={addr | (reg)}]
                  [,EPLIST={addr | (reg)}]
                  [,UFLAGS=(addr | (reg) | value}]
                  [,COPY={YES | NO | (reg) | (addr,mask)}]
                  [,MODIFY={YES | NO | (reg) | (addr,mask)}]
                  [,FENCE={YES | NO | (reg) | (addr,mask)}]
                  [,ERROR={addr | (reg) | 'ABEND' | *}]
                  [,CALLTYP={PROGRAM | EPLIST |
                          SUBCOM | NONUCXE |
                          NONUCXT | FUNCTION |
                          CMS | value | (reg)}]
```

label	optional assembly language label
PLIST	specifies the location of the plist
EPLIST	specifies the location of the eplist
UFLAGS	specifies a one byte value to be saved in the user save area (USERSAVE)
COPY	specifies whether CMSCALL should relocate the plist and/or eplist if it is above 16 megabytes and the called program is amode 24.
	If (reg) is specified, it is tested and if it is nonzero, the lists are moved.
	If (addr,mask) is specified, the byte at addr is tested with the mask and if the result is nonzero, the lists are moved.
MODIFY	specifies whether the parameter list will be modified by the call program. If the called program does modify the lists, CMSCALL passes those changes back to the caller. (reg) and (addr,mask) behave as in COPY, above.
FENCE	specifies whether the last token of the plist is to be followed by a CMS fence. (reg) and (addr,mask) behave as in COPY, above.

Figure 1-7 CMSCALL parameters.

CMSCALL Macro (continued)

ERROR   specifies the action to be taken if the called
        program returns an error.

       'ABEND'   specifies the caller should abend.

       addr   specifies an address that should
                   receive control.

       (reg)   specifies a register which contains an
                   address that should receive control.

       *   the next instruction following the
                   CMSCALL should receive control.

CALLTYP specifies the type of call.

       PROGRAM   only the plist is passed to called program

       EPLIST   both the plist and eplist are passed
                   to the called program.

       SUBCOM   the called program is a subcommand specified
                   via the SUBCOM interface. An eplist is passed.

       NONUCXE   Bypass nucleus extensions to find and
                   execute the called program. Both plist and
                   eplist are passed.

       NONUCXT   The same as NONUCXE but only the plist is
                   passed.

       FUNCTION   Call a REXX function or subroutine. An eplist
                   is passed.

       CMS   Call a command as if it were invoked from
                   the console. Both plist and eplist are passed.

       value   specifies a one byte constant to represent
                   the call type. All call types have equivalent
                   numeric values.

       (reg)   specifies that the low order byte of register
                   reg contains the numeric value of the call
                   type.

Figure 1-7 (continued) CMSCALL parameters.

Since IBM considered these internal services part of the internal workings of CMS and not part of any published interface, they modified and enhanced these services as was appropriate for the internal needs of CMS from release to release. This required applications that used these internal services to be modified to work with the changes. Waiting for applications to be modified from VM release to VM release slowed the process of migrations.

In bimodal CMS IBM has formalized many of these services. While this is a good sign in general for CMS developers, it can also be viewed as a bad omen as IBM considers the removal of source code availability. The removal of source code is further troubling in light of the fact that the new interface still does not provide a straightforward means to do wildcard lookups of files.

The formalization of the interface has resulted in system services being classified into one of three classes. They are:

The CMS Preferred Interface — This is list of about 70 macros that are either new with bimodal CMS or have been upgraded to support the new 31 bit addressing environment. They provide all of the functionality of the macros and services that were documented in previous versions of CMS.

Bimodal CMS provides improvements to the handling of interrupts and the invocation of user exits based on these interrupts. Lacking from the interface is a means to front end supervisor calls (SVCs) used to invoke CMS commands and functions. Some applications front end SVCs so that they can add features to the existing CMS functionality and other front end SVCs simply to account for which CMS functions are used. Applications that front end CMS SVCs will still need to provide a first level interrupt handler (FLIH) for SVC interrupts.

The CMS Compatibility Interface — This is a list of 16 macros and services that continue to be supported but have not been improved for handling 31 bit addressing. They continue to be supported for existing applications that will be ported to bimodal CMS. For all but three of the macros (TEOVEXIT, DMSEXS, DMSKEY), preferred interface macros and services exist.

For the TEOVEXIT macro, which manages the setting and clearing of the tape end of volume exit, applications will need to use the nucleus extension facility to front end DMSTVS which now provides this service.

For the DMSEXS and DMSKEY macros, which changed the protection key in the PSW used to access memory in varying storage keys applications, will need to continue to use these macros (from addresses below 16 megabytes) or use the equivalent 370 instruction Set PSW Key from Address (SPKA).

In previous versions of CMS it was sometimes necessary for applications to change PSW keys between a key of zero (to access system storage) and a key of x'0E' (to access user storage). Since key zero storage survived abends, applications that utilized the nucleus extension facility to enhance CMS found it necessary to enter and leave PSW key zero. Bimodal CMS's new global subpools provide the equivalent function to key zero storage but with storage that is in user key. This should eliminate much of the need nucleus extensions generated for changing keys.

Bimodal CMS still uses storage in key zero for internal control blocks (such as the nucleus constant or NUCON area from location x'0' to x'5000'). But since these internal control blocks are not part of the preferred interface or compatibility interface, their modification by applications is frowned on by IBM. Applications that wish to disregard IBM's objections can continue to use DMSEXS and DMSKEY from addresses below 16 megabytes, or use the SPKA instruction.

I/O Improvements   When bimodal CMS is running in an XA virtual machine, bimodal CMS uses a new I/O subsystem that takes advantage of 370-XA I/O instructions. This provides for enhanced I/O performance.

Conclusion

It should be clear that VM/XASP is a competitive offering for large-scale interactive computing in the 1990s. Some will say (and rightfully so) that many of the new features are long overdue and are at best contemporaneous.

IBM has stated to developers that there will be two VMs in the future: VM/SP for the small 9370 class systems and VM/XASP for the larger system. HPO will be phased out.

One has to wonder, however, what IBM will do when users who have made large investments in 9370 networks run out of addressability. Clearly, either new, cheaper XA capable systems will need to appear or IBM will need to provide XA capabilities on the existing 9370 family. (At the time of this writing, IBM has stated that it will make its new Enterprise Systems Architecture [ESA] available on 9370s. ESA is a superset of 370-XA that provides for even more addressability for MVS/XA users.)

And there still is the problem of interconnectivity. APPC, IBM's great hope for seamless peer-to-peer connectivity, is finally a partial reality with VM/SP Release 5 and a complete reality of its integration with VTAM, and hence the rest of the SNA family, with the availability of VM/SP Release 6. But there's the rub: IBM has not announced plans for APPC/VM availability with VM/XA SP. It should be noted that this unavailability prevents VM/XA SP users from being participants in distributed SQL/DS databases.

In the final analysis the problem is this: Can IBM develop a single VM that provides all of the services a contemporary operating system should offer? VM/SP Release 6 provides most if not all of the support services including the all important networking. VM/XA SP provides the addressability and high-performance environment. When one VM supports both, we'll know that VM has entered its own. As a long-time VM bigot, I just hope it all happens before UNIX and the ilk obsolete my favorite operating system.

About the Author

Thomas J. Foth is a senior software developer with RELAY Communications, Inc., a leading manufacturer of PC communications and micro-to-mainframe linking software based in Danbury, Connecticut. Tom designs PC-to-mainframe communications software for RELAY.

During his 14 years in data processing, Tom has worked for a leading Silicon Valley-based computer and systems manufacturer, state government, and small entrepreneurial ventures. He is responsible for founding one of the top ten PC user groups in the United States and co-founding a PC special-interest group in one of the leading mainframe user groups.

Tom has published several pieces of popular public domain software that enhance end-user computing and program development. He is an international speaker and has written articles on cooperative processing, computer conferencing, and mainframe and PC technology, which have appeared in *BYTE*, *PC Week*, *Softalk*, *Mainframe Journal*, and *Systems User*, as well as in a PC Expo Directory.

2

VM Data Communications

by Edward Sterling

Introduction

It has been said that VM was killed by IBM; yet today VM is stronger than ever, and has an equal place beside MVS. Many people view the two operating systems as black and white, wanting one to be better than the other. In reality, each operating system does a good job in a specific major area, and VM is best known for its interactive timesharing support. The mention of timesharing immediately suggests users on terminals, wanting to connect into and out of a VM system, on many different media. It also means users wanting to exchange data with one another, between large systems, minicomputers, and personal computers. It's the connectivity game, and it is very complex. Yet in some ways, it's a nice problem to have: There are so many choices, it's difficult to know which is the best one.

In the early years of VM (the 1970s), data communications support was very primitive. Card image files could be transferred between hosts, a long-time IBM traditional communications path. Print files could be sent to remote printers. Users on 2741 "Selectric" typewriter terminals, as well as ASCII terminal users, could logon in "line-by-line" (teletypewriter) mode. In the first release of VM/370 (ca. 1971), there was no 3270 support!

By 1980, IBM realized VM could not be killed, and moved to make it a "strategic" product. Today, VM's data communications capabilities are certainly on-par with MVS, especially since SNA/VTAM is available in both operating systems. The importance of the VM system as a premier application development platform, and as a migration vehicle for new releases of CICS, IMS, and even MVS, requires the full scope of communications support used by these subsystems. Because the VM environment is so conducive to development, and so much control can be given to the developer, without compromising system integrity, VM becomes an obvious choice for data communications research and development.

VM Data Communications: Past and Present

VM Almost Killed by IBM

VM is nearing the end of its second decade of commercial existence. During the "early years" VM/370 (as it was called in the '70s) was often run on a separate machine, as something of an outcast or a non-conformist. If the MVS group regarded the VM system with disdain, the feeling was usually mutual. The VM programmers delighted in their new-found extended control and improved interactive response. As a result, VM systems were usually not part of the corporate mainstream network and thus, simple communications were generally regarded as adequate. In fact, because VM was regarded in many ways as experimental, even inside IBM, many installations spent their days making (often extensive) modifications and debugging problems for themselves, other installations, and IBM. Networking was generally minimal.

Early VM Networking: RSCS

The earliest networking package available for VM was (and still is) RSCS, the Remote Spooling Communications Subsystem, introduced as an integral part of VM/370 Release 2 in 1974. RSCS might be thought of as a simple VM version of HASP, the time-honored remote spooling system from the 1960s. It consisted of a virtual machine with its own operating system. This was done primarily to simulate multi-tasking, which VM does not support in a single virtual machine. RSCS could communicate with a remote VM system, a

HASP system, or a non-programmable 2780 workstation which performed remote printing. The links used binary synchronous protocol (bisync or BSC), and while each link was operational, the line was polled every 2.5 seconds to ensure the other side was operational. However, there was an inherent "master/slave relationship" between the sender and the receiver, instead of a more logical peer-to-peer especially between two VM systems. Another major problem was that all communications were point-point: There was no ability to pass files on to a more distant third system using network routing. But, for simple remote printing, and exchange of punched-card images, RSCS cost nothing and did an acceptable job.

As VM grew in popularity, and VM installations began to grow internally, the need for some RSCS networking upgrades became evident. The idea of logging in to a remote VM system from your own terminal was still the "stuff dreams are made of," but the primary need of the day was for "store and forward" networking. This would allow the establishment of a true "network web" of processors, and for each VM system to see the other as equals. Better performance and lower overhead were also becoming important.

Various short-lived experimental systems appeared to fill the gap. Several large VM installations decided to "go their own way," and created an informal consortium called the *Common System*. Besides sharing VM modifications with each other, they designed and built a significant networking system called RASP (something of a merge between RSCS and HASP) based on the then-current RSCS. RASP addressed many of the concerns VM installations had voiced at the SHARE Users' Group, which had not yet been addressed by IBM. RASP ran successfully at about a dozen installations in the late 1970s.

VM Becomes a Strategic Product

To be sure, a lot was going on inside IBM concerning VM during the mid to late 1970s. IBM internal interest in VM was growing sharply, and IBM's own internal SUN network (Subsystem Unified Network) was based on the IBM internal RSCS. To distinguish it from the regular RSCS, this internal version of RSCS was named VNET. Started in 1972, VNET continued to be developed, and was finally available to VM customers as a PRPQ (i.e., special controlled release) in 1976. VNET addressed many of the SHARE requirements. It offered peer-to-peer networking, low overhead during idle periods, full CMS file support, store and forward networking, channel to channel adapter (CTCA) support for linking VM to other systems in the same physical complex, and remote 3270 workstation printing. Yet despite the extended capabilities VNET offered, its price was simply too high for most companies to justify, and its use at customer sites was never significant. Finally, as VM's status improved and IBM moved to create VM/SP from VM/370, VNET was also revised for a regular Program Product release. In 1979 it became available as RSCS/Program Product (RSCS/PP) at a very reasonable monthly cost. The old RSCS, RASP, and VNET quickly disappeared as everyone adopted the new Program Product as the "standard."

VM Networking Extends to Terminals

Concurrent with the creation of VM/SP came another long-sought communications offering: the ability to logon to a remote VM system as if it were part of your local CPU. This was achieved using an elegantly simple subsystem added to VM's Control Program called Logical Device Support Facility (LDSF), and a new networking product called VM/PASSTHRU (also called VM/PassThrough Facility). VM/PASSTHRU became an essential tool in VM system maintenance, with the introduction of the tiny 4331 processor. Being one of the first "departmental" processors in the mainframe class, the 4331 required mainframe systems programmers, but the cost could not be justified. VM/PASSTHRU was the solution, because it brought the remote VM 4331 system right to the system programmer's terminal. Now, in conjunction with an RSCS link to send fixes, modifications, and maintenance procedures to one or more of these remote systems, "SYSGENs" could be performed without traveling to another terminal, dialing-up remotely, or even physically going to the remote site for such maintenance. The combination was superb, and paved the way for effective remote site maintenance from a central location. Like the new RSCS/PP, VM/PASSTHRU treated VM systems as peers, used either BSC or CTCA links between systems, and was very reasonably priced.

The First Attempt at SNA for VM

Reeling from the delight of IBM "blessing" VM in the form of VM/SP, and the advent of RSCS/PP and VM/PASSTHRU providing low-overhead, high-function networking, VM installations' networking needs seemed well addressed by 1980. Yet one could not ignore SNA, IBM's true corporate networking strategy. The specter of two separate corporate networks loomed large: SNA for the MVS systems, and RSCS and PASSTHRU for the VM systems. Clearly, while this might have delighted the equally bigoted systems programming groups, neither IBM nor its major customers could tolerate this. VM was winning its case as a highly effective development platform, and the success of the PROFS electronic mail system was selling VM processors by itself. Somehow, VM had to link into the corporate SNA network.

IBM's quick answer was to move the MVS version of VTAM into a virtual machine, and have it controlled by a "guest" operating system; OS/VS1 was the obvious choice, since it had a special "VM handshaking" feature to reduce duplication of effort in paging. From IBM's standpoint, this new package called VM/VCNA was an easy way to address the SNA link-up problem. VCNA used mainly off-the-shelf components, and the only major change to VM was the addition of IUCV Console Services (CCS). CCS seemed to duplicate the Logical Device Support in some respects, although it allowed for a more general concept of remote logons (3270 and ASCII) for remote SNA users.

In practice, VCNA was a square peg in a round hole. Early users had a very difficult time installing and running it, and many "VM purists" would have nothing to do with a VS1 system running on their CPU. The 1976 design specification for VCNA could not foresee the popularity of VM and the many CMS-intensive installations that would exist three years later. Most installations regarded the overhead of running a VS1 guest system as too high a cost to simply link terminals to the SNA network. VS1 expertise was required, as well as a knowledge of traditional OS, JCL, etc. The requirement still stood for a "native" SNA implementation, with VM-like installation procedures and maintenance tools.

VM Goes Native with SNA Networking

Finally, with the advent of VM/SP Release 4, IBM announced native VM/SNA support. A new "operating system" was provided by IBM in VM/SP called the Group Control System (GCS). GCS is like a miniature version of MVS, whose sole function is to provide all the required OS services to make ACF/VTAM operate in a virtual machine. Major changes were made in the VM Control Program, to allow for the emulation of MVS's CSA, so that common storage can be shared by members of the group running the GCS operating system. A new version of VTAM for VM was developed, and is required for the operation of VM/SNA. It forms a custom fit with the GCS to provide SNA networking. All maintenance procedures and files are done using native CMS-like files and "EXEC" procedures. VM/SNA effectively replaces VM/VCNA; only installations still running VS1 for production might still wish to run VCNA.

Thus, VM/SP now has a full complement of networking products, to satisfy both the VM "purist" and the MIS director, who need full connectivity to the corporate network.

VM/SP Support for Data Communications Hardware

You can attach any kind of device to a VM system. The question becomes whether Control Program (CP) has support for it or if you have a device driver in a virtual machine which can control the device. It is, therefore, pertinent to review which devices are supported directly by CP. SNA support is detailed in the next section under *IBM Data Communications Products: VM/VTAM*.

37x5 Front-End Communications Processor Support

The 37x5 (3705, 3720, 3725, and 3745) front-end processors provide sophisticated communications support for SNA, non-SNA, and certain Local Area Network (LAN) connections. Traditionally, VM's Control Program has had support for the 37x5 Emulator Program (EP), as well as real 2703 type transmission control units (the few that exist today are usually DEC PDP-11s emulating the 2703 or the venerable Memorex 1270). EP supports asynchronous (ASCII) terminals, and "bisync" (BSC) lines for RSCS and remote 3270 terminal clusters. When running EP, the 37x5 is "owned" by the VM Control Program, as opposed to a virtual machine such as VTAM. The EP is stored in a saved segment (DCSS), and the CP NET LOAD command is issued by the operator after IPL to load the 37x5 with a specified version of the EP. For SNA operation, ACF/NCP is required. Because CP does not support this itself, the 37x5 must be loaded and controlled by either the VCNA or VM/VTAM virtual machine; the CP NET LOAD command does not apply under SNA.

3270-Family Display Station Support

CP supports both local and remote BSC 3274 controllers, with full device support including extended highlighting, colors, and GDDM graphics. A "D" model local controller is channel-attached, and is normally defined on a block multiplexer channel. A "B" or "C" model remote 3274 controller attaches to the 37x5 via a BSC line, under the direct control of CP. The speed of the line concerns only the 37x5 controller, and not CP itself. An SNA "A" model remote 3274 runs under SDLC line control, and is controlled by a 37x5 running ACF/NCP.

Virtual machines run in one of two modes of screen display: a traditional "VM" mode, controlled by CP, with the last 2 rows of the screen serving as a single command-line input area; and, a "full-screen" mode defined and solely controlled by an application program, such as CICS under VM, or a text editor like XEDIT. To simplify the interface to the real 3270 terminal, generic channel command words (CCWs) are defined for the virtual screen I/O operations, which are later translated into the correct CCWs for the actual terminal being used. Control of a 3270 terminal can be given to a virtual machine in several ways: permanently, via a directory entry linking it to a certain virtual machine; or temporarily, via an OPERATOR-level CP ATTACH command, or the self-initialed CP DIAL command.

For non-SNA operation, a single group of remote 3270 terminals controlled by a 3274 is termed a "cluster," and there may be a total of 256 remote clusters. The maximum number of terminals supported in a single cluster is 32. Note too that "multidrop" configurations, where several controllers share the same telephone line, are not supported. This is a somewhat arbitrary decision, made long ago, because it probably meant less work. CP takes the responsibility for the required BSC polling of each "cluster" of terminals, and therefore the active use of many clusters imposes some overhead on CP. Another small criticism lies in the design of the CP code for remote 3270 support, which causes each full-screen input to be processed twice: The initial input is effectively disregarded, while CP scrambles to switch the smaller input buffer to a larger one. In many cases, this is totally unnecessary. Two alternatives exist: Switch to VM/VTAM and use SDLC protocol (a sizable undertaking); or, use the remote 3270 support introduced in VM/PASSTHRU Release 3. There are also cases where the entire VM system will ABEND ("crash") due to a sequencing error in remote 3270 flow. While one can argue that this identifies an integrity problem, the entire user population suffers from a problem on a single line. In summary, having a virtual machine, such as PASSTHRU, responsible for remote 3270 communications appears to be a more logical approach to VM architecture. For SNA operation, most of the above limitations do not exist. SNA supports a very large number of remote 3270 controllers and allows multidrop connections.

Asynchronous Communications Support

CP has always supported asynchronous ASCII communications. However, the support is generally regarded as minimal, and notably self-serving, especially in the face of a large "real world" of many types of ASCII terminals. This is not isolated to VM alone, but can be said for ASCII support in most IBM communications products. Fortunately, there are various hardware and software add-on products which make ASCII terminals function very capably in a VM environment. ASCII communications support exists both in native CP and VM/VTAM.

ASCII terminals normally run in "line by line mode," where output appears at the bottom of the screen, and scrolls off the top of the screen. A "dot" (.) character is the normal prompt, which includes an XON character to enable any terminal expecting XON/XOFF flow control. Support for this mode of input/output is generally quite limited in applications that normally run in "full-screen" mode. In recent years, IBM has made several enhancements to VM/SP to improve scrolling and PF key usage, but it applies only to their own 3101 ASCII terminal. Hence, there is widespread use of ASCII-to-3270 protocol conversion products which make the ASCII terminal appear as a regular 3278 terminal. This removes the "problem" of limited ASCII terminal support once and for all.

Asynchronous communication can also link a VM system with an X.25 packet switched network, such as TELENET or TYMNET. IBM offers this capability only through VM/VTAM, but COMM-PRO Associates sells a very well-known enhancement to the 37x5 Emulator Program which creates multiple virtual asynchronous lines from a single X.25 connection. This can be a very cost-effective alternative to VM/VTAM, if no other SNA capabilities are required.

As mentioned above, ASCII-to-3270 protocol converters are usually the best vehicles for productive access to VM applications. There are two types of protocol converters which can be installed: hardware and software. IBM's major protocol converter is the 7171. It supports up to 64 concurrent users on many types of ASCII terminals, and the unit is defined to VM/SP as a local 3274 channel-attached controller. An optional SYSGEN keyword, called EMUL3270, can distinguish the 7171 from a real 3274; and allows an application program to reference a control block to determine if the terminal is really connected to a 7171. This information may be useful for extra security checking or to enable a file transfer program to a PC attached to the 7171.

Because the 7171 physically appears to be an IBM PC with a large expansion cabinet, it can run standard PC DOS software, and thus 7171 maintenance is performed using PC software. A set of approximately 12 brands of ASCII terminals is included with the system, and PC-based software is included which allows the customer to modify ASCII keyboard mapping to 3270 functions; or define new terminal types as required. The 7171 also recognizes a special transparency string which disables 3270 emulation, and allows "raw ASCII" characters to be sent directly to the terminal or PC to drive plotters, ASCII printers, or perform PC file transfer. The transparency string, an invalid 3270 addressing command, is placed at the head of a 3270 output command buffer, and the "raw ASCII" follows behind it. For example, to send "raw ASCII" to the terminal, the 3270 output sequence would be EBCDIC 05C3115D7F110000 followed by the (already translated) ASCII data. Upon seeing the 115D7F110000 string, the 7171 stops all EBCDIC to ASCII translation as well as 3270 protocol conversion (but just for that output data stream on that terminal). A second code, EBCDIC 115D7F110001 performs this same function, but also allows "raw ASCII" input from the terminal. This code is most often used for PC file transfers, allowing the PC to send ASCII file data up to the mainframe transparently.

Earlier IBM attempts at protocol conversion include the venerable Series/1 minicomputer, running the "Yale 3270 Emulation IUP"; and a Series/1 variant called the 4994 Host-Loaded Protocol Converter (both packages are no longer marketed). In an SNA environment, IBM also offers the 3708, which attaches directly to the 37x5. With few exceptions, most non-IBM units emulate 3274 remote BSC or SNA controllers, and thus require a 37x5 front-end processor. Because this set-up entails two separate communications links (ASCII, and then BSC or SDLC), response can be sluggish, and an echo-delay may be noticed. However, for a group of users at a remote location, using inexpensive ASCII terminals with a protocol converter can be a very cost-effective way to link to a headquarters mainframe.

Local Area Network Controllers

VM supports two local area network (LAN) interface controllers: the 7170 Device Attachment Control Unit (DACU) and the 8232 LAN Channel Station (LCS). The 7170 DACU is no longer marketed and was recently replaced by the 8232. These units provide a high-speed direct link between a local area network and the IBM mainframe channel. Each of these units, like the 7171, are variants of the IBM PC, with large expansion cabinets. The 8232 has a slightly different appearance, because it is an industrial IBM PC/AT in a rack mount cabinet, with an industrial display monitor. As of this writing, the 8232 is still in RPQ limited availability status, requiring some extra effort by your local IBM branch office to place an order. The alternative to these controllers is to have a LAN with a "gateway" PC, on which you would run the IBM 3270 Workstation Gateway Program. PCs on the LAN would request a session with the host, and the gateway PC would attach to the 37x5 as a remote 3274 controller. At best, the speed of the gateway link would not exceed 19.2 KBS in such a configuration. Therefore, for practical high-volume local area networking, a channel-attached LAN controller is essential.

The 7170 DACU supports the well-known Ethernet and PRONET by Proteon Corp.; the 8232 supports the IBM Token-Ring LAN and also Ethernet. Both units, to date, are supported only by the TCP/IP local area network protocol, which is available as Program Product 5798-FAL, TCP/IP for VM. TCP/IP is a widely supported protocol, especially in the Ethernet world, and is one of the few protocols which has been widely accepted throughout the industry for local area networking. VM's Control Program does not directly support the 7170 or the 8232. Instead, these controllers are dedicated to the TCP/IP virtual machine, which performs all initialization, I/O operations and error handling.

Special Notes for the 4331, 4361, and 9370

The 4331 processor (now obsolete) and its replacement the 4361, as well as the 9370, employ integrated communications controllers to reduce space, power consumption, and cost. These units are known as the Display Printer Adapter (DPA), the Integrated Communications Adapter (ICA), and the Work Station Adapter (WSA). The DPA/WSA are essentially built-in 3274 controllers, and the ICA is a built-in 37x5 communications controller. The DPA provides basic System/370 operator console support, system printer support (for the 326x family of low-speed printers), and a small base of additional 3278 ports. The ICA provides telecommunications support for up to eight ASCII, BSC, or SDLC lines, running either microcoded EP, or a subset of VTAM called VTAM/E. The WSA allows up to four 3299 multiplexer units, each of which expands a WSA 3270 port to eight ports. The advantages to these integrated adapters are obvious. No external controllers are required, reducing overall system costs and, in particular, they keep valuable system channel slots open for other equipment such as disks and tape drives.

The 9370 takes a giant technological leap ahead of the 4361 by providing virtually all of the data communications capabilities of the external controllers, using its own internal subsystem controllers. These subsystems function as scaled-down 37x5, 3274, 7171, and 8232 controllers, providing full RSCS, PASSTHRU, and ASCII communications, as well as a VTAM, X.25, 3270, and local area network support. Although the 9370 has been marketed as a "departmental" distributed computing mainframe, it may in fact become the new breed of "front-end controller," replacing a large number of different controllers with a single integrated system providing full networking and connectivity. The 9370 may thus become the "gateway" to the mainframe.

IBM Data Communications Software Products for VM/SP

RSCS/PP

RSCS is the Remote Spooling Communications Subsystem. It is a VM system's data link to other mainframes, providing both file transfer and remote printing, and allows a VM system to join a network supporting Network Job Interface and Network Job Entry (NJI and NJE). RSCS uses a spool file handling concept called store-and-forward. This means that it will accept files as an intermediary, store them locally, and transmit them to their remote destination when the link is operational and ready to accept them. The advantage to this system is that the entire route between two nodes does not have to be operational at the time of file transmission. RSCS Version 1 supports BSC telecommunications and channel-to-channel adapter (CTCA) links. RSCS Version 2 also supports SDLC telecommunications links to an SNA network, and requires VM/VTAM to be installed and operational.

Outbound files are placed in the VM spooling system by users (virtual machines), in such a manner that RSCS sees them as input "card reader" files. Each file must be properly identified using the CP TAG command, which names the remote destination, and possibly a userid on that remote system to receive the file. For example, if a user wished to send an assembler source file named TESTASM

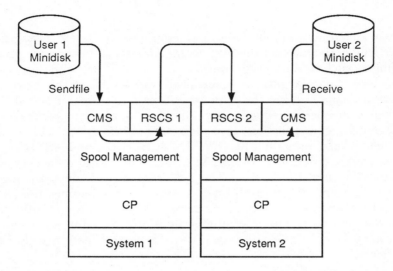

Figure 2-1 With RSCS, a user can initiate the transfer of a file from one system to another.

ASSEMBLE to a friend named SYSPROG at network site VMBOSTON, the commands to send the file would be:

```
CP TAG DEV PUNCH VMBOSTON SYSPROG
CP SPOOL PUNCH TO RSCS
PUNCH TESTASM ASSEMBLE (or, DISK DUMP TESTASM ASSEMBLE)
```

Assuming that our user's friend is really named Mary Jones, we might assume that this friend's name and node are stored in our user's private NAMES file under the nickname MARYJ, such as:

```
:nick.MARYJ
:name.Mary Jones
:node.VMBOSTON
:user:SYSPROG
```

Thus, the three earlier commands would be replaced by the much simpler command SENDFILE TESTASM ASSEMBLE TO MARYJ. SENDFILE would generate the required CP TAG, CP SPOOL, and PUNCH commands. We trust that RSCS would find node VMBOSTON as either a direct or indirectly routed link in list of remote nodes, and it would then queue the file for transmission.

A master directory, named RSCS DIRECT on the main RSCS 191 disk, identifies the local system name, all direct-link remote names, and all indirect (routed) remote names. In addition to the link name, each direct link is defined with a link address (BSC line or CTCA address), a driver type (HASP, VM peer link, JES2-compatible, etc.), and a default spooling class. Indirect routed links are specified by the name of direct-link on the "first hop." A sample RSCS DIRECT might appear like this:

LOCAL	NYCVMSYS					
*	LINK	DRIVER	LINE	TIME	TASKE	SPOOL
*	NAME	TYPE	ADDR	ZONE	NAME	CLASS
LINK	VMBOSTON	DMTVMB	05C	5	BOST	*
LINK	LAMVS1	DMTNJI	061	8	LAMV	A
LINK	WASHHASP	DMTSML	06D	5	WASH	*
LINK	OURVMNO2	DMTVMC	500	5	CTCA	*
ROUTE	LONDON	VMBOSTON				
ROUTE	SANDIEGO	LAMVS1				

RSCS is unusual in that it runs its own unique operating system, the sole purpose of which is to receive local spool files and transmit them to remote links, and receive files from the remote links, and either pass them on to other remote links or create a local spool file for the recipient. This operating system is stored and IPLed from the RSCS 191 disk; it is not stored in a saved segment such as CMS. The nucleus of this operating system performs time-slicing, driver activation and deactivation, storage management, spool-file management, line-driver I/O, and CMS-like disk file support. But the real flexibility of the RSCS system is in its driver architecture. Line drivers are dynamically loaded by name, allowing several versions (production and test) to exist. The major drivers used by most installations are:

```
DMTVMB - VM to VM peer link over a BSC line
DMTVMC - VM to VM peer link over a CTCA
DMTNJI - VM to a JES2 or JES3 MVS complex
DMTSML - VM to a programmable remote such as HASP or Model 20
DMTNPT - VM to a non-programmable remote such as a 2780
DMTPOW - VM to a DOS/VSE POWER system
DMTRPT - VM to a remote 3270 cluster (3287, 3289) printer
```

The driver architecture also allows for easy modifications when required. Some installations have written modifications to drive unusual hardware, which appears somewhat like a CTCA, while others have developed fancy banner-page modifications that make print identification much easier for users and operators. Even complex multiple-link balancing, or route-name aliasing can be easily accomplished. Third-party RSCS drivers are available which support ASCII printers, including sophisticated HP Laserjet fonts.

System overhead is kept to a minimum on VM peer links, where all polling activity quiesces when the queues empty on each end; however, on the 2780 and HASP links, binary synchronous protocol requires the line to be polled every 2.5 seconds to ensure that the other side is operational.

There are several methods of user and operator interfacing to RSCS. The most common way to command or query RSCS is via the CP SMSG command: This is a message which arrives as a data interrupt, instead of a simple console message. RSCS has a special trap for these messages, and knows which user sent it. The message can be a QUERY, wherein RSCS will reply to the user such information as active links, specific routing "hop" names, the number of files queued for a certain link, the details about a certain file being sent or received, etc. The VM operator, or a similarly authorized assistant, can start, stop, or drain a specific link, as well as perform spool file operations such as class and form changes, file purging and flushing, and redirecting to another link. In addition, RSCS can be controlled from its own console, or via a secondary userid allowed to "speak" for RSCS; this would most often be the OPERATOR userid.

RSCS Version 2 is a major revision of the RSCS Program Product Version 1. It is designed specifically to integrate RSCS within an SNA network, which is much more common today than BSC links in most corporate environments. Unlike Version 1, RSCS Version 2 uses the VM/VTAM Group Control System (GCS) operating system, so that it can participate as a member of the VTAM group. RSCS Version 2 no longer IPLs its own operating system. Instead it runs as a VTAM application, retaining its identity as a virtual machine. The VTAM master virtual machine performs all real I/O, and communicates with the RSCS application using new system service calls. As a result, most of the line drivers have been reorganized and rewritten for VTAM. All non-SNA NJE line drivers have been consolidated in a single new driver. Those BSC links which are required can still be supported, but the 37x5 EP must be retained; the Partitioned Emulator Program (PEP) feature of NCP must, therefore, be installed.

The traditional VM peer-to-peer VM-to-NJE drivers have been replaced with the Multi-system Networking Facilities of VTAM

(MSNF), an integral VTAM component. This offers faster throughput and multiple parallel paths, which improves service to users by opening priority paths based on file size. Large files no longer congest the link for long periods. The option of establishing direct paths between nodes eliminates the store-and-forward work of intermediate nodes, which also improves file transfer time. Although Version 1 is still supported, the time will come when most new functions will only be available in Version 2.

VM/PASSTHRU

VM/PASSTHRU (also known as VM/PassThrough Facility) is a terminal networking package designed specifically for VM non-SNA networks. PASSTHRU provides the ability to logon to a remote VM system as if it were part of your local CPU. The ability for PASSTHRU to create a 3270 terminal session for a remote user is achieved using a simple subsystem added to VM's Control Program called Logical Device Support Facility (LDSF). Like RSCS Version 1, PASSTHRU is a multi-tasking system with line drivers for BSC and CTCA links; however, it does not run its own operating system. Unfortunately, there is no integration of RSCS and PVM; hence, they *cannot* share a BSC or CTCA links between each other (whereas under VM/VTAM, this sharing *would* occur). PASSTHRU's multitasking is simulated by series of OS-like macros, all controlled by a central dispatcher. The PASSTHRU virtual machine is referred to as PVM, and this

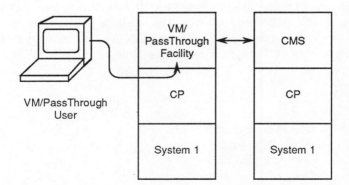

Figure 2-2 With VM/PassThrough Facility, a user can access two physical processors from one terminal, connecting from one virtual machine to a virtual machine on the second processor.

acronym is used extensively to reference PASSTHRU and its associated products.

To use PASSTHRU, a VM user has a choice of connecting to a remote system whether logged on to the local system or not. In the case of not being logged on locally, the user clears the VM logo from the terminal screen, types CP DIAL PVM, and the PASSTHRU welcome menu appears. This menu lists all active nodes in the PASSTHRU network, as well as showing the how to return to normal VM terminal mode. Operational nodes are shown as highlighted words; non-operational nodes appear in regular intensity. If the user is logged on already and wishes to use PASSTHRU, one needs only to type the word PASSTHRU, optionally specifying parameters such as the remote destination name, a PF key with which to capture screens, a disconnect string, etc. The connection is made simply by placing the cursor on the name of the desired remote node name and pressing enter. To disconnect from the remote system, a string of four number signs (####) signals the end of session. This is especially useful if one cannot gracefully exit from the remote application. A CP LOGOFF will also end the remote session.

While using PASSTHRU from CMS, the user's local CMS session is suspended during the remote terminal session. When the remote session ends, the screen clears and the user is right back in CMS. The PASSTHRU command is an EXEC on the public disk, which invokes module DVMUSI to take control of the user's screen and communicate with the PVM virtual machine.

A master directory, named PVM DIRECT on the main PVM 191 disk, identifies the local system name, all direct-link remote names, and all indirect (routed) remote names. In addition to the link name, each direct link is defined with a link address (BSC line or CTCA address), a driver type (BSC, CTC, or SIM) and a time zone code. A sample PVM DIRECT might appear like this:

```
     LOCAL      NYCVMSYS
   *            LINK      DRIVER    LINE    TIME    TASKE
   *            NAME      TYPE      ADDR    ZONE    NAME
     LINK       VMBOSTON  DVMBSC    04C     5       BOST
     LINK       LAMVS1    DVMSIM    04D     8       LAMV
     LINK       VMSYSNO2  DVMCTC    480     5       WASH
     ROUTE      LONDON    VMBOSTON
```

PASSTHRU's design is similar to RSCS in that line drivers are dynamically loaded by name, based on a link directory. PASSTHRU has three line drivers:

```
DVMBSC - VM to VM peer link over a BSC line
DVMCTC - VM to VM peer link over a CTCA
DVMSIM - VM appears as a remote 3274 BSC controller to a host
```

DVMSIM allows VM users to link to a remote system which supports 3270 BSC protocol, such as DOS/BTAM or possibly even a minicomputer. Line activity must follow normal remote 3270 BSC rules, which require a line poll every 2.5 seconds. It is worth mentioning that DVMSIM uses an uncommon channel command, called ADDRESS PREPARE, to ensure that it receives only the traffic from a specific controller on a potential multidrop line. In most cases this is quite unnecessary, and ADDRESS PREPARE may not be supported (or enabled) on some older front-end controllers.

There is also a separate field-developed product from IBM called PVM-3101 (5796-PPF). This is a very inexpensive set of modifications to PASSTHRU which permits an asynchronous logon, which is assumed to be from an IBM 3101 block-mode ASCII terminal. A new driver named DVMUTY allows some remapping of the PF keys at logon, and then provides 3270 protocol conversion. The modules which perform this are written in IBM's internal PL/S language, and cannot be easily modified to support another type of ASCII terminal. Despite the fact that only IBM 3101 terminals are supported, the product works quite well. There are signs that IBM is probably not going to support this product much longer, as there have been no upgrades to fit this product into PASSTHRU Release 3.

VM/SNA

The term VM/SNA stands for "native VM/SP SNA support," and it describes both Control Program enhancements and optional MVS-like software called VM/VTAM. Together these provide true SNA networking for VM/SP. VM/SNA replaces VM/VCNA, which was IBM's first attempt to provide VM with SNA support.

VTAM is the mainframe component of SNA networking, whereas NCP is the 37x5 component of SNA. The prefix ACF (Advanced Communication Function) has been added over the years to distinguish ACF/VTAM and ACF/NCP from earlier "no-fee" versions of each component; however, you can be sure that the terms VTAM and NCP imply the current ACF/VTAM and ACF/NCP versions. In order to implement support for VTAM under VM, IBM had to enhance VM/SP to provide critical system functions found only in DOS and MVS, such as multitasking and shared common storage between tasks. In particular, one can see that RSCS and PASSTHRU required multitasking support, and each of these subsystems had to provide that capability for itself. IBM wisely chose to implement these functions in the base VM product, in a way that would not impact existing subsystems.

The development of native SNA support in CP took place over three major releases of VM/SP. The earlier Virtual Machine Communication Facility (VMCF) was not suited to allow data exchange between CP and a service virtual machine, so IBM developed a new virtual-machine-to-CP data transfer facility, called Inter-User Communication Vehicle (IUCV). This was better suited for handling complex inter-virtual machine data transfer with heavy traffic flow. The LDSF 3270 emulation used by PASSTHRU was too limited for VTAM, and here IBM developed a special IUCV service called *CCS (Communications Console Services, with the * denoting an IUCV service), which is capable of handling all types of terminal data and all aspects of terminal I/O. JCL "PROCs," used by VM/VCNA and MVS/VTAM maintenance and installation, were eliminated by using REXX, an advanced version of the CMS EXEC procedure language. And finally, IBM developed a new storage concept called shared writable storage, which allows a group of virtual machines to share a common storage area without the normal interference of VM storage protection. This facility lets VM/SNA provide the special VM version of VTAM with an MVS-like "CSA" (common storage area). Once these major enhancements were in place, IBM could now proceed with the development of a control system which would run the actual VTAM supervisor.

IBM chose to develop a completely new VTAM supervisor program for VM/SNA, which they called Group Control System, or GCS. GCS is the implementation of a specialized operating system, similar in many respects to MVS, which hosts the VM version of ACF/VTAM. It has some CMS-like characteristics, in that it is a VM "saved system," which can be IPLed by name; has a start-up PROFILE; and can process REXX EXECs instead of JCL. However, its essence has many "OS" standard features like multitasking, multiprogramming, and an I/O supervisor. IBM has made it quite clear in their announcements that customers should *not* expect to develop non-SNA applications using GCS; nor should anyone misconstrue it as an alternative to MVS for regular batch work.

In operation, GCS embodies a VTAM *super virtual machine* with a number of associated *group members* providing additional VTAM services. Most group members run a single VTAM application program such as RSCS Version 2; NCCF; NPDA; and numerous non-IBM vendor offerings such as network managers, multiple session managers, PC file transfer managers, etc. In order to run a new VTAM application program, you simply add a new virtual machine member to the group, and add the name to the master list of applications in the VTAM virtual machine. The (new) application virtual machine communicates with the VTAM service machine using the common writable storage, and VTAM manages all real I/O on the network.

The GCS group's identity is primarily defined by the act of IPLing the GCS operating system. Thus, in a passive way, the VM system directory defines the GSC group, in that each group member will have an IPL statement naming the GCS operating system, in lieu of the usual CMS. Whenever a virtual machine IPLs GCS, it then becomes an active member of that GCS group. Though it is not normally done, a VM system could run several groups, each having its own *separate* GCS saved system, perhaps with the names GCSPROD, GCSTEST, etc. GCS is a *saved system* like CMS, defined in the CP saved system table (DMKSNT) with a special parameter indicating that part of its storage is to be shared in a read/write mode among the users of the group. This special storage feature allows emulation of the MVS "CSA" storage concept. When the GCS system is "SYSGENed," several parameters define both a "supervisor" virtual machine (usually named VTAM), and a recovery virtual machine which acts like a guardian if anything should happen to VTAM (i.e., an ABEND occurs). Thus, a number of different parameters creates the group and links its members together as a whole.

Converting from a traditional RSCS, PASSTHRU, and remote 3270 BSC network to a VM/SNA network is a significant undertaking. In addition to the use of GCS on the mainframe and NCP on the 37x5, a special version of ACF/VTAM, *Version 3 for VM*, is required for VM/SNA networking. Previous MVS or VCNA versions will not work properly. Concurrent operation of the old network and the new VM/SNA network is possible during the installation and test period; but only if the 37x5 EP is retained. It is very important to remember that control of the 37x5 is taken away from CP, and placed in the hands of VM/VTAM. Therefore, concurrent operations are only possible if the Partitioned EP (PEP) option of NCP is installed. Concurrent operation will also incur some temporary costs in the form of duplicated telecommunications lines, and there must be adequate real memory in the 37x5 to support both PEP and NCP.

It is not intuitively obvious that the visual and operational interface to the system, seen by end-users, will be completely changed once you convert to VM/SNA. The familiar VM logo is replaced by an Unformatted System Services (USS) message. USS messages are de-

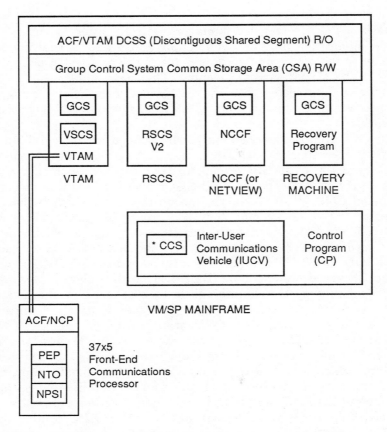

Figure 2-3 Overview of VM/VTAM.

fined in USS tables, stored in the VTAM main library (SYS1 VTAMLIB). USS tables are effectively macros, which allow a single word like "VMSYS2" to mean "LOGON APPLID(VMSYS2)." However, lengthy messages, logos, greetings, new user information, etc., cannot be output due to the fairly strict limitations in the USS definitions. Instead of the limited capabilities of USS tables, many installations prefer the increased flexibility and security available in a VTAM network solicitor package, the most popular of which are sold by third-party software vendors. These packages are also known as VTAM network access managers or VTAM session managers. In addition to USS tables, an installation may specify a specific VTAM application to be invoked when a terminal power-on.

VM/SNA allows terminal bidirectional access to the system. Using a standard application name called "VM," users on SNA terminals can access the VM system from either local SNA controllers, or from distant remote systems via a *cross-domain logon.* "VM" is really a synonym for the terminal handling program which runs as an internal application in the VTAM service machine. This program, called VTAM SNA Console Services (VSCS), is the "other end" of the IUCV *CCS link between VTAM and CP. VSCS receives 3270 data streams from CP over the *CCS link; although the data comes from CP, it originally could be the output from the XEDIT editor, PROFS mail, the RDRLIST spool file lister, etc. Yes, the path lengths for a VM/SNA session can be quite long!

There is also the reverse requirement, to allow local VM/CMS users on non-SNA terminals to access local or remote SNA services and VTAM applications. This is achieved using the CP DIAL command, by which the user temporarily attaches his/her non-SNA terminal (on a non-SNA controller, or as a Logical Device session) to connect to the VTAM service machine. VSCS manages these outbound sessions as well, which would not involve *CCS if the user is requesting a remote cross-domain logon.

With care and planning, the "shock" of converting to a VM/SNA network can be eased. One way to retain the familiar VM logo would be to specify the standard VTAM application named "VM" in the terminal definition table called SYS1 VTAMLST. Instead of presenting a USS table message, VTAM would automatically connect the terminal with a specific application, in this case named "VM." The "VM" application supplied by IBM with VM/VTAM calls for a standard VM logon on the local system. Some VTAM session managers provide an automatic logon facility using *scripts,* which run like a VM/CMS EXEC and perform typing and response scanning. Such scripts can eliminate confusing logon steps for inexperienced users or data entry clerks. While numerous options and capabilities exist, they can be quite confusing, and the transition period requires thorough preparation and education for all parties involved.

Some initial concerns most existing VM installations will have are the high costs of VM/SNA, compared to traditional VM networking; the overall complexity of VTAM and the need for SNA and VTAM technical training; as well as the possible negative impact of VTAM on overall VM performance. VTAM itself is a larger system than all of VM/SP CP and CMS combined! The training issue is very important and must not be overlooked. Recommended subject areas include:

- SNA, VTAM, and NCP Overview
- VTAM Installation and Maintenance

- NCP Installation and Maintenance
- VTAM and NCP operation for system operators
- VTAM trace analysis and problem determination (optional)
- VTAM performance and tuning (optional)
- VTAM application programming (optional; for programmers)
- VTAM and NCP internals (optional; for senior programmers)

The performance issue is installation-dependent, and depends on the type of CPU, the amount of real memory, the number of interactive users and their workload characteristics, the presence of a guest operating system such as MVS, and its workload, etc. Many of the early "war stories" from VM/VCNA installations and the early hysteria about the impact of VTAM performance on VM is quite unjustified today. While there are still copious numbers of "bugs" in the IUCV and *CCS portions of CP, and VTAM regularly has its share of problems, relatively speaking, this is nothing to be overly cautious about nor should it delay a necessary conversion to VM/SNA.

One of the major inefficiencies of running both RSCS and PASSTHRU to common network nodes is the lack of multiplexing. Under VM/SNA, all types of data are multiplexed over a single SDLC telecommunications line. VTAM becomes the central telecommunications manager, combining RSCS, PASSTHRU, and the internal CP support for asynchronous and bisynchronous terminals. VM/SNA will also relieve your mainframe of the burden of polling binary synchronous terminals. Under SNA, polling becomes a front-end processor function, which makes a lot of sense especially on smaller 4300 class CPUs. The limitation of 256 remote clusters does not exist under VTAM, and VTAM will be able to run virtually any terminal IBM makes, including sophisticated workstations.

In addition to the benefits of improved line discipline provided by SDLC, and the multiplexing of all data types on a single SDLC telecommunications line, VM/SNA also supports X.25 packet switched networks, such as TYMNET, TELENET, and Canada's DATAPAC. As well as those public networks, there are increasingly more and more private X.25 packet networks being implemented by governments and large businesses. VM/SNA supports X.25 networks through the use of IBM's Network Packet Switched Interface (NPSI), an optional software component of the 37x5 NCP.

One final consideration of VM/SNA is *future networking*. Clearly, SNA is IBM's *strategic* networking architecture, and the one system you can count on to support all their telecommunications and workstation hardware. If your company is planning some serious local area networking (LAN), LAN-to-mainframe links, or cooperative processing involving sophisticated applications which treat workstations as more than simple terminals, then you will soon require VM/SNA. Most of IBM's significant hardware and software developments in communications will likely be implemented using SNA.

Program to Program Communications: LU6.2, TSAF, and APPC/VM

Until recently, there have been two general types of communications links between IBM computers: peer-to-peer, in the style of VM/PASSTHRU VM-to-VM; and host-to-slave, in the style of a VM mainframe controlling a remote 3270 cluster. The VM peer-to-peer link connects two mainframes, running the same operating system, with the same System/370 instruction set, with the same communications software. The host-to-slave link has two distinctly different machines, running completely different "control-ware" (software on the mainframe, and firmware on the 3274 controller), with the VM side in absolute control of the communications session.

Enter the personal computer, and new opportunities and problems arise. Now we have machines similar in size and cost to the 3274 controllers, yet capable of mainframe-like computing. This is a new hybrid situation, with distinctly different hardware and machinery; with the possibility of running identical communications software, especially via mainframe emulation on the personal computer side. With local area networking, these microcomputers could have sessions between each other, without any intervention or permission from the mainframe. Further, instead of specific communications tasks on the host such as RSCS and PASSTHRU, why not allow applications to communicate with each other directly, instead of using "batch" file transfers? The microcomputer has spawned a new requirement to open up IBM communications architecture, and IBM's response is *application program-to-program communications (APPC)*.

Because SNA is IBM's strategic networking architecture, a new development such as APPC requires an SNA definition so that it fits into the SNA scheme. IBM chose to extend an earlier concept of linking two CICS systems together via a Logical Unit 6 protocol. The new APPC extension is called Logical Unit 6.2 (LU6.2), and it broadens the scope beyond CICS to any system capable of supporting LU6.2 communications, to include mainframes, System 3x, and IBM personal computers. The notion of peer-to-peer might now also be thought of as *any-to-any*, in that APPC does not link only similar mainframes, but it links similar communicators, each with an equal stature in the network, and capable of initiating sessions with any size machine, without permission from a larger machine.

At the highest levels, APPC support is available using application program interfaces (APIs), either through a series of assembler language macros, or through the Common Programming Interface for Communications defined by IBM's new Systems Application Architecture (SAA). These two APIs comprise the VM support package called *APPC/VM*. The API helps isolate the application from the specific and detailed requirements of establishing and maintaining the actual communication between programs, in that it consists of a series of commands which later translate to specific communications functions. The actual APPC communication functions take one of two paths: an SNA path, using VM/SNA and LU6.2; and the non-SNA path, using Transparent Services Access Facility (TSAF) and traditional communications media. TSAF is a virtual machine which emulates SNA LU6.2 APPC functions over bisynchronous lines and channel to channel adapters.

Because LU6.2 is implemented as (just) another SNA Logical Unit, it does not represent any major change to VM/SNA support. GCS virtual machines, representing VTAM applications, may open an LU6.2 session just as easily as a typical 3270 LU2 session. However, it was necessary to provide an interface to translate APPC/VM commands into real SNA LU6.2 requests, which was achieved by creating a new VTAM application, thus adding a new virtual machine to the GCS group, named APPC VTAM Services (AVS). TSAF on the other hand uses the same communications media types as PASSTHRU and RSCS V1 (BSC line and CTCA), making it a non-SNA equivalent to the AVS virtual machine, yet achieving the same results. In a general sense, applications written to use the APPC/VM API for communications can migrate easily from a non-SNA TSAF environment to an AVS VM/SNA environment. This is one of the goals of IBM's SAA: to isolate and remove all specific communications functions from applications.

TCP/IP for VM

TCP/IP is one of the hottest connectivity strategies available today. Although it is almost 20 years old, only in the past few years has TCP/IP "come of age," particularly in the commercial world. TCP/IP seems to be the one, if not the only, connectivity protocol which can link almost any vendor's equipment to an IBM mainframe, especially in a local area networking (LAN) environment.

TCP/IP stands for Transmission Control Protocol (TCP), Internet Protocol (IP). Basically, IP defines a way to link computers and workstations together, so that data can be properly routed between (usually) very heterogeneous systems. Once the data reaches its destination, free of errors, TCP defines how the data can be used. TCP is really a suite of several networking functions: FTP (File Transfer Protocol, such as VM's RSCS); TELNET (virtual terminal sessions similar to VM/PASSTHRU or a VTAM cross-domain logon); SMTP (Simple Mail Transfer Protocol, such as VM NOTE or PROFS); and several other minor functions for control and message passing. In other words, once IP gets your data to the proper remote system, TCP defines how it is handled.

For an IBM shop, TCP/IP does not replace SNA, but instead provides a much more realistic local area networking (LAN) protocol than trying to push SNA onto a workstation. Without TCP/IP, there would have to be a specific interface for each type of local area network. Certainly, those options do exist. If you were only interested in connecting your VM mainframe to a DECNET system, you could purchase a specific IBM-to-DEC interface package. While IBM's SNA and Digital's DECNET both appear to be comprehensive solutions, the proprietary nature of each protocol prohibits any real integration of the two, and the understandable selfish interests of each vendor will always keep them separate and distinctly different. While Open Systems Interconnect (OSI) might someday be *the* international inter-system communications protocol, it is largely experimental at the moment. In contrast, TCP/IP has a relatively long and successful history (for this industry) and has shown itself to be a widely accepted, sensible, and usable protocol, offering much of OSI's capabilities plus a proven track record. Therefore, the benefit of considering TCP/IP is that it offers connectivity to many different types of systems, and leaves your options open.

As TCP/IP popularity soared in concert with the growth of local area networks, pressure increased on IBM to develop a more comprehensive and internally-supported TCP/IP product. Also, the DACU was proving to be somewhat unreliable and slow, compared to other similar offerings from smaller vendors. Taking an early TCP/IP product, developed at the University of Wisconsin, IBM rewrote most of the original offering to provide support for the 9370 integrated LAN adapters, as well as the DACU's replacement: the 8232 LAN Channel Station. This new product is called TCP/IP for VM, and it has a product code of 5798-FAL (the product code has lent itself to the nickname FAL by which the product is also commonly known). FAL is now at release level 1.1, as many of the bugs from the initial release have been fixed.

A userid named TCPIP manages all the TCP/IP activity and is responsible the DACU or 8232 LAN attachment unit. Similar to the way the VTAM userid controls the various GCS virtual machines, this TCP/IP virtual machine is the controlling focal point for a number of other virtual machines providing TCP/IP services. Userid FTP manages file transfer requests from remote users on other systems. ARP helps the TCPIP userid resolve complex network addressing, particularly when one LAN type bridges to another (e.g., PRONET to Ethernet to Token-Ring, etc.). SMTP handles network mail, acting like a post office to distribute the mail.

Remote logons are handled centrally by TCPIP. A local user wishing to do a remote logon issues the TELNET command, which is a CMS MODULE. Similar to the IBM PASSTHRU EXEC, the user seems to "escape" from his/her current CMS session, though it actually remains connected, and any remote terminal I/O is passed through the network back to the TELNET module, which takes over the user's screen and keyboard. When the remote session ends, the user "pops" back into CMS. Remote users logging onto the local VM system are handled by the TCPIP virtual machine's internal TELNET support. TCPIP will create either an LDSF Logical Device session or a *CCS line-by-line session for those ASCII terminals which cannot use 3270 protocol conversion services.

IBM quietly offers a PC support program with "FAL" as a program feature; you really have to know it's there to ask for it! This program is used on a Token-Ring network, with Token-Ring equipped PCs, to provide a 3270 emulation program using TN3270 protocol. If you have Ethernet instead, many other vendors offer a wide variety of hardware and software to help link your Ethernet PCs and workstations to each other, and to your mainframe.

It is worth a closer look at the new 8232. The older (and now unavailable) DACU only supported Ethernet and Pronet local area networks, which left IBM without a mainframe link to its Token Ring LAN. To make that significant link, in the summer of 1987, IBM announced the 8232 LAN Channel Station (LCS) as a general-purpose high speed LAN attachment unit supporting both Token-Ring and Ethernet. The 8232 is, in fact, an industrial version of the IBM PC/AT; however, for various marketing and technical reasons, the unit was "bolstered" by using an industrial-grade version of the PC/AT, placed in a standard rack-mount chassis. Obviously, the channel attachment adapters in this PC are quite special, and distinguish the 8232 from a normal industrial PC/AT. Model 1 has one AT system unit, and Model 2 has two, the latter offering concurrent Ethernet and Token-Ring support from the same physical box. A recent presentation at SHARE by IBM claimed file transfer speeds approaching 150,000 bytes per second under optimal conditions; 90 to 100K bytes per second is more the norm.

The 8232 has tremendous potential. Because it is a real PC/AT, it can be programmed for special functions and unique applications. As well, it suggests this unit may have multiple personalities: channel-to-channel adapter, LAN attachment, etc., merely by the switch of a PC program. At present, that programming will be done only by IBM, as they are keeping the covers on specific details about the 8232. The 8232 does not run normal PC-DOS; it has its own specialized operating system.

Clearly, any connection of a non-IBM communications link to an IBM mainframe demands some attention to 3270 display emulation. Because TCP/IP has generally linked UNIX systems long before IBM's entry, there had not been a need to address 3270 emulation. Hardware and software protocol converters have traditionally provided this function for async dial-up, but the unique nature of TCP/IP demands some integrated function to provide better connectivity to IBM hosts. This was recently provided thanks to the efforts of the University of California at Berkeley, in creating TN3270, a yet unpublished TCP service (meaning no RFC exists to officially define it). TN3270 is a combination of the TELNET protocol for remote terminal sessions, and a 3270 emulation subsystem, rolled into one neatly packaged program. Typically it is obtained as a standard offering in Berkeley's UNIX operating system. However, because it is a publicly available protocol, many vendors have picked up TN3270 and integrated it into their hardware and software.

TN3270 creates or decodes 3270 data streams, and uses one or more ASCII terminal definition tables (i.e., UNIX "TERMCAP" files) to map 3270 functions to the appropriate ASCII terminal such as VT100, ADM3A, etc. Because it sends and receives 3270 data streams, it is more easily adapted to an IBM environment than using traditional protocol converters. TCP/IP's TELNET defines a mode of passing "binary data" transparently, meaning the actual 8-bit EBCDIC 3270 data is sent between IP nodes; TN3270 then does all the conversion necessary to change the data to ASCII, and perhaps add VT100 screen formatting. The protocol conversion is done outside of the IBM host, and the network traffic is optimized by using large packets of data. By comparison, the character-mode full-duplex nature of UNIX and DEC systems results in the local area network being flooded with single-character packets, which is highly inefficient. Aside from Berkeley UNIX, you can also find TN3270 implemented in various software programs for the IBM PC (DOS), the Macintosh, DEC's VMS, as well as on workstations such as SUN, APOLLO, and MASSCOMP.

The dilemma of many mixed-vendor installations is that Token-Ring is a safe bet on the IBM side, yet Ethernet is the most commonly supported LAN protocol in the mini- and microcomputer world. Like the SNA versus DECNET issue, there can only be coexistence in the end; no side wins everything. As IBM customers look at both LAN protocols, TCP/IP appears to be the one protocol which will support both Token-Ring and Ethernet, and which does not force a commitment to a particular vendor. TCP/IP is not meant to replace SNA in IBM mainframe shops. Rather, it can coexist with SNA and provide very effective local area networking, as well as micro to mini to mainframe connectivity to and from all points in the LAN.

Third-Party Data Communications Software Products for VM/SP

Protocol Converters

Because of the elegant simplicity of the Logical Device Support Facility used by VM/PASSTHRU, it is quite easy for an application to create virtual 3270 sessions. As a result, several software-only protocol conversion packages have been developed. Unlike other similar products, Simware's SIM3278 can make almost any type of ASCII terminal or PC terminal emulation package appear as a local 3278. Simware also offers PC software which makes an IBM PC or Macintosh appear as an ASCII 3278 terminal. Similarly, Relay Communications' RELAY GOLD is an excellent IBM PC communications package which provides 3278 emulation, as well as concurrent file transfer during the terminal session. The advantage of software-only systems is that they are often less expensive than hardware, especially for a large number of casual users. On PCs, extra communications layers can be added to provide an SNA-like protocol to detect transmission errors and lost blocks of data.

Outbound Access from Your 3270 Terminal

As protocol converters allow the remote ASCII terminal user to conveniently access mainframe 3270 applications, there can also be a need for a reverse connection, where the 3270 user needs to access a remote computer via a "dial-up" asynchronous connection. There are several vendor offerings for such "outbound access." TSS from Adesse Corp. and TRAX from TRAX Softworks are two VM-specific programs which allow a VM/CMS user at a 3270 terminal to dial a remote service. They do not require nor use VM/SNA services. Typically, an asynchronous line is attached to the user's virtual machine, and the vendor program takes control of both the 3270 terminal and the communications line. The actual dialing of the telephone number of the remote service can be done via an auto-call unit (a special 37x5 feature which accepts a special call-out request), a "Hayes" compatible modem which understands the "AT" modem command language, or an interface to an X.25 public network through the 37x5 or a PC dedicated to communications support. These packages usually can capture screen output to a CMS disk file.

When VM/SNA is available, and the X.25 NPSI program is installed on the 37x5, two other vendor packages support SNA outbound dial. Simware's SIM/DIALOUT and Dusquene Software's STX are VM/VTAM application programs which use the X.25 network interface in NPSI to call a specific network address. Note there is no telephone number involved, as it is assumed that your 37x5 has a direct connection to an X.25 network such as TYMNET or TELENET. Both of these programs provide *reverse* protocol conversion, allowing your 3270 terminal to appear to be a VT-100 or Hewlett-Packard terminal to a remote minicomputer.

The 9370 and Its Role as a VM Communications Front End

The 9370 comes in four models: 20, 40, 60, and 90. While not yet "PC" sized, the model 20 is about the size of a dormitory refrigerator. The other models are hardly bigger than a large refrigerator. The truly amazing packaging feature of the 9370s is that *everything* really does fit inside the single columnar unit. The 4331 was significant in that the CPU, channels, and control units all fit in a single box, but there were still a few armchair-sized DASD and tape units that had to be hooked up. Now IBM has neatly placed the DASD and tape in rack-mounted units, making the 9370 a true "office" mainframe.

The critics currently see the 9370 in two roles: a mini-mainframe addressing computing needs below the capabilities, costs, and space requirements of the 4361; and, as a significant player in IBM networking, acting as a server or communications processor. The 9370 does not appear to compete with the 3725 front-end processor. Its internal black boxes obviously contain variations on the 3174 terminal control unit (for 3270 and PC support), the 4361 Integrated Communications Adapter (for telecommunications support of async, bisync, and SDLC/SNA lines), and the 7170 Device-Attach Control Unit (for local area network and "unusual device" interfaces). Internally, the 9370 contains new I/O support systems that are as unique and perhaps as revolutionary as the integrated control units of the 4331/4361. It appears that 9370 I/O will treat the channel and control unit as one gray area, rather than the two distinct and hierarchical entities they are in the normal System/370 architecture.

The system console takes a departure from the usual 3270-like terminal found on the larger mainframes. The 9370 uses a "standard" PC/AT as the processor support console, on which the keyboard has been customized for 9370 operator functions. This PC takes the place of standard console display such as the 3278-2A.

3270 terminals, 3270-PCs, and PCs with "Irma" emulation boards connect through an integrated 3174-like control unit called the Workstation Subsystem Controller (WSC). The WSC relies on the IBM 3299 multiplexer to provide an adequate number of access ports, so that four basic "root" ports with four 3299s allow up to 32 3270-family terminals. It is encouraging to find that even sophisticated 3179/G color graphics terminals are fully supported, because earlier integrated adapters, such as the 4331 "DPA," had been restricted to text-only terminals.

Local area network (LAN) support is provided for both the IBM Token-Ring LAN and the DEC/XEROX Ethernet LAN, via a Telecommunications Subsystem Controller (TSC). The TSC also supports other traditional types of telecommunications and, thus, serves as a miniature (3725-like) front-end processor. The 9370 can also connect to other System/370 mainframes in your computer room by using an optional block-multiplexer channel. However, it does not directly offer a channel-to-channel adapter (CTCA), so the connection is made by joining into a 3088 outboard CTC coupler. For those companies with a ROLM digital telephone system, the 9370 provides ISDN connectivity to ROLM CBX via the async communications adapter. Various ROLM interface modules can be used to connect the async communications line to the CBX, allowing ROLM terminals to logon to the 9370.

The above-mentioned Telecommunications System Controller (TSC) supports traditional IBM networking. Remote 3270 terminals can connect over synchronous lines using bisync or SDLC protocol. As the 9370 is being promoted as a VM machine, the native 3270 bisync support in VM Control Program (or alternatively VM/

PASSTHRU) would provide excellent remote access with very little overhead. Connections to other VM systems will use a combination of VM/PASSTHRU and RSCS peer-to-peer links. These "native" VM favorites should be a clear choice over SNA links, based on their low overhead. Data exchange between MVS systems and the 9370 will use regular RSCS NJE/NJI connections over bisync lines, and VM/PASSTHRU can be used to connect 9370 VM terminals to MVS systems. It remains to be seen how well VM/VTAM will perform on the smaller 9370 models, such as the Model 20 and 40; in general, it would appear to be unadvisable.

What also remains unclear is the role the LAN support may provide in linking 9370s to each other and to 3725 controllers in a single building or campus location. You may see more of this in the newer technology links providing application-to-application program connectivity (APPC), where terminal types and data structures become irrelevant. A good example of this is TSAF, the Transparent Services Access Facility for VM, which provides such an APPC service. TSAF running on a 9370 will support both Token-Ring and Ethernet LANs, and it will also support SNA Logical Unit 6.2 connections. Thus, the 9370 will be able to serve as an APPC (i.e. LU6.2) gateway, bridge, or server between a local area network and an SNA network. Hopefully, in practice, such a 9370 gateway will provide very high bandwidth (i.e., speed and capacity measured in megabits per second) between PCs on the LAN and mainframes running SNA/VTAM. The current "band-aid" for such a desirable connection is a gateway PC running a 3274 emulator, linking the LAN to the mainframe at a comparatively poor data rate of 9600 bits per second.

Dial-up synchronous and asynchronous communications is supported via the TSC. I suspect that the TSC is really just a rack-mounted version of the 3174, and, thus, has all of its capabilities such as ASCII-to-3270 protocol conversion. This will eliminate the need to purchase a separate 7171 or 3708 (IBM) protocol converter unit for dial-up users. Future releases of VTAM will also support synchronous dial-up connections in the SNA network to and from 9370 processors (running VTAM of course) with auto-call and auto-answer features installed. This should allow for independent remote 9370s to link to a larger host for data exchange and support, without the need for permanent leased lines.

Finally, the increasing important area of X.25 packet-switched networking has not been forgotten in the 9370 offerings. The 9370 will support X.25 connectivity using a new release of VTAM which specifically supports the 9370's X.25 adapter. The new X.25 support in VTAM will allow SNA-to-SNA system networking over the packet-switched network, as opposed to a traditional SDLC link between two such systems.

Diagnosing Data Communications Problems in the VM Environment

Although VM's Program Event Recording facility (PER) is great for tracing the logic flow in user programs, it cannot trace the real CP operating system; thus, it is of little value when dealing with input/output problems. Looking into CP itself, one finds that all major events are recorded, however briefly, in the CP trace tables. A VM systems programmer who has read enough CP dumps gets to know the trace codes and formats quite well. Each storage "get" and "release," each scheduler call, each internal SVC, and both start-I/O and I/O interrupts are all recorded in the trace table. There are over two dozen different codes. For this discussion, we are interested in what the I/O trace entries can offer. Hex 0B codes trace start-I/Os (SIOs), where a list of channel command words (CCWs) are given to a device for various I/O operations. Hex 18 is an SIO Fast-release, a variation of SIO that assumes the hardware devices are not likely to be already busy. Hex 05 is an I/O interrupt code, which indicates the I/O request (0B or 18) is now complete and the hardware is signaling completion to CP. There are several other codes for test-I/O, halt-I/O, clear-I/O, etc. The trace entries offer limited information: the real device address; the condition code (important for SIO); and the channel status word, which gives some indication of why an I/O interrupt comes back with an error. But there is no data, nor any list of the CCWs to tell us what was being read or written to the device.

The dilemma in relying on CP trace codes is that you have to either take a CP dump (force an ABEND) or you have to work *very* fast to dump the CP trace area where these entries are being recorded. Since they exist only in memory, they often have a lifetime of one second or less, depending on how active your VM system is and how large your trace table area has been declared. Products like VM Systems Group's V/SNAP allow a CP dump to be taken without bringing the system down, which is a possible compromise. However, a CP dump represents a large and complex single snapshot of time. The real requirement is to have selected CP trace entries kept in a private area where they do not disappear.

In VM/SP Release 2, IBM implemented a CPTRAP command which allows specific CP trace entries for certain userids and devices to be collected in a spool file. Yet even with CPTRAP, you still do not seem to have enough data to solve most hardware problems. There is no CCW list, no time-stamp, and no data related to the I/O operation. For example, you do not know what the I/O operation was (such as a POLL, SEEK, SENSE, ENABLE, etc.) and you have no idea what is being read or written.

Fortunately there is an answer for this problem. It is an IBM "on-request" facility called CCWTRACE. CCWTRACE provides highly detailed tracing of the real hardware devices attached to the mainframe. The trace information helps to diagnose difficult hardware and timing problems, giving both the customer and the vendor a permanent record of the interactions between the VM operating system and the hardware. Although VM provides Program Event Recording, virtual tracing, and a CPTRAP command, CCWTRACE is in a class of its own. CCWTRACE consists of several modifications to the VM Control Program which collect detailed I/O information, as well as a CMS program which formats and prints the collected data for the systems programmer. Unfortunately, because it is not a part of the regular VM/SP product, it is unknown to many new VM systems programmers. You can obtain CCWTRACE from your IBM support center, and it comes with the usual caveat of "use at your own risk"; however, there is virtually no risk in installing or using it. CCWTRACE is not yet part of the official VM/SP product, though it may eventually be included in Release 6 or 7. The good news for VM/XA/SP is that it has a DATATRACE command which does essentially the same thing as CCWTRACE.

CCWTRACE is a privileged CP command, activated by the systems programmer, as required, which takes control of the CP tracing systems. It turns off normal tracing and uses the trace tables for its own data collection area. Thus, one drawback is that if your system "abends," the normal trace data in the dump will not be there if CCWTRACE was running. The systems programmer can trace one or more devices, along with a variable amount of data tracing. In some cases, your hunt for a bug may require maximum data tracing in the case where you believe bad data is going to the device. At other times you may be concerned more about the actual I/O operations, in a case where there may be missing interrupts, or exceptional status from the device. Once tracing is completed, the data can be formatted and printed using the CCWTRPRT CMS module, which locates and reads the real CP trace tables. The printout will show the device address, a millisecond-accurate timestamp, the channel command words, and then a variable amount of data pertaining to the I/O operation. The CCWTRACE output can then be discussed by both the vendor and the customer to review the validity of the I/O operations, the content of the data, and timing aspects of the I/O operations. It becomes a definitive record of device operation, and can prove a point for either side. In case you were wondering, CCWTRACE takes no measurable overhead during operation. My estimate is that it adds about 300 to 500 extra instructions per event, which is really insignificant on a 30XX-class processor. By comparison, simply pressing your ENTER key on a 3270 generates thousands of instructions in the VM operating system.

Normally the CCWTRACE data is placed in the CP trace tables in a circular fashion, wrapping over and over based on the number of devices being traced and their activity. For a problem that can be recreated easily, it is adequate to start CCWTRACE, produce the failure, stop CCWTRACE, and then run the CCWTRPRT formatting program. When the need arises to trace a device all day long (i.e., once a day at random a device drops off-line for no reason), CCWTRACE has an option that allows the trace information to be written to a tape drive dedicated to CCWTRACE. CCWTRPRT can then be run against the tape instead of the in-memory CP trace tables.

Appendices

Non-IBM Sources of Data Communications Information

Technical Aspects of Data Communications; McNamara, John;
   Digital Press: 1982

SNA: IBM's Networking Solution; Martin, James; Prentice Hall: 1987

Micro to Mainframe: Creating an Integrated Environment; Durr, M.
   and Walker, D.; Addison Wesley: 1985

KERMIT: A File Transfer Protocol; da Cruz, Frank; Digital Press:
   1987

Networking with TCP/IP; Comer, Douglas; Prentice Hall: 1988

Recommended IBM Manuals for Data Communications

GG22-9386: SNA Networking Product Overview
GC30-3072: SNA Concepts and Products

GC30-3073: SNA Technical Overview
GG24-1568: X.25 SNA Guide
GG24-1592: 9370 Connectivity
SC24-5287: TSAF Reference Guide
GG24-3016: IBM Asynchronous ASCII Guide
GC09-1203: IBM TCP/IP for VM Installation Guide

CP Internal Modules and Their Relation to Data Communications

DMKCNS: handles ASCII line-by-line communications
DMKGRx: handles local 3270 communications
DMKRGx: handles remote 3270 BSC support
DMKHPx: handles Logical Device Support
DMKRNx: handles 37x5 EP support (LOAD, DUMP)
DMKIUx: handles IUCV and CCS VTAM console support
DMKVCx: handles virtual 3270 console traffic and the virtual full-screen interface for CMS

About the Author

Ed Sterling is a principal founder and past president of Simware, a leading data communications software development company with a broad product line for VM, MVS, GCS, and the IBM PC. Before joining Simware, he was manager of VM Systems Programming at Bell-Northern Research in Ottawa, Canada. Ed is now vice-president of U.S. Operations for Simware and is currently developing communications software in the TCP/IP environment at Simware's Boston area office. The Simware Inc. main office is located at 20 Colonnade Road, Ottawa, Canada, (613) 727-1779.

Service Virtual Machines

by Gabe Goldberg

Introduction

This chapter describes service virtual machines, sometimes called servers, service machines, SVMs, DVMs (for disconnected virtual machines), or (less frequently) demons. They are referred to as SVMs throughout the chapter. This chapter's information facilitates evaluating and maintaining vendor products and public domain offerings which use SVMs; it also provides background, perspective, and details useful in designing and implementing SVM-based applications.

SVMs provide operating system function (security, automatic operation, terminal protocol conversion, etc.) outside the operating system (CP and CMS). The virtual machine architecture allows SVM-based functions to use rigid and well-defined interfaces to communicate with human users, other SVMs, or system services. These interfaces isolate SVM function and operation from other SVMs and system operation, providing compartmentation that improves overall system reliability. SVMs can be virtual machines with no special system privileges, which accept requests from users and return information or perform actions on their behalf. SVMs can also be highly privileged virtual machines which act as "trusted assistants" to the operating system.

This chapter begins with detailed descriptions of SMART and CMSBATCH, two common SVMs, and continues to discuss the following aspects of SVM:

- advantages
- architectural decisions
- building blocks
- input (e.g., transactions, data, system status)
- output (e.g., messages, files, actions)
- control, initialization, and termination
- performance and accounting
- maintenance and debugging
- security

The chapter concludes with brief descriptions of other common SVMs (used as examples throughout the chapter), with rules and recommendations for SVM construction and operation. A bibliography lists sources of additional information.

Advantages of SVMs

SVM functions and typical implementations include resource serialization (SQL/DS), work scheduling (VMUTIL), batch job processing (CMSBATCH), resource allocation and control (DIRMAINT), automated system operation (AUTOOP), system monitoring (SMART), CP extensions (Resource Access Control Facility, RACF), and communication (Remote Spooling Communications Subsystem, RSCS; VM/Pass-Through, PVM). Implementing operating system function outside traditional operating system (CP and CMS) boundaries offers:

Localized function protected from users: An SVM makes software available without compromising its integrity. An application executing in a user's virtual machine can be compromised by CP commands such as PER, STORE, and DISPLAY. No security or accounting based on user virtual machine software is reliable. SVM execution is impervious to user penetration, except through the SVM's interfaces. If well designed, these disallow inappropriate user actions.

Enforcement of standard interfaces: An application which executes in a user's virtual machine to control access to linked minidisks can be subverted, providing direct and unrestricted access to the minidisks. SVM-owned resources are invisible to users, and can only be acquired through SVM interfaces. SVM interfaces usually confine problems within a single SVM, preventing corrupted data from being shared with other SVMs, and keep programming errors in specialized functions from causing total system failures.

Centralized control of resources: An installation with multiple links to other sites would hardly want an operator to attach a telecommunication line to users wanting to transmit a file, confirm that transmission was complete, retrieve the line, and allocate it to the next waiting user. Similarly, it would not be practical to control access to multi-user data base resources with passwords, because authorized users would likely imbed passwords in application software. There would be periodic needs to change passwords, breaking many applications and imposing inconvenience on users. Centralized control allows a single SVM file or data repository to specify system-wide rules governing access, or granting specific user privileges. This allows the SVM owner to easily monitor and change access to SVM resources.

History

When first introduced (announced August 1972, available November 1972), VM/370 lacked many features and options, such as PVM, RSCS, remote 3270 support and more, which are now taken for granted. Even worse, tools for building virtual machine applications were limited, lacking today's VMCF and IUCV for inter-virtual machine communication, the TAG command for routing SPOOL files, the DIAGNOSE to determine virtual memory size and, not least, the capability of DIAGNOSE 8 to capture responses from CP commands for interpretation.

Many installations implemented new function in CP which today would be placed in an SVM. An example of that was RASP, a large system for sophisticated cross-processor SPOOL file communication, which imbedded file routing control in CP. While IBM initially supported remote 3270 terminals in CP, under VM/XA these terminals are controlled by the VM/Pass-Through SVM. Similarly, while some (3203 or equivalent, 3800-1, etc.) printers are directly supported by CP, the trend in printer management is more function provided by SVMs. IBM, other vendors, and users recognize benefits of SVM implementation of operating system-like functions.

Sample Service Machines

Before introducing SVM building blocks, architectures, input/output, control, and the like, it is instructive to examine two common SVMs: SMART and CMSBATCH. These are described in detail to illustrate SVM operation and interfaces. For readers not familiar with SVM concepts, the external characteristics of these SVMs illustrate the elegance, power, and flexibility of providing operating system functions in SVMs.

SMART

IBM's SMART (more formally, VM Real Time Monitor, Program Number 5796-PNA) is a widely-used tool that provides an observation window into the performance of a running CP system. SMART (the name of the monitor program and the userid in which it typically runs) is a large assembler language program that periodically samples data within CP with the privileged DIAGNOSE 4 interface (described later in this chapter), processes the data in its virtual memory, and (on demand or at predefined intervals) displays or prints it. Requests for data and commands to control operation are sent to SMART from users via VMCF (Virtual Machine Communication Facility, described later in this chapter). The program performs no minidisk I/O (after initialization is complete) and minimizes use of other CP and CMS services, to avoid affecting the system performance being measured.

While some SMART commands are non-privileged and available to all users, other commands affect SMART operation and are restricted. SMART usually executes disconnected, although it will display data on a console to which it is connected. Data is more commonly displayed on user terminals in response to specific requests. SMART can function as an early-warning system for VM problems. More than 20 key system conditions are monitored; default values and conditions are defined which can be overridden by privileged commands. SMART can detect real I/O devices requiring manual intervention, limits exceeded for values such as CPU utilization or CP overhead, disconnected and disabled users (which will automatically be forced off by CP after 15 minutes), and many other potentially dangerous conditions. Out-of-bounds values are (at a minimum) logged; SMART can also be told to notify a specific user for each condition, either by message or VMCF. Finally, SMART can be authorized to remove, from the system, users who are idle (consuming no resources) for a specified time period.

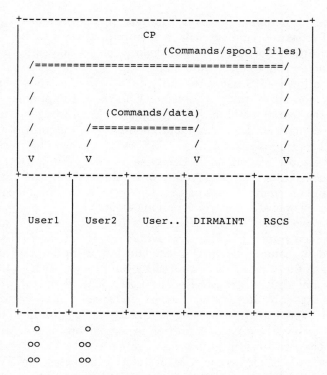

```
+-----------------------------------------------+
|                          CP                   |
|                                               |
|                       (Commands/spool files)  |
|  /==========================================/ |
|  /                                          / |
|  /                                          / |
|  /                                          / |
|  /              (Commands/data)             / |
|  /         /================/               / |
|  /        /                /                / |
|  V        V                V                V |
+--------+--------+--------+----------+--------+
|        |        |        |          |        |
|        |        |        |          |        |
| User1  | User2  | User.. | DIRMAINT | RSCS   |
|        |        |        |          |        |
|        |        |        |          |        |
|        |        |        |          |        |
|        |        |        |          |        |
|        |        |        |          |        |
|        |        |        |          |        |
+--------+--------+--------+----------+--------+
    o        o
    oo       oo
    oo       oo
```

Figure 3-1 Typical user interactions with SVMs. User1 communicates through CP spool with RSCS to send and receive files. User2 uses CP's VMCF to submit requests to DIRMAINT. Human users control the Usern virtual machines while DIRMAINT and RSCS operate disconnected.

CMSBATCH

The CMS Batch Facility is defined in the *VM/SP Library Guide, Glossary, and Master Index* (GC19-6207) as "A facility that allows a user to run time-consuming or noninteractive CMS jobs in another CMS virtual machine dedicated to that purpose, thus freeing his own terminal and virtual machine for other work." This facility, more commonly called CMSBATCH (the userid in which it usually executes) is described in the *VM/SP CMS User's Guide* (SC19-6210). CMSBATCH in this chapter refers to the facility provided with VM; several vendors (including IBM) offer enhanced batch job processors, and several improved public domain implementations also exist.

Because CMS's interactive user interface is one of its greatest strengths, the term "CMS batch" seems oxymoronic. Some CMS applications and functions, however, do not capitalize on CMS's interactivity. If executed connected to a terminal, these can be disruptive if they inhibit normal terminal tasks such as accessing personal files or responding to electronic mail.

CMSBATCH allows CMS users to "multi-task"—that is, to execute more than one computer task at a time. This is accomplished by submitting to the batch SVM a "job" (a spooled card-image punch file) containing control cards, normal CMS commands, a subset of CP commands, and (optionally) data files. CMSBATCH reads the punch file, notifies the job's submitter or designee of the job's initiation, interprets control cards, executes commands, directs output where specified by supplied commands, and provides notification of job completion. No user or operator control functions exist.

Input (source programs, object decks, data files, etc.) can be supplied in the spooled punch job file, or provided on minidisks LINKed and ACCESSed by commands in the job. Output (compiler listings, object decks, data files, etc.) can be routed by commands in the job or placed directly on a minidisk LINKed and ACCESSed writable by commands in the job. Returning output in spool files requires slightly greater overhead than placing it directly on a minidisk, but can be used whether the minidisk owner is logged on or not, and, more importantly, prevents minidisk damage caused by two userids with simultaneous WRITE access. CMSBATCH illustrates the SVM concepts of localized function (all users typically submit jobs to the same batch SVM) and defined interfaces (the batch SVM reads job files sequentially, executes commands, produces output).

Architecture

SVM architecture can be open, robust, general, and use standard interfaces. It can also be closed, fragile, over-specific, and use undocumented interfaces. These attributes are often not chosen explicitly, but are imposed by design and implementation decisions. This chapter describes CMS-based SVMs. SVM applications can also be stand-alone (run without any virtual machine operating system) or based on another operating system like MVS or VSE.

Open/Closed

An "open" SVM provides documented external and internal interfaces, and is easily extended to provide unanticipated functions. It uses structured code with minimal dependencies between seemingly unrelated functions. An open SVM may have a main function driver, triggered by arriving transactions or timer events, which invokes specific functional action routines. Localized function and formalized interfaces simplify understanding operation, and facilitate adding or removing function or changing event processing without side effects. The openness may extend to packaging, so that functions are isolated in separate files, whether EXECs or other source files.

A "closed" SVM is a black box, presenting a set of actions and functions which cannot be easily changed. SMART is a closed SVM because it was written as a single 17,000+ line assembler program, in which it is difficult to identify and change specific function.

Robust/Fragile

A robust SVM is insensitive to trivial (or larger) changes in operating environment. An SVM should not fail because it is executing on a new userid or processor, or under a new version of VM. Misadventures like a full minidisk, a virtual machine program check, or invalid command received should be noted without interruption of SVM operation.

General/Specific

A general SVM provides an engine for implementation of specific functions without itself being application specific. RSCS is general in that it supports a variety of communication functions with a single nucleus which supports protocol-specific line drivers. Most earlier communication SVMs (and some today, e.g., VM3812) required separate virtual machines and software for each communication line or protocol.

Standard/Non-Standard Interfaces

Standard interfaces are documented in IBM manuals. While sometimes changed without notice, they are an attempt to create a formal definition of services and protocols which applications can use. Examples are: command syntax, message responses, and DIAGNOSE code parameters. SVMs should, as much as possible, use only standard interfaces.

Non-standard interfaces include direct use of data from operating system control blocks and undocumented side effects of standard system services. SVMs sometimes must acquire information not available from a defined interface, perform an action not supported by standard facilities, or rely on continuation of undocumented system behavior. Use of these non-standard interfaces makes an SVM (or any other application) vulnerable to IBM changes. Therefore, their use should be explicitly documented and grouped in one or a few modules to simplify future maintenance. SMART's use of DIAG-NOSE X'4' to read CP storage is a standard interface, but its interpretation of CP control blocks and vulnerability to changes in CP is a non-standard interface.

Types

Different SVM characteristics satisfy different operational requirements.

Connected/Disconnected

"Connected" refers to virtual machine execution with a real terminal (virtual machine console). "Disconnected" describes execution with no virtual machine console. Most SVMs execute disconnected since their purpose is hands-off automation. Disconnected SVMs are usually LOGged on with the AUTOLOG command, though they can be LOGged on and then disconnected. Disconnected SVMs should execute with console spooling started and directed to the SVM owner or (better) an SVM central repository for console files (see LOGFILE, in the list of example SVMs).

In special cases (e.g., critical service provider, debugging, monitoring security violations) an SVM may execute connected. An MVS guest, for example, may execute connected to simplify operational tasks. Special care is needed to prevent a terminal MORE or HOLD-ING condition from blocking execution or delaying desired output. Public domain CP enhancements, which provide flexible handling of MORE and HOLDING, are available from sources such as VMSHARE and the University of Waterloo (see Acknowledgements and Resources, at the end of this chapter).

Always/Sometimes Logged On

An SVM can be logged on whenever VM service is offered, at certain time intervals, or only on demand. Most SVM services (e.g., terminal access, file transfer, data base functions) are expected to be constantly available. SVMs like these are usually AUTOLOGged by AUTOLOG1 or another system-initializing SVM when CP is IPLed. See AUTOLOG1 for a description of CP and SVM startup.

Some SVMs (e.g., a private SQL data base server) may be best logged on only when needed, to avoid their holding unused resources. This can be accomplished manually, by requests to or instructions for the system operator. It can also be accomplished by time-of-day processing by another SVM, or even by allowing any user who knows the password to AUTOLOG a requested SVM. AUTOOP, described in the list of example SVMs, provides time-of-day processing and a straightforward means of making AUTOLOG an unprivileged command. A userid which is LOGged or AUTOLOGged periodically to execute a predefined application with no external interactions is a disconnected batch job rather than an SVM.

Synchronous/Asynchronous

Synchronous communication requires that requestor wait for the SVM response. Synchronous communication is simple, requires minimal handshaking, and is relatively impervious to the user's virtual machine environment. On the other hand, it tends to be application-specific and (should be) limited to servers that respond quickly. Synchronous execution couples the requesting user to the SVM until the requested function is complete. During this time, the requesting user's virtual machine is dedicated to waiting for completion and cannot perform any other tasks. SMART's synchronous execution provides mostly instantaneous execution of commands. For this reason, when the SMART SVM is hung (logged on and partly functional, but not able to process requests), issuing a SMART request can hang a user's virtual machine. SVC and DIAGNOSE requests are synchronous, in that the issuer waits until the requested function completes.

Asynchronous communication uncouples the requestor's execution from the SVM response. Asynchronous communication is more general in nature and can be extended to support new applications. It is, however, more complex than synchronous communication, requiring overhead and handshaking transactions. It can be affected by changes in the user's virtual machine environment. Asynchronous execution allows a request to be submitted and normal interactive tasks to continue, with the SVM providing notification when the request is complete. CMSBATCH's asynchronous execution allows users to submit jobs without regard for the number of jobs awaiting execution. CMSBATCH notifies the person who submits a job when it starts and ends execution. The CP MSG command is asynchronous, in that it completes instantly for the sender, but the message will not be displayed until the target user's terminal is available (i.e., not in MORE/HOLDING state or in full-screen mode).

Single-Thread/Multi-Thread

An SVM's level of "threading" is the number of transactions it can handle simultaneously. Threading is a synonym for "tasking," the number of tasks in simultaneous execution. Most simple SVMs like CMSBATCH and SMART are single-threaded. This requires arriving transactions to be queued until preceding transactions have completed. SMART transactions take hardly any time, so SMART appears to handle all requests instantly. An installation with a single CMSBATCH SVM and many users submitting jobs may find that queue length and service waits become unacceptable. Since CMSBATCH is, architecturally, single-threaded, a solution can be to create multiple batch servers (with different userids, of course). Users can then be allocated to a particular server or servers, or another SVM can be created to receive batch jobs and route them to available servers.

Most SVMs that provide end-user functions like protocol conversion, file transfer, or data base access (VM/Pass-Through, RSCS, and SQL/DS) are multi-threaded. Up to a point, this provides better overall service. However, if an SVM is too overloaded, maintaining task queues and internal dispatching can be costly. A tradeoff would be to provide a maximum level of multi-threading, after which transactions are queued and wait for previous transactions to complete.

Building Blocks

Programmable Operator (PROP)

PROP, part of VM, can automate VM operation by intercepting messages and requests directed to its virtual machine and handling them according to preprogrammed actions. PROP commonly runs in the system operator's virtual machine to log selected messages, filter (ignore) common informational messages, and act on designated commands from authorized users. PROP activity is controlled by a routing table, a CMS file containing user authorizations, command definitions, and option specifications. Action routines are programs or EXECs invoked by the match of a message and a routing table entry. PROP can also be the foundation of non-system operator transaction-based applications.

REXX

REXX (Restructured EXtended eXecutor), also called the System Product Interpreter, is the language of choice for many CMS applications. Replacing the older EXEC and EXEC 2, it is particularly suited for command procedures (EXECs), user defined XEDIT subcommands, prototyping, and general personal computing. Similar to PL/I, it has extensive debugging facilities.

CP SET xxxx IUCV

Several classes of virtual machine console output (CPCONIO, EMSG, IMSG, MSG, SMSG, VMCONIO, and WNG) can be retrieved via IUCV. This allows programs to intercept and act on messages or interruptions generated by their own or other virtual machines.

EXECIO

EXECIO is a general data transfer utility frequently used in SVMs. It reads from disk or reader files to the program stack or EXEC variables, writes from the program stack or variables to disk or spool files, and executes CP commands with optional retrieval of resulting output.

Interrupt Handling

Interrupts are asynchronous events presented by CP. Since SVMs typically run disconnected, the assorted facilities for manually interrupting a virtual machine from the terminal (PA1, PA2, HX, HT, CP ATTN, etc.) are not available. Other virtual machine interrupts (program check, IUCV, VMCF, external, I/O, etc.) may occur as part of normal operation or errors. SVMs must handle anticipated interrupts without interfering with normal virtual machine operation and must avoid or not be damaged by error interrupts. Interrupts can be processed at a low architectural level (by replacing a new PSW with an SVM-specific PSW), an intermediate level (with interrupt-specific macros), or a high level (capturing results of an interrupt without dealing with the interrupt protocol).

PSW Manipulation: The PSW (Program Status Word) is 64 bits of information which represent and control virtual machine execution and status. An interrupt causes the current PSW to be saved and a new interrupt-specific PSW to be loaded. It has been traditional to manipulate appropriate PSWs to direct specific interrupts (I/O, external, etc.) to application-specific interrupt handlers. This is no longer advisable for two reasons:

Many more flexible facilities have been added (assembler language macros, commands, language facilities, CMS subroutines) that are easier and more reliable to use.

Complex SVMs use interrupts for multiple communication tasks or paths and use diverse interrupt types. PSW manipulation can disrupt this coexistence.

CMS Macros:

HNDEXT — traps external interrupts and passes control to a designated routine.

HNDINT — traps interrupts for one or more specified I/O devices and passes control to designated routines.

HNDSVC — traps interrupts for one or more specified SVC instructions and passes control to designated routines.

WAKEUP and SUPERMSG: These commands simplify SVM interrupt handling. They suspend virtual machine operation until a designated event occurs. WAKEUP is part of IBM's VM/IPF product which is described later. It can detect and report time-of-day and time interval events; or console, external, I/O, VMCF, IUCV, and unit record interrupts. Options control interrupt processing and reporting. Since multiple events and interrupts can be awaited simultaneously, WAKEUP resumes execution when the first specified event/interrupt occurs, indicating what resumed execution. WAKEUP is used by the IPF VMUTIL SVM machine for event processing.

SUPERMSG is a command available on the Waterloo Tape. Written by Barry Leiba at IBM Gaithersburg, it intercepts terminal output through the IUCV *MSG system service. CP SET command options direct some or all virtual machine console traffic (messages from other users, warnings from other users, error and informational messages, CP console output, virtual machine console output, or SMSGs) to *MSG, to be retrieved by SUPERMSG and processed by an EXEC or program. Output can be retrieved from commands (e.g., LISTDS, MACLIB, TXTLIB, etc.) which do not have a STACK option. SUPERMSG includes sample applications, documentation, and source code.

CP Spool Commands

Many SVMs process, are driven by, or create spool files. CP commands which manipulate VIRTUAL spool resources (files or devices) are CHANGE, CLOSE, DEFINE, DETACH, FREE, HOLD, NOTREADY, ORDER, PURGE, QUERY, READY, SPOOL, SPTAPE, TAG, and TRANSFER. A general-user virtual machine can use these commands to manipulate files and devices which it owns. Operator command privileges are required to affect non-owned resources. Privileged CP commands which manipulate REAL spool devices are BACKSPAC, DRAIN, FLUSH, HALT, LOADBUF, LOADVFCB, QUERY, REPEAT, SPACE, and START.

VM/Interactive Productivity Facility (IPF)

IPF, IBM Program Product Number 5664-318, provides interactive panels and utility programs. Only the utility programs are of interest in this chapter. Its commands supplement those of CP and CMS, providing such functions as DCSS backup and restore, and spool file manipulation, without loss of printer carriage control. It also includes WAKEUP, described above.

Virtual Machine Communication Facility (VMCF)

VMCF, part of CP, lets a virtual machine exchange data with other virtual machines without performing I/O. It is commonly used by SVMs to receive requests from and return answers and data to users, though is it obsoleted by IUCV. VMCF includes data transfer and control functions, a special external interrupt code, and a special external interrupt message header.

Inter-User Communications Vehicle (IUCV)

IUCV, part of CP, lets a virtual machine communicate with other virtual machines, CP system services, and itself. It is the tool of choice for programmed exchanges of data between SVMs and clients. IUCV functions create and dismantle communication paths, send and reply to messages, receive or reject messages, and control the sequence of IUCV events.

VM/SP and HPO DIAGNOSE Codes

In general, CP creates virtual machines by emulating real hardware facilities (i.e., equipment that exists in the real world, even if not on a particular VM system). An exception is the DIAGNOSE facility, used by virtual machines to request CP services. (When executed on the real CPU in supervisor state, the DIAGNOSE machine instruction controls REAL hardware configuration and diagnostic functions.) DIAGNOSE instructions are sometimes called "hypervisor calls," since they request service from CP, the system hypervisor. The CP module that handles DIAGNOSE services is, therefore, named DMKHVC. DIAGNOSE instructions are often used in SVMs to communicate with CP, request CP services, or to extract CP information. The DIAGNOSE instruction has no assembler language mnemonic, and thus must be created with

DC X'83xycccc'

instructions or macros such as DIAG, supplied in CMSLIB MACLIB. "83" is the DIAGNOSE operation code and "cccc" is the 4 hexadecimal digit (DIAGNOSE codes are always identified in hex) DIAGNOSE code. DIAGNOSE codes are multiples of 4. IBM reserves DIAGNOSE codes 0 - FC (hex); installation-defined DIAGNOSE functions start at 100. A subcode parameter selects a function for DIAGNOSE codes, such as X'14', which perform multiple functions. Not all DIAGNOSE codes are used. Sometimes a function (or particular subcode) is implemented only on some VM versions, so the associated DIAGNOSE code is missing from other VM versions. The x/y digits identify virtual machine registers which contain parameters for the DIAGNOSE code. Some codes use more than two register parameters by defining the contents of the "x+1" and "y+1" registers. DIAGNOSE codes can return data in registers or in virtual storage addressed by registers; status information is available in the PSW condition code after execution.

Some DIAGNOSE codes can be executed directly from REXX programs, with appropriate notation for supplying parameters and receiving answers. While many DIAGNOSE functions are available to all users, some are restricted to users with particular command privileges. Execution of a privileged DIAGNOSE without proper privileges results in a virtual operation exception (program check); invalid DIAGNOSE parameters may cause virtual specification, protection, or addressing exceptions.

Release 5 DIAGNOSE code information is provided in *VM / SP System Facilities for Programming* (SC24-5288). If the "User Class Restructure" facility has redefined privileges required for DIAGNOSE codes, the command class requirements listed in the manual may be misleading. The CP COMMANDS command displays the commands and DIAGNOSE codes available to a user. The following list of DIAGNOSE codes includes those defined up through Release 5; codes X'A0' and above are new in Release 5.

DIAGNOSE 0 — retrieves information about the CP version, real CPU, and userid in use. This facilitates writing robust SVMs.

DIAGNOSE 4 — examines real CP storage, and is used by SVMs that monitor CP status or performance.

DIAGNOSE 8 — executes a CP command and (optionally) retrieves any response. This is a common way for SVM software to change the state of its virtual machine or the real system, communicate with users, or interrogate CP.

DIAGNOSE C — stores timer information and is used for generating SVM accounting, performance, or statistical data.

DIAGNOSE 10 — releases virtual memory pages, signaling CP that the contents of specified areas in virtual memory are no longer needed, allowing CP to free corresponding real memory or paging areas.

DIAGNOSE 14 — manipulates reader files, a common source of SVM input transactions or data.

DIAGNOSE 18 — performs standard DASD I/O, and is primarily used by the CMS file system.

DIAGNOSE 1C — clears error recording cylinders, and is used by software that processes hardware error data.

DIAGNOSE 20 — performs general I/O, and is primarily used internally by CMS.

DIAGNOSE 24 — returns virtual I/O device type and features, and facilitates writing SVMs that handle a variety of I/O devices.

DIAGNOSE 28 — modifies executing channel programs, typically in teleprocessing applications.

DIAGNOSE 2C — returns the DASD location where LOGREC (the hardware error log) starts, and is used by software that processes hardware error data.

DIAGNOSE 30 — reads one page of LOGREC data, and is used by software that processes hardware error data.

DIAGNOSE 34 — reads a system dump spool file, and is used by dump processing software.

DIAGNOSE 38 — reads the system symbol table, and is used by software that monitors real CP memory.

DIAGNOSE 3C — updates the VM directory, a common SVM function.

DIAGNOSE 40 — cleans up after virtual IPL by device, not usually needed by CMS-based SVMs.

DIAGNOSE 48 — issues SVC 76 from second-level VM, and is not usually needed by CMS-based SVMs.

DIAGNOSE 4C — generates accounting records in various formats, often used by SVMs to place accounting information in the CP accounting file.

DIAGNOSE 50 — saves a 370x control program image.

DIAGNOSE 54 — controls operation of the PA2 key, not usually needed by CMS-based SVMs.

DIAGNOSE 58 — controls the 3270 virtual console interface, and is used more by single-user screen intensive applications than SVMs. In Release 5 the CMS CONSOLE macro provides a similar function.

DIAGNOSE 5C — edits error messages, and is used to customize by user whether an entire message, a message code, a message text, or no message is to be displayed.

DIAGNOSE 60 — determines virtual machine storage size, and should be used if an SVM requires a particular minimum size for execution.

DIAGNOSE 64 — manipulates named segments (DCSSs), and is used by individual applications to acquire and release resources.

DIAGNOSE 68 — controls the Virtual Machine Communication Facility (VMCF), one of the common communication techniques between virtual machines.

DIAGNOSE 6C — requests shadow table maintenance for guest MVS virtual machines.

DIAGNOSE 70 — activates the time-of-day clock interface for a guest operating system virtual machine.

DIAGNOSE 74 — saves or loads a 3800 named system.

DIAGNOSE 78 — controls MSS (Mass Storage System — 3850) communication.

DIAGNOSE 7C — creates and manipulates logical devices. Logical devices are program-created 3270 sessions and are often supported by both specialized and generalized SVMs.

DIAGNOSE 80 — controls the 3081 Monitoring and Service Support Facility (MSSF).

DIAGNOSE 84 — updates the directory in-place, a common SVM function.

DIAGNOSE 8C — returns device-dependent information about terminals, for use in screen formatting.

DIAGNOSE 94 — requests a dump of virtual storage, and is used by SVMs for tracing or (more commonly) after a severe problem.

DIAGNOSE 98 — is a privileged function to manipulate real channel programs.

DIAGNOSE A0 — returns the ACI (Access Control Interface) group to which a user is assigned in the system directory with the ACIGROUP statement. IBM's RACF product adds subcodes to DIAGNOSE A0, and uses group membership to evaluate logon, link, and spool file requests.

DIAGNOSE B0 — retrieves diagnostic information for a virtual machine under the "protected application facility" (that is, with SET CONCEAL ON in effect) being reIPLed. This DIAGNOSE, typically executed in the application's PROFILE, returns the reason for reIPL, such as "disabled wait PSW," "paging error," or "shared page altered," along with supplemental information such as a specific PSW or the name of the shared system whose page was altered. Under VM/SP Release 6, DIAGNOSE B0 also retrieves the issuing user's IPL statement from the system directory.

DIAGNOSE B4 — controls "external attribute buffers" (XABs) associated with virtual printers. XABs, used by AFP (Advanced Function Printing) products, contain arbitrary information to be used in processing spool files; an XAB is copied to a spool file when the file is closed. IBM suggests use of a standard XAB layout to allow coexistence of IBM and other vendor products, along with local applications.

DIAGNOSE B8 — controls XABs associated with files.

DIAGNOSE BC — opens the next file of the correct class for the specified virtual reader and returns information on the file to a buffer. If a file is already open on the device, information on it is returned. This DIAGNOSE is similar to, but more structured than, DIAGNOSE 14.

DIAGNOSE C8 — selects a national language for CP messages by storing the address of the language's message repository in the issuers VMBLOK.

DIAGNOSE CC — saves a CP message repository in space allocated by a NAMELANG macro in CP module DMKSNT.

DIAGNOSE D0 — tells CP the volume serial (VOLSER) of a volume mounted on a 3480 tape device which is attached to the issuer. The VOLSER will be recorded in I/O statistical or error information.

DIAGNOSE D4 — lets a privileged virtual machine specify a worker machine userid and an end-user machine for whom the worker will act. The worker machine can then imitate or act for the end-user machine.

DIAGNOSE D8 — (HPO Release 5 only, because of major changes to spool support) returns SFBLOK information for all files, regardless of what user or queue (reader/print/punch) they belong to.

DIAGNOSE DC — under VM/SP Release 6, defines a buffer within a service virtual machine which CP will sample and record in system monitor data.

DIAGNOSE E4 — returns information about another user's minidisk or dynamically defines a full-pack minidisk.

VM/XA SP DIAGNOSE Code Changes

DIAGNOSE codes 1C, 2C, 30, 38, 50, 6C, 78, 84, 98, B4, B8, C8, CC, D4, and D8 are not available in VM/XA SP Release 1. Some of these will be added as XA function evolves to the level of VM/SP and HPO, while others will not be carried forward. SVMs now being implemented should avoid dependence on function not committed to XA.

The following codes are unique to XA at the time of writing:

DIAGNOSE 44 — notifies the VM/XA SP scheduler that a spin lock exists in a virtual machine and to signal voluntary time slice end.

DIAGNOSE 90 — returns the address of a specific symbol in the system symbol table.

DIAGNOSE A4 — performs synchronous I/O in either 370- or XA-mode to a disk device used by CMS and supported by VM/XA SP.

DIAGNOSE A8 — performs synchronous I/O in either 370- or XA-mode to all fully supported devices except channel-to-channel adapters and consoles.

DIAGNOSE C4 — creates, deletes, and validates class override system data files, and uses them to override the privilege class structure.

DIAGNOSE E4 — only returns information about another user's minidisk.

Some DIAGNOSE functions are changed subtly from SP/HPO to XA. Refer to documentation when developing SVMs for multiple environments.

HPO/XA Spool Structure and Function

Under VM/SP with HPO and VM/XA SP, each user may have (subject to limitations of checkpoint and storage space) up to 9900 spool files. Under earlier systems, 9900 spool files could exist system-wide. CP commands that manipulate spool files accommodate this change by disallowing the SYSTEM option with a spool file number, and class D command responses displaying a six digit number when referring to the system-wide number of files changed, purged, queried, or transferred. Programs which parse command responses or examine spool file control blocks will need modifications to support new structures.

System Services

System services are a special form of IUCV that provide communication between virtual machines and CP. They allow SVMs and CP to present asynchronous messages to each other, and support a reasonably high transaction rate. For example, CP uses *RPI to request authorization from an access control SVM such as RACF or ACF2 for LOGON, LINK, and other resource-related transactions. CP functions required by installation-written SVMs can be added as new system services. CP module DMKIUC contains a table of system services, and DMKIUB lists modules which support system services. System service names begin with "*" to indicate communication with CP instead of another virtual machine.

*BLOCKIO — provides device-independent access to minidisks with support for multiple concurrently pending I/O requests.

*CCS — (SNA Virtual Console Support) provides VM console capabilities to SNA terminals through a VTAM service machine (VSM) that acts as an interface between an SNA network and CP.

*CRM — allows an authorized virtual machine to connect to the Collection Resource Management System Service and become the TSAF virtual machine.

*IDENT — allows authorized TSAF virtual machines to identify themselves to CP as resource owners and to revoke resource ownership.

*LOGREC — lets an authorized virtual machine receive a copy of records written to the CP Error Recording Area.

*MONITOR — is a VM/XA system service which provides system performance and resource utilization data to an SVM. It replaces spool files or tape volumes for data collection.

*MSG — allows incoming messages and responses from CP to be read by a program instead of being displayed on a user's terminal.

*MSGALL — receives incoming messages in classes not directed to the *MSG system service.

*RPI — provides a communication path over which an access control SVM (RACF, ACF2, etc.) can receive requests and return authorizations and rejections.

*SIGNAL — allows members of a virtual machine group to signal each other.

*SPL — lets an authorized virtual machine handle logical printer functions.

Some system services are of most use to IBM-provided software (*CCS and *CRM), some may be used by IBM and non-IBM software (*IDENT, *RPI, *SIGNAL), and some are of great use in IBM and non-IBM SVMs (*BLOCKIO, *LOGREC, *MSG, *MSGALL, *SPL).

Input Transactions

Input transactions can be categorized by source (where they originate) and type (how they arrive at the SVM). Some SVMs handle multiple transaction sources and/or types.

Sources

Timer: Powerful SVMs exist which are driven purely by the passage of time. SMART is an IBM SVM which gathers system statistics and verifies system status at predetermined intervals. Several commands (described in the "Building Blocks" section) allow applications to suspend execution until a specified time is reached. To guard against invalid calculations causing too-soon or too-late execution, or execution resumed by extraneous interrupts, timer-driven SVMs must verify the time when execution resumes. Timing anomalies such as leap year, the year 2000, and repeated execution at the same time of day should be considered. Timer-driven SVMs should allow "escape" from application code without requiring LOGOFF or CMS reIPL.

System Status or Events: An SVM connected to CP via a system service must react asynchronously to events or changes in system status. For example, a member of a virtual machine group must respond to *SIGNAL input, and an SVM supporting logical printers must respond to *SPL input. Most SVMs which appear to be driven by system status or events (system spool occupancy too high, a critical userid disconnected and disabled, CP free storage extended, etc.) are really timer-driven to interrogate and report their area of interest.

User Requests: User requests are functions invoked by a user at a terminal or a user-initiated process. Under VM/SP Release 6, a user accessing Shared File System (SFS) resources will generate implicit requests to the SFS SVM. User input (as opposed to input generated by an application front-end or automatic process such as SFS) requires thorough validation.

Types

Virtual Machine Interrupts (I/O, Timer): SVMs written in high-level languages (EXEC2, REXX, PL/I, C, etc.) cannot handle interrupts directly, but use tools such as WAKEUP or the VM/SP Release 6 Callable Services Library. Assembler language SVMs can either use these tools or handle interrupts directly with appropriate CMS macros. The technique of replacing virtual machine new PSWs with application code PSWs ("PSW stealing") is largely unnecessary (should be avoided for XA compatibility) with availability of standard interrupt handling facilities provided by the HNDxxx macros described earlier.

Secondary Console: The Single Console Image Facility (SCIF) allows a user (or SVM) to control one or more disconnected SVMs. The controlling (secondary) user uses the CP SEND command to provide console input to (primary) SVM(s). Console output from primary SVMs is prefixed with the originating userid. While SCIF is a limited interface (only one userid can be the secondary console for a given SVM), it allows one userid to control multiple SVMs. The controlling userid can, in fact, be automated, submitting transactions with SEND and receiving responses and asynchronous primary user console output with a combination of CP SET CPCONIO and SUPERMSG (see "Building Blocks") or equivalent. A disadvantage of SCIF is that secondary users must be defined in the system directory.

User Requests (MSG, SMSG, VMCF, IUCV):   User requests can be detected immediately by one of the interrupt-handling programs described in "Building Blocks."

Spool Files: The CP spooling system was the first communication path between virtual machines. Spool files are easily understood, created, transmitted, detected by an SVM, read, and purged. Transactions in spool files are automatically queued by CP in an SVM's virtual reader, independent of the SVM's status or activity level. This allows asynchronous transaction creation, processing, and purging. CMSBATCH receives transactions—batch jobs—in spool files. Spooling, however, can cause system overhead out of proportion to the amount of data transmitted; creating and purging even small spool files causes the system spool checkpoint to be updated. Spool files are an adequate input mechanism for low-volume SVMs which need not provide crisp response.

Spool file arrival can be detected immediately by one of the interrupt-handling programs described in "Building Blocks." The originator and characteristics of spool files should be validated; files can be processed immediately or queued for later handling. Alternatively, if an SVM need not react instantly to arriving files, a timer-driven SVM, which checks for new spool files periodically, will probably serve.

Problems can be caused by spool files not arriving as expected (if an SVM looks for files while spool is being backed up by SPTAPE, which makes groups of spool files invisible while they are processed) or arriving in the wrong order (if spool files are restored by SPTAPE or the system is started CKPT).

Dialed-In Terminal: Function is sometimes provided by multi-user SVMs which handle user terminals as dedicated or DIALed devices. A user-written alternative to SMART, CPWATCH (available on the Waterloo Tape) provides CP performance information to terminals which DIAL the CPWATCH SVM. Interactive end-user computing is provided by systems such as MUSIC and AIX/370 to users whose terminals are connected to the appropriate SVM instead of being logged on to VM. In these cases, other than providing SVMs with virtual machine functions and supporting connected terminals, CP is not involved in handling SVM input or output transactions. This technique provides perhaps the most secure implementation of SVM function, because a user connected to the SVM is completely under the SVM's control and cannot directly invoke any CP or CMS functions to escape or subvert the SVM application.

Validation

Input provided to SVMs must be validated to prevent accidental or deliberate abuse of SVM applications.

Source: The source of transactions must be reliable. An application front-end executing in a user virtual machine can be used to impersonate another (perhaps more highly privileged) user. Use CP identification of the sender of VMCF, IUCV, SMSG, and spool file transactions, rather than information provided by the user's virtual machine.

Function: Unknown function types must be detected, rejected, and logged. Even a minimal SVM must filter commands based on SVM-specific specification of privileges.

Data: Similarly, all other aspects of input transactions must be validated. An SVM must detect invalid command syntax, conflicting options, and invalid data types without any problem (e.g., program check or EXEC branch error). Transactions containing invalid information should be rejected and logged, rather than partially processed or repaired.

Output

Most SVMs provide some form of output, rather than simply accepting user input with no resulting action or feedback.

Actions

SVM actions range from running a batch job (CMSBATCH or MVS), creating a logical terminal session (VM/Pass-Through), or executing a time-of-day set of commands. An SVM should provide the requesting user confirmation of action taken and results accomplished. Certain actions should be reported to the system operator or other authority, in the form of messages, electronic mail, or audit files.

Responses

Responses include reports of actions taken, data base output, and answers to queries on system behavior. The form in which responses are provided (VMCF/IUCV transactions, message, message-noheader, spool file) should be tailorable on a system-wide or individual user level.

Files

Data provided by SVMs should be available as spool, minidisk, or SFS files, as alternatives to programmed interfaces like VMCF/IUCV. Data in files can be processed at user convenience, and permits asynchronous requests and output processing.

Validation

Most SVMs validate input transactions only, assuming that acceptable input transactions will produce proper output. An extremely sensitive application could post-process output to ensure that actions taken, responses issued, and files transmitted were appropriate to the environment (userid involved, day of week, time of day, system load, etc.).

Initialization

SVM initialization should ensure that the environment is correct and understood (minidisk configuration and space available, virtual machine size, virtual and real devices, other required SVMs) before beginning to accept transactions. Some adaptation may be required; for example, buffer allocation may depend on virtual machine size. If conditions are incorrect and cannot be corrected, an SVM should report initialization failure and log off or at least reject arriving transactions with, of course, messages explaining the problem to transaction submitters. An SVM should guard against repeated failures to initialize in a short time interval. SVM console activity should be collected by issuing:

CP SPOOL CONSOLE START

A specialized use of an "internal file" (described later) during initialization is a "profile" capability. An SVM profile is similar to a user's PROFILE EXEC or XEDIT, which are executed after CMS IPL or when entering a file in XEDIT. Instead of being processed directly by CMS, the SVM profile is read by SVM application code during SVM startup. An SVM profile can execute CP and CMS commands, and execute an initial set of SVM commands to start communication links, define virtual I/O devices, synchronize action with other SVMs, and perform other SVM-specific actions. The SVM profile is distinct from the SVM's PROFILE EXEC, which can also issue CP/CMS commands but cannot perform SVM-specific functions.

It is inefficient to allocate multiple SVM minidisks, each of which contains nothing but an SVM-specific PROFILE and, perhaps, a few additional files. A single minidisk can serve as several SVM's 191 disk, by controlling execution of the (one) PROFILE EXEC with the userid under which it is executed. This is especially useful for managing multiple SVMs which run the same software, or groups of otherwise related SVMs. Under VM/SP Release 6, an IPL command option can direct CMS to execute a PROFILE from an SFS file pool, which eliminates the need for SVM 191 minidisks.

Parameters used (by default or specified at startup) should be logged. Userids identified as owning or monitoring the SVM should be notified of startup, any problems, and availability for service. Some SVMs may need to recognize whether they are being restarted under a running VM system or being started as part of normal system startup. This can be done by passing a special parameter during system bringup, or by the SVM comparing its log-on time with CP IPL time.

Operational Control (Parameters and Commands)

All but the simplest SVMs require some amount of operational control; for example, identification of privileged users, definition of communication nodes, choices of problem handling techniques, or specification of spool file classes to handle. Initial and changed parameters and date/timestamps of parameter files should be logged in an SVM audit trail. Any means of providing parameters and commands to an SVM should allow inclusion of comment lines beginning "*" which will be ignored by the SVM. SVM parameters can be provided in a variety of ways, with differing amounts of flexibility.

At Startup

Simple parameters (e.g., spool file class) can be provided on the CP AUTOLOG command which starts an SVM. The command:

   AUTOLOG SPOOLER FEB31 EXEC SPOOLPRG CLASS P

would start an SVM called SPOOLER, with password FEB31, and execute SPOOLPRG with parameters "CLASS P." The EXEC would presumably parse and act on the parameters. This technique is most suitable for a "private" SVM which is occasionally logged on by an individual user. It is too error-prone to be appropriate for "system" SVMs which must be reliably started with specific options. In addition, if SVMs are started by a set of AUTOLOG commands (perhaps executed by AUTOLOG1), changing parameters can be burdensome and unauditable.

External Commands

Parameters can be specified on commands accepted from authorized users. These commands (often sent by SMSG) can be handled by normal transaction processing in the SVM, and can take effect immediately. The command:

   SMSG RSCS START LINKWEST CLASS Z

tells an RSCS SVM to process class Z files on communication link LINKWEST. All commands and, for most SVMs, all transactions should be logged. Since SQL/DS and PROFS servers do not accept external commands, it can be difficult to automate their operation. The combination of Single Console Image Facility (SCIF) and Programmable Operator (PROP) can allow authorized users to submit commands to these and other SVMs. PROP, running in the OPERATOR virtual machine, can detect messages from users submitting SVM commands and use routing tables and action routines to validate authorizations. Valid commands can be submitted to SVMs through SCIF.

```
CP SLEEP 10 MIN
&STACK VMC SMART SET LOGM 1 ON USER OPERATOR LIMIT 1
&STACK VMC SMART SET LOGM 6 OFF USER OPERATOR LIMIT 1
* USERS TO NOT FORCE WHEN IDLE -- KEEP ALPHABETICAL
&STACK VMC SMART SET ULIST AUTOSP AMSBATCH DATASETE
&STACK VMC SMART INTERVAL DISPLAY 3
```

Figure 3-2 Sample external SMART initialization commands. These commands, executed from a privileged user, set SMART SVM options because SMART has no "profile" capability.

Internal Commands

Internal commands are executed from SVM-owned files. These files specify actions to take at SVM startup, specified intervals, or particular times of day.

External File(s)

External files exist on non-SVM minidisks linked Read/Only. If an SVM reads parameter files from the minidisk only at startup or upon command, parameters in external files are easy to change.

An authorized user can change files and signal the SVM to reACCESS the minidisk and read and process the parameter file. (The reACCESS is required for the SVM to obtain the minidisk directory as updated by the user.) This puts the new parameters into effect with no interruption in SVM availability. If the minidisk is Read/Only but the SVM cannot be told to process new parameters during operation, changes will take effect only when the SVM is restarted. If continuous operation of the SVM is not critical, it can be FORCed and AUTOLOGged.

```
CP ATTACH 708 RSCS 308
CP SPOOL CONSOLE START TO CONSAVE
START F4000
START HPLASER
```

Figure 3-3 Sample RSCS initialization PROFILE. This file provides commands executed only at initialization.

```
00 23 SPOOL CONSOLE START CONSAVE
00 00 CLOSE CONSOLE
00*23 AUTOLOG SERVLOG1 CHAIRLEG RESTART
00 23 AUTOLOG OUTFO TABLEA
*****************************************************************
* Daily backup runs Monday night thru Friday night         *
* Execution days are Tue-Sat since command runs at midnite *
*****************************************************************
00 00 2 AUTOLOG BACKDOWN TABLEA DAILY 580
12 12 R CMS EXEC QDROPERS
```

Figure 3-4 Sample AUTOOP command file. This file contains commands executed at specified times of day. The columns of numbers indicate the first and last hour of the day in which the commands should be executed. An asterisk between the columns indicates that a command should be executed every hour in the range; otherwise, the command will only be executed once, either when AUTOOP is started or when the time range arrives.

Internal files

Internal files exist on SVM minidisks. If the parameter minidisk is accessed Read/Only, parameters can be handled as if they were in external files. If the SVM accesses the disk Read/Write, files can only be changed from the SVM (with normal operation interrupted) or from another userid with the SVM logged off.

Imbedded in Code

SVM options should not be specified in SVM software, whether it is an EXEC or compiled language. Such options can only be changed by taking the SVM out of service, and such changes blur SVM maintenance history.

Reconfiguration and Maintenance

Ideally, it should be possible to completely reconfigure or apply maintenance to an SVM without disrupting service. This is, in practice, usually impossible. Some reconfiguration can be done by externally changing parameters as described earlier. Allowing an SVM to execute CP and CMS commands at the direction of authorized users provides an added degree of external control permitting, for example,

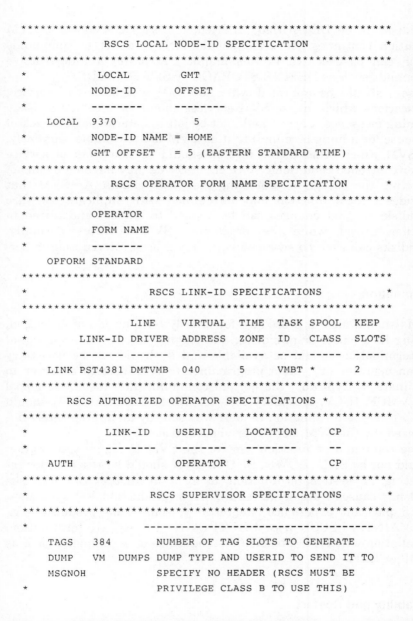

```
*************************************************************
*               RSCS LOCAL NODE-ID SPECIFICATION           *
*************************************************************
*           LOCAL        GMT
*           NODE-ID      OFFSET
*           --------     --------
   LOCAL  9370            5
*           NODE-ID NAME = HOME
*           GMT OFFSET   = 5 (EASTERN STANDARD TIME)
*************************************************************
*               RSCS OPERATOR FORM NAME SPECIFICATION      *
*************************************************************
*           OPERATOR
*           FORM NAME
*           --------
   OPFORM STANDARD
*************************************************************
*                   RSCS LINK-ID SPECIFICATIONS            *
*************************************************************
*               LINE    VIRTUAL  TIME  TASK SPOOL  KEEP
*       LINK-ID DRIVER  ADDRESS  ZONE  ID   CLASS  SLOTS
*       ------- ------  -------  ----  ---- -----  -----
   LINK PST4381 DMTVMB  040       5    VMBT *      2
*************************************************************
*     RSCS AUTHORIZED OPERATOR SPECIFICATIONS *
*************************************************************
*           LINK-ID    USERID     LOCATION    CP
*           --------   --------   --------    --
   AUTH    *           OPERATOR   *           CP
*************************************************************
*                   RSCS SUPERVISOR SPECIFICATIONS         *
*************************************************************
*           ------------------------------------
   TAGS    384       NUMBER OF TAG SLOTS TO GENERATE
   DUMP    VM   DUMPS DUMP TYPE AND USERID TO SEND IT TO
   MSGNOH            SPECIFY NO HEADER (RSCS MUST BE
*                    PRIVILEGE CLASS B TO USE THIS)
```

Figure 3-5 Sample RSCS Version 1 parameter file. This file is processed at initialization to determine the number and type of communication links, users authorized to control RSCS, and other options. Lines beginning "*" are comments.

minidisks to be DETACHed, LINKed, or reACCESSed while SVM execution continues. An SVM should include a list of commands which can be executed in this manner, excluding self-destructive commands such as DEFINE STORAGE or SET ECMODE.

Users should be informed when an SVM will be out of service; applications which invoke SVM services should be disabled or issue warning messages. Users should not be left to determine from lack of response (or a hung terminal) that an SVM is unavailable. Similarly, an SVM which other SVMs rely on should be taken out of service under controlled conditions, since client SVMs may have no means of detecting the outage or protecting their own clients. An SVM that provides critical function may be defined with duplicate software minidisks so that changes can be applied to one set and tested in another userid while the production SVM operates normally. Minidisks can then be swapped with only a brief interruption in service.

Termination

SVMs should have a procedure for orderly termination of operation, closing files (spool or minidisk), and logging off. An external signal for termination should be available and it should not be necessary for an operator or system programmer to reconnect to a server to terminate it. Typically, the normal communication technique (spool file, VMCF, IUCV, secondary console) will be used; the SVM should verify that the termination request was sent by an appropriately authorized (by the SVM, not CP privileged) user.

The command or function sent to the SVM to signal termination should not be SHUTDOWN. SHUTDOWN should be reserved for requesting CP system termination; using it in another context risks (and has caused!) accidental shutdown of production VM systems—not a pleasant experience. Regrettably, some IBM products (e.g., DIRMAINT, RSCS) use SHUTDOWN to signal termination; installation-written SVMs should standardize on a command such as STOP or EXIT.

Reliability and Restart

Disabled Wait

Program checks in critical CMS modules, some CMS file system errors, paging errors, and program interrupt loops cause CMS to load a disabled wait PSW. This stops virtual machine execution and prevents any internal (timer interrupts, etc.) or external (user requests, I/O interrupts, etc.) event from causing it to resume. Nothing can be done within a virtual machine to prevent or recover from disabled wait conditions. The SMART SVM, however, can be instructed to monitor critical SVMs and, if they become DISConnected and disabled, notify the system operator or other designated user. SMART can notify another userid of such conditions via VMCF, which allows automatic recovery by FORCEing and reAUTOLOGging the disabled SVM.

Program Check

Through programming or data errors, SVM software can encounter program checks or other application ABENDs. Normal CMS processing of these conditions results in program execution ending and a read being issued to the virtual machine console. These actions are fatal to an SVM. The CMS ABNEXIT macro can establish an exit routine which receives control in the event of an application ABEND. This exit can log the problem, collect diagnostic information, take corrective action, and either restart the SVM or (in the case of unrecoverable problems) log it off. OS macros STAE and SPIE are also available for intercepting SVM application failures, though native CMS macros such as ABNEXIT are preferred.

Disk Full

An SVM which creates or maintains disk files (even if only for log, audit, or accounting data) may fail if a minidisk fills. Minidisk occupancy must be monitored at time intervals or when transactions start or complete. If occupancy is too high (or, alternatively, if not enough space remains free), an SVM should recover space by erasing or compressing files or (as a last resort) temporarily storing files in CP spool. Any of these actions should be reported to the system operator and other appropriate users. If no minidisk space can be recovered, an SVM should cease operation before a minidisk fills completely, since errors writing to full minidisks can corrupt data.

Missing/Invalid/Duplicate Input

SVMs can encounter problems with internal data, such as control files, or external data, such as spool files. All assumptions about data should be validated; no data should be trusted without validation.

The unexpected must be anticipated and handled. Required files will not always arrive, or will arrive in the wrong order, or will be duplicated. An SVM must ensure the correct origin, time/date, size, data type, and other attributes of data files. The data type of information provided must be verified. Within an installation, standard facilities should be used for controlling and processing SVM files, to ensure consistency and facilitate implementation of new SVMs.

Conceal

The SET CONCEAL ON command or CONCEAL directory option instruct CP to "protect" a virtual machine. In a protected virtual machine, terminal activity such as attention or break key interrupts will not enter CP, a disabled wait PSW will result in an automatic virtual machine reIPL, and CP will attempt to continue execution if a shared memory page is altered. Protecting an SVM greatly increases the reliability of the service it provides.

Notification

SVMs should automatically report problems they encounter to the proper authorities, typically the system operator and one or more persons responsible for SVM maintenance. If the list of userids to be notified is stored in a CMS "NAMES" file, an SVM can use the TELL or SENDFILE commands to notify one or several users simultaneously. In many cases both commands should be used: TELL provides immediate notification with a message; SENDFILE provides an electronic note if a user to be notified is not logged on when a problem occurs. As an external file, the NAMES list can be changed without impacting the SVM, though the SVM must reACCESS the minidisk containing the NAMES file to ensure that the most current copy is used. Alternatively, if problem messages only appear on an SVM's console, the system operator or other userid running PROP can be made a secondary SVM console with SCIF. Messages can then be handled or redirected by PROP action routines.

Debugging

Detect Being (Re)connected

SVMs that handle errors by dumping their virtual machines and/or logging off or reIPLing should detect when they are operating connected and suppress normal error handling. When operating connected, SVMs should report errors to the virtual machine console and enter a debugging mode where virtual machine activity is displayed on the console. SVM commands should be provided to end debugging mode and to begin disconnected operation.

Console

An SVM's spooled console file is often the most useful tool for problem analysis. All SVMs should start console spooling early in initialization. When many SVMs are used, printed console logs become burdensome. A simple SVM can receive and archive spooled console files so that they need not be printed but remain available for debugging. The archiver can maintain several days or weeks of console files, erasing files as they age or as storage disks fill. The benefit of the archiver SVM can be increased by having all SVMs close their consoles at least once a day, so that in case of a system failure, console files covering many days or weeks will not be lost.

Performance

SVM performance can affect overall system behavior and response to individual SVM transactions.

Measurement

The load an SVM places on the system can be observed from any VM performance monitor (SMART, VMMAP, etc.) or reported by the SVM itself. An SVM can use the CP QUERY TIME command periodically to determine its resource consumption, and responses can be recorded with SVM activity statistics to measure the resources used by specific or average transactions. By timestamping input and responses, an SVM can measure elapsed time for user requests. Statistics can be useful in reporting service levels to users or countering complaints about service unavailability or delays.

Tuning

SVM performance can be affected by external factors to and within the SVM. An SVM cannot deliver satisfactory service if it is denied adequate CPU, I/O, or memory resources. A critical SVM (typically, one on which interactive users depend) on a heavily loaded system

must be designated for improved processing. CP commands SET FA-
VORED, SET PRIORITY, SET RESERVED, SET QDROP OFF, and
LOCK can improve SVM performance but can degrade operation of
other virtual machines. Critical SVM minidisks can be cached to improve I/O service.

Internal SVM operation can be changed to minimize resource demands. SVM software can be made resident (to avoid repeated fetch-
ing from minidisk) with EXECLOAD and NUCXLOAD. SVM applications can be implemented or operated with performance in mind:
databases can be compressed or reorganized periodically; data files
can be retained in virtual memory to avoid repeated reads, since CP
paging is much more efficient than minidisk I/O.

Security

Audit Trail

An SVM's spooled console log can be an audit trail if the SVM logs
arriving transactions, actions performed, and problems. It has disadvantages of not being directly under the SVM's control, being at risk
of CP spool difficulties, being somewhat free-form, and occupying
more space than needed. CMS files are a more efficient and accessible location for an audit trail, allowing fixed-format data to be stored
compactly. An audit trail is useful only if it is used; exceptions (errors, access violations or attempts, etc.) should be highlighted to
allow easy manual or automatic detection.

Command Authority

At least two classes of authority should be defined: general user and
privileged. Only privileged users should be able to invoke functions
that reconfigure an SVM or affect other users' service or data. Complex SVMs may require multiple levels of authorization.

SVM-specific authorization should be required for privileged SVM
functions, rather than granting SVM privileges based on CP command privileges (as SMART does). If privileges are granted to users
designated in the system directory as members of an ACI group, an
SVM can use DIAGNOSE X'A0' to verify group membership. If users
can request an SVM to issue CP commands (and this should be carefully considered and implemented, since it can compromise SVM

integrity), destructive commands (LOGOFF, DEFINE STORAGE, some SET options) must be disallowed. In addition, checks must be made for illicit execution of multiple commands in a single transaction, for example, by imbedding X'15' (the line end character) in a CP command.

Accounting

SVMs should gather transaction and resource consumption information to allow charging for service. Even if SVM service will not be charged, planning for or actually gathering accounting information greatly simplifies charging later.

DIAGNOSE X'4C'

This facility places information in the CP accounting file. It integrates SVM and other accounting data in time sequence, and can simplify processing of aggregate data.

Internal

Instead of, or in addition to, placing SVM data in the CP accounting file, SVM data can be kept in SVM-managed storage (minidisk or SFS). This simplifies detailed analysis of an individual SVM's data, but can complicate integration into system-wide reporting. In addition, SVM retention of the data requires space management and, ultimately, disposition of data to avoid space exhaustion.

More SVM Examples

IBM

AUTOLOG1: AUTOLOG1 is one of the very few userids known specifically to CP. When CP is IPLed, AUTOLOG1 is AUTOLOGged if it is defined in the system directory. A PROFILE EXEC on AUTOLOG1's A-disk can serve as a system-wide PROFILE, AUTOLOGging assorted other SVMs and issuing CP commands. After the PROFILE completes, AUTOLOG1 can log off or remain available as an SVM.

DIRMAINT: The VM Directory Management Program Product, more familiarly known as DIRMAINT, manages the VM system directory. It can automate directory changes, including minidisk allocation and password maintenance.

PVM: VM/Pass-Through provides terminal connectivity between VM systems or between VM and MVS or VSE systems. It allows VM terminals to log on to remote VM, VSE, or MVS systems.

RACF/VM: RACF enforces security access rules for LINK and LOGON commands.

RESLIM: The VM Resource Limiter (RESLIM) is an SVM-based IBM product that automates computer load management functions and detects and reports situations requiring intervention. RESLIM periodically examines system and user-specific resource consumption, and applies rules to ensure proper resource allocation.

RSCS: Remote Spooling Communication Subsystem (RSCS) provides file transfer services between VM systems or between VM and MVS or VSE systems.

SFS: Under VM/SP Release 6, CMS files can be stored in Shared File System (SFS) file pools, in addition to traditional personal and shared minidisks. Each file pool is owned and managed by an SVM which processes user and administrator requests.

SQL/DS: Structured Query Language/Data System (SQL/DS) is an IBM data base management system implemented as an SVM. SQL/DS provides data sharing between users, multiple concurrent updates, different views of data for different users, access control, and data recovery. SQL/DS servers communicate via IUCV.

VMUTIL: VMUTIL, part of IBM's VM/IPF product, is a general time-of-day event processor. It is controlled by the WAKEUP module with a parameter file giving specific actions to perform.

Non-IBM

Accounting: Accounting data is usually collected and processed by an SVM (the alternative being manual interactive processing, an unreliable technique). While collection techniques differ between VM/SP (and HPO) and VM/XA SP, the issues are the same. Accounting data often represents data center revenue, and must be reliably processed. At the same time, this function is overhead, and so must be done as efficiently as possible. Processing usually consists of accepting arriving data immediately to avoid risk of loss, and batching it for later reporting.

AUTOOP: AUTOOP, available on the University of Waterloo Tape, provides system and user event scheduling, centralized control of I/O resources, and general-user AUTOLOG command. System events are defined in an internal file, and can be executed at specified hours and days of the week. User events can be scheduled up to a year in advance. A table of shared I/O resources authorization allows users to acquire I/O devices without operator intervention, including tape drives during unattended operation. Requests are submitted to AUTOOP in spool files.

Error recording: Hardware error information is captured by CP. Under VM/SP and HPO, it is written to CP owned DASD space and can be monitored as it is collected by an SVM via the *LOGREC system service. Under VM/XA SP it is only available to an SVM, which must record it for later processing. This processing, similar to that of accounting data, is controlled by the RECORDING command.

Dump processor: While dump analysis is not yet suitable for automation, some dump-related tasks may be implemented in an SVM. The destination userid for dump files is specified in VM module DMKSYS. If this is not an individual's userid, dump files can collect without being noticed, especially on systems which are sometimes unattended or which can take a dump without restarting. If the dump destination userid is periodically AUTOLOGged, it can detect newly arrived dump files and alert the proper staff. New dumps may be processed automatically with data extraction tools to provide basic problem determination information and load the dump onto disk before manual analysis begins.

LOGFILE: Many installations have implemented a LOGFILE SVM to receive, process, archive, and dispose of SVM console files. At its simplest, LOGFILE simply reads all reader files it receives onto disk, assigning fileids to facilitate retrieval (for example, the sending SVM's userid as filename, the date/time as filetype). More elaborate functions include compression, grouping arriving files in disk files by day or week of arrival, and analyzing the content of console files.

Special Examples

GCS: Group Control Subsystem (GCS) is a virtual machine supervisor. It manages subsystems (SVMs) that support a Systems Network Architecture (SNA) network. SVMs in a GCS group can share common read/write virtual memory and communicate with each other. Some GCS-based SVMs are VM SNA Console Support (VSCS), which lets SNA network terminals be virtual machine consoles; and Remote Spooling Communication Subsystem (RSCS) Version 2, described above.

MVS: MVS is IBM's "other" major operating system. While sometimes used without VM, it often operates as a virtual machine under VM. See the chapter "VM and MVS Working Together" for a description of MVS as a VM guest.

SRPI: CMS can provide a different kind of service machine when connected to a PC providing host services to it. Enhanced Connectivity Facilities (ECF) is a method for sharing resources between personal computers (PCs) and 370 computers. The Server-Requestor Programming Interface (SRPI) allows PCs to access host servers.

TSAF: The Transparent Services Access Facility (TSAF) provides access to SVM resources within a VM processor or across VM processors. The TSAF SVM handles communication between systems by letting APPC/VM (Advanced Program-to-Program Communication/VM) paths span VM systems.

Future Developments

Many new interfaces for SVMs have been created in the last few years. VMCF, IUCV, SMSG, TSAF, and GCS are all relatively new VM terms. New facilities will continue to be introduced, primarily (as always) to support IBM function and products, but will be available, as well, for non-IBM innovation.

Intra-system interfaces (VMCF, IUCV, spool files) are well understood and widely used. Cross-system facilities such as TSAF, however, have yet to be exploited. Cooperative and distributed processing are just beginning to reach production applications. Perhaps ECF and SRPI will replace the multiplicity of techniques now used for PC-host communication and cooperation. Interfaces such as TSAF, SRPI, and ECF will be better understood and may be the foundation for enterprise-wide applications and applications that capitalize on the best aspects of PC and host architectures.

Rules and Recommendations for SMV Construction

1. Do not rely on software executing in user virtual machines for security, accounting, or data integrity.
2. Do not grant users SVM privileges based on CP command privileges (as SMART does); require SVM-specific authorization for privileged SVM functions.
3. Create open, robust, general SVMs that use (when possible) standard interfaces.

4. Localize and document any non-standard interfaces used.
5. Verify SVM environment attributes and any required resources during initialization.
6. Begin spooling the SVM console early in initialization.
7. Consider XA architecture in SVM development and maintenance.
8. Validate the identity of clients and verify any assumptions about data received in user transactions.
9. Provide complicated or critical SVMs with duplicate software minidisks to simplify applying maintenance and testing.
10. Gather statistics on SVM transaction service times for capacity and performance analysis, or for evaluating user complaints about SVM availability and performance.
11. Gather transaction and resource consumption information to allow charging for service.

Bibliography

William T. Fischofer: presented SHARE session O615 on "CP Support for Hidden Servers" in July 1985.

Gabriel Goldberg: presented SHARE session B623 on "Automatic Operator and Modified CMSBATCH" in March 1982.

Gabriel Goldberg: presented "COUNTER—A Data Collector" at the 1983 VM Wichita Workshop.

Gabriel Goldberg: presented SHARE session O557 on "Automating Software Operation and Data Collection Under VM" in August 1987.

John Nolan: presented SHARE session B867 on "Use of the Programmable Operator Interface (PROP) as an Operator Interface" in August 1984.

Michael Roegner: presented SHARE session O611 on "VM: May I Be of Service" in March 1987.

Linda Tyler and John Dooman: presented SHARE session O672 on "Can SQL/DS Run (Well) on VM?" in August 1988.

Michael Wagner: presented SHARE session O558 on "Using the Programmable Operator in Service Virtual Machines" in August, 1986.

T. D. Wilson and T. E. Potok: presented SHARE session O601 on "VM Service Machine Performance" in March 1987.

IBM manuals for VM/SP are listed. Other VM versions (VM/SP HPO, VM/IS, VM/XA SP) are described in equivalent manuals.

VM/SP Library Guide, Glossary, and Master Index (GC19-6207): explains the organization of, and provides a master index to, the VM/SP library; contains a glossary of VM terms.

VM Real Time Monitor (SMART) PDOM (SH20-2337): describes operation and installation of IBM's SMART SVM.

VM/SP Using Release 6 Enhancements (SC24-5369): provides a detailed description of changes to VM/SP function and use introduced in Release 6. It will be withdrawn after all manuals are updated with Release 6 information.

VM/SP CMS Shared File System Administration (SC24-5367): documents (for VM/SP Release 6) management and control of the SFS.

VM/SP CMS User's Guide (SC19-6210): provides information and examples regarding the CMS file system, CMSBATCH, XEDIT, and REXX.

VM/SP CMS for System Programming (SC24-5286): provides system programming details about CMS functions such as interrupt handling, storage maps, assembling and executing programs, creating commands and message files, and simulation of OS services.

VM/SP CMS Command Reference (SC19-6209): describes privileged and general user CP commands.

VM/SP CMS Macros and Functions Reference (SC24-5284): describes CMS assembler language macros and functions.

VM/Interactive Productivity Facility System Reference (SC24-5321): describes IPF modules and EXECs of use in building SVMs.

VM/SP System Facilities for Programming (SC24-5288): describes VM facilities such as IUCV, VMCF, DIAGNOSE instructions, CP system services, and programmable operator. It is intended for system programmers and others with experience in assembler language and programming concepts and techniques.

VM/SP CP Command Reference (SC19-6211): describes CMS commands.

VM/SP CP for System Programming (SC24-5285): is a reference for system programmers who implement and extend CP functions.

Acknowledgments and Resources

SHARE is a leading national group for users of IBM computers. It provides a framework for formal, informal, technical, and introductory presentations. Much of the information in this chapter was gathered at SHARE; and the technical review of the chapter took place at SHARE. Call (312) 822-0932 for membership information.

The University of Waterloo collects and distributes VM tools and enhancements in the form of the University of Waterloo Library. The University also distributes Workshop Tools Tapes. SUPERMSG and AUTOOP, mentioned in this chapter, are available on the Waterloo tape. Call Jack Hughes at (519) 888-4621 for information.

VMSHARE is a world-wide bulletin board devoted to VM topics. Used by VMers with a variety of skills and experience, it is a place to get fast answers to questions and a forum for sharing VM experience. Many VMSHARE users provided information used in this chapter.

The Annual VM Workshop is usually hosted by a university. Volunteer staff coordinates local arrangements, housing, and transportation. The technical program is coordinated by other VM community volunteers. Attendees give presentations on various topics of current interest, including contributions to the "tools tape," a collection of public domain utilities, application systems, and VM enhancements. The tools tapes contain many facilities useful in constructing SVMs.

Reviewers helped shape this chapter and avoid technical and logical pitfalls. Special thanks to John Foley, Dave Gomberg, Tom Kumpf, Barry Leiba, Pat Ryall, Jeff Savit, and Phil Smith.

About the Author

Gabriel Goldberg is the Director of Technology with VM Systems Group, responsible for product planning, development, and support, in addition to internal computer operations. VMSG develops and markets data center and end-user software for VM installations. Before joining VM Systems Group, he was a senior member of The MITRE Corporation's technical staff. His involvement with VM began at MITRE in 1972, when he coordinated conversion from MVT to VM; he has been a VM enthusiast ever since. Before joining MITRE, he worked in IBM's OS System Design Department in Poughkeepsie, New York. Gabe has consulted for clients such as The World Bank, The University of California, and the Association for Computing Machinery. He obtained a B.S. degree in mathematics in 1968 from The Polytechnic Institute of Brooklyn.

Gabe is active in many IBM user groups; he is a founding member and elected director of MVMUA (Metropolitan New York VM Users Association, the oldest and largest local VM user group), a member of the Hillgang (Washington, DC, area VM user group) steering committee, and has held several offices in SHARE (a major national IBM user group), most recently serving as CMS Project Manager. He has given dozens of presentations to these and other groups and contributes regularly to various trade journals.

Gabriel Goldberg
Director of Technology
VM Systems Group
901 S. Highland Street
Arlington, VA 22204
(703) 685-1314

B

Optimal VM Performance

Keeping the operating system running at peak performance requires close attention to the three areas that are discussed in Section II: I/O management, problem diagnosis, and maintenance.

I/O management is a critical performance consideration in the VM environment, with multiple users and operating system guests all competing for a slice of the CPU. Kim Cooper's "VM I/O Management" (Chapter 4) first discusses I/O issues from a unique VM perspective, followed by a practical approach to managing I/O in the VM environment. Cooper also discusses I/O as it relates to VM performance.

Accurate problem diagnosis, and subsequent resolution, can be a deciding factor, not only in whether the system runs at its peak, but whether it runs at all. Jim Bergsten's "Problem Diagnosis in VM" (Chapter 5) focuses on the process of operating system debugging. Bergsten describes major problems that can occur, such as system crashes, and presents potential solutions. Bergsten also discusses the use of the VM dump and other tools for debugging the VM system.

Maintenance is a key to assuring the integrity of the VM system and is a basic task of the systems programmer. In "VM Maintenance" (Chapter 6) Jeff Savit describes both methodology as well as an overall strategy for maintaining VM's CP and CMS components. Savit provides practical guidelines for the installation of new VM releases and fixes.

4

VM I/O Management

by Kim Cooper

Prologue

Many papers have been written on the subject of VM I/O. Managing the I/O subsystem is a large topic due to the varied genre of application. Some of the environments using VM as a vehicle include PICK/370, AIX, MVS/SP, and VSE/SP.

Many view the CPU as driving the I/O in the system. I approach this concept a little differently. Using the analogy that a CPU is like a car engine that runs on fuel and that data is the fuel that drives the CPU, then the I/O subsystem becomes the driver of the CPU.

I have included information not readily available in manuals, and glossed over the more available information, since the manuals go into greater detail than can be presented in this writing.

In excursions to different companies, I have witnessed a lot of approaches—some failures and some successes. I wish I could take credit for the information we have gathered; unfortunately, in many cases I can't even give credit where it is due. I have asked directors for permission to use their names and have been denied that permission.

I believe that my viewpoint, as an employee of a hardware vendor, tends to vary slightly from other software technicians. This writing carries a slight complexion of a hardware person. I certainly don't believe the solution to every problem (bottleneck) is hardware, quite the contrary. I'm hoping that the reader will find this viewpoint refreshing rather than offensive. Naturally, I've weeded out any vendor bias (right!).

The scope of this discourse will involve the DASD I/O subsystem. Topics covered include an introduction to the I/O subsystem, what components make up the time involved in providing the data to the processor, how VM massages the data before handing it to its guests, and some basic information on the I/O infrastructure of VM/SP/HPO itself. Some performance issues are addressed, as well as some performance management techniques as they relate to the I/O subsystem.

Storage subsystems get a lot of attention these days with IBM touting their SMS. It is obvious the I/O subsystem is moving off the CPU and out to other devices. The migration is analogous to that of the 3705, a processing subsystem that removed polling and many network control functions from the mainframe CPU and placed them outside of the system. The 3705 helped revolutionize teleprocessing. We are seeing the same event. Some of IBM's non-compatible vendors are already marketing a database driving processor to isolate that function and optimize parallelism.

Some of the technological changes that have occurred in the past three years put VM into a unique position. To be sure, the lean VM code is eclipsed by the massive synoptical paths of the MVS system; but both systems are capable of taking advantage of the I/O processors that exist outside the main computer and still within the computer complex.

At this writing we are gently easing into the era of quad porting. For those of you new to data processing, dual porting, the ability to transfer data concurrently from any two actuators on a string, was an innovation provided by PCM vendors in the early years and capitalized by IBM with their DLS (Device Level Selection) feature. This feature was purported to increase efficiency by 5–15%, depending on the environment. Today we are looking at four concurrent transfers simultaneously from solid state PCM DASD or the new IBM 3900-2 and by the time this publication is released we will see cached four path transfer.

Although this paper deals with VM software, I am addressing the matter from the perspective of hardware. Software is the taskmaster of hardware—software provides us with the ability to easily capitalize on hardware features. Knowing the hardware we are trying to maximize is necessary to properly capitalize on the resource.

There are four primary groups of DASD:

1. Cached rotating storage
2. Semiconductor DASD
3. Rotating storage
4. Optical Disk

Each type of storage media has its own performance and economic position in the hierarchy of peripherals. Using the analogy of the CPU being an engine that needs fuel (data) to run it, then fuel or data is being provided by a carburetor or channels. For those who are less mechanically inclined, the carburetor mixes air with fuel and controls the flow of that mixture into the engine. Some carburetors are very small and spray little fuel-air mixture into the cylinder(s). Often designers put two barrels into carburetors, allowing for reliable transfer of greater amounts of fuel—all the way up to the three deuce carburetors of the late sixties (six barrels all together).

Different fuel apparatus contribute to the productivity of an engine in their own economic/performance niche. There are turbo chargers that force air into the engine for a greater boost than the vacuum created by the engine. Additionally, electronic fuel injection allows for smoother response from the engine.

The purpose of these variations is to allow us to better utilize the same engine. By upgrading the fuel system we can make our existing engine run more efficiently and produce more power.

The same tenet holds true in computers. Our primary concern is to drive the machine to its maximum potential. By doing this we have absolutely no concern for fuel economy as it is more expensive not to feed the machine faster.

Obviously, in our analogy the data is the fuel. It is our responsibility, as technical people, to get the data into the machine at the highest possible rate. Instead of barrels we have channels (with the exception of expanded storage, which is still classified as an I/O device). The more channels, the more concurrent I/Os we can push into the machine simultaneously. There are fast channels such as in the NAS processors, transferring at 6MB per second, or the 4.5 M transfer of the IBM 3090, or the three megabyte rates of the older machines, down to the 1.8 and below found on the 4300 series processors. There are also byte channels, which transfer at 100 kilobytes per second.

The transfer rate has different degrees of importance, depending on the type of data. Examine swap data. Swapping is the block paging of selected pages grouped by USERID. Swapping allows for faster page transfer but there is the likelihood of more page movement than would take place by paging strictly as needed, or on demand.

Swapping is often specified to 19 pages at a time. The reason for this is that, on 3380 equipment, 10 pages fit onto one track. On IBM's 3380s there isn't time to switch heads; thus, it costs one revolution if the second I/O doesn't have a one page delay. This doesn't seem to have been a problem on the 3350s.

During the swapping process, a "lot" of pages is transferred with one I/O and the "hard" functions of the device are a smaller percentage of the overall time. Swapping need not be on a semiconductor device to gain its benefit, as the transfer time is the greatest component of I/O time and rotating devices transfer just as fast as semiconductor devices (on 3MB channels).

Let's review the components of I/O time. I/O time is comprised of the instruction time required to process an I/O, combined with the channel speed, or how much data can be transferred in a given unit of time. This is combined with the parallelism, or the number of channels the system has, and then combined with device characteristics such as access arm motion speed and rotations per minute. Finally, this amount is combined with CPU dependent factors such as the size and speed of the memory into which the data will flow.

First we must deal with the instruction time it takes the processor to process one I/O. In the XA world, these instructions are minimized by placing the I/O instructions into the channel subsystem and performing a start subchannel from the operating environment. XA systems (VM and MVS) need only be generated with a device specification. The path are all handled by the I/O subsystem, which is specified in the IOCP.

Keep in mind that processors like the 4381 and 4341 with integrated channels are hybrid systems. These systems do not have totally separate channel processors and must perform these functions by interrupting the CPU processing. This can be a performance problem. IBM has documented the performance ramifications of the channel interference in the 4381 Channel Characteristics guide.

Many are unacquainted with the fact that the only place that data can be manipulated by the instruction processor is in the processor's high-speed buffer. The high-speed buffer, or cache, is similar to the chamber in the automobile engine. The chamber is where the gasoline and air mixture combine for combustion. It is in the high-speed buffer that memory speeds are high enough to feed the instruction processor. This special, very high-speed memory. Naturally, the more of this memory there is, the faster the processor can obtain data from the storage subsystem.

Moving out from the processor, and the memory and channels, we have devices hanging on the system. It would be nice if all of our data were in main storage, but as of yet (and I suspect this will be shortlived) memory is much too expensive and volatile to keep real data. So the data that feeds the processor must reside on either rotating devices (disk or tape) with intelligent memory to pre-buffer the data, or solid memory.

Let's keep the data portion of this discussion away from cards. I am familiar with a lot of data centers that still maintain their operations around card readers and card punches. They are not by design, and I hope to see them done away with shortly. Teleprocessing equipment can serve to feed the CPU, but I would consider this mostly in the control function. Teleprocessing paths rarely exceed 56 kilobytes per second, a processor simply could not be overwhelmed by these small amounts of data.

The primary components of I/O time exist outside the central processing unit. What are the components that make up the time it takes for an I/O to reach the channel? First, the rotating disk devices must do a seek to access the data on the disk. All disks (except 3370/75s) spin at 3600 revolutions per minute. This may seem fast until you consider that race car engines typically max out somewhere around 10,000 revolutions per minute, and have much more complex internal mechanisms. The heads of the disks, however, tend to move at approximately the same speed. There are some design differences, but in general, it appears the limits of this technology have been reached.

Some vendors have been using linear actuators (piston-like movement), others have been using a rotary arm (like a phonograph arm). The fact is that seek time runs in a range from 11ms to 17ms in the 3380 compatible world.

When dealing with seek times we want to minimize the distance seeked, the total number of seeks, and maximize seek overlapping. Seek overlapping is the ability to start seeks down multiple paths to multiple devices; then return and "scoop up" our rewards in incoming data. When examining seek times, refer to the hardware vendors' specifications.

After the seek, we wait for the data to come around to the head. The time is easily calculated. Based on 3600 revolutions per minute, it takes 16.7 milliseconds for the disk to rotate. On the average, logically, we wait 8.2ms (1/2 of a full rotation) for the data. Remember, on a 3370/75 device we deal with a 22.2 millisecond rotation.

Surprisingly enough, neither seek nor latency (formerly referred to as rotational delay) are the greatest components of the time involved

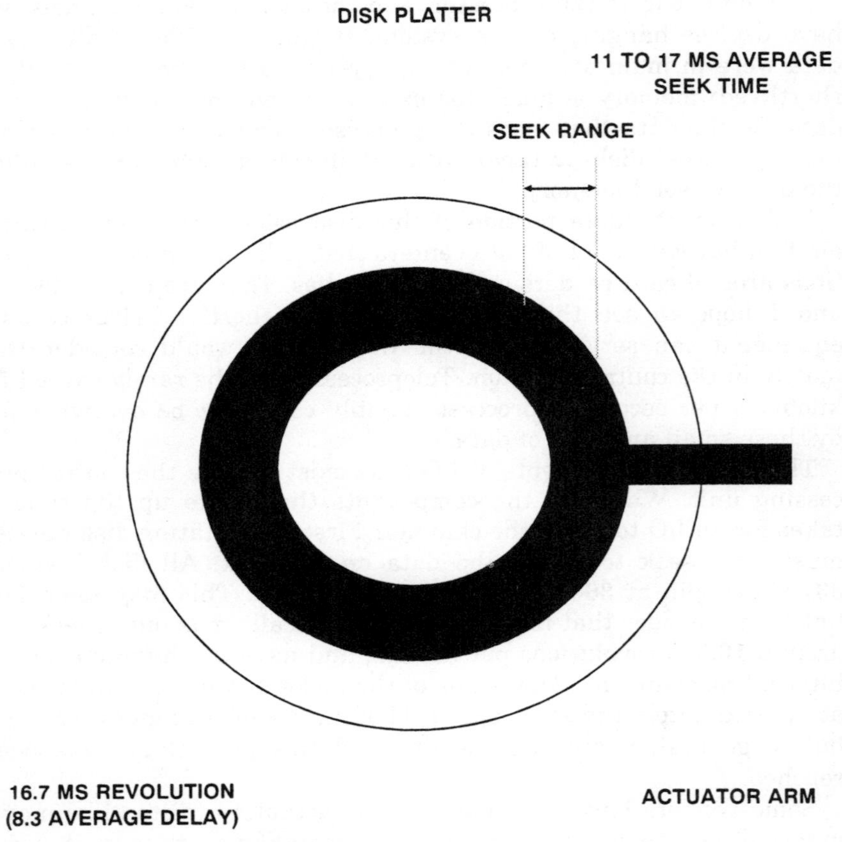

DISK PLATTER

11 TO 17 MS AVERAGE
SEEK TIME

SEEK RANGE

16.7 MS REVOLUTION
(8.3 AVERAGE DELAY)

ACTUATOR ARM

Figure 4-1 The direct access storage device.

in getting the data to the mainframe. Potentially, our biggest enemy
is a clogged carburetor. That is, too much fuel being pumped down.

We pay a very high price for channels that exceed a busy threshold. Why don't we want to fully utilize our channels? Because we are
overlapping our seeks and our latency. How do we do this? By dis-
connecting from the channel and allowing another I/O to get into the
channel while we perform our seek and our set sector (latency).

The problem occurs when we have disconnected from the channel
and wish to reconnect to transfer the data. If another I/O is busying
up the channel with its data transfer, we are then unable to perform
our transfer. This means we must wait at least one full rotation before the data comes back underneath the heads. One full rotation
will cost us 16.7 (or 22.2) milliseconds. This is a higher price than

either the seek or the waiting for the data to come under the heads. We must, therefore, take care not to drive our channels too high. If the channel becomes too high, then we need another channel (and corresponding control unit director).

How high can we drive our channels? When we look at this question, we are looking at the laws of probability. If our channel is 33% busy, then 1/3 of all our reconnects will be met with a busy; therefore, 1/3 of all our I/Os will cost us 16.7 milliseconds. The result of an RPS miss is an average of 5.6 milliseconds added to the cost of an I/O. If the channel becomes 40% busy, then two out of every five I/Os will require another rotation. This results in a 6.6ms increase overall. Because of probabilities, this response is not linear, and results in a very large knee in the curve at about 35% busy. If a channel exceeds this busy, the delays are too costly. Typical documentation for a non-XA system indicates that 30% busy is the limit. Some of the newer documentation targets the online network and response time as the primary reason for computing. These indicate 20% channel busy to be the limit.

One of the things that is most unfortunate about IBM's VMMAP is that it does not allow you to report on channels by time. Therefore, you are forced into the average for the collection period. This figure is preposterous. If this indicates 25%, for example, we may be, and probably are, looking at 40% during peak hours of the day; an unacceptable time.

We have taken a look at the rotating devices. Cached rotating devices are the next fastest concept. It might be noteworthy to mention that there are software solutions to caching that may be more amenable in many circumstances. One thing, currently VM/SP does not support cache.

A cached controller powers up with cache on all volumes; thus, you may be able to utilize cache. However, being on for every volume causes a lot of pollution of the cache memory and is far less effective then the results that can be obtained by utilizing the selective caching feature of VM/HPO.

It is also noteworthy that some vendors do not require IBM compatible cache commands to selectively cache devices. Also, the IBM commands required are relatively simple and there exists at least one no-charge software product that allows selective caching in the VM environment. Additionally, the members of Guide have proposed cache support for VSE/SP and it appears IBM is listening to this request. A lot of VM/SP only users have VSE/SP as a guest.

Before looking at the usage of a cached controller, we need to become educated on what the controller can and cannot provide. First of all, a cached controller can only address read requests from the processor. There are two distinguishable types of read requests. One request is a random read, the other is a sequential read.

Random reads will cause a track of data to be read into memory on most vendors' cache. There is a difference in design sophistication here. We find that some vendors have only one processor per director in a cached unit. This precludes that controller from transferring simultaneously from the device to the controller, and from the controller's memory to the channel. This lack of ability causes the reading of an entire track to unacceptably tie up the director's processor. Therefore, an entire track slot (piece of memory) is allocated; however, the track is only read from the point where the data exists to the end of the track. On the average, this causes 50% more storage to be allocated than is actually used.

IBM's announced 3990 will have this feature, but at this writing simultaneous transfer of data is only available from PCMs. Additionally, some vendors use the cache memory for the program directory or for the program itself, again making a percentage of the memory unavailable. All these need to be examined.

VM never uses a sequential read to a cached controller, but it is interesting to note that some vendors read a different number of tracks at a given time. There are performance ramifications to this also, if the chief user of the VM system is an MVS guest controlling the cache.

How do we know if we can benefit from cache? Almost any computer complex can make use of the benefits of a cached controller, and in some instances, this is the only way to drive the processor economically. Faster processors require more data to feed the instruction processor. The XA channel subsystem is well designed to assist this, but other methods must be employed by the 370 system.

Several vendors have software tools that enable us to determine whether we can use a cached controller or not. There are two primary criteria for determining the need for cache. The first is a read-to-write ratio. A read-to-write ratio of 80% is generally considered a good criterion. Locality of reference is the second criterion. Locality of reference is an indication of "clustering" of data—how closely the data is physically located by frequency of reference.

I've also noted another undocumented phenomenon. I've termed it a "moving locality of reference." This occurs when there is a locality of reference at isolated instances of time, but it varies over the course of a sample period. The final reports indicate that data access is distributed consistently over the database but, in fact, moving clusters of access mask this. Regardless. These reports need to be reviewed and a determination made.

If your data center prefers not to involve a PCM, then a rough guess can be made using the seeks analysis from VMMAP. The seeks analysis on VMMAP 1.4.1 and VM/HPO 4.0 and above will show a read-to-write ratio. The problem is, this data does not take into consideration time and because of this, you cannot determine a locality of reference. Nonetheless, a high read-to-write ratio would certainly indicate a trial of cache.

Generating I/O under VM is probably the single most overlooked area. Until the last few years, most data centers I visited used the alternate pathing mechanism which exists within VM's logic. Unfortunately, this mechanism is extremely rudimentary, with high overhead, and quite ineffective. Years ago, it was even less effective than today. The newer processors are equipped with start I/O fast queu-

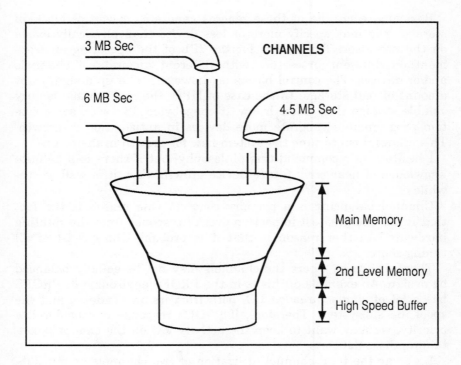

Figure 4-2 The high-speed buffer is like the combustion chamber in an internal combustion engine.

ing. This is the ability of the processor to give a 0 return code to the operating system even if the path is busy. When the path is free, the I/O is started. This is great. The only problem is that VM doesn't see any channel overactivity, and doesn't schedule I/O down the alternate path until the queue is tied up. Notice on your monitor reporting, I/O queuing is very low. If it is not, there is a probably a serious bottleneck problem on the subsystem. This same phenomenon will show up as a high page chaining on VMMAP.

In order to overcome the queuing problem, we must make an attempt to balance the I/O ourselves. VM lends itself well to this endeavor, with device flexibilities.

Three macros come into play on a device gen. They are:

1. Rdevice
2. Rctlunit
3. Rchannel

Basically, each one of these macros generates a control block in storage. You may specify more or less device than physically exists on the processor. This allows for the IPL of the operating environment on different processors with different amounts of channels and/or devices. The control blocks do, however, take up a significant amount of real storage. In the case of HPO, the real storage is very voluble storage that exists below 16 megabytes. I've seen some system programmers generate more devices in anticipation of growth. This allows them to tune the system now for growth in the future.

I hesitate to recommend this philosophy, but if there is a definite knowledge of near term future device growth, then it is well worthwhile.

Channel balancing is a primary concern. One reason is the fact that it has the greatest impact on overall response from the rotating hardware. Another reason is that it is probably the easiest of all tuning chores.

There are cases where the channels may not be equally balanced by design. An example of this is in the PROFS environment. PROFS has a lot of single threaded I/O, both from its own indexes and the spool file subsystem. Therefore, if PROFS response is considered a priority, we may want to keep the activity low on the channels containing these datasets.

Let's say the total channel utilization of two channels on our subsystem (the only two channels) is 65%. We discussed previously that our goal was to keep the channel utilization below 30% per channel. This obviously is impossible in this case, so we have to look at which files must be sacrificed. The obvious answer is to penalize the files that do not inhibit the total system performance.

For our example, let's consider the system having two DASD channels and eight total devices. This is a highly conservative system, but a very good one for making examples. We know that our spooling subsystem uses temp storage (or PS in HPO) and we must checkpoint these files for recovery purposes. The first file we need to look at is the checkpoint dataset. Up until release 5, this file must exist on the IPL device. Now we have the capability of moving the file.

Let's say the checkpoint dataset is on device 1A0 and the spool file storage is on 1A4 and 1A5. A gen to isolate these three devices on their own channel might be as follows:

```
RDEVICE   ADDRESS=(1a0,1),DEVTYPE=3380,ALTCU=2A0
RDEVICE   ADDRESS=(2A1,3),DEVTYPE=3380,ALTCU=1A0
RDEVICE   ADDRESS=(1A4,2),DEVTYPE=3380,ALTCU=2A0
RDEVICE   ADDRESS=(2A6,2),DEVTYPE=3380,ALTCU=1A0


RCTLUNIT ADDRESS=(1A0),FEATURE=32-DEVICE-FEATURE
RCTLUNIT ADDRESS=(2A0),FEATURE=32-DEVICE-FEATURE
```

In this scenario we can keep the channel busy low to our spool files and to our checkpoint dataset. It would be a good idea also to include the paging areas here. Paging bottlenecks can bring a system to its knees.

Let's add another controller and eight additional devices to our configuration. Now we have channels 1, 2, 3, and 4. Each of these channels is connected to a director attached to a string of eight devices. Now we can start playing some fun games.

Let's assume we have a parasite operating system (VSE or MVS or even a guest VM system). In the case of VSE, which is my most familiar environment, we make an attempt within the operating system to balance the I/O subsystem. If VSE (version 1.3.5 and above) is generated with the secondary path option, then VSE counts the number of I/Os going from one device to the next and tries to schedule the I/Os on the least used path. Unfortunately, when it encounters a busy, only the lower channel number is allowed to reschedule on the other path. It is for this reason the secondary usually reports slightly higher numbers.

When running under VM, we are faced with a problem. If the device is defined as minidisk, then VM will handle all paths to the individual device; thus, we are unable to take advantage of perhaps a more capable scheduling system (this is not an endorsement). What we can do is define each device twice.

```
RDEVICE ADDRESS=(1b0,1),DEVTYPE=3380
RDEVICE ADDRESS=(3b0,1),DEVTYPE=3380


RCTLUNIT    ADDRESS=1B0,DEVTYPE=3880,FEATURE=32-DEVICE
RCTLUNIT    ADDRESS=3B0,DEVTYPE=3880,FEATURE=32-DEVICE
```

When VM is IPLed, the second device address occurring numerically will be varied offline due to equal volid. It may then be varied online again and attached to the appropriate guest. Thus, the guest has two paths and can control its own I/O.

This presents another problem. Now we can efficiently schedule the I/O to the device from the guest, but we are unable to look at the device from a CMS userid or another guest. It must be defined as a minidisk for this purpose and a minidisk is on a non-dedicated device.

In comes some creativity—remember we have four directors. We are permitted to come out of the back of one director and into the front of another. This gives us another path to the device, so we may define it thusly:

```
RDEVICE ADDRESS=(1b0,1),DEVTYPE=3380
RDEVICE ADDRESS=(3b0,1),DEVTYPE=3380
RDEVICE ADDRESS=(2b0,1),DEVTYPE=3380


RCTLUNIT    ADDRESS=1B0,DEVTYPE=3880,FEATURE=32-DEVICE
RCTLUNIT    ADDRESS=2B0,DEVTYPE=3880,FEATURE=32-DEVICE
RCTLUNIT    ADDRESS=3B0,DEVTYPE=3880,FEATURE=32-DEVICE
```

The volume at 2B0 can be attached to the system Any minidisk volid reference to that volume will allow total access. It can even be accompanied by an alternate.

```
RDEVICE ADDRESS=(1b0,1),DEVTYPE=3380
RDEVICE ADDRESS=(3b0,1),DEVTYPE=3380
RDEVICE ADDRESS=(2b0,1),DEVTYPE=3380,ALTCU=4B0
RCTLUNIT    ADDRESS=1B0,DEVTYPE=3880,FEATURE=32-DEVICE
RCTLUNIT    ADDRESS=2B0,DEVTYPE=3880,FEATURE=32-DEVICE
RCTLUNIT    ADDRESS=3B0,DEVTYPE=3880,FEATURE=32-DEVICE
RCTLUNIT    ADDRESS=4B0,DEVTYPE=3880,FEATURE=32-DEVICE
```

Remember, there are really only two directors to the device. The other two channels, 2 and 4, are on the secondary or ("b") interface of the same director.

VM Paging I/O Subsystem

Let's take a quick review of paging, the time elements involved, and how it affects overall systems performance. All virtual machines in VM run in virtual storage. CP itself, pageable or non-pageable, runs outside of the virtual storage allocated for guests. When a page fault is taken for a guest, a page handling routine is called which stacks a request for a page on the CP request queue. Unless the guest machine supports PAGEX, or one of the newer HPO parameters is specified for the guest, the machine will go into a wait and will not be redispatched until that page request has been satisfied.

PAGEX introduces a very important performance concept if the guest is doing multiprogramming. Leaving a multiprogramming guest non-dispatchable until a page has been satisfied, has a great opportunity cost associated with it.

Let's look at an example. A typical 4K page response could be looked at as 23ms. Let's say a guest has a paging rate of 10 pages per second on its behalf. These requests will more than likely be single threaded. VM overlap seeks and does chaining on pages, but in all likelihood, this would probably not occur on behalf of a single guest without PAGEX. This means that the guest would be non-dispatchable (.023 sec. x 10) = .23 of every second. This is an astonishing 23% loss of productivity. If, during this timeframe, the guest is the only runable workload, then it has forfeited the right to overlap processing 23% of the time. I don't believe ten pages per second is very high. I know of one data center that was running on a processor approximately twice the speed of a 370-158 that paged an average of 60 pages per second and frequently peaked above 100 pages per second.

The moral of the story is that a multiprogramming guest should not be allowed to wait on pages. VSE now sets PAGEX ON itself to insure this isn't a problem. On the contrary, the PAGEX parameter can be utilized to favor the online response and inhibit batch in that environment, since the online generally has the highest demand for virtual storage.

VM probably has the most advanced paging subsystem of any of IBM's operating systems. All of VM's code is probably equal to just

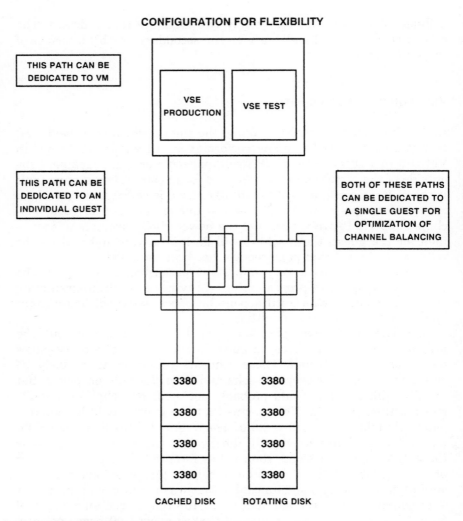

Figure 4-3 Configuration for flexibility.

the I/O code in MVS, but MVS doesn't have PAGE MIGRATION or PREFERRED PAGING AREAS.

In VM you can specify preferred paging areas. These are areas that VM will go to before going to any other area. They may be defined as TYPE=PP on the SYSPAG macro. What does this mean to us? It means we can capitalize on faster devices.

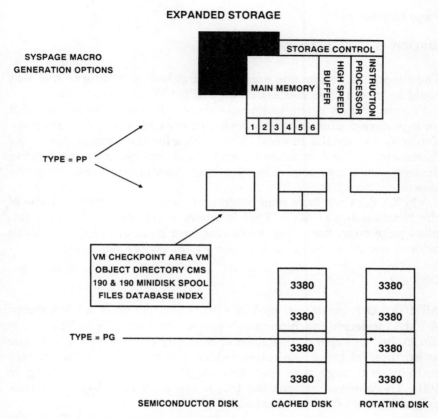

Figure 4-4 Maximizing I/O throughput.

As we mentioned before, many vendors other than IBM have solid
state disk emulation devices. These devices can greatly enhance paging workloads. Although not as fast as expanded storage, they may
be carried from CPU to CPU, thereby making them an investment
above and beyond the depreciable investment in expanded storage.
Additionally, they allow the flexibility of placing other datasets on
the device, such as making a second copy of the system "S" disk at
IPL time, or copying out a read-only minidisk which may be a single
thread bottleneck in a system.

Multiple SYSPAG macros may be specified. Each of these macros
will generate areas for paging that will form a hierarchy. That is, the
areas specified in the first SYSPAG macro will be filled before moving onto the areas specified in the second SYSPAG macro.

Page Migration

IMPLICIT vs. EXPLICIT Definitions

The concept of having one area filled first before moving to the next could be looked at as IMPLICIT vs. EXPLICIT page migration.

Page migration is the technique where VM moves pages allocated on a preferred area to a less preferred area at a specified interval. You may specify the interval. This allows for the highest use pages to remain on the fastest device and the slower pages to move off to devices which my have a heavier load elsewhere or are physically slower.

VM/XA does not have page migration, as it is approaching some of the functionality of MVS. That is where I first heard the term Implicit page migration. This is allowing your most active user to logon prior to the other users, such as the VTAM service machine.

Disk I/O

All disk I/O is performed by VM with the exception of a PMA guest. A PMA (preferred machine assist) guest, whether MVS or VSE/SP, is dispatched in supervisor state and basically only re-enters VM code at an interval timer expiration (which means the operating system occupies real page zero with the program check PSW pointing to VM). There are exceptions but this is the principle. Because of this, only the guests CCWs are executed.

A brief bit of information for those not familiar with a CCW. On the larger mainframes the channel may not only be thought of as a separate processor—it is a separate processor. As a separate processor, it has its own instruction set, both internally and user controlled. CCW, or channel command words, are the user controlled interfaces with the channel subsystem.

In normal operations (non-PMA) a start I/O is attempted by the guest operating system. This causes a privileged operation exception allowing VM's interception of the operation. Upon examination, VM determines the operation is an I/O and passes the I/O to other routines which determine whether the I/O is to a minidisk or not.

The pages associated with data transfer in the CAW must be locked prior to transfer to or from the disk device. Because the guest operating system isn't aware of the real page, address translation must also occur. CP handles all the busy conditions associated with channel, control unit, and device, as well as scheduling on multiple paths.

Minidisks

This is a sort of misnomer, since CMS is perfectly capable of using an entire volume itself. We generally see CMS using minidisks, but the data can just as well be dedicated, as with any other guest operating system. CMS initially was a standalone operating environment, but now relies on CP for I/O scheduling, thus eliminating double coding, as in a normal guest.

CMS performs I/O using the diagnose vehicle provided by VM. If you are coding in straight assembler under CMS, you can perform a direct I/O via a diagnose, or you can use CMS's built-in SVC interface to perform CMS I/O on your behalf. The SVC 202 and 203 usage are interesting. SVC 202 is hexadecimal "CA." Cambridge University initially wrote CMS.

CMS minidisks may be formatted in either 512, 1024, 2048, or 4096 byte blocks. The reason for the difference is obvious. As we discussed earlier, the technology hasn't grown very much in the area of actuator speed or rotation—its transfer rate. In order to take advantage of the transfer rate, increasingly larger block sizes were implemented in CMS to reduce the number of actuator movements (seeks) and rotational delays (latency).

On the new architectural standards (3380 type devices) 4K blocks are the premium performance decision. We can pay quite a price, however, for using 4K. Very small files, files which consume less than 4K, will require an entire 4K block due to the internal architecture of CMS, so it is possible to greatly waste space. In most cases, however, the change to 4K, or the default implementation of 4K, is not difficult.

As a side note in our discussion, notice that IBM hasn't changed the architecture of the drive for almost ten years. It used to be that many programs would have to be reassembled (rewritten) for device type changes. Supporting code, whether it be VSAM or a third party vendor, took a long time to catch up to new device types 2311 to 2314 to 3330, 3340, 3350, FBA, 3375. With the 3380 type devices, these major concerns have become a thing of the past. All of the devices, 3380 standards to 3380 D/E to 3380 J/K, have the same structure, the same number of bytes per track, the same number of tracks per cylinder. This is a productivity saver. Rumors had it that the FBA (fixed block architecture) would be the device of the future. If these come to fruition, then we have one more major hump to overcome in the magnetic media area.

Each CMS minidisk used for CMS file allocations is formatted and a directory written at the beginning of the minidisk. Two directories are used. At each file write the directories are switched. This makes it possible to "unerase" a file by changing one bit and backing off to the previous director. The directories are actually maintained in CMS storage and written out at file write time. This can cause some consideration for linked disks.

CMS allocates space on the minidisk in a similar fashion to that of the PC and MVS partitionable datasets. Data is written sequentially. When datasets are deleted, that space becomes available in the directory and is used by subsequent writes.

This causes fragmentation and increased seek activity over a period of time. Benchmarks have demonstrated that a typical 3% performance boost may be realized by backing up files, reformatting the disk, and restoring them.

With Release 6 of VM/SP, file sharing has been implemented for CMS. Once again, IBM has implemented a service machine to manage I/O to shared minidisks. A pool of space may be allocated and an individual CMS user can participate in any pool. Space is allocated in blocks. No actual space is consumed until files are "committed"; thus, a tremendous space savings can be realized for the price of single threading through a service machine. The implementation strongly resembles the implementation used by one of IBM's major non-compatible competitors and also feels a tad like the directory system used by MS-DOS.

Using I/O as a Measuring Stick of Performance

One of the handiest methods of discerning performance is through the user of I/O. If you consider what our goal is in driving a computer—online response and batch turnaround—what unit of measurement can we use to determine whether we have improved this or not. The obvious answer is online transactions and batch jobs.

This is of no consequence if the online system supports data collection of transactions and the batch work is easily delineated into jobs. The workload we are likely to find on a VM system doesn't necessarily lend itself well to these criteria, nor are we necessarily in a position to collect this information, due to lack of the necessary software tools.

One unit of measurement that sometimes alludes technical support personnel is that an I/O can be looked at as a unit of work. The same batch job that processes the same files day in and day out is always going to use roughly the same amount of CPU time per I/O. The same CICS, IDMS, or even CMS transaction is also going to roughly use the same amount of CPU per I/O.

CMS is a much more dynamic workload and the amount of CPU can vary greatly, especially in a small shop environment with changing people. Nonetheless, the data plotted over a period of time will result in roughly the same amount of CPU per I/O.

In VM, if we want to take a look at these figures, we can use Virtual I/O (I/O performed on behalf of a guest) and virtual CPU time (CPU time less any time used by CP). If we take these two numbers and divide the latter by the former, we get a rough estimate of one CPU second per I/O. This can be carried to further extremes by doing it by guest, classifying guests into different groups, based on their type of workload. For instance, five SQL users may be classified together. Ten programmers may be classified together. All PROFS users may be classified the same.

REXX programs may provide a mode of operation for this type of data. I like using my PC, as I can manipulate the data and add graphics a little easier than using the interfaces on the mainframe.

I also favor keeping this data in ratio form and running a continuous Spearman Co-efficient of Correlation to make certain we have

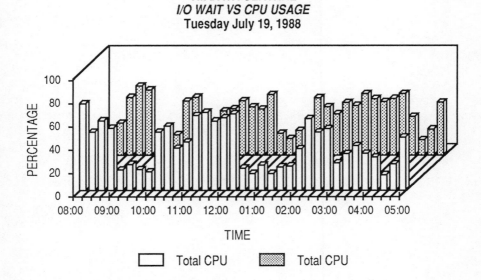

Figure 4-5 CPU usage plotted against I/O.

some linearity. I like to see a co-efficient of correlation of at least .7 to establish some linearity between CPU consumed and I/O performed.

About the Author

Kim Cooper is a systems engineer for National Advanced Systems. His background includes technical support for manufacturing, as well as development and teaching VM/HPO Internals for National Advanced Systems.

Kim is currently acting as a district capacity planning specialist in the North Coast District of National Advanced Systems and also serves on the board of trustees for the Midwestern VM Regional Users Group.

5

Problem Diagnosis in VM

by James R. Bergsten

Chapter Summary

This chapter presents an overview to help you to diagnose problems and debug a VM system and the applications that run under it.

We begin by introducing the problem analysis process. Next, we look at some of the common problems you may encounter and at some of the evidence you can obtain to help debug these problems. Then, we show you some ways to solve the problems, and finally, we discuss some of the tools that are available to make the debugging task easier.

Please remember that the debugging process covers a lot of ground. Like a television private eye, you can never tell how much information and effort will be involved in solving your problem. What's more, you probably won't even get paid for expenses. So, don't expect this short introduction to teach you everything you'll ever need to know. You should, however, be able to use this data as the basis for becoming a debugging pro.

Some terms used in this discussion which may be unfamiliar to you are defined in Figure 5-1.

Why Debug?

Although you may be tempted to ask, "Why do I want to debug at all?," there are several compelling reasons below for developing strong debugging skills.

You simply cannot develop any piece of software without testing it. It is one of the cardinal rules of the universe that ANYTHING THAT ISN'T TESTED DOESN'T WORK. A major part of testing anything is fixing the problems you encounter. This process of fixing problems is what debugging is all about.

You cannot always depend on your software suppliers to solve your problems promptly. It is pleasant to believe that anyone providing software is capable of an instantaneous problem resolution. This is never the case however, no matter who the vendor is. There are several reasons for this. Something you consider to be a problem, the vendor may consider to be a standard feature. Also, it is very difficult to debug a problem remotely — a vendor cannot easily gather timely information and isn't as intimately familiar with your facility as you are. In addition, you tend to get far better response from a vendor when you call armed with a reproducible problem and a fix. And finally, your problem may be more important to you than it is to a vendor who may be dealing with hundreds of other problems at the same time.

You learn much more about your systems and applications during the debugging process. There are several benefits to this. An obvious one is that your value and career opportunities are enhanced as your knowledge and skill levels increase. Also, you learn more, and this learning helps you to find similar problems faster and produce applications and systems of higher quality.

Debugging can (sometimes) be fun. You may find this hard to believe, especially when three hundred managers are standing behind you waiting for a solution, but debugging is just like detective work. If you are a natural problem solver, debugging is for you. If you like to get to the bottom of things you will enjoy the challenges of debugging.

How Do I Go About Debugging?

Watching a seasoned debugging expert working sometimes seems like magic. The all-time greats seem to arrive at a fix intuitively, apparently with little or no information.

Bug	A specific problem or set of problems. This term allegedly was coined long ago when an insect lodged itself into some wiring causing one of the first computer malfunctions.
Control blocks/ Data areas	Data structures containing information about a particular system process or resource. For example, a VM RDEVBLOK contains information about a particular Real I/O device. Control blocks are usually linked to one another in a hierarchical fashion, so that one can find a particular block by chaining through other blocks. Control blocks are usually documented in data areas manuals and their source is usually in system macro libraries.
Debugging	The process of investigating and hopefully solving a problem.
Dump	A snapshot of a system at the time the system detected a problem. Dumps generally contain a copy of system storage and registers.
Loop	A system or application that appears to be in an endless, infinite loop of program code.
Registers	Special, fast access locations in computer hardware where data, storage addresses and control information are kept.
Standalone dump	A dump, created by an independent utility, taken in cases when the system is unable to dump itself.
Storage	The memory of a computer. Three kinds exist: fast electronic temporary memory, on line permanent memory such as disks, and off line memory such as tapes.
Trace table	A circular list of logged important system events. This table shows a recent history of system actions and exists in one fashion or another in all major systems.
VMDUMP	A dump of a virtual machine, requested by a user, taken by the CP operating system.

Figure 5-1 Common debugging terms.

Truthfully, however, debugging really comes down to a few simple skills, virtues and disciplines.

Patience and Perseverance. Given enough time and information, any problem can be solved. It is frustrating at first to view what appears to be an insurmountable problem. One of the things that separates the good from the great is the ability to stick to a problem until it is resolved.

Intelligence gathering. It is impossible to arrive at a solution with no information. Over time, you learn what information should be gathered and what information is simply noise to be discarded.

One of the skills seasoned user support personnel learn is to look behind questions and problems to see what the real issue is. Knowing why a question is asked is often more important than the question itself.

Familiarity with the software. All the information in the world is useless if you don't know how to apply it. Surprisingly, most systems are, in general, very similar. Knowledge derived from one can be easily applied to another. For example, most VM systems contain *trace tables*, circular lists of important system events.

A good memory. One of the magic tricks the experts use is applying their experience to new problems. You begin to have an "I've seen this before" feeling when presented with a new bug. While there can be an infinite number of potential problems, most fall into a few categories. Your ability to limit the possibilities is a function of your knowledge and experience.

In the remainder of this chapter, we will give you specific details about how to begin debugging. For now, let's look at the steps involved:

1. Get a good description of the problem.
2. Gather appropriate evidence—information that is relevant to solving the problem.
3. Use your available tools to search through the information.
4. If the problem is obvious, create a fix to it if possible. If not, attempt a circumvention.
5. Report the problem to those responsible for the software in question.

What Problems Can I Expect?

This section tells you a bit about the kinds of problems you may meet in your debugging travels. It also gives you some of the reasons for these problems and tells you what sort of information to gather to solve them.

The following section goes through some of the information gathering process. You might want to refer between to both sections when debugging a specific problem.

System Crashes

Hopefully, system crashes aren't the most common problem you'll encounter.

System *crashes*, as the name implies, are conditions that are so unexpected that the system is completely disrupted by the error. They are serious events, because all of your computer users may be affected.

In VM/SP, VM/HPO and VM/XA systems, the following events generally occur at a system crash:

1. The system displays a message to the operator's console giving the *abend code*, a three-letter and several-digit code giving the expected cause of the error.
2. The system attempts to take a dump.
3. The system attempts to restart.

For most CMS utilities and application programs, an error message is displayed and the software terminates, leaving you in CMS command level (back at the ready prompt).

How to Deal with System Crashes

For VM/SP, VM/HPO, or VM/XA systems, look up the message in the appropriate Messages and Codes manual. This will give you a short description of the problem, together with a small amount of information suggesting further research. The first three letters of the code are the last three letters of the CP module that detected the error and caused the system to restart.

In most cases, a system dump will be taken, although sometimes the error is so severe that a dump cannot be taken. In such cases, you may have to take a *standalone dump*—that is, a dump generated by a special IPLable utility. Between the dump and the abend code, you should be able to determine the cause of the abend quickly. This is not necessarily the error condition, simply the result of it. Further study will be needed to find out why the error occurred.

Figure 5-2 shows some, but by no means all, of the common CP abend codes. You will note that many of the three-letter codes give you a good idea of the problem right away.

Some CP abend codes are caused by relatively benign conditions that only affect one user. There are add-on products that trap these conditions and prevent the entire system from crashing.

Application programs are also susceptible to abend conditions and, interestingly, some of the same ones as system software. CMS usually gives a textual message describing the condition. You can use the CMS DEBUG command to look at the failing registers and storage right after the abend. You can also use the CP VMDUMP command to create a dump of the CMS machine for later analysis.

A common application abend is a *program check*. This is a hardware detected programming error condition, such as an attempt to address nonexistent memory or use a privileged instruction. Figure 5-3 shows some common program checks.

There is one particularly nasty CMS abend message which ends in "908T." This indicates that a file system error occurred in one of your accessed CMS minidisks. If this occurs, be very careful what you do next because you may loose the data on your entire disk. It is beyond

FRExxx, **FRTxxx**	An error involving free storage management.

PAGxxx,
  PGTxxx,
  PGUxxx
	An error involving paging.

PRGxxx	A program check. "xxx" is the program check code. See the list of program checks in Figure 5-3.
LOKxxx	An error involved with multiple processor interaction.
PSA002	The system was manually restarted by a command on the processor operator's console.
SVC003	An error caused by the inability of CP to bring in one of its pageable modules. This is usually caused by DASD hardware errors and is one of the cases where a dump may not be taken (if the disk powered off, for example, the dump cannot be written).

Figure 5-2 Some common VM abend codes.

001	Operation exception—attempting to issue an invalid machine instruction. Usually caused by a wild branch to memory that doesn't contain valid instructions. A wild branch to location zero usually indicates a call to an undefined routine.
004	Protection exception—attempting to store into protected memory. Usually caused by the corruption of a storage pointer.
005	Addressing exception—attempting to address nonexistent memory. Usually caused by the corruption of a storage pointer.
006	Specification exception—basically using a machine instruction incorrectly. Usually caused by program error or the corruption of a data value or storage pointer.
007-015	Various arithmetic errors (overflows, underflows, divide by zero, etc.)—usually caused by program error or the corruption of a data value or storage pointer.

Figure 5-3 Some common program checks.

the scope of this chapter to discuss how to recover from this sort of error and, in all fairness, it occurs very infrequently, but you should be aware of it.

Wait States

Wait states are conditions so serious that the system is placed into a *disabled wait state*. Wait states normally only occur during system initialization when the system hasn't enough resources to send messages to the operator or during hardware errors.

The symptom of wait states is that all work stops and the program status word (PSW) has its wait bit set with no interruptions enabled (00020000 xxxxxxxx or 000A0000 xxxxxxxx). Note that the wait state code is contained in the right part of the PSW (where the x's are).

Since the system is unusable, this PSW must be displayed from the processor's operator console. This display varies from machine to machine but usually involves stopping the machine and entering a command to display the PSW. Figure 5-4 shows a few common VM/SP and VM/HPO wait states.

001, 00A, 00B	Unrecoverable machine (processor) hardware error.
002	Unrecoverable channel hardware error.
003	Fatal error when attempting to restart the system.
005	No operator's console. Usually a system generation error.
006, 008	When the system is shut down.
00C	Attempting to IPL from a disk with no VM system on it.

Figure 5-4 Some common VM wait states.

Loops

Loops are conditions where the entire system locks up inside a usually small piece of code. As an example, assume that there is a chain of data in storage, each entry of which points to the following entry, and the last entry's pointer is zero denoting the end of the chain. If the last entry weren't zero (say it points to itself or the top of the chain), a program could conceivably run forever around and around the chain.

Another cause of loops is status from hardware devices saying, in effect, "I'm busy right now, but should be free almost immediately," but they lie and never come free.

Loops manifest themselves by taking large amounts of processor time. A loop in the system causes users to be locked out, while the system light on the processor remains solidly lit.

A loop in an application program may not cause the processor to lock up, but it does cause that user to soak up inordinate amounts of processor time. It also causes performance problems as described in the following section.

When the system is in a loop, try to determine if the loop is I/O related. Is it in an I/O module such as DMKIOS? Check R12 to see if it points to DMKIOS or DMKIOT. Also check to see if the trace table is full of I/O entries to a single device. If you can narrow it down to a single device or control unit, stop the processor, reset the device or control unit, start the processor, and see if the problem clears. If you reset a device, you will want to cause it to present an interrupt to the system so that the system doesn't wait for it forever. On disk drives you do this by pressing the attention switch. Other devices, such as tapes, cannot be made to present an interrupt. Clearly, some device knowledge goes a long way when handling this sort of problem.

For other loops, a system restart may be in order. Stop the system and do a system restart from the processor's operator's console. A PSA002 abend should occur. By examining the resulting dump, you should be able to determine the cause of the loop. Note that some loops are small and obvious; others are large and convoluted. The VM trace table may help here—look for groups of repeated entries.

For virtual machine or application program loops, use an online software monitor, if one is available, to determine the user causing the problem. Contact this user if possible, to see what is going on before simply forcing him off the system (it might be the application that prints your pay check).

Performance

Problems with performance are an entire endeavor unto themselves. Basically, the procedure for optimizing performance consists of:

1. Determining what appropriate and realistic performance is.
2. Using accurate tools to compare desired and actual performance.
3. Modifying or adding resources to solve the performance problem.

There are several kinds of performance problems—one-time, short-length problems, such as users in loops, and long-term problems such as insufficient processor power or a poor I/O configuration. Sometimes, a hardware problem disguises itself as a performance problem; for example, a disk pack that drops ready may cause only certain users to stop running.

The biggest problem in debugging the one-time problem is that it may be gone by the time you look at it. In general, it is best to be aware of the entire situation when investigating a performance problem by asking questions like:

• What is the nature of the application?
• What is the specific performance issue: response time? turnaround?
• What resources are involved?

Remember, performance problems are the most nebulous and subjective kinds of problems, unless you have a set of optimum performance guidelines to work against.

Security Problems

Security problems are a relatively new concern among businesses today. As companies recognize the value of information and the potential losses resulting from destruction or misuse of this information, security issues will become high priority problems.

Some security problems are due to system shortcomings; however, the vast majority are due to human error.

We cannot begin to tell you how to prevent security problems. Each installation has different needs and requirements. The simple rule of thumb is to consider security aspects before a break occurs, not after. Also, without causing undue hardship to legitimate users, don't make it easy to break into your system. Some things to consider:

- Don't use common, easily guessed passwords such as the standard passwords that come with the system.
- Don't allow unrestricted access to facilities, computer rooms, tape storage, and/or telephone dial-up lines.
- Don't leave terminals unattended.
- Prevent unauthorized access to secure information.

Incorrect Results

Incorrect results (such as $1 + 1 = 7$) are the most common problems encountered in debugging, and can be the most frustrating. Unless you take specific action to prevent it, the environment is long gone before you get to gather information. When you tackle this sort of problem, you need to do the following:

Come up with a reproducible case. Obviously, if it occurs once and only once, it will be nearly impossible to track down and correct. (Of course, the result of the error determines the amount of effort involved to find it—for example, a space mission crashed because of a period used in a FORTRAN statement where a comma was needed.)

Place diagnostic traps where you expect that the error is occurring. When these occur, compare intermediate data to isolate the origin of the failure. If we use our $1 + 1 = 7$ analogy, you might stop a program where the addition is to see which of the 1s is really a 6 (or maybe something changed both to 3s).

Work backward interactively until the single origin of the problem is found. Remember, there may be multiple small problems that compound into one big problem.

Just about all system and application crashes and abends can be traced back to their initial cause by use of the above process.

Hung Users

Hung users are VM users who, due to some error condition, can neither run nor be forced from the system. This is a specialized case of incorrect results, but is common enough in VM systems to merit individual attention.

The VM operating system was originally written as a research project. While it is an excellent, low-overhead system, VM either doesn't handle, or will gloss over, many types of error recovery. This is why some abend conditions can be cleaned up by add-on products. It is also why cases occur where you have hung users.

For the most part, a *hung user* is a user who is stuck— cannot run, and cannot be forced off. This condition is almost always caused by the system waiting for an event that will never occur, such as a missing device interrupt.

There are several things that can be done here. One is to find the offending device and reset it (this doesn't always help, because if the system is waiting for an interrupt from this device, resetting it ensures that one will never arrive). Another is to restart the system. This is not recommended since you lose all users to save one (of course, if the one is your VP. . .).

There are available add-on products that are designed to specifically unsnarl hung users. These go through VM's control blocks and clean the user off the system, a potentially complicated process.

Conversions

A final potential source of new problems—we, of course, now call them debugging opportunities—is a system conversion.

Recently, a new and very different VM system has become available supporting 370 extended, or XA architecture. This system is anticipated to become the VM system of the future; so even if you aren't using it today, you may well encounter it soon.

Converting the CP System

Despite some incompatibilities, XA CP provides similar function to VM/SP and VM/HPO CP. When you look at XA CP source code, however, you will see that it is significantly different from the system 370 CP code.

Don't be discouraged. XA CP was derived from VM/370 Release 3.8. If you understand the principles and inner workings of VM/SP and VM/HPO, you should have little trouble adjusting to XA CP. The modules begin with HCP instead of DMK and most of the control block names have been changed, but their functions and interrelationships are almost identical. Needless to say, if you have local CP modifications, these will need to be reworked—it may even be a good time to throw some away if you're not using them any more.

Converting to XA CMS or CMS Release 6

Here we have good news and bad news. The good news is that XA CMS is based on VM/SP CMS Release 5 and consequently isn't very much different. CMS Release 6 is based on XA CMS, sometimes called CMS 5.5. The bad news is that almost any application that is written in assembler or uses semi-documented CMS interfaces has to be carefully checked.

Here are some of the things to look for when converting CMS systems applications:

- Any instructions or operands that use three byte areas as storage addresses.
- Any load address instructions used specifically to clear the upper byte of a register.
- Any 370 specific instructions, such as TIO.
- All CMS macros that call system services now use SVC 204. This isn't supported in old CMS, so be sure that you don't assemble any program that needs to run in the old CMS under the new CMS.
- CMS storage services have been vastly improved, but at a price. The new CMSSTOR service generates a much larger parameter list—watch out for addressability problems. Also, to release stor-

age, an additional register is needed; R1 can't be used, as it points to the CMSSTOR parameter list.
- Many control blocks have been changed and in a rather nasty way—new fields are inserted into the middle of blocks, causing familiar locations to shift. Because of this, be sure that you don't have any hard-coded control block offsets in your applications.
- Test your application in various CMS operating environments—the CMS code may function differently. Try:

— Old CMS if your application needs to run under both old and new CMS.
— New CMS in 370 mode.
— New CMS in XA mode residing under the 16 megabyte line.
— New CMS in XA mode residing above the 16 megabyte line.

What Evidence Can I Gather?

Before any problem can be solved, information relating to the problem must be collected. In this section, we are going to discuss some of the data that can be gathered so that a particular problem can be diagnosed.

Dumps

Dumps are the programmer's crowning glories and nightmares. Although dump reading can be a highly paid occupation, it is also extremely time consuming and frustrating.

Not very long ago, dumps were massive collections of paper—some towering six feet high. Those were the days of paper clips and dog-eared pages (to mark places in the pile), and yellow markers.

More recently, coinciding with the large increase in computer storage size (we calculate that a full dump of a 2**31 bit machine would be about a mile high), dumps are almost always kept in binary disk files and specialized utilities are used to display them interactively in a variety of formats.

Dumps come from a variety of sources and are in several formats, as shown in Figure 5-5.

How Do I Read a Dump? Unfortunately, asking "How do I read a dump?" is just like asking "How do I learn to speak Japanese?" We can't possibly tell you everything you will ever need to know, but here are a few important tips:

CP dumps   These come from the VM/SP, VM/HPO, or VM/XA system it-
                    self. In most cases, these are generated as a consequence of
                    the system crashing, although VM/XA can take soft abend
                    dumps and some add-on products allow dynamic dumping of
                    the system without a system restart.

VM dumps   These contain data from virtual machines and are generated
                    by either the VMDUMP command or by a system or applica-
                    tion itself using the VMDUMP command or diagnose X'94'.
                    Internally, VMDUMPs are formatted differently than CP dumps
                    but contain similar information.

Standalone   These are generated by independent, standalone utilities that
dumps   run from tape or disk and create the dump on tape. VM/SP,
                    VM/HPO, VM/XA, MVS, and MVS/XA all come with stand-
                    alone dump utilities—each creates an output tape in a differ-
                    ent format.

Printed dumps   These dumps are generated by use of the CP DUMP com-
                    mand. These dumps are in readable printed format. These
                    can also be generated by either a user or by a program inter-
                    nally. Some older or less enlightened software still generates
                    paper dumps.

Figure 5-5 Common dump types.

CP Dumps

1. First look at the abend code. This should give you some idea of
   the nature of the problem and will help eliminate the obvious.
2. If the abend was the result of a program check, examine the
   offending instruction and its operands, and at R12 check to see
   which module the code is in and the function being performed.
   Usually, R11 will point at the VMBLOK (VM) or VMDBK (XA)
   which contains the USERID for whom services are being performed.
      The instruction and its operands will tell you the exact rea-
   son for the program check, NOT what caused the operands to
   be faulty. Lacking faulty code (use of the wrong register or instruction, for example), you will have to trace back to find why
   the operands are incorrect.
      Many times, the nature of the incorrect value will become
   readily apparent (such as a character string in a register that

should contain an address). The value of an incorrect operand can often point you to the original problem.

3. For other errors, look at the trace table. This table will show recent system events and tell you what the system was doing right up to the error in question. Again, you are gathering information on the environment leading up to the detected error.

4. Investigate the *control blocks* associated with the operation in question. Look for inconsistencies—corrupted fields, missing or incorrect values or bit flags, incorrect inter-block linkages, and so on.

5. If the problem has occurred before, compare the current dump with previous dumps to see similarities and differences. For example, problems caused by storage overlays may be more benign in one dump than another. Compare unrelated dumps, and the running system also—this will show you "good" vs. "bad" conditions.

6. If you're getting nowhere, leave the problem for a while and come back to it. Sometimes this gives you a fresh perspective on the problem.

VM Dumps

To read VM dumps, you use many of the general analysis techniques described above; however, things can be a bit more complex. This is because unlike a CP dump, which is always a dump of VM/SP, VM/HPO, or VM/XA, a VM dump can be a dump of anything from a subsystem such as RSCS or PVM, to an abending CMS user application, to a single page showing invalid data from a full-screen operation.

For the most part, you need to determine the nature of the problem—program check? loop? incorrect results? Then examine the dump for clues that lead to the cause of the problem.

Because this sort of dump can be a bit more unstructured than a CP dump, you need to look at the dump based on the structure of the failing software. Look for the following:

• Low-storage PSW contents, especially the program check old PSW.
• The contents of registers.
• The contents of data areas/control blocks.
• The application's trace table.

We will talk about some of the qualities of a good dump analysis tool in "Tools for Debugging Dumps."

Console Listings

Most often when debugging, a dump is not enough. You need to see the user's and/or operator's interactions with the system and the system's responses prior to the error condition. Was the console full of device I/O error messages before the system crash? Did the operator attempt to FORCE a user from the system?

Because of the way VM works, you can find some portions of this information in a dump, such as the most recent console activity (if the console was spooled) and the last few commands entered (if the user had a retrieve key). Needless to say, console spooling and a retrieve key are good things to set up if you are trying to recreate a problem.

User's Perceptions

This is the most subjective evidence, yet it has validity. Vast quantities of time can be saved if you can get a user to acknowledge what he or she "only" changed.

We recommend:

Listen carefully. Don't assume anything from half of the story.

Always look for the real question or issue. Many times, users like to "help" by asking questions that anticipate a fix. For example:

User	How do you turn off printed output for my application?
You	*Why?*
User	Because it's creating these huge dumps in my virtual printer.
You	*Why?*
User	Because my program is full of divide by zero errors that I don't care about.
You	*Why?*
User	Because some of the monitor record's time intervals are zero.
You	*Why?*
User	Beats me.

Try to get a good comparison of the before and after issues, especially in the case of performance problems. For example:

User	Response time is really crummy lately!
You	*Compared to what?*
User	Compared to my home PC.

Never assume anything. Often, a user's module doesn't match his object deck which doesn't match his source. Be polite and diplomatic, but check everything out yourself. Many times, the fact that a user cannot solve his own problem is because he is working based on incorrect assumptions.

Secondary Storage

Another potentially necessary piece of information is a system's or application's input data and output results. There is an old saying "garbage in, garbage out." You should always be sure that a problem is not being generated by incorrect input.

Here's another very important fact: **The vast majority of programming errors are not caused by faulty processing code, but by inadequate error recovery.** Since you cannot rewrite all of the world's code, you should carefully check that input data is valid.

Incorrect output data is also a clue pointing to specific problems. When did it go bad? From the beginning, somewhere along the line, or right before the crash?

Source Code

Much has been written about the pros and cons of providing systems source code. We will avoid the issue, except to state the obvious: **The source code is the final authority when you need to determine how something actually works.** Also: **You can't fix a problem unless you have the resources to fix it (such as modifiable, compilable source).** Suffice it to say that you need to know how something works to fix it and the best "source" is the source.

Other Information

Other information might also be handy, for example:

- Load maps from the CP and CMS systems and/or other products and applications.

- CPEREP listings (hardware environmental reporting records).
- System monitor data.
- System accounting data.
- Changed code due to newly applied service.
- Microcode levels of peripherals and the processor.
- EC (engineering change) levels of peripherals and the processor.
- Environmental information (air conditioning outages, power brown-outs, etc.).

What Tools Can I Use?

Now that we've gone through some of the data you need to collect in order to solve problems, let's look at some of the tools we can use.

Tools for Debugging Dumps

Dumps can be debugged in one of two ways. The first is to chop down a forest, mill it into paper, print off the dump, sit down and go through the mass of paper by hand with lots of colored markers, paper clips, eye drops, and coffee.

The second way is to use an interactive dump analysis tool. Although, in their current state, these tools make dump analysis easier, they do not find the problems for you (at least not ALL the problems).

Here are some of the things a good dump analysis tool does:

- Display dump storage and registers in a variety of formats.
- Display formatted control blocks.
- Display trace tables in formatted and unformatted versions.
- Locate data in storage.
- Allow symbolic expressions such as the names of modules to be used to locate storage addresses.
- Chain through control blocks.
- Locate commonly used control blocks.
- Remember important storage locations, your comments about the dump, the last time you looked at it, the problem tracking number, and so on. Provide mechanisms for easy extension of the tool; for example, allow EXEC/REXX macros to be written so that they automatically search control blocks for internal consistency.

```
PRB00002 D1  KPROBE Release 2 - Storage/Register Display Menu
COMMAND=>
ADDRESS 00000868              MODULE DMKPSA+0868   INCREMENT 000010  SHIFT 000000
00000860   00000000  00000000  9110034A  47100898  *........j..¢...q*  GENERAL
00000870   900F0500  D2030374  08949180  069A4780  *....K....mj.....*  00000040
00000880   088E5810  06605820  03745021  037458C0  *.....-....&.....*  00C889F8
00000890   0B5807FC  D7E2C102  95FF0860  47800870  *....PSA.n..-....*  00BFF600
000008A0   90BF052C  58C00B5C  07FC0000  00BCE000  *.......*........*  40000000
000008B0   43F02001  54F004A8  478008C4  1EFF1EFF  *.0...0.y...D....*
000008C0   58FFB0B0  43102002  88100002  541004B8  *........h.......*  00000000
000008D0   478008D8  5EF1B0B0  41100FFF  54102000  *...Q;1..........*  90BBCBA0
000008E0   4111F000  07FE9540  20004740  08FC9580  *..0....n ... ..n.*  00C88850
000008F0   20004740  08B01FFF  47F008C4  43102001  *... ......0.D....*  0007C798
00000900   950E2000  4780091C  541004A8  078E1A11  *n.........y....*
00000910   1A115811  B0B04110  100007FE  88100002  *............h....*  00076320
00000920   541004B8  5811B0B0  41101000  9500092C  *............n....*  00DF55F0
00000930   07FE0000  00000000  50E00ADC  45E00AA8  *........&......y*  00FF62E0
00000940   58E00ADC  54F0049C  078E4300  B0A947F0  *.....0.......z.0*  00FF62E0
00000950   096450E0  0ADC45E0  0AA858E0  0ADC54F0  *..&......y.....0*
00000960   049C078E  50E00AE0  45E00AA8  58E00AE0  *....&......y....*  00014C10
00000970   54F004BC  540004BC  47800988  150F4780  *.0.........h....*  00C003C0
00000980   09889500  098207FE  180F9101  034A4710  *.hn..b....j..¢..*  00C88A28
00000990   099E58F0  06649101  F34A4780  09D69108  *...0..j.3¢...Oj.*  00FF64B8
   PF2-Display 5-BRLOff 6-Cursline 7-Backward 8-Forward 9-Mode 10-Left 11-Right
```

Figure 5-6 Dump analysis tool screen showing storage display.

We've included a couple of full-screen displays (see Figure 5-6 and Figure 5-7) to show what you might see when you use a dump analysis tool.

Tools for Debugging Running Systems

Problems in running systems usually take two forms:

• Performance (something/everything is running too slowly).
• Something is working incorrectly or not at all.

When a performance problem occurs, you must look into the running system and check indicators to see what is going on. This can be done manually using the CP DCP or XA DISPLAY H commands; semi-automatically by using an interactive dump analysis tool that

```
PRB00002 D1  KPROBE Release 2 - Format CP Trace Table
COMMAND=>
Start Address 00BCE000 End Address 00BFE000 Next 00BD31B0 Last 00BD3300 Len 10
A RUNUSER VMBLK WTF01     RUN  PSW 07ED0E00 0046628E                  BD31C0
  I/O INT C62            REAL CSW 00C97F20 0C000004 I/O OPSW+4 0002C002 BD31D0
  UNSTACK VMBLK SYSTEM     FROM DMKPAHIO     ST BF001000 IOB/TRQBLOK 00C97EA0
  FRET    VMBLK LOGONAB1   FROM DMKDSPWI+0136 G0 0000000A G1 00C1C180  BD31F0
  RETURN  TO DMKSVCIN+0488 FROM DMKPTRAN+06C0 CC=0                     BD3200
  FREE    VMBLK LOGONAB1   FROM 70BBC354     G0 00000018 G1 00DF55F0  BD3210
  CALL    TO DMKQCOFT+0068 FROM BBC368                                BD3220
  FREE    VMBLK LOGONAB1   FROM DMKQCOET+0188 G0 0000000A G1 00C1C180  BD3230
  SCHED   VMBLK LOGONAB1 STAT 84000200 LVL 0000 IOINT 0000 PEND 00 G14 002840
  FRET    VMBLK LOGONAB1   FROM DMKDSPWI+0136 G0 0000000A G1 00C1C180  BD3250
  RETURN  TO BBC368        FROM DMKQCORD+03D2 CC=2                     BD3260
  FREE    VMBLK JJL00      FROM DMKLOCK+0010  G0 00000003 G1 00C465E0  BD3270
  FRET    VMBLK JJL00      FROM DMKLOCKD+0020 G0 00000003 G1 00C465E0  BD3280
  CALL    TO DMKQCOFT+0068 FROM BBC942                                BD3290
  FREE    VMBLK LOGONAB1   FROM DMKQCOET+0188 G0 0000000A G1 00C1C180  BD32A0
  SCHED   VMBLK LOGONAB1 STAT 84000200 LVL 0000 IOINT 0000 PEND 00 G14 002840
  FRET    VMBLK LOGONAB1   FROM DMKDSPWI+0136 G0 0000000A G1 00C1C180  BD32C0
  RETURN  TO BBC942        FROM DMKQCORD+03D2 CC=2                     BD32D0
  FRET    VMBLK ........   FROM 40BBCB8A     G0 0000004C G1 00FE9780  BD32E0
  ABEND   LOK003           FROM DMKLOKTR+008C                         BD32F0
PF2-Display 5-BRLOff 6-Mformat 7-BAckward 8-FOrward 9-MSwitch 10-MENUSEL 11-CUR
```

Figure 5-7 Dump analysis tool screen showing VM trace table.

allows you to view the running system; or automatically via a performance monitor. A typical performance monitor display is shown in Figure 5-8.

Once you have identified the source of the performance problem you can take standard debugging measures. Some common performance problems include:

• Excessive CPU utilization, such as a user application in a loop.
• Excessive I/O utilization, such as a looping user application, or a device giving hot (continuous) I/O interrupts.
• Excessive storage utilization, such as an application in a large virtual machine accessing arrays one byte per page—the worst possible way.

When something is working incorrectly, you need to do one or two things:

1. Gather information, then correct the immediate problem. Obviously, this isn't always possible. For example, hardware devices can be reset, but the act of resetting them may cause them never to respond again.
2. Attempt to recreate, then solve the problem. Again, this is harder than it looks, but there are some techniques for doing it:

   • Insert traps into the system at suspected strategic points; for example, at a place in the code that you should never get to.

     If possible, create a test VM system that runs under the native VM system. This way, you can use CP commands such as ADSTOP and PER to trap code instead of source modifications. This also decreases the number of real system outages.

     Because of real device availability and timing issues, you may not be able to recreate a problem *second level* (running VM under VM). If you can't, and must patch the live system, you can gather information without necessarily taking the system down, by:

     a. Stopping the trace table by clearing the trace table entry enabling bits in the PSA. Then, you can use your dump analysis tool to look at the frozen trace table.
     b. Installing an add-on product which allows you to dump the running system at an error point without causing a restart.
     c. Using the CCWTRACE command for I/O related problems. This causes special tracing information to be placed into either the CP trace table or onto a tape. This information can subsequently be examined to see each command and response from one or more devices.

   • Debug using the real system's operator console. Based on the processor model, this gives you many of the same condition-trapping that you'd get from PER. Needless to say, stopping the machine in the middle of the day is frowned on in most

```
+--------------------------------------------------------------------------------+
|                                                                                |
| VM/370 CPU9375 SERIAL 00977  7988K DATE 10/09/88 START 16:29:53 END 16:32:54   |
|                                                                                |
| <-- ACTUAL DATA -->  < IO SAMPLE > <------ 19% SAMPLED TRACE TABLE DATA ------> |
|                                                                                |
| CH TYPE IOREQST SEC MXB MXW MXQ %DVB %CUB %CHB %PC %CUX IOCC0 %BMX %ERR %CNT    |
|                                                                                |
| 00 BMPX      19   0   0   0   0 .... .... .... ... ....    4 .... .... ....     |
|                                                                                |
| 01 BMPX    *** CHANNEL IDLE ***                                                |
|                                                                                |
| 05 BMPX     384   2   0   0   0 .... .... .... ... ....   80 .... .... ....     |
|                                                                                |
| 07 BMPX     113   0   0   0   0 .... .... .... ... ....   16 .... .... ....     |
|                                                                                |
| 11 MPX     *** CHANNEL IDLE ***                                                |
|                                                                                |
| 12 BMPX      21   0   0   0   0 .... .... .... ... ....    4 .... .... ....     |
|                                                                                |
|              *                                                                 |
| USERID-> %CPU %CP %USR ISEC PSEC WSS RES USEC DRUM PRI VMSIZE Q EXCTN-STATUS    |
|                                                                                |
| PVM      3.6 2.5  1.1  2.1  .0   37  37  .0    0  20 1024K . CMS,IDLEWAIT       |
|                                                                                |
| USER1    2.5 1.9   .6   .0  .0  117 112  .0    0  64 2048K . CMS,IDLEWAIT       |
|                                                                                |
| SMART    1.1  .8   .3   .0  .0  141 141  .0    0  64 2048K 2 CMS,INSTWAIT       |
|                                                                                |
| USER2    .98 .41  .57   .0  .0  205 205  .0    0  64 2048K . CMS,IDLEWAIT       |
|                                                                                |
| SYSTEM   .30 .30  .00   .0  .0    0 694  .0    0   0   0K . ...,SYSTEM          |
|                                                                                |
|               <-- 00 LOG ACTIONS INDICATED -->                                 |
|                                                                                |
| %CPU %CP %USR %TWT %PAG %I/O %IDL %STO ISEC PSEC XPG PPAG USR IQ WQ ACT Q1SEC   |
|                                                                                |
| -> 10   8   2   90    0    0   90    8    2    0    0 1711  16  1  0   5  .04    |
|                                                                                |
| <- 14  10   4   86    0    0   86    8    1    0    0 1711  16  1  0   4  .06    |
|                                                                                |
+--------------------------------------------------------------------------------+
```

Figure 5-8 Sample performance monitor output.

installations, so this sort of debugging should be reserved for only the most severe problems.

Tools for Debugging Applications

Just as applications come in many flavors, so do the tools used to debug them. The gamut runs from built-in CP facilities to full-screen systems. We will touch on some of these in this section.

In general, you debug applications using the same techniques you've developed for debugging systems that is, information gathering, exploration, fix.

CP Facilities

CP provides several commands to help you to debug virtual machine systems. Since CP knows nothing about your application, these tools

ADSTOP   stops the machine at a specific address.

BEGIN   starts the machine at a specific address.

DISPLAY   displays virtual storage, registers, protect keys, etc.

DUMP   dumps virtual storage, registers, protect keys, etc., in a printed, readable format.

PER   takes an action (such as stopping the virtual machine) based on one or more program event recording (PER) events; for example, the modification of a storage location or register.

STORE   modifies virtual storage, registers, protect keys, etc. STORE STATUS saves the machine's status into low storage.

SYSTEM   performs system restart, clear, or reset.

TRACE   takes an action (such as stopping the virtual machine) based on one or more software detectable events; for example, an I/O operation.

VMDUMP   dumps virtual storage, registers, protect keys, etc., into a dump file for later analysis.

Figure 5-9 CP debugging commands.

are restricted to a set similar to those provided by a real processor; for example, stopping the machine, starting at specific addresses, displaying and modifying storage, restarting the machine, and so on. Figure 5-9 shows some of those commands.

DEBUG   provides very rudimentary debugging commands. This command has been removed from CMS as of release 5.5.

EXEC tracing   provides the ability to debug EXEC routines such as displaying lines from the EXEC as it runs.

SVCTRACE   provides a printed list of CMS SVC calls.

Figure 5-10 CMS debugging commands.

CMS Facilities

CMS also provides some facilities to help in debugging, although these are somewhat basic or specialized and aren't often used. Figure 5-10 shows those commands.

Program Product Facilities

While it isn't within the scope of this chapter to cover all program products that run under VM, suffice to say that most of these contain some commands and facilities to assist in debugging their problems. Figure 5-11 shows some examples.

CPTRAP

CP has a facility which allows you to add your own entries to the CP trace table. Also, the trace table can be written to a special spool file for later analysis.

Three kinds of records can be written into a CPTRAP file—standard trace table entries, user generated virtual machine entries, and user generated CP entries. GCS, for example, can create trace table entries containing VTAM trace information. The CMS TRAPRED command can be used to display data from CPTRAP files. Also, some dump analysis tools support CPTRAP files.

AVS	AGW SET ETRACE, AGW SET ITRACE.
GCS	GDUMP, ETRACE, ITRACE.
PVM	AUDIT, DUMP, QUERY, SNAP, STATUS, TRACE.
RSCS	DUMP, QUERY, TRACE.
SFS	ETRACE, ITRACE.
TSAF	RUNTSAF n ETRACE.
VSCS	TRACEON, TRACEOFF.
VTAM	F TRACE, F NOTRACE.

Figure 5-11 Program product debugging commands.

High-Level Language Debuggers

Again, this is a topic beyond the scope of this chapter. Suffice it to say, there are packages that assist in debugging COBOL, FORTRAN, PASCAL, and PL /I. The current versions of these compilers come equipped with their own debugging systems.

Application Debugging Systems

One of the problems in debugging an application using CP services is that the CP services live outside the operating environment of the application. Consequently, one cannot specify symbolic addresses (such as statement or storage labels). Also, one cannot take advantage of the CMS system services when a breakpoint is taken.

To solve this problem, there are application debugging systems that allow you to debug applications in a CMS environment. Similar in function to a dump analysis tool, these systems also allow you to start and stop your application just like using the CP ADSTOP, PER, and TRACE commands. There are, however, two important and useful differences:

- You can specify program variable and statement names, rather than storage addresses.
- You remain in the CMS environment when the event occurs. This allows you to examine CMS files (such as your source), look at the status of your minidisks, issue additional FILEDEFs, and so on.

We have included a few examples of a CMS full-screen debugging system to show you what such an environment might be like. These are shown in Figure 5-12 and Figure 5-13.

Here are some of the features you might want in application development, testing, and debugging:

- A simple means for executing repetitive tasks, such as compiling, linking, and running an application.
- The ability to do unit *testing*, that is, to test individual parts of an application before integrating the pieces together.
- The ability to interrupt an application if it:
  - — Abends
  - — Program checks
  - — Modifies a particular storage location
  - — Reaches a particular instruction

```
          BP XDEBUG Release 2.00 — TYPE Mode Menu
COMMAND=>
Breakpoint name: ASTOP001
Breakpoint at: 00020008  Module: BR14  Label: BR14


Type          Old Psw      Int Code  (Current) New Psw
XDEBUG   FFE40001 40020008  00020001  FFE40001 4002000A


Program Status Word fields:
CC: 0   IL: 2   Key: E0   I/O: Enabled   Mask: FE
External: Enabled   Machine Checks: Enabled   Problem: Off   Wait: Off
Fixed point Overflow: Off   Decimal Overflow: Off
  Exponent Underflow: Off        Significance: Off


G0-G7   00000E08 0B000850 00000850 0000DF40 00F01332 00000006 80F14BBC 0B000850
G8-G15  40F148B8 00F158B8 E3404040 00E61000 00020008 0000DF40 00F01332 00000000


00020008 SR     R15,R15                   1B F F

PF2-Display 5-Go 1 6-Mformat 7-Backward 8-Forward 9-Brkpoint 10-HI 11-Retline
```

Figure 5-12 Debugging system showing a taken breakpoint.

>   — Issues a system call (SVC)
>   — Sets a register to a specific value, etc.
> • The ability to reference and change data in a symbolic fashion.
> • The ability to display storage in a variety of formats and to format
>   data areas/control blocks.
> • The ability to be extended via a macro system.

Fixing or Reporting the Problem

Once you've found a problem, you have several possibilities:

Ignore it. This is not the best choice, but possible for smallimpact, seldom-occurring problems.

Circumvent it. Again, not the best choice but perhaps the only possible solution if you lack the resources to repair the damage. For instance, if you don't have the source code for the offending module.

Report it to the supplier or owner. This is somewhat better, but you are still at the mercy of an outsider's schedule and priorities.

Repair it.

```
          CL XDEBUG Release 2.00 — Subroutine Call Interface
COMMAND=>


Subroutine                      Parameters
CALL MDSPRD    1 NUMBER    2 RETCODE    3 KEY       4            5
               6           7            8           9            10


Registers                  Condition code 0
  G0-G7   00000E08 0B000850 00000850 0000DF40 00F01332 00000006 80F14BBC 0B000850
  G8-G15  40F148B8 00F158B8 E3404040 00E61000 00020008 0000DF40 00F01332 00000000


          Declarations
Name  Type Length       Value
NUMBER  F  4     0
RETCODE F  4     0
KEY     C  8     ENTER
LONG    D  8     +0.1234567890123457 E+006
LLONG   L  16    +0.12345678901234567890123456789012 3 E+009
FLONG   F  8     9223372036854775807



PF2-Display 5-Loader 6-Call 7-Backward 8-Forward 9-Brkpoint 10-Disks 11-Delete
```

Figure 5-13 Debugging system showing a subroutine call test.

Repairing VM Problems

When repairing VM problems (in system software provided with source), it is the convention to make changes via the CMS UPDATE process. This process uses lists of fixes to individual modules which contain individual fixes for specific problems or functions. The standard practice is to:

- Create your own *control file*. This file lists your locally created AUX files.
- Create a local AUX file pointing to your fix.
- Use XEDIT's CNTRL option to create the fix. You can also manually generate a fix, but using XEDIT is generally easier and less prone to error.
- Assemble the module. Check the listing to ensure that the fix went in correctly.

- Build a test system and attempt to recreate the problem to ensure you've really fixed it.
- Put the fix into production.

Since it is likely that the vendor will also fix the problem eventually (especially if you've reported it), you must check that your fix is still valid *every time you put on system maintenance*.

Under VM/XA SF and VM/SP Release 6, a new set of procedures exists to help you keep track of your local fixes.

Reporting VM Problems

If you report a problem to a vendor, it makes everyone's life easier if you follow these few simple suggestions:

Always keep copies of anything you send, so that you can refer to it as needed.

Attempt to have as much information at hand as possible. This should include:

- A simple description of the problem, together with specific information relevant to the type of problem, such as an abend code, a wait state code, loop, performance, or incorrect results (sometimes called INCORROUT, or incorrect output).
- Supplemental information such as program listings, dump files, console listings, and so on.
- A list and the nature of local modifications.
- Your system's hardware and software configuration.
- The product and system's version, release, and last modification level.
- Information on recent changes. Did the problem occur only after something (however small) changed?
- The smallest program or sequence possible that reproduces the problem.
- The problem's severity (from "the entire computer's down" all the way to "just thought you'd like to know").
- The name and number of your local expert best equipped to deal with this problem.
- Who to contact, when, where, and how.

Have a place to keep the information, plus any information you receive from the support group, so that you can refer to it during subsequent calls. You should also note who you've spoken with, the date, time, and duration of the call, what was decided/accomplished, and what actions are to be taken and by whom.

The process of resolving a problem with a vendor can vary from being extremely smooth to extremely exasperating. Usually, a support organization first checks its problem database to see if your problem has already been resolved. This is why it is important to gather information to improve your chances of finding a database match.

If this doesn't work, the next step is to use the information you've provided to debug the problem. This debugging is done using the same steps we've discussed in this chapter, with the added disadvantage of not having your environment readily available.

Once (and if) a fix is worked out, you will receive it for local testing. Usually, the problem will remain open until you are satisfied that it solves your problem. Be sure to let the support people know how it works out so that they can integrate it into the system and, thus, potentially avoid having it affect other users.

By being accurate, thorough, understanding, and level-headed, you will establish credibility with your vendor's support people. This is important, because when you are viewed as an expert, your vendors will give far more credence and attention to your problem reports.

For Further Information

For more information on debugging and system internals, look through product diagnosis, diagnostic reference, data areas, and logic manuals. There are also seminars and classes given on systems internals with an eye toward problem analysis and resolution.

Conclusions

Debugging, like other simple activities such as brain surgery, gets easier the more you do it. At first, you may feel overwhelmed, but over time you will almost know what a problem is before you even look into it.

Remember, the key skills are patience, persistence, and experience. Almost all problems can be solved once you've discovered enough information about them.

One day you will be the old timer, telling the young sprouts your own horror stories, such as the computer system that crashed every day at 6 P.M. for completely different reasons. Turns out, that's the time the place next door tested their microwave transmitters (which pointed straight at the computer center).

Acknowledgments

I'd like to thank Gabe Goldberg of VM Systems Group for letting me crib some of his previous writings and thoughts about system debugging.

I'd also like to thank Wilt Byrum of VMSG and Charles Reinking, my original partners in Kolinar Corporation, for pioneering some of the world class system and debugging software.

Finally, I'd like to thank Jean Lockwood, technical writer extraordinary, for editing this chapter into something resembling English, and Wilt Byrum and Tom Kumpf for technical editing.

About the Author

James R. (*Jim*) Bergsten, is vice-president of VM Systems Group, Inc. (VMSG), a Virginia corporation specializing in the development of systems and applications software for the IBM VM operating system.

Jim was a founder, and the chairman and president, of Kolinar Corporation, a California corporation that also developed and marketed VM software. Kolinar, a six-year-old profitable company, with sales exceeding $1 million, merged with VMSG in June of 1988.

He is well recognized within the industry for his development of computer graphics, diagnostics, applications and systems software, and is consultant to several major corporations in the areas of design, development, systems analysis, and computer performance. Jim has given many presentations, seminars, lectures, and talks worldwide.

Jim authored Kolinar's *XMENU/E*, an ICP award winner, widely considered to be a *de facto* industry standard. He also wrote and designed *SQL/MENU*, *SQL/EXEC*, and parts of *KPROBE, XDEBUG, K3101*, and *KDES*. Jim is responsible for the design and management of over 250,000 lines of debugged product software and documentation. All of his products have a reputation for excellent reliability, function, and ease of use.

Jim has held management positions in program development, data center management, customer support, and software testing at Amdahl Corporation, Storage Technology, National Aeronautics and Space Administration, and General Electric. He studied electrical engineering at Cooper Union in New York City.

6

VM Maintenance

by Jeffrey B. Savit

What Is System Maintenance?

VM/CMS is the primary method of delivering interactive computing services on IBM 370 family computers and has become vital to many business, academic, and research institutions. Since VM reliability is extremely important to these firms, preventing system outages is a major responsibility of the VM systems programmer.

The goal of VM maintenance is to improve system integrity by safely upgrading system software to more reliable and functional versions. Applying software improperly can create a system that performs poorly, produces incorrect results, crashes frequently, or doesn't run at all. This makes system maintenance the most critical of all systems programmer jobs.

Systems programmers have other important tasks: performance tuning, system debugging, and installing new products and hardware. However, maintenance is the process by which the system is updated to perform these tasks, and is thus central to all systems programmer activities. Systems maintenance is the heart of systems programming, and is the task that best defines the systems programmer's role.

IBM and other vendors continually write new VM code to fix bugs and add new facilities. The new software is sent to systems maintainers on both a periodic and on-request basis. Finally, the systems programmer creates system changes: software changes, to update the system's configuration, are among the most critical changes.

VM can be installed and maintained "cookbook style" by mechanically following the procedures in the IBM installation manuals. However, these manuals don't fully explain how a VM system can subsequently be maintained safely and unobtrusively. This chapter discusses methodology and strategy of maintenance for VM's CP and CMS components. The examples and techniques used are for VM/SP Release 5 and VM/SP Release 5 with the High Performance Option (HPO).

Skills Needed for VM Maintenance

First and foremost, the VM systems programmer must be familiar with VM concepts and must be experienced using CP and CMS commands. This permits judging consequences of new software that alters the user interface or affects critical applications.

VM systems maintenance also requires some level of skill in System/370 assembler language, at least at the level of knowing assembler syntax, because VM is written in assembler and is customized using assembler macros. VM internals knowledge and system debugging abilities are not needed, though they are extremely helpful.

The role also requires that the systems programmer have discriminative abilities for judging how to manage the contents of the software and the risks associated with instituting change.

VM System Maintenance Overview

VM maintenance results in an updated software base from which the running system is built. VM system software resides on maintenance disks from which a "live" system is constructed. These are normal CMS minidisks, containing source and object code, macro libraries, and control files which configure and deliver the actual system.

VM maintenance is applied via a series of conceptually simple steps, using normal CMS commands. IBM provides "all-in-one" maintenance EXECs, such as SPGEN and GENERATE, but it is simpler to use the fundamental CMS commands they invoke, and apply the output from each step of maintenance in the succeeding steps.

VM system maintenance can be roughly subdivided into the tasks of creating individual program modules and combining them to produce either a CP or CMS system "nucleus." A nucleus is an executable copy of CP or CMS, loaded from disk when bringing up a VM system or when a CMS session begins.

Some CP and CMS modules are used to build runable CMS command files (files with filetype MODULE), or create IPLable programs that can run "standalone" on the bare hardware, such as the DDR (Disk Dump Restore) utility program. Each module consists of an assembler program, updates to the "base" version of this program, and object code (TEXT file) produced by assembling (compiling) the updated source module.

Source and object code files are provided by IBM on the system distribution tape and on service tapes. CP modules have sixcharacter names beginning with the letters "DMK," and (often) ending with three characters that suggest the function of the module. For example, DMKIOS is the central module of the CP I/O Supervisor. CMS modules have six-character names beginning with "DMS." DMSFOR, for instance, is the module that is used to create the CMS FORMAT command.

A CP or CMS nucleus is built by appending TEXT files to a "bootstrap loader" program. A "load list" EXEC specifies the names and order of modules to be placed in the loader deck. The resulting file can be "IPLed" (Initial Program Load) to build a memory image of the CP or CMS system and save it on disk. The VM system can then be reloaded using the new software copy.

Systems programmers allocate and format disk areas that receive the CP system nucleus when the system is first installed and create the nucleus and write it to disk whenever the system is changed. Several nucleus areas can be allocated, allowing use of one area for a production system and other areas for testing and emergency fallback copies of CP. This facility is new in VM/SP Release 5 with or without HPO.

CMS consists of an IPLable portion and a public CMS minidisk containing system command files and libraries. Instead of residing in a CP formatted disk area, a CMS nucleus is stored on reserved disk space at the end of the CMS S-disk. When the S-disk is formatted, the RECOMP option of FORMAT is used to reserve disk space at the end of the minidisk.

It is good practice to reserve sufficient space for several CMS nuclei, to allow test, production, and fallback versions, just as with CP. The new CMS nucleus can then be used by issuing the command "IPL 190," perhaps specifying the cylinder address of a new nucleus, instead of "IPL CMS." The SAVESYS parameter can be used, when IPLing CMS by device address, to make a new CMS nucleus accessible to all users after it has been tested.

Definitions

Like other disciplines, system maintenance defines new words and adds meanings to words used more generally. The following words have special meanings in VM maintenance:

Release — A release of VM introduces new functions and facilities. Most new functions added to VM are introduced at the release boundary. For example, VM/SP Release 5 CMS added National Language Support (system messages can be in French, German, and other languages, as well as English), and the CMS full-screen windowing environment. VM/SP Release 5 CP added support for the alternate IPLable nucleus and added the Transparent System Access Facility (TSAF).

A new release of VM is built upon the previous release, incorporating bug fixes available when it is built.

Version (verb) — A module is "versioned" if it exists in a standard version and an altered form for a different VM system. The HPO (High Performance Option) of VM/SP adds new modules to CP and "versions" existing ones by changing them to add support for new facilities.

Module — A module is an individual program file. CP and CMS are composed of many program modules and are combined in the system generation process into an executable system.

Don't confuse "program module" with the filetype MODULE, which is the filetype used for executable CMS commands created by the LOAD and GENMOD commands.

Source — CP and CMS are written in System/370 assembler language, except for a few modules written in PL/AS, IBM's proprietary systems programming language, a dialect of PL/I. VM is distributed with source code for most modules written in assembler.

Object — Object code is the binary representation of a program, produced by running the assembler language source code through the system assembler. Object code usually has the filetype TEXT; other types are possible to identify test or custom versions of the object code.

APAR — APAR stands for "Authorized Program Analysis Report," and is a "bug report," in which an IBM customer reports a software defect. Every VM APAR has a name of the form "VMnnnnn," where "nnnnn" is a sequence number assigned by IBM. The fix software itself is frequently called an APAR. The IBM support center might ask "Have you applied APAR so-and-so?"

PTF — A PTF is a Program Temporary Fix, actually a misnomer since it is the permanent representation of a program fix. In VM there is generally a one-to-one relationship between an APAR and the PTF that fixes it for a specific release of VM. Unique PTF numbers are assigned for each version of VM that the PTF applies to. For example, APAR VM30287 is PTF UV32319 under VM/SP4 and UV32320 in VM/SP5. VM systems programmers normally think in terms of APARs, but the IBM support center may occasionally refer to a fix by its PTF number instead.

PUT — A PUT is a Program Update Tape, frequently and redundantly referred to as a PUT tape. IBM periodically distributes PUTs to VM licensees. PUTs are named by the year in which they are issued and a sequence number, for example, PUT 8801.

SLU — SLU stands for Service Level Update, and identifies the version of VM provided on a given PUT tape. An SLU is a three digit number: The first digit is the release of the software (e.g., 5 for VM/SP5); the remaining digits are a sequence number starting with 00 when the release is shipped, and incremented with each PUT.

SPE — SPE stands for Small Programming Enhancement and is an APAR that adds new functions to VM, instead of correcting a problem. IBM sometimes adds new facilities to already-released versions of VM via APAR, if they are important enough to be delivered before the next "release" is available. SPE APARs frequently support new IBM software or hardware products.

ZAP — A ZAP is a method of patching object code by overlaying the compiled code with new contents. ZAPs are applied using the CMS ZAP and ZAPTEXT commands. ZAP subcommands specify an offset into a module's object code and the original and replacement hexadecimal contents. ZAP subcommands are used when the source code to a module is unavailable.

ZAPs are especially complicated when code must be inserted into a program. The usual technique is to change the instruction where code is to be added to a branch instruction to a "patch area," where the overlayed instruction and the new code are executed. Finally, a branch instruction jumps back to where the code was logically added.

Support Center

IBM's Support Center, accessible via a toll-free phone number 24 hours a day, provides software support for problems and installing service.

When you call the Support Center, the dispatcher asks for your IBM customer number, and then routes you to a "Level 1" Program Support Representative (PSR). The Level 1 PSR searches IBM's problem databases for previously recorded incidents with symptoms similar to yours. Quite frequently, there will be a good match with a problem at another site. If the problem has been solved, the PSR will ship you the fix.

If the problem cannot be "closed" in this manner, Level 1 transfers your problem to the Level 2 queue for the affected system component or section of code. The Level 2 PSR calls you back, usually by the next day, to help diagnose and correct the problem. Level 2 PSRs work with the code, dumps, the customer systems programmer, and the code's developers to create new fixes.

IBM maintains a comprehensive system to track open problems. Each problem is assigned an "incident number" for tracking and a "severity level," between 1 and 4, to specify the seriousness of the problem. You, not IBM, specify the severity of the incident. Severity 1 is normally used for emergencies where immediate assistance is needed and the systems programmer remains on site for callback from IBM. Severity 1 incidents move to the front of the Level 2 queue and the local IBM branch is notified. Most incidents are opened at Severity 2; less critical problems can be opened at Severity 3 or 4.

The Maintenance USERID

VM system maintenance is customarily done from a standard VM userid named MAINT, which has minidisks that contain the maintenance files and the live CP and CMS disk areas.

A standard disk set up, using the IBM recommended configuration, includes the following minidisks:

295 —   Local customization files. Many sites simply use the MAINT 191 disk.

294 —   CP source updates and current PUT tape's version of object code and macro library files.

194 —   Base version of CP object code and macro libraries.

394 — Base version of CP source code.

293 — CMS source updates and current PUT tape's version of object code and macro library files.

193 — Base version of CMS object code and macro libraries.

393 — Base version of CMS source code.

190 — CMS S-disk, containing CMS commands, EXECs, and library files.

If HPO is installed, additional disks, 296, 196, and 396, contain HPO-versioned files corresponding to those on 294, 194, and 394. The disks should be accessed in the order: HPO, then CP, and finally CMS.

This configuration can be used without change, but it is safer to add extra minidisks for test and fall-back versions. For example, CMS maintenance updates the 190/S-disk accessed by all logged on users. If a separate disk is used to load new S-disk contents, maintenance can be applied without requiring users to logoff. More importantly, if there are problems with the new version of CMS, the old version is still intact and can be used to fix the problems.

Alternate minidisks can be created on the same userid or a secondary userid can be set up with duplicate minidisks. In either case, current production minidisks would be copied to the second set, service would be applied to auxiliary disks, and new systems created from them. Once the new software has been in production long enough to be considered trustworthy, new disk contents can be copied over the previous version to make them identical again.

Naming the MAINT USERID

It is not necessary for this userid to be called MAINT, or that it be a single userid at all, though IBM manuals and this chapter assume that it is. The main advantage of using the traditional name is that it matches the standard documentation. Installation EXECs for some products assume the name MAINT is used.

There are also disadvantages to the standard userid name. Product install EXECs from IBM and other vendors often assume it is safe to write to, or even format, the contents of MAINT minidisks. This can cause serious damage if the system is altered during normal processing hours or if new software doesn't work. Renaming MAINT makes it more difficult for a runaway install EXEC to change the running system without your knowledge and prior preparation.

Using the standard name can open a security breach. The maintenance userid normally has privilege classes and security access to control most aspects of the VM system and access the contents of any minidisk. A hacker seeking to penetrate a VM system would try to logon to MAINT, perhaps using the original password IBM provides when distributing a system. Renaming MAINT (or at least changing its password on a timely basis!) defeats this security risk.

Using the standard MAINT name also makes it awkward to install and operate different software levels simultaneously. Many sites install new versions of software one component at a time. For example, an installation could convert from VM Release 4 to Release 5 by first installing the CP component of Release 5, and then the CMS portion.

This is prudent, since it is much easier to diagnose a problem when only a portion of the system software has been changed. It is difficult to do this kind of incremental maintenance using a single maintenance userid. Different versions of VM should not be kept on the same maintenance userid, even though it is generally safe to operate a system containing different versions. For this reason, it is a common practice in experienced VM installations to separate their maintenance userids by system component (e.g., separate userids for CP and for CMS) or by system version or PUT level.

Module Maintenance Philosophy

VM maintenance is unlike that of most other operating systems, since VM is distributed and maintained using source programs that comprise it, and object code files generated by assembling (compiling) them. VM/SP is written largely in System/370 assembler language.

Source based maintenance has major advantages over the kind of maintenance necessary for software distributed in object code only (OCO) format. Source code availability has become a controversial subject in the last few years, due to IBM's recent policy of moving to OCO for its products. VM is still largely distributed and maintained in source form, which increases safety and ease of maintenance, even for installations with no local modifications or internals experience.

A VM system is shipped with a complete set of object code and with source code to most of its modules. Fixes are shipped as source updates to prior versions of system modules, as well as the re-assembled object code.

VM's source based maintenance is sometimes called "base plus delta" maintenance, since all maintenance activity starts with the original (base) version of a module and applies incremental updates ("deltas") to produce the current version. This method contrasts with the "moving base" method used in IBM's MVS systems, which replaces earlier versions of modules with new copies. The advantage of "base plus delta" is that a prior version of a module can always be recreated if the latest version doesn't work.

The VMFASM command creates an object module by reassembling a temporary copy of the source module, constructed by applying updates to the module's base version. After assembly, the temporary source file is erased to prevent accidental misuse. The update history of the module is placed in the object code "TEXT" file. The service record of a program can be determined simply by browsing it. When a MACRO or COPY file is changed, a new MACLIB is created by applying updates to base versions of affected files, by using the VMFMAC command. Affected modules are reassembled to pick up the changed definition.

This method can be used with the IBM Support Center when resolving a problem. The IBM PSR can read an emergency fix over the telephone to the systems programmer, who can type it in, assemble it, and test it in minutes.

A different method must be used when a module is not distributed with source code. Instead, ZAP commands are used to replace incorrect object code. It is extremely easy to make a transcription error typing the replacement data, since they consist solely of hexadecimal values and are subject to little validity checking. Source level updates, in contrast, are processed by the UPDATE command, which validity checks its sequence numbers, and by the system assembler, which syntax checks them along with the rest of the module. ZAPs are provided by IBM. An APAR is provided as a ZAP until a replacement TEXT file is shipped as part of a PTF.

Module Maintenance Mechanics

The building block of VM maintenance is the individual program module. Each module consists of its original source code in System/370 assembler language, updates to create later versions of the source, and object code files produced when they are combined and the resulting file assembled (compiled). MACRO and COPY files are similarly combined with updates to create new macro libraries (MACLIBs).

VMFASM Command

Object modules are created using the VMFASM command, which is of the form:

```
VMFASM module-name cntrl-name
```

where "module-name" is the name of the source module being assembled. The "cntrl-name" specifies the CNTRL file that selects which updates are to be applied to the module, and the filetype to assign to the resulting TEXT file.

VMFMAC Command

Updated MACRO and COPY files are placed in a new MACLIB by the VMFMAC command:

```
VMFMAC maclib-name cntrl-name
```

where "maclib-name" is the name of the MACLIB to be produced and also names an EXEC file containing names of files to be placed in it:

```
&1 &2 RBLOKS COPY
&1 &2 VMBLOK MACRO
```

VMFMAC creates a MACLIB containing updated versions of the specified files. When a MACRO or COPY file has been changed, the assembler modules that use it must be reassembled via VMFASM.

Both VMFMAC and VMFASM are based on the CMS UPDATE command, documented in the "VM/SP CMS Command and Macro Reference." The same method used to maintain CP and CMS modules can be used for applications programs written in PL/I, Fortran, or COBOL.

Update Files

Update files consist of "update commands" beginning with "./," intermingled with replacement or added source code. Update commands are:

```
./ *     - comments
./ D     - deletes a line or range of lines
./ I     - inserts new lines of code
./ R     - replaces a line or range of lines with new code
```

The file identifier of the update file correcting an APAR includes the APAR number, making it easy to determine if a fix for a particular problem has been applied. The filetype is built by concatenating a one-letter prefix that designates the VM version to the APAR number and the characters "DK" for CP modules (since CP modules begin with "DMK") or "DS" for CMS modules. The prefix character for a VM/SP Release 5 fix is "O," while "A" is used for VM/HPO5. Thus, HPO5 APAR 28728 applied to module DMKDMP is contained in the file DMKDMP A28728DK. This APAR corrects a low-storage overlay in HPO5, by replacing, deleting, and inserting lines of code:

```
./ R 14924710          $ 14924715 5
        MVC    EXTCPTMR,CPUTIMR      CPU TIMER                @VA28728
./ R 14924740          $ 14924745 5
        MVC    TRQBVAL-TRQBLOK(L'TRQBVAL,R3),CLOCKCMP         @VA28728
./ D 14953480  14953670
./ I 14955950          $ 14955980 30
                                    SPACE
        SPX    ATTPSA        SET PREFIX REG TO NON-IPL PSA @VA28728
        BAL    R6,SAVECTOR   SAVE VECTOR USER, IF ANY      @VA28728
        SPX    ALLZEROS      SET PREFIX REG TO ZERO        @VA28728
                                    SPACE
./ I 14977990          $ 14978020 30
                                    SPACE
        SPX    MAINPSA       SET PREFIX REG TO IPL PSA     @VA28728
        BAL    R6,SAVECTOR   SAVE VECTOR USER, IF ANY      @VA28728
        SPX    ALLZEROS      SET PREFIX REG TO ZERO        @VA28728
                                    SPACE
```

Update commands used sequence numbers in columns 73 to 80 of each assembler program line. The first ./ R statement replaces the line with sequence number 14924710 with a line with a unique, new sequence number. The ./ D command deletes a range of lines and the ./ I command inserts new lines. Numbers after the "$" sign in the ./ I and ./ R statements specify the line number of the first new line and the increment to be used calculating sequence numbers for following lines.

Each new line of code has an "eyecatcher" containing the APAR number in the comment portion of the line. This makes it easy to identify the origin of source statements when reading an assembler listing.

Creating update files would be extremely tedious if the update commands had to be created manually. Fortunately, XEDIT's "update mode," documented in the "VM/SP System Product Editor Guide," creates these files automatically.

Aux Files

Updates to be applied by VMFASM are listed in an "auxfile." The first word (sometimes called a "token") in each line not beginning with an asterisk (used for comments) is the filetype of the update to be applied, with the filename obtained implicitly from the VMFASM command line. The remainder of the line is used for comments. For example, DMKHVC AUXSP, contains:

```
029147DK 510 UV32160 OLTSEP FOR D/T3480 FAILS WHEN RUN IN VIRT MACH
028249DK 505 UV29262 SPLIT DMKDRD TO ADD DMKDRE
027226DK 504 UV28023 CORRECT DIAG28 PROCESSING FOR TCAM USERS
026824DK 502 UV26599 INTEGRITY PROBLEM
026273DK 502 UV26836 PEVM20688 LOOP IN DMKVMC VMEXWAIT TURNED OFF
```

This auxfile specifies that the SLU 510 version of DMKHVC is built by applying update files DMKHVC O29147DK, DMKHVC O28249DK, and so on. Updates are applied "from the bottom up," with the recent fixes at the top of the auxfile. A new fix is added by inserting a new line at the top of the auxfile and issuing VMFASM. A fix can be removed by deleting or commenting out its line.

IBM uses the comment field to identify the SLU of each APAR (e.g., APAR VM27226 was added at SLU 504), the PTF number associated with this APAR, and a brief description of the problem being corrected. The notation "PEVM20688" seen in the auxfile entry for APAR VM26273 indicates that it corrects a "PTF in Error" (PE), VM20688.

VMFASM inserts the contents of the auxfiles it used in the resulting TEXT file, so the APAR history of the module is always available.

CNTRL Files

CNTRL ("control") files specify which auxfiles are used to update a module, the MACLIBs to use during assembly, and the filetype to use for the resulting TEXT file of object code (it needn't remain TEXT).

Two control files are needed for CMS: DMSSP for ASSEMBLE files and EXECs, and DMSMSP for MACRO and COPY files. DMSMSP CNTRL has an entry for an auxfile type AUXMSP, instead of AUXSP, and is needed because there is both an assembler module and a MACRO named DMSABN.

CP control files exist in different formats for HPO and non-HPO versions, for different types of CPU VM can run on, and for optional inclusion of the CP "FREE trap" for debugging:

```
CP CNTRL file               VM/SP5       VM/SP HPO5

-------------               ------       ----------

Uniprocessor                DMKSP        DMKH50

With FREE trap              DMKSPT       DMKH50T

Attached-processor (AP)     DMKSPA       DMKH50A

AP and FREE trap            DMKSPAT      DMKH50AT

Multi-processor (MP)        DMKSPM       DMKH50M

MP and FREE trap            DMKSPMT      DMKH50MT
```

The standard CNTRL file for VM/SP CP, DMKSP CNTRL, consists of the following lines:

```
TEXT MACS DMKSP DMSSP CMSLIB OSMACRO
TEXT AUXSP
```

The TEXT MACS line lists the MACLIBs needed for assembly. The TEXT AUXSP line tells VMFASM to apply updates contained in an AUXSP file with the same name as the module being assembled, and to name the resulting object code file with filetype TEXT (the standard name in CMS). If you issue "VMFASM DMKIOS DMKSP," VMFASM will search for DMKIOS AUXSP, apply updates specified in it, and name the resulting file DMKIOS TEXT.

DMKSP CNTRL can be made more flexible by adding a MACLIB and lines for additional levels of auxfile, for example:

```
TEXT MACS DMKLCL DMKSP DMSSP CMSLIB OSMACRO
LCL  AUXLCL
TMP  AUXTMP
TEXT AUXSP
```

This control file (which would be saved on the A-disk, leaving the original file intact) simplifies installation of temporary files or local modifications. When multiple auxfiles are present, they are processed from the bottom up: AUXSP, then AUXTMP, and finally AU-

XLCL. This allows more fundamental updates to be applied first, followed by temporary or custom updates. DMKLCL MACLIB, at the beginning of the list of MACLIBS, provides a place for MACRO and COPY files updated by local changes or temporary fixes.

VMFASM remembers which auxfile contains the "topmost" update applied to the module. The word preceding the auxfile type specifies the filetype to name the object deck produced by assembly. If it is not "TEXT," then the TEXT file is renamed to "TXT" followed by the word. If a temporary fix is listed in DMKHVC AUXTMP, the resulting file would be named DMKHVC TXTTMP. If a local modification is provided in an AUXLCL file, the file would be named DMKHVC TXTLCL.

Renamed TEXT files help identify a text file. When building a nucleus, VMFLOAD searches for object code files using the filetypes in the control file in top-to-bottom order: TXTLCL, then TXTTMP, then TEXT. This is VM's mechanism for selecting the proper version of a module for inclusion in a CP or CMS nucleus.

This scheme is slightly more complicated for HPO, as shown by DMKH50 CNTRL:

```
TEXT   MACS DMKH50 DMKSP DMSSP CMSLIB OSMACRO
H50    AUXH50
TEXT   AUXSP AUXH50
```

When several auxfiles are listed in a single line, the leftmost auxfile's updates are applied only if none of the other auxfiles exist for the module being updated. This technique, called "preferred auxfiles," selects the correct updates to a module that exists in different versions.

For example, DMKRGE is not versioned by HPO5 and VMFASM uses updates in DMKRGE AUXSP to produce DMKRGE TEXT. Module DMKIOS is versioned by HPO5 and has an AUXSP and an AUXH50 file: Only HPO5 updates are applicable. VMFASM uses AUXH50 updates, and not those in AUXSP, to produce DMKIOS TXTH50.

The object code filetype identifies the version of the code contained inside it and makes it possible to conveniently deliver either an HPO or a non-HPO nucleus.

Loadlists

The "loadlist" is used by the VMFLOAD command to select the modules used to create CP or CMS nucleus. There is only one CMS loadl-

ist EXEC, CMSLOAD EXEC, but there are CP loadlist versions for
each type of VM system that can be created:

```
CP CNTRL file                    VM/SP5     VM/SP HPO5
-------------                    ------     ----------
Uniprocessor                     CPLOAD     H50CPLOD
Attached Processor               APLOAD     H50APLOD
With V=R area                    VRLOAD     H50VRLOD
AP with a V=R area               AVLOAD     H50AVLOD
"small nucleus option"           CPLOADSM   not used with HPO5
```

Loadlists consist of lines like:

```
CPLOAD EXEC                     CMSLOAD EXEC
-----------------------        -----------------------
&1 &2 &3 DMKLD00E LOADER        &1 &2 &3 DMKLD00E LOADER
&1 &2 &3 DMKPSA                 &1 &2 &3 DMSNUC
&1 &2 &3 DMKACR                 &1 &2 &3 DMSZNR
&1 &2 &3 DMKACS                 &1 &2 &3 SLC L00E000
&1 &2 &3 DMKCCH                 &1 &2 &3 DMSZAT
&1 &2 &3 DMKCCW                 &1 &2 &3 SLC L020000
...and so on...                ...and so on...
```

The tokens after the "&1 &2 &3" name object code files are named
in order of appearance in the "IPL deck" to be created by VMFLOAD:
first the bootstrap loader, then modules to create the nucleus file.

If a filetype is not present, VMFLOAD searches for files with that
name and the filetypes specified in the CNTRL file, searching in top-
down order. For example, with our updated DMKSP CNTRL,
VMFLOAD would search for DMKPSA TXTLCL, then TXTTMP, and
finally TEXT. This allows selection of the right version of the TEXT
file for that CNTRL file's version of CP.

"SLC" stands for "Set Location Counter"; these files adjust the
starting address of the following object code.

IBM may occasionally direct you to add a module to the loadlist or
change its position. The CP nucleus consists of both a resident and a
pageable portion. Resident modules precede DMKCPE in the loadlist
and resident modules are after it, but before module DMKCKP. It is
safe to make a pageable module resident by moving its loadlist entry
before DMKCPE, due to CP coding conventions, but not the other
way around. New CMS modules can be added to the loadlist before
module DMSSIG.

Corrective Service

VM service comes in two forms: "corrective service," in which individual fixes are applied to eliminate a problem, and "preventive service," in which a collection of fixes is applied to prevent problems from ever arising.

Corrective service is usually obtained by contacting the IBM Support Center and describing a problem. If the problem's symptoms match an APAR in their databases, they can send a fix by shipping a tape or reading it over the telephone. If it is a new problem, IBM will assign an APAR number, debug the problem, and write new code to fix it.

Corrective service usually updates a small number of files. IBM provides updates containing the APAR fix and the systems programmer creates the new TEXT file by adding an auxfile entry for it and issuing the VMFASM command. If the fix doesn't work properly, the APAR can be backed off by renaming or erasing the offending TEXT decks.

In the example below, an APAR is added to DMKXST, using a DMKH50 CNTRL that includes a line for AUXTMP files, and a nucleus is built including the new DMKXST TXTTMP. Note that the load map is saved on the A-disk; this file will be needed for IPCS dump processing if the resulting system has a crash.

```
.listfile dmkxst
DMKXST AUXTMP    A1
DMKXST A30589DK A1
Ready;


.type dmkxst auxtmp a

A30589DK Invalid ALOCBLOK chain for PAGE or DUMP when other
           processor in MP grabs control, in HPO 5.0


Ready;


.type dmkxst a30589dk a

./ R 11010000      S 11014990 4990     02/16/88 15:40:00
         CALL DMKMHCCP,AFFINITY ISSUE THE SERVICE CALL    @VA30589
Ready;


.spool prt *
```

```
Ready;

.spool pun *
Ready;

.vmfasm dmkxst dmkh50
UPDATING 'DMKXST ASSEMBLE I1'
APPLYING 'DMKXST UPDTHP50 I1'
APPLYING 'DMKXST A26706DK G1'
APPLYING 'DMKXST A30589DK A1'
ASMBLING DMKXST
ASSEMBLER (XF) DONE
NO STATEMENTS FLAGGED IN THIS ASSEMBLY
DMKXST TXTTMP A1 CREATED
PRT FILE  3015  TO MAINT    COPY 001   NOHOLD
Ready;

.vmfload h50aplod dmkh50
SYSTEM LOAD DECK COMPLETE
PUN FILE  3017  TO MAINT    COPY 001   NOHOLD
Ready;

.q v 123
DASD 123  3380  VMSRES R/W    1770      CYL
Ready;

.q r all *
ORIGINID FILE CLASS RECORDS  CPY HOLD DATE  TIME     NAME  TYPE    DIST
MAINT    3017 B PUN 00047470 001 NONE 07/15 18:19:36 LDT   DMKSAVNC HOME
Ready;

.ipl c cl
NUCLEUS LOADED ON VMSRES -- STARTING CYL/BLK=0080, LAST CYL/BLK USED=0083
CP ENTERED; DISABLED WAIT PSW '00020000 00000012'

.ipl cms
PRT FILE  3019   TO MAINT    COPY 001   NOHOLD
VM/SP RELEASE 5
Ready;
read cpnuc map a
CPNUC MAP A1 created
Record length is 132 bytes
Ready;
```

Preventive Service

Preventive service (also called periodic service) protects systems against failure by applying fixes before problems arise. Sites avoid suffering from known and solved problems by applying packaged, pretested fixes.

IBM creates preventive service by packaging new fixes and placing them on a Program Update Tape (PUT). The PUT is tested on a small number of systems. This helps identify problems that might occur when fixes interact with one another and many errors are caught before the software is sent to the general VM population.

VM PUT tapes are normally cumulative with each PUT tape containing all of the service contained on the previous tape, plus new fixes, going back to the first service distributed for that release of VM. This is very useful, since it allows an installation to skip PUTs and reduces the maintenance work needed to keep a VM system current.

IBM, recognizing that most installations do not install each PUT, allows customers to elect to receive "PUT on request," in which PUTs are only shipped at customer request. This reduces tape handling and storage, but should not be selected, even if most PUTs are skipped. If you have PUTs onsite, you can pull an emergency APAR from the tape, instead of waiting for Support Center to ship it to you.

Infrequently, IBM may designate a PUT as "mandatory." This usually happens when the number of fixes on the tape has grown so large that they cannot fit on a single reel of tape recorded at 1600 BPI, the lowest tape density IBM uses for shipping software. Such PUT tapes must be applied before installing subsequent service, since later tapes will not include older fixes from the earlier tapes.

PUT tapes are customized for each customer and contain service for licensed products. Products are identified by a seven-digit product number, often followed by a letter indicating the release of the product. For example, 5664167 is the product number for VM/SP. A suffix of "C" indicates Release 4 and "D" indicates Release 5.

Each product version is also identified by a "service level update" (SLU). For example, the 8801 PUT tape contains the ninth service update for VM/SP Release 5, called SLU 509. It also contains the twenty-fourth service update for VM/SP Release 4, called SLU 424, if the customer profile for the installation shows that it is still in use. A documentation file on the PUT tape, "PUT DOCUMENT" includes a table that matches the SLU number of a product with the PUT tape number. Sometimes an IBM support representative will ask you the most recent PUT tape you've applied, sometimes the service level.

Applying a PUT tape fixes bugs, but is itself a risk, since the software is being changed. A PUT contains fixes for bugs, but potentially contains bugs as well.

Some fixes are added because they solved a problem for a small number of users, but haven't been thoroughly tested before being placed on a PUT. IBM may not test the new code in the wide range of environments in which it will be applied. SPE APARs exacerbate this situation, since they add completely new code, which is unlikely to have been as well exercised as the surrounding VM code. It is quite possible that applying a new PUT will reduce stability instead of increasing it.

It is generally accepted that a PUT cannot be safely run without obtaining "follow on" fixes for problems discovered by its beta-site testers and other early users. A PUT can be applied with a good level of confidence by "aging" (waiting before applying it) and cautiously applying it after other users have reported problems with it. The IBM support center keeps a list of problems reported against a PUT, called "buckets," and ships fixes for these problems on request.

The systems programmer can determine when the rate and severity of new problems with a PUT has decreased to a level that he or she feels comfortable with, by periodically calling IBM Support Center for new buckets. Even after the new PUT has been installed, it is a good idea to call the Support Center for buckets, to see if any new problems have arisen.

The Value of Remaining Current

Most systems programmers are very much aware of the negative consequences of installing bad service and the small immediate consequences of postponing system upgrades. Users rarely greet the systems programmer in the hallway and say "Wonderful! The system didn't crash today!" However, they certainly make their feelings known in the opposite situation.

Users, and data center management, rarely understand why the programmer would take an apparently sound system and "worsen" it by applying software changes that risk its stability. In many ways, systems maintenance is a game of chance in which the very best you can do is to break even, you can never gain credit. Maintenance is best when it is unnoticed.

Because of these negative perceptions of system change, many installations avoid installing service until some event makes it absolutely necessary. The maxim "Don't fix it if it ain't broke" is applied instead and no fixes are installed on a stable system.

Such a conservative approach is attractive for a site experiencing no software outages, but has dangers that ultimately make it unworkable. An old problem could surface at any time on a back-level system, even if it has already been solved by IBM. Alternatively, one might need a function recently added to VM as an SPE APAR. For example, IBM added software support for their new 3990 disk controller, a replacement for the industry standard 3880, and 3380 Model CJ2 disk drives at the 8802 PUT level.

Consider what must be done to apply a recent APAR to a back-level system. The APAR that is needed might have a long chain of prerequisite fixes that must be installed first.

Suppose your system is at the 8606 PUT level and you are now installing a 3990 controller. Support for the 3990 is introduced by APAR VM29507, which appears on the 8802 PUT tape. However, VM29507 requires VM25672, VM26518, VM27455, VM27560, VM28400, VM28977, and VM29096 which must be installed first. These prerequisites might themselves have prerequisites, and so on. This can easily result in a "family tree" of fixes covering several sheets of paper. These fixes could all be applied manually, but only through updating dozens or hundreds of files, a tedious and error-prone process.

If this collection of fixes were successfully applied, it would almost certainly result in the only VM system with that combination of software. These fixes normally would be present in conjunction with other fixes contained on the unapplied PUT tapes. You might discover a bug-causing interaction or prerequisite relationship between fixes that no other site encounters.

It is much easier to apply the latest PUT tape and upgrade the system's service level in the customary manner. However, applying so much service in a single update (in this example, the effects of a dozen PUT tapes) would add hundreds of fixes to your system. Such a massive change would update most of the system and increase the likelihood of several parts of the system suddenly being broken or behaving differently. With so much change, determining which module caused the problem would be significantly more difficult.

The systems programmer must balance the risk of introducing bad code from the service tapes against the risk of large instability when it finally does become necessary to upgrade. It is better to incur small amounts of risk on a planned schedule, than a large risk at an unplanned moment. It is also likely that a problem reported to IBM will be responded to, and rightly so, with a recommendation to "come 'up-level'" and see if the problem persists.

Part of the systems programmer's task is to remain current enough to exploit new software functions and bug fixes, yet not so current as to discover new bugs.

Before Applying the PUT Tape

If sufficient disk space is available, it is best to first apply service to a separate maintenance userid (like MAINT in most respects) reserved for testing and development. This userid can be used for testing new PUT levels, typically by running VM under VM. When testing VM under VM, ensure that the test VM userid does not have system command privileges in the first level system. Specifically, don't give the test userid privilege class "A"; this class would make it possible to accidentally SHUTDOWN the live VM system instead of the one being tested!

The test system can be run on the real hardware if its systems residence disk is a minidisk starting on real cylinder 0 of a disk pack. This can be used for realistic testing and also as an emergency system, in case the normal systems residence volume suffers hardware damage. It is impossible to overstate the additional safety provided by having separate IPLable VM system, for testing and emergencies.

When the new software is proven to be reliable, it can be copied to the production system or the production and test minidisks can be swapped. Ensure that the production maintenance disks are backed up before their contents are replaced.

Applying the PUT Tape

To apply the PUT tape, logon to MAINT and attach a tape drive containing the PUT as MAINT's virtual 181. Then prepare the disks for running VMSERV, the maintenance install EXEC.

VMSERV normally writes updated CMS material to the live system S-disk, MAINT's 190 minidisk. This is very dangerous and will disrupt the sessions of logged on users. Worse, it can result in a disabled VM system if the new version of CMS doesn't work the first time! It is safer to apply the PUT to a duplicate copy of the 190 disk, which preserves an uncorrupted S-disk if the new software level fails. Copy the S-disk to a new location before running VMSERV and apply service there.

VMSERV has other service functions, but is unreliable performing them and should not be used to do more than load service from the PUT. Some VM "purists" avoid VMSERV altogether and directly VMFPLC2 LOAD files from tape to the service disks. This is a matter of choice; VMSERV simplifies positioning the tape and loading the files to disk.

The DDR utility produces a byte-for-byte identical copy of the S-disk. In the example below, DDR copies from the 190 disk to the 390 disk. DDR displays an error message when the end of the 190 minidisk is reached, because the COPY ALL command was used. COPY ALL normally copies an entire disk volume, not a minidisk. The message could be avoided by keying in the amount of space to copy, but the method in the example removes the possibility of omitting part of the minidisk.

It is good practice to define disks that are visible to the public as "read-only," by defining their MDISK statements in MAINT's directory entry as "RR" instead of "MR" as IBM specifies them. This helps prevent inadvertently altering these disks, because they must explicitly be re-LINKed to become writable.

It is very easy to accidentally update a system minidisk. A disk can be altered merely by being ACCESSed in read/write mode and then RELEASEd, because the RELEASE command rewrites the file directory in filename sorted order. If this is the S-disk, then all users will get the "S-STAT unavailable" message when they logon. If either the S-disk or Y-disk is changed, CMS must be resaved to eliminate the messages and the associated performance degradation. It is best to LINK these disks read/only until it is necessary to write on them.

In contrast with the treatment of the 190 disk, in the example below, the 19D "help" disk is linked to in write mode. Any user logging on will get a warning message telling him or her that the disk is write-linked. It is also possible that a HELP command would fail, while or after service is applied, since the "live" help disk is being changed. In practice, service should be applied to a separate HELP disk as well.

```
.query v 190
DASD 190 3380 VMSRES R/O     40 CYL
Ready;
.* Note that users are linked to the production S-disk
.query link 190
MAINT     190 R/O, MELINDA    190 R/O, GABE      190 R/O, BRENNER    190 R/O
```

```
KENT       190 R/O, GOMBERG   190 R/O, BERGSTEN  190 R/O, RYALL     190 R/O
ALVORD     190 R/O, CHASE     190 R/O, SIMCHA    190 R/O, WALKER    190 R/O
COWLES     190 R/O, ROMNEY    190 R/O, SERGE     190 R/O, DANEY     190 R/O
ARTY       190 R/O, ARNY      190 R/O, JEFF      190 R/O, KEARNEY   190 R/O
Ready;


.query v 390
DASD 390 3380 VMSRES R/O     40 CYL
Ready;


.* Note that a 'w' link would fail if any users were linked to this
 .* disk.
.link * 390 390 w
Ready;
.* An 'MR' link gets read/write status even when other users are
.* linked in read/only mode.
.link * 19d 19d mr
DASD 19D LINKED R/W; R/O BY 017 USERS
Ready;


.ddr
ENTER:
.sysprint cons
ENTER:
.input 190 3380 sp5cms
ENTER:
.output 390 3380 scratch
ENTER:
.copy all
COPYING SP5CMS
COPYING DATA 07/01/88 AT 21.14.50 GMT FROM SP5CMS TO SCRATCH
INPUT CYLINDER EXTENTS        OUTPUT CYLINDER EXTENTS
       START      STOP        START      STOP
DMKDDR705E IO ERROR 0190 CSW 0002C7D00E000000
SENSE 80000000
INPUT 000000280000 OUTPUT 000000280000 CCW 0702C3CA40000006
       0000       0039        0000       0039
END OF COPY
ENTER:
.

END OF JOB
Ready(00004);
```

The PUT can now be applied; PUT 8802 is on the tape drive. The VMSERV service EXEC must run from the "C" disk, since it ACCESSes disks at filemode "A" (and, potentially, "B" as well).

The first step is to load the first file from the PUT tape, which includes service programs, and the documentation files for the PUT itself.

```
.cp rewind 181
REWIND COMPLETE
Ready;
.release a
Ready;
.access 191 c
Ready;

.vmfplc2 load * * c
LOADING.....
PUT      8802      C1        -- identifies the PUT tape
PUT      DOCUMENT  C1        -- contains install directions
VMSERV   EXEC      C1        -- service install EXEC
VMFSTK   MODULE    C2        -- utility module for VMSERV
END-OF-FILE OR END-OF-TAPE
Ready;
```

The first time VMSERV is run, it "maps" the tape by seeing which products are contained on it. VMSERV also loads the documentation files for each product to the 191 disk, and asks you if you want to print them. It's not necessary to print these files—you can save paper by using XEDIT or BROWSE to read them.

```
.vmserv

PUT001I: YOU WILL BE REQUIRED TO REPLY TO QUESTIONS REGARDING THE
APPLICATION OF SERVICE. THE ACCEPTABLE RESPONSES WILL BE SHOWN IN
PARENTHESES. A RESPONSE SHOWN WITHIN DASHES: -YES-, IS THE DEFAULT,
AND MAY BE SELECTED WITH A NULL RESPONSE.

IBM VM/SYSTEM PRODUCT RELEASE 5 - 5664-167

IBM VM/SYSTEM PRODUCT RELEASE 4 - 5664-167

OVERLAY GENERATION LANGUAGE FOR VM VERSION 1 RELEASE 1

5664173 - VM/SYSTEM PRODUCT HIGH PERFORMANCE OPTION - RELEASE 5
```

```
5664173 - VM/SYSTEM PRODUCT HIGH PERFORMANCE OPTION - RELEASE 4.2

ENGR SCIENTIFIC SUBROUTINE LIBRARY 5668-863

PUT005I: PLEASE NOTE:
*
*   THE MEMO-TO-USERS SHOULD BE REVIEWED PRIOR TO INSTALLING SERVICE.
*
*  IF YOU HAVE OTHER PUT VOLUMES TO MAP; WHEN YOU HAVE THE NEXT
*     VOLUME MOUNTED, ENTER: VMSERV
*
*  WHEN YOU HAVE REVIEWED THE MEMOS AND ARE READY TO APPLY SERVICE,
*     MOUNT THE CORRECT PUT VOLUME AND ENTER: VMSERV
*
PUT006R: SHOULD THESE 'MEMO(S)-TO-USERS' BE PRINTED? - ( -YES- | NO )
.no                -- save a tree
Ready;
```

The tape is now mapped. VMSERV also ACCESSed the 194 disk
as the A-disk and produced a "TAPE MAP" file showing the files it
loaded from disk. The MEMO files describe the service contained on
this tape for the corresponding product.

```
.q disk a
LABEL CUU M STAT CYL TYPE BLKSIZE FILES BLKS USED-(%) BLKS LEFT BLK TOTAL
194SP5 194 A R/W 30 3380 4096 578 2184-49 2316 4500
Ready;
.t tape map

LOADING.....
5664167D 051040    C1
5664167D MEMO      C1
5664167C 042439    C1
5664167C MEMO      C1
5664293  010103    C1
5664293  MEMO      C1
5664173G 051012    C1
5664173G MEMO      C1
5664173F 042412    C1
5664173F MEMO      C1
5668863  010103    C1
5668863  MEMO      C1
END-OF-FILE OR END-OF-TAPE

Ready;
```

VMSERV also updates SERVICE DISKMAP and VMPUT SERV-
ICE on the 191 disk, which contains status for each PUT tape that
has been applied.

```
.type service diskmap c

*  *

*  *  VM SYSTEM PUT 8802

*  *  TAPE LAYOUT AND SERVICE STATUS

*  *

*  *

*  *   RELATIVE      PROGRAM  NUMBER   FIRST    SERVICE   COREQ

*  *   TAPE - POS    NUMBER   FILES    FILE     LEVEL     FLAG

*  *

       01     01     5664167D   39       003      051040    ---

       01     02     5664167C   38       042      042439    ---

       01     03     5664293    02       080      010103    ---

       01     04     5664173G   11       082      051012    ---

       01     05     5664173F   11       093      042412    ---

       01     06     5668863    02       104      010103    ---

*  *

*  *  END OF RELATIVE TAPE 01

*  *


Ready;


.type vmput service c

*  *

*  *

*  *  VM SYSTEM PUT 8708

*  *  TAPE LAYOUT AND SERVICE STATUS

*  *

*  *

*  *   RELATIVE      PROGRAM  NUMBER   FIRST    SERVICE   COREQ

*  *   TAPE - POS    NUMBER   FILES    FILE     LEVEL     FLAG

*  *

       01     01     5654260B   04       003      030205    ---

       01     02     5668981D   03       007      040204    ---

       01     03     5664167D   39       010      050840    ---

*  *  *  *  *  STATUS OF VM/SP REL5 CP SERVICE: LOADED

*  *  *  *  *  STATUS OF VM/SP REL5 CMS SERVICE: LOADED

*  *  *  *  *  STATUS OF VM/SP REL5 TSAF SERVICE: LOADED

*  *  5664167D APPLY RETURN CODE 4
```

```
     01      04    5664167C      38      049     042239     ---
     01      05    5735XXBC      03      087     040404     ---
     01      06    5664289A      03      090     020604     ---
     01      07    5664280A      03      093     010804     ---
     01      08    5735XX7       03      096     040204     ---
     01      09    5664280       03      099     011704     ---
     01      10    5664289       03      102     011204     ---
     01      11    5664173G      11      105     050812     ---
* * 5664173G APPLY RETURN CODE 4
* *
* * END OF RELATIVE TAPE 01
* *
* *
* * VM SYSTEM PUT 8801
* * TAPE LAYOUT AND SERVICE STATUS
* *
* *
* *   RELATIVE     PROGRAM     NUMBER    FIRST    SERVICE    COREQ
* *   TAPE - POS   NUMBER      FILES     FILE     LEVEL      FLAG
* *
     01      01    5664167D      39      003     050940     ---
* * * * * STATUS OF VM/SP REL5 CP SERVICE: LOADED
* * * * * STATUS OF VM/SP REL5 CMS SERVICE: LOADED
* * * * * STATUS OF VM/SP REL5 IPCS SERVICE: LOADED
* * 5664167D APPLY RETURN CODE 4
     01      02    5664167C      38      042     042339     ---
     01      03    5664293       02      080     010103     ---
     01      04    5664173G      11      082     050912     ---
* * 5664173G APPLY RETURN CODE 4
     01      05    5664173F      11      093     042312     ---
     01      06    5668863       02      104     010103     ---
* *
* * END OF RELATIVE TAPE 01
* *

Ready;
```

Now VMSERV applies the new software level. VMSERV issues prompts to select the products to update and for the minidisk addresses to load the new service to. Default responses are indicated by hyphens and are selected by hitting the ENTER key without typing any text. Default responses are shown in this example as "<enter>."

```
.vmserv

PUT001I: YOU WILL BE REQUIRED TO REPLY TO QUESTIONS REGARDING THE
APPLICATION OF SERVICE. THE ACCEPTABLE RESPONSES WILL BE SHOWN IN
PARENTHESES. A RESPONSE SHOWN WITHIN DASHES: -YES-, IS THE DEFAULT,
AND MAY BE SELECTED WITH A NULL RESPONSE.


IBM VM/SYSTEM PRODUCT RELEASE 5 - 5664-167


PUT012R: DO YOU WISH TO APPLY SERVICE FOR 5664167D? ( YES | -NO- | QUIT )
.yes


   VSP201R: CREATE A COMBINED LIST OF ALL THE FILES LISTED IN THE
TAPE MAPS INTO ONE FILE CALLED ' 5664167D MAP8802 C '? ( -NO- | YES )
   ( THIS IS A BIG FILE. BE SURE YOU HAVE DISK SPACE FOR THIS FILE. )
.yes


VSP113R: ENTER CP SOURCE SERVICE DISK ADDRESS ( -294- | CUU )
. . . . ( CP SOURCE, MACRO, COPY, AUX, UPDATE FILES )
.<enter>


VSP112R: ENTER CP SERVICE DISK ADDRESS ( -294- | CUU )
. . . . ( CP TEXT, MACLIB, EXEC FILES )
.<enter>
VSP111R: ENTER CP BASE DISK ADDRESS ( -194- | CUU )
(NEEDED TO VERIFY IF AP TEXT FILES WILL BE LOADED)
.<enter>


VSP121R: ENTER CMS BASE DISK ADDRESS ( -193- | CUU )
(CMS BASE REQUIRED TO REGENERATE ASSEMBLE MODULE)
.<enter>


VSP122R: ENTER CMS SERVICE DISK ADDRESS ( -293- | CUU )
. . . . ( CMS TEXT, MODULES, EXEC, XEDIT FILES )
.<enter>


VSP124R: ENTER CMS SYSTEM DISK ADDRESS ( -190- | CUU )
. . . . ( SYSTEM DISK TEXT, MODULE, EXEC, MACLIB FILES )
.390


VSP125R: ENTER CMS-IPCS SERVICE DISK ADDRESS ( -496- | CUU )
. . . . (CP-CMS / IPCS INTERFACE FILES)
.<enter>
```

VSP123R: ENTER CMS SOURCE SERVICE DISK ADDRESS (-293- | CUU)
. . . . (CMS SOURCE, MACRO, COPY, AUX, UPDATE FILES)
.<enter>

VSP128R: ENTER INSTALL SAMPLES SERVICE DISK ADDRESS (-PASS- | CUU)
. . . . (SAMPLES DMKRIO, DMKSNT, DMKSYS FILES)
.<enter>

VSP126R: ENTER HELP DISK ADDRESS (-19D- | CUU)
. . . . (SERVICE FOR HELP FILES)
.<enter>

VSP127R: ENTER IOCP SERVICE DISK ADDRESS (-PASS- | CUU)
. . . . (IOCP TEXT FILES)
.<enter>

VSP132R: ENTER IPCS SERVICE DISK ADDRESS (-496- | CUU)
. . . . (IPCS TEXT, MODULE, MACLIB, EXEC FILES)
.<enter>

VSP133R: ENTER IPCS SOURCE SERVICE DISK ADDRESS (-496- | CUU)
. . . . (IPCS SOURCE, MACRO, COPY, AUX, UPDATE FILES)
.<enter>
VSP145R: ENTER GCS-IPCS SERVICE DISK ADDRESS (-496- | CUU)
. . . . (GCS / IPCS INTERFACE FILES)
.<enter>

VSP142R: ENTER GCS SERVICE DISK ADDRESS (-596- | CUU)
. . . . (GCS TEXT, EXEC, XEDIT FILES)
.<enter>

VSP155R: ENTER TSAF-IPCS SERVICE DISK ADDRESS (-496- | CUU)
. . . . (TSAF / IPCS INTERFACE FILES)
.<enter>

VSP152R: ENTER TSAF SERVICE DISK ADDRESS (-494- | CUU)
. . . . (TSAF TEXT, MODULE, EXEC FILES)
.<enter>

VSP707I: POSITIONING TAPE TO CP TAPE FILES . . .

VSP311I: NOW LOADING CP AUX FILES AND UPDATES TO 294
VSP312I: NOW LOADING CP MACLIBS TO 294

```
VSP314I: NOW LOADING CP TEXT AND TXTAP TO 294
VSP315I: NOW LOADING CP CNTRL AND EXEC FILES TO 294
VSP316I: NOW LOADING NEW CP SOURCE FILES TO 294
VSP350I: STATUS OF VM/SP REL5 CP SERVICE: LOADED
VSP321I: NOW LOADING CMS AUX FILES AND UPDATES TO 293
VSP323I: NOW LOADING CMS-RELATED CP TEXT FILES TO 293
VSP324I: NOW LOADING CMS TEXT FILES TO 293
VSP325I: NOW LOADING CMS EXECS AND CNTRL FILES TO 293
VSP326I: NOW LOADING CMS XEDIT FILES TO 293
VSP327I: NOW LOADING NEW CMS SOURCE FILES TO 293
VSP328I: NOW LOADING CP-CMS/IPCS INTERFACE FILES TO 496
VSP381I: NOW LOADING CMS MACLIBS TO 390
VSP382I: NOW LOADING CMS TEXT FILES TO 390
VSP383I: NOW LOADING THE IPL'ABLE UTILITY FILES TO 390
VSP384I: NOW LOADING CMS EXECS AND CNTRL FILES TO 390
VSP385I: NOW LOADING CMS MODULES, DDR, IOCP AND XEDIT FILES TO 390


VSP051R: PUNCH NEWLY LOADED STANDALONE SERVICE PROGRAMS? ( -YES- | NO )
.no                          -- it's more convenient to load
                                them to tape later.


VSP391I: NOW LOADING NEW HELP FILES TO 19D
VSP371I: NOW LOADING NEW IOCP FILES TO 192
VSP350I: STATUS OF VM/SP REL5 CMS SERVICE: LOADED
VSP331I: NOW LOADING IPCS AUX FILES AND UPDATES TO 496
VSP332I: NOW LOADING IPCS MACLIBS TO 496
VSP333I: NOW LOADING IPCS TEXT TO 496
VSP334I: NOW LOADING IPCS CNTRL AND EXEC FILES TO 496
VSP335I: NOW LOADING NEW IPCS SOURCE FILES TO 496
VSP350I: STATUS OF VM/SP REL5 IPCS SERVICE: LOADED
VSP341I: NOW LOADING GCS TEXT, CNTRL, EXECS, MACLIBS TO 596
VSP346I: NOW LOADING GCS/IPCS INTERFACE FILES TO 496
VSP350I: STATUS OF VM/SP REL5 GCS SERVICE: LOADED
VSP351I: NOW LOADING TSAF TEXT, EXECS, MODULE TO 494
VSP355I: NOW LOADING TSAF/IPCS INTERFACE FILES TO 496
VSP350I: STATUS OF VM/SP REL5 TSAF SERVICE: LOADED


IBM VM/SYSTEM PRODUCT RELEASE 4 - 5664-167


PUT012R: DO YOU WISH TO APPLY SERVICE FOR 5664167C? ( YES | -NO- | QUIT )
.no             -- because we're updating VM Release 5 and this
                   is Release 4 service.
```

```
5664173 - VM/SYSTEM PRODUCT HIGH PERFORMANCE OPTION - RELEASE 5

PUT012R: DO YOU WISH TO APPLY SERVICE FOR 5664173G? ( YES | -NO- | QUIT )
.yes              -- HPO service must be kept 'in sync' with the
                     base VM/SP service.
VHP021R: ENTER VM/SP HPO RELEASE NUMBER TO BE SERVICED ( -REL5.0- |
. . . WITH 'N' THE APPROPRIATE RELEASE NUMBER.
.<enter>


VHP101R: ENTER VM/SP HPO STAGING AREA ADDRESS ( -196- | CUU )
.<enter>


VHP103R: ENTER VM/SP HPO SERVICE STAGING AREA ( -296- | CUU )
. . . . . ( AUXFILES AND PTFS )
.<enter>


VHP104R: ENTER VM/SP HPO SOURCE STAGING AREA ( -396- | CUU )
. . . . ( OPTIONAL ASSEMBLE AND SOURCE UPDATE FILES )
.<enter>


VHP105R: ENTER VM/SP HPO MACLIB DISK ADDRESS ( -296- | CUU )
.<enter>


VHP106R: ENTER CONTROL / EXEC DISK ADDRESS ( -196- | CUU )
.<enter>


VHP107R: ENTER CMS SYSTEM DISK ADDRESS ( -190- | CUU )
.390                        -- use the duplicate S-disk

VHP108R: ENTER HELP FILES DISK ADDRESS ( -19D- | CUU )


296 replaces A (19D)
396 replaces A (296)
296 replaces A (396)
196 replaces A (296)
196 replaces A (196)


390 replaces A (196)
VHP207I: THE 390 MINIDISK HAS BEEN CHANGED BY SERVICE.
IT WILL BE RE-ACCESSED AS 'G'. IF IT IS YOUR NORMAL CMS SYSTEM DISK
IT WILL BE NECESSARY TO RE-IPL IT AND RE-SAVE ANY SHARED CMS SYSTEMS.
THE FILES THAT WERE ADDED/REPLACED ON THAT DISK ARE:
```

```
LOADING.....              FILE STATUS   FORMAT LRECL  RECORDS DATE     TIME
DMKLD00E LOADER   A2 CHANGED FILE  F       80      152 03/01/88 08:06:28
DDR      MODULE   A2 CHANGED FILE  V    65535        5 03/01/88 07:58:55
DIRECT   MODULE   A2 CHANGED FILE  V    24224        2 03/01/88 07:59:14
DMKDDR   TEXT     A1 CHANGED FILE  F       80     1023 02/29/88 18:32:49
DMKDIR   TEXT     A1 CHANGED FILE  F       80      480 02/29/88 18:44:08
DMKFMT   TEXT     A1 CHANGED FILE  F       80      657 02/29/88 18:57:13
DMKLD00E TEXT     A1 CHANGED FILE  F       80      242 02/29/88 19:29:59
IPL      DDR      A2 CHANGED FILE  F       80     1428 03/01/88 07:59:58
IPL      DIR      A2 CHANGED FILE  F       80      483 03/01/88 08:00:00
IPL      FMT      A2 CHANGED FILE  F       80      660 03/01/88 08:00:02
DMKMES   TXTAMENG A1 CHANGED FILE  F       80      753 02/01/88 11:16:08
END-OF-FILE OR END-OF-TAPE
```

```
19D replaces A (390)
PUT016I: PLEASE NOTE:
* * * * * * * * * * * * * * * * * * * * * * * * * * * * * *
* * * *    THE CMS SYSTEM DISK HAS BEEN CHANGED.     * * * *
* * * *    THE CMS SYSTEM DISK SHOULD BE RE-IPL'D.   * * * *
* * * * * * * * * * * * * * * * * * * * * * * * * * * * * *
Ready(00004);
.ipl cms
VM/SP RELEASE 5
Ready;
```

The PUT tape is now loaded. SERVICE DISKMAP on the 191 disk has been updated to record that the service disks now contain the PUT's contents. You can now remove the PUT tape and hold it for later reference or to apply the auxiliary products on the tape.

```
.t service diskmap c

* *
* * VM SYSTEM PUT 8802
* * TAPE LAYOUT AND SERVICE STATUS
* *
* *
* *    RELATIVE   PROGRAM  NUMBER  FIRST  SERVICE   COREQ
* *    TAPE - POS NUMBER   FILES   FILE   LEVEL     FLAG
* *
       01     01  5664167D    39    003   051040    ---
* * * * * STATUS OF VM/SP REL5 CP SERVICE: LOADED
```

```
* * * * * STATUS OF VM/SP REL5 CMS SERVICE: LOADED
* * * * * STATUS OF VM/SP REL5 IPCS SERVICE: LOADED
* * * * * STATUS OF VM/SP REL5 TSAF SERVICE: LOADED
* * 5664167D APPLY RETURN CODE 4
     01      02    5664167C     38    042  042439    ---
     01      03    5664293      02    080  010103    ---
     01      04    5664173G     11    082  051012    ---
* * 5664173G APPLY RETURN CODE 4
     01      05    5664173F     11    093  042412    ---
     01      06    5668863      02    104  010103    ---
* *
* * END OF RELATIVE TAPE 01
  * *
Ready;
```

The easy part is complete. It is now time to remove "reachahead" fixes applied from the previous PUT tape's buckets, or from corrective service, now contained on new PUT tape. This process is sometimes called "regressing old fixes." Temporary copies of the APARs, now in the PUT, are erased along with associated TEXT (probably "TXTTMP") and AUX file entries.

If a private version of a module is still needed, for local modifications or an APAR too new to be on the PUT, it must be reassembled to ensure that the latest APARs from the PUT are picked up. It is also a good idea to reassemble the local customization modules (DMKRIO, DMKSNT, DMKSYS, and DMKBOX) in case the MACROs they reference have been changed.

The first step is to access the service minidisks for VM/HPO CP (if your site has it), VM/SP CP, and VM/SP CMS, in that order.

The disk search used is very important. Use alphabetical search order to locate the most recent version of a file. ACCESS disks containing your local maintenance in front of the disks updated by VMSERV, the "standard" IBM minidisks (19x, 29x, and 39x, where x is 3 for CMS, 4 for CP, and 6 for HPO). NEVER change a file on these disks. If one of the files must be updated, it is best to copy it to a "local" disk that is maintained manually. This makes it possible to undo your change reliably or to determine afterwards what had been altered.

In the scheme used here, standard IBM PUT minidisks are accessed after minidisks that contain local mods (192 disk), vendor products (292 disk), and temporary fixes from IBM (392 disk). You may instead choose to keep all your maintenance files on a single disk or use a different arrangement. IBM documentation shows a

295 disk for all locally created files. This is a matter of choice and there are numerous valid possibilities.

All disks are accessed as read-only extensions of themselves to prevent accidental destruction or erasure of files. A disk is accessed read-write only when it is to be changed; for example, to remove a temporary fix now on the permanent IBM disk managed by VMSERV.

```
.type cpmaint exec

/* CPMAINT EXEC */
'SET CMSTYPE HT'
'ACCESS 192 D/D'  /* local modifications to CP and CMS */
'ACCESS 292 E/E'  /* Vendor supplied CP and CMS mods   */
'ACCESS 392 F/F'  /* IBM provided CP and CMS fixes      */

/* The disks below should not be updated by anything other
   than the IBM service EXECs: */
/* HPO 5 */
'ACCESS 296 G/G'  /* HPO Updates */
'ACCESS 196 H/H'  /* Object code and MACLIBs */
'ACCESS 396 I/I'  /* Source code */
/* CP 5 */
'ACCESS 294 J/J'  /* CP Updates */
'ACCESS 194 K/K'  /* Object code and MACLIBs */
'ACCESS 394 L/L'  /* Source code */
                  /* CMS 5 */
'ACCESS 293 M/M'  /* CMS Updates */
'ACCESS 193 N/N'  /* Object code and MACLIBs */
'ACCESS 393 O/O'  /* Source code */
'SET CMSTYPE RT'
Ready;

.cpmaint
Ready;
.q disk
```

LABEL	CUU	M	STAT	CYL	TYPE	BLKSIZE	FILES	BLKS USED-(%)	BLKS LEFT	BLK TOTAL
191SP5	191	A	R/W	45	3380	4096	186	5058-75	1692	6750
LOCAL	192	D/D	R/O	10	3380	4096	244	686-46	814	1500
VENDOR	292	E/E	R/O	10	3380	4096	76	259-17	1241	1500
FIXES	392	F/F	R/O	10	3380	4096	343	1162-77	338	1500
SP5296	296	G/G	R/O	25	3380	1024	1392	5404-46	6221	11625
196SP5	196	H/H	R/O	20	3380	4096	610	1770-59	1230	3000

```
396SP5 396 I/I R/O  35 3380 4096    555    3222-61   2028   5250

294SP5 294 J/J R/O  25 3380 2048   1497    5600-83   1150   6750

194SP5 194 K/K R/O  30 3380 4096    578    2184-49   2316   4500

394SP5 394 L/L R/O  97 3380 4096    728   12747-88   1803  14550

293SP5 293 M/M R/O  30 3380 2048    945    4051-50   4049   8100

193SP5 193 N/N R/O  30 3380 4096    744    2497-55   2003   4500

393SP5 393 O/O R/O  80 3380 4096    654   10126-84   1874  12000

MNT319 319 P/P R/O 110 3380 4096   1242   15214-92   1286  16500

SP5CMS 190 S   R/O  32 3380 4096    219    3009-63   1791   4800

MNT300 300 U/U R/O  50 3380 4096    149    2820-38   4680   7500

MNT31A 31A X/X R/O  15 3380 4096    367    1397-62    853   2250

MNT19E 19E Y/S R/O  55 3380 4096    375    6022-73   2228   8250

Ready;
```

The disk containing buckets and corrective fixes is now accessed read-write so its obsolete contents can be removed. We will illustrate the process with modules DMKGRT and DMKJRL. This process would be done for each disk containing CP or CMS code not upgraded by VMSERV.

In practice, one would inspect each module on these disks, checking off each to ensure that no back-level modules remain. This is critical: A back-level module could mean that an important APAR was not applied; or worse, that an APAR was only partially applied. The results are likely to be totally unsatisfactory!

In the example here, the F-disk contains locally applied APARs, the G-disk contains HPO5 service, and the J-disk contains CP5 service. The temporary fix on the F-disk is removed so the permanent copy from the PUT can be used. The process of removing temporary fixes is repeated for every fix now present on the PUT.

```
.access 392 f
392 replaces F (392)
Ready;

.* See what disks VM26835 is on.
.listfile * *26835dk *(d
FILENAME FILETYPE FM FORMAT LRECL RECORDS BLOCKS DATE     TIME
DMKGRT   A26835DK F1 F        80      22      1 11/04/87 09:13:51
DMKJRL   A26835DK F1 F        80     849     17 11/04/87 09:14:18
DMKGRT   O26835DK F1 F        80      22      1 11/04/87 09:14:01
DMKJRL   O26835DK F1 F        80     849     17 11/04/87 09:14:44
DMKGRT   A26835DK G1 F        80      22      2 10/16/87 14:54:13
DMKJRL   A26835DK G1 F        80     849     67 10/16/87 15:07:31
```

```
DMKGRT    O26835DK J1 F        80       22        1 10/16/87 14:52:28
DMKJRL    O26835DK J1 F        80      849       34 10/16/87 15:05:59
Ready;


.* We can erase the now-redundant temporary fixes
.erase * a26835dk f     - the HPO versions of the fix
Ready;
.erase * o26835dk f     - the SP5 versions of the fix
Ready;


.* Now see if the AUX and TXT files can be removed.
.listfile dmkgrt * f(d
FILENAME FILETYPE FM FORMAT LRECL RECORDS  BLOCKS DATE    TIME
DMKGRT    AUXTMP   F1 F        80        1      1 01/04/88  12:50:00
DMKGRT    TXTTMP   F1 F        80       62      2 01/04/88  12:55:29
Ready;
.type dmkgrt auxtmp f

A26835DK 8801 buckets PEVM23495 SECURITY SPE EXPOSURES

Ready;
```

The AUXTMP file shows that the only temporary fix applied to DMKGRT is VM26835. We can therefore remove the AUXTMP and TXTTMP files.

```
.erase dmkgrt * f
Ready;
```

VM26835 also affected DMKJRL. Its auxfile is inspected to determine if its temporary fixes can be removed.

```
.type dmkjrl auxtmp f

A29738DK 8801 buckets PEVM26835 invalid data in type04 acct recd. pf
A26835DK 8801 buckets PEVM23495 SECURITY SPE EXPOSURES
Ready;


.listfile * *29738dk *(D
DMKJRL A29738DK F1 F    80    4    1 04/07/88 11:38:13
DMKJRL O29738DK F1 F    80    4    1 04/07/88 11:38:21
Ready;
```

VM29738 is still not on the PUT, so we must edit DMKJRL AU-XTMP, delete the now-redundant line for VM26835, and issue VMF-ASM, just as if we were re-installing it as corrective service. This produces a new DMKJRL TXTTMP file that includes recent fixes from the PUT, as well as VM29738. This process would be repeated for every previously installed corrective service fix.

Applying the Bucket

The IBM Support Center should be contacted to obtain buckets before the new PUT is placed into production.

The first file on the buckets tape is named "VSPnpppp BUCKET," where "n" is the release of VM and "pppp" is the PUT number. For 8802, the VM Release 5 bucket is named "VSP58802 BUCKET." The contents of this file must be carefully read to determine last minute corrections in service instructions, as well as recent fixes. The abstract of each fix should be read to see if it corrects a problem relevant to the installation. If it does, then the fix should be applied using the same techniques as corrective service.

When the buckets have been applied, CP and CMS have been upgraded to a new service level and are ready for testing.

Allocating Disk Space for CP

Providing disk space for CP functions is not specifically part of software maintenance, but is an error-prone task that deserves mention.

Most sites have software to ensure that minidisks added to the CP directory do not overlap and destroy one another. Users of packages like IBM's Directory Maintenance (DIRMAINT) or VM Software's VMSECURE can allocate disk space, since the directory manager selects unused disk extents. If a site does not use a directory manager product, the DIRMAP (available with IBM's IPF product) or DIS-KMAP (provided with CMS) commands can locate free space not currently allocated to a minidisk.

CP uses disk areas for its nucleus, checkpoint and warmstart areas, saved systems, paging and spooling, T-disk, and for the CP directory. CP does not use the CP directory to specify the locations of these disk areas. Instead, the locations for these areas are specified in two places: the allocation map in cylinder 0 of each DASD volume, created by the IPL FMT utility, and in the SYSRES and SYSPAG macros in DMKSYS ASSEMBLE. Furthermore, CP areas must be on

CP-owned volumes, specified in the SYSOWN macro, and are format-ted by IPL FMT.

CP does not ensure that its areas do not overlap minidisks. If such an overlap occurs, user data will be destroyed and it is quite possible that VM will crash as well.

To prevent such a disaster, define "cover" minidisks for each CP area, using fake userids like "$PAGE$" for page areas, "$TDSK$," and so on. The extent checking performed when adding a minidisk can then be used to ensure that no data is being overlaid.

Additional caution must be used when preparing a new disk vol-ume for VM use. Cylinder 0 should be reserved for the system, by allocating a dummy minidisk over it, since the IPL FMT program writes the CP allocation map there. Making that cylinder available to a user would also cause the real volume serial to change when the user CMS-formatted his or her minidisk. Disk volumes should ini-tially be allocated with all cylinders marked as PERM space. If you omit this step and add this volume to SYSOWN, CP will use the default allocation of TEMP (spooling and overflow paging) and at-tempt to spool on the entire volume.

A new CP disk area must be properly formatted (except for tempo-rary disk cylinders) and allocated BEFORE CP might try to use it. IPL FMT is used to put it in 4K page format (the CMS FORMAT command cannot be used for this) and allocate the cylinders as TEMP, PAGE, TDSK, DRCT, or OVRD. Finally, the disk area is added to the SYSPAG macro in DMKSYS and a new VM nucleus is created.

If these changes are made in a different order, and VM is brought down and up again while they are being done, CP may try to spool or page onto an area that is not yet prepared for it, resulting in a sys-tem crash. Also, new volumes must be added to the end of the SYS-OWN list (or, at least, after the last volume containing TEMP space), or a COLD start will be necessary at the next VM IPL.

Other precautions are necessary when working with an existing volume. Normally, changes to the CP allocation map can be specified by typing the cylinder extent of the changed area. If you specify the cylinders used for the CP directory, even if no change is made, CP will "release" the directory area and you must reissue the DIRECT command immediately.

If disks are being converted from single density 3380 to dual or triple density disks, the allocation map cannot be copied, via DDR, from the original volume to the new one. IPL FMT must be run again, so the allocation map can be adjusted for the additional cylin-ders.

Precautions

Extreme caution must be applied when implementing system changes. New software may be faulty or may conflict with other programs. It is possible to install a fix and produce a system that is totally unusable: a VM system that won't IPL or a CMS that fails immediately after LOGON. These problems can be avoided or reduced by careful application of maintenance and by proper testing.

Always ensure that there is a spare working copy of CP or CMS, in case the updated system doesn't work. The very worst thing that can happen is to generate a new version of the system and suddenly have a totally inoperative CPU. Some sites resolve this by backing up the working system and restoring it in case of emergency. Backups are very important, but they are not enough for smooth handling of emergencies. All too often, the recovery procedure is untested and the restore tapes can't be found or prove unusable. Also, DDR, which can be IPLed from a tape drive to restore disks when VM is not up, is unreliable when run "standalone." Don't depend on it for your emergency restore process.

A safer and faster form of recovery can be provided for a bad copy of CP by using the alternate nucleus facility of VM. The alternate nucleus makes it possible to load a new CP system to a different volume than the VM system's residence volume. Prior to this capability, each new CP nucleus overlaid the prior nucleus; the only copy of CP known to work! This danger prompted VM users to modify CP to allow it to be IPLed from different volumes, yet still use the same checkpoint, warmstart, directory, and SPOOL areas as if the "primary" nucleus on the system volume had been IPLed. IBM adopted this modification in VM/SP Release 5.

A new CP system nucleus is loaded to a different DASD volume than the current nucleus. The new volume should be CP owned (listed in the SYSOWN macro in DMKSYS) and the same DASD locations used for the normal CP nucleus reserved and CP-formatted.

To test the new nucleus, SHUTDOWN VM and IPL the system using the device address of the new nucleus's disk. If the new CP fails, it is easy to revert to the working version by IPLing the prior version device address.

A common scheme is to maintain production, test, and fallback versions for CP. The fallback version should be a trusted version of the software, guaranteed to be a reliable system in case the new version is flawed. Usually, the current CP becomes the fallback version when a new copy is installed.

A similar scheme can be provided for CMS by maintaining alternate S-disks. When a new version of CMS is being created, it should be installed on a separate minidisk. A separate CMS saved system (e.g., CMSTEST) can be used to IPL this S-disk. To put this CMS into production, change the DMKSNT entries and switch directory entries for every user's 190 disk to point to the new S-disk. Additional flexibility can be gained by defining the CMS saved system without the "VSYSRES=" and "SYSCYL=" parameters. This makes it possible to switch S-disks just by swapping directory entries: Make the new disk the MAINT 190 disk and resave CMS.

For additional safety, many sites maintain emergency VM systems that can restore the entire production environment. This VM system can also be used for development and testing, provided it is always kept in a state where it can run on the computer hardware even when the usual VM system is "down." An emergency system should be a self-contained VM system, residing on a single disk volume. It need not occupy the entire volume, though the minidisk containing the "virtual sysres" pack of this system should start at cylinder 0 of the real DASD volume.

The emergency system requires sufficient space for CP nucleus, checkpoint, warmstart, and directory areas, and enough TEMP space for one user's paging and spooling. The emergency system should also have an S-disk, a minidisk for a small work area, and a small USER DIRECT file. The directory should include an MDISK statement that points to the live system's source directory. This makes it possible to repair software on the failed system by defining and LINKing to its minidisks.

Emergencies like this can be avoided by careful application and testing of service. It is useful to change only one software component at a time to ease problem isolation and to be prepared to remove any change that is made. Good test and recovery plans require considerable effort, but are well rewarded when problems do arise.

Conclusions

This chapter describes methods for maintaining VM systems. There is no single technique that is the only right way to do VM maintenance. Other arrangements are possible, and can be quite successful, if they provide the ability to control the introduction of new software.

Acknowledgments

Anyone writing about VM system maintenance owes a debt to Melinda W. Varian, of Princeton University. Her tutorial, "What Mother Never Told You About VM Service," available on the Waterloo VM Modifications tape and on the annual VM Workshop Tools Tape, has educated hundreds of VM systems programmers. I wish to thank her, not only for the sage advice in her guide, but for the many other services she has selflessly provided to the entire VM community.

I also wish to thank Gabriel Goldberg and other early reviewers of this paper.

About the Author

Jeffrey B. Savit is manager of VM Technical Services at a major financial institution. Formerly an independent consultant, he advised corporate clients on VM systems and performance, and served on a computer science delegation to the People's Republic of China. He teaches The Adesse Corporation's "Performance and Tuning" and "Problem Determination" classes and is the author of Adesse's Modula-2/370 and Multiple Volume Tape products. Mr. Savit is vice-president of the Metropolitan VM Users Association and is a frequent speaker at the VM Workshop, SHARE, and Modula-2 Users Association meetings. He has an M.S. in computer science from Cornell University and a B.S. in computer science from the Polytechnic Institute of New York.

C

VM in the User Environment

An impetus for the phenomenal growth of VM has been its adaptability to the demands of users, providing an interactive, virtual machine environment to large numbers of simultaneous users. Accompanying this "usability" are issues that must be addressed to maintain both data integrity and overall resource economy. Part C addresses these issues.

DASD is an economic resource, and the rapid growth in DASD, that results from user demand, translates into real budget dollars. Todd Margo and Ron Kral provide a practical approach to managing this resource in "VM DASD Management" (Chapter 7). They discuss the major CP DASD requirements and how DASD is allocated. Margo and Kral also describe the issues that must be considered in formulating the DASD management strategy and provide practical solutions.

Accounting and chargeback in VM is a means of monitoring overall resource use while making users more aware of what they are individually consuming. Julie Tray's "VM Accounting and Chargeback" (Chapter 8) describes the CP accounting records, which provide raw accounting data in native VM. Tray outlines the information included in each of the accounting records, how these records are handled in native VM, and guidelines for the use of the CP accounting records.

System security must be carefully managed to maintain the integrity of data in the VM environment. In "VM Audit and Security" (Chapter 9) Michael Lude begins with an overview of security concepts. He then discusses the security provisions of native VM beginning with the VM directory. Lude also presents security and audit concerns vis-á-vis the areas that must be considered in designing a comprehensive approach to securing the VM system.

7

VM DASD Management

by Todd J. Margo and Ronald P. Kral

Introduction

An IBM 3380K Direct Access Storage Device (DASD), with a retail
cost of about $110,000, stores about 7.5 gigabytes of data. Factoring
in overhead costs such as floor space, installation and maintenance,
controllers and cable, and system staff administration, the cost of
online storage has declined to about $15 per megabyte. By 1991,
hardware advances should drive this cost down to less than $10 per
megabyte.

While the cost per megabyte declines, VM/CMS users are growing
at about 20% to 25% annually. These trends combine to give many
VM data centers annual online storage growth rates of 30% to 35%.
At this rate, online storage doubles every two to three years. This
growth is accompanied by a discomforting sense that the DASD
hardware is not being used as effectively as it should.

The hardware costs of this growth are enormous and many sites
try to actively manage it. But this management is accompanied by a
disturbing growth in expert human administrative costs. Well-managed data centers are more frequently implementing systems software to reduce the expert labor component of their DASD management costs and still optimize their DASD hardware usage.

What solutions are these VM data centers finding? This is the major topic of this chapter. Before diving into it, let's review some of the basics of VM DASD management.

Basic Concepts

Managing any resource means first understanding the market of consumers. Under VM, the "consumers" of DASD fall into two major categories: virtual machines and the VM operating system itself. VM has three different and independent ways to allocate DASD: one for virtual machines and two for the VM operating system. It is extremely important to properly coordinate the different DASD allocations or serious and unpredictable problems will develop.

Before we start, a little terminology. VM consists of two parts, *CP* (the Control Program) and *CMS* (the Conversational Monitor System). CP controls the real machine and *end-users* use CMS under CP to do their work. There are two types of virtual machines: CMS and *guests*. Guest virtual machines run operating systems other than CMS, such as MVS or DOS/VSE. In this paper, we assume all virtual machines are end-users using CMS.

One final point. There are several ˙"flavors" of VM including VM/SP, VM/IS, VM/HPO, and VM/XA. In VM/XA, the way CP DASD is allocated is changed. This paper describes the way DASD is managed when using VM/SP, VM/IS, and VM/HPO. The CMS portions of the paper are common for all versions of VM.

CMS End User DASD

Under VM, users are enrolled by defining a virtual machine. A virtual machine (synonymous with "VM userid" and "end user") stores data—normally CMS files—on one or more *minidisks*. As virtual machine *devices*, minidisks are the logical equivalent of real disks. This means they consist physically of a portion of a real disk but appear to a virtual machine as a complete piece of hardware, similar to a PC hard disk. Thus, minidisks can be as small as one cylinder or as large as one real disk volume. For example, a user's minidisk may be defined as a full 3380K triple density disk, about 1.6 gigabytes.

Minidisks are defined in a VM userid's directory entry via the MDISK directory control statement. Below is a userid directory entry with an MDISK statement.

```
USER BERT STOVE 2M 3M G
ACCOUNT FINANCE JONES
SPOOL 00C 2540 READER A
SPOOL 00D 2540 PUNCH A
SPOOL 00E 1403 A
LINK MAINT 190 190 RR
LINK MAINT 19D 19D RR
MDISK 191 3380 874 5 VMPK01 MR
```

For this discussion, we will ignore all the control statements in the above example except for the last, the MDISK statement. Let's discuss this control statement in detail:

```
MDISK 191 3380 874 5 VMPK01 MR
```

191 is the virtual address of the minidisk. The "191" virtual address is a VM convention; most CMS virtual machines have at least a 191 minidisk. They may have additional minidisks at other virtual addresses. A minidisk has a virtual address because it is a virtual *device*.

3380 is the device *type* of the real DASD volume on which the minidisk resides.

874 is the starting location of the minidisk on the real DASD volume.

5 is the length of the minidisk in device dependent units. In this case, it's the number of 3380 cylinders (a 3380 cylinder holds about 600K of data). This means the minidisk is about three megabytes in size (600K x 5 = 3 Meg).

VMPK01 is the *volume serial number*, or name, of the real DASD volume the minidisk is defined on.

MR is the default access mode of the minidisk. "MR" means the owner gets read/write access unless another user already has read/write access.

Because minidisks are the basic unit of end-user DASD space, VM DASD management is necessarily tied to VM directory management. A directory manager allocates minidisk space when enrolling a new userid on the system. The above MDISK statement typifies a VM user's DASD allocation. When the CMS end-user logs onto the VM system, his 191 minidisk is automatically made available. The directory manager is also responsible for increasing or decreasing the size of user's minidisks as necessary.

On a typical DASD volume, several hundred small minidisks and a few large ones are defined. CP manages access to the minidisks similar to the way the hardware manages access to real DASD volumes. This security prevents virtual machines from reading or writing to DASD areas outside the bounds of their minidisks. In this sense, the userid *owns* the minidisk and the real DASD space within its bounds.

CP's Use of DASD

CP has two DASD allocation mechanisms:

- CP system generation areas ("DMKSYS" and "DMKSNT")
- FORMAT/ALLOCATE areas, or "volume allocations" (allocated using the DMKFMT program)

DASD volumes containing one or more CP areas are known as *CP-owned* volumes. Volumes which do not have CP areas on them are known as *CP-system* volumes. CP-owned volumes are defined and identified by putting them into a list (known as the *sysowned list*) during CP system generation (*sysgen*). Putting a volume in this list is a required first step in allocating DASD areas for CP's use. Once a volume is in the sysowned list, there are two ways of actually allocating CP space on that volume. Some CP areas are allocated via other parts of the CP sysgen and some areas are allocated using the DMKFMT program. All of these areas must be properly coordinated with each other and with the VM directory to prevent allocation errors.

CP-system volumes contain only minidisks and are never used by CP. With the proper coordination, however, CP-owned disks may be set up to contain end-user minidisks.

CP System Generation Areas   Some CP DASD areas are reserved and defined during CP system generation. These areas are specified by IBM System 370 Assembler language *macros* in the DMKSYS ASSEMBLE system generation control file. These DASD areas must be physically located in PERM space on a CP-owned volume; they are not allocated by the CP FORMAT/ALLOCATE program.

A CP-owned volume is defined to CP by a list specified in the SYS-OWN Assembler macro, also in DMKSYS. The example below specifies various CP DASD areas on the VM "system residence" volume "VMSRES."

```
SYSRES SYSVOL=VMSRES,
    SYSRES=123,
    SYSTYPE=3380,
    SYSCLR=YES,
    SYSNUC=(1,4),
    SYSWRM=(6,2,VMSRES),
    SYSERR=(8,2,VMSRES)
    SYSCKP=(10,2,VMSRES)
```

SYSVOL the volume serial number (label) of the disk which contains the CP nucleus.

SYSRES the real address of the disk where the sysres is mounted.

SYSTYPE the type of the sysres disk.

SYSCLR signals that, for security reasons, T-DISK should be reformatted to zeros before allocating it to another user.

SYSNUC is the allocation for the CP nucleus. The number pair specifies the start and length for the nucleus. It is important to allocate enough space since CP does not check for overflow when writing the nucleus.

SYSWRM is the allocation for spool file warmstart data. During system SHUTDOWN and after system ABENDs, CP "remembers" key information about the network, spool files, and accounting in the warmstart area. It is important to allocate enough DASD area to contain all of this data. If the warmstart area is too small, CP will be unable to checkpoint all of the necessary data very slow CHECKPOINT start will be necessary to prevent loss of spool files. Another problem with a too-small warmstart area is that CP cannot automatically restart and requires manual intervention to restart the system after an ABEND.

SYSERR is the allocation for IBM's Environmental Recording Editing and Printing (EREP) program data.

SYSCKP is the allocation for the spool file "checkpoint" area. It is important for this area to be large enough to checkpoint all of the spool files in the system.

CP FORMAT/ALLOCATE Areas   CP FORMAT/ALLOCATE areas, or "volume allocations," are one type of CP DASD use. When a new disk is installed, a program called DMKFMT (CP FORMAT/ALLOCATE) must be run. DMKFMT initializes the disk by writing a label record on cylinder zero and zero records on the rest of the disk. After the disk is initialized, DMKFMT allocates the space based on parameters given to it. The allocations may be for end-users (PERM) or for a variety of CP uses such as spooling, the user directory, paging, temporary disk, and others. The allocations are encoded into a special record termed the *volume allocation map* and written on real cylinder zero of the disk. An example of FORMAT/ALLOCATE allocations for a 3380K DASD volume is:

```
DRCT 025 004
PERM 029 277
TDSK 306 400
TEMP 706 179
```

DRCT 025 004 reserves an area beginning at real cylinder 25, extending 4 cylinders, for the compiled version of the VM user directory. The number of cylinders allocated should always be an even number, since the area is logically divided in half and new versions of the directory are alternatively written to the currently unused half.

PERM 029 277 Reserves an area beginning at real cylinder 29, extending 277 cylinders, for virtual machine minidisks.

TDSK 306 400 reserves an area beginning at real cylinder 306, extending 400 cylinders, for temporary disk allocations.

TEMP 706 179 reserves a second area beginning at cylinder 706, extending 179 cylinders, for spooling and overflow paging.

Note: Since there was no specification given for cylinders 0 to 24, DMKFMT by default assigns them to "TEMP."

When creating a CP-system volume for minidisk use, it is strongly recommended that the allocation be set to "PERM." Remember,

DMKFMT defaults to "TEMP." If the volume is allocated "TEMP," used for minidisks, and subsequently added to the sysgen CP-owned list, CP destroys the minidisk data by using the volume for spooling.

System Name Table (DMKSNT) CP provides a mechanism for re-entrant programs to be shared among virtual machines. This eliminates the need for each userid to have a personal copy of the program loaded into private virtual memory, thereby reducing system paging and potentially improving overall performance. Programs are shared by putting them into a named *DisContiguous Shared Segment* (DCSS). The most common DCSS is CMS.

The NAMESYS macro is used to define shared programs the CP Assembler program DMKSNT.

The NAMESYS macro parameters are shown below:

```
NAMESYS SYSNAME=CMS,
  SYSVOL=VMSRES,
  SYSSTART=(006,1),
  SYSPGNM=(0-8,14-34,3824-4095)
  SYSPGCT=302,
  SYSHRSG=(239-255),
  SYSSIZE=256K,
  VSYSADR=190,
  SYSCYL=502,
  PARMRGS=(0,15),
  VSYSRES=VMSRES
```

It is beyond the scope of this discussion to detail each of the parameters of the NAMESYS macro. (In addition, as this article later points out, VM/XA SP eliminates the DMKSNT control file in favor of simplified CP commands that dynamically manage shared programs.) It is enough to review a few of the parameters:

SYSNAME specifies the name of the shared program.

SYSSTART specifies the location of the shared program on the DASD volume.

SYSVOL specifies the real DASD volume the shared program is allocated on.

SYSPGCT specifies the size of the program in 4K-pages.

From a DASD management standpoint, note two things about this DASD allocation:

1. "SYSSTART=(006,1)" specifies that the program named CMS is stored on page 1, cylinder 6 on the volume named VMSRES. Unlike minidisks, saved programs on CKD devices do not have to reside on cylinder boundaries. If the saved program is allocated on an FBA disk, SYSSTART is specified in units of 4K-pages. In contrast, FBA minidisk directory allocations are specified in units of 512-byte blocks.
2. "SYSPGCT=302" specifies the length of the shared program. Regardless of the DASD device type, this is always specified in units of 4K-pages. Depending on the size of the program, SYS-PGCT is actually equal to the size of the shared program plus up to three CP *information pages*.

System Reserved Area Minidisks   As distributed by IBM, VM does not provide any programmatic protection to prevent overlapping DASD allocations. Thus, in order to minimize the chance for error and to coordinate the CP allocations and minidisk allocations, "fake" (non-end-user) minidisks are conventionally set up to cover the CP DASD areas. There are many programs available which *map* the VM directory and highlight free areas. The fake MDISK statements make the CP reserved areas appear as used and unavailable for allocation.

Typically, there is a separate *pseudo userid* and a set of MDISK statements covering each type of CP allocation. The example shows pseudo userid allocations for the volume allocation maps ($ALLOC$), spool space ($TEMP$), and temporary disk space ($TDSK$). Other pseudo userids are typically defined for the CP online directory ($DRCT$) and the DMKSYS allocations. For saved systems, one or more MDISK statements normally map a group of saved systems:

```
USER $ALLOC$ NOLOG
MDISK AO1 3380 000 001 VMSRES R
MDISK BO1 3380 000 001 VMPKO1 R
MDISK EO1 3380 000 001 VMPKO4 R


USER $TEMP$ NOLOG
MDISK A09 3380 100 200 VMSRES R
MDISK D09 3380 200 100 VMPKO1 R


USER $TDSK$ NOLOG
MDISK A02 3380 500 100 VMSRES R
```

A Summary of CP DASD Allocations The following table summarizes
the types of VM DASD allocations. The next section discusses several issues in VM DASD management.

Use	Allocation method		Allocation parameters and types	
CMS	Directory		MDISK	MiniDISK. A CMS end-user DASD storage allocation
CP	FORMAT/ALLOCATE		TEMP	Spooling space. Intermediate holding area for printer files and virtual card and reader files. Also used for alternative virtual paging.
			PAGE	System PAGing for virtual storage management.
			OVRD	User class OVeRriDe. Storage for tables for customized CP command privilege classes.
			DRCT	DiReCTory. Storage for the compiled version of the VM user directory.
			TDSK	Temporary DiSK. A pool from which temporary minidisks are allocated.
			DUMP	Reserved areas for storing CP ABEND DUMPs. This space is optional. If it is not defined, TEMP space is used for CP ABEND DUMPs.
	SYSGEN	DMKSYS	SYSNUC	Storage for the CP SYStem NUCLeus.
			SYSERR	Storage for recording hardware ERRors.
			SYSWRM	Storage for system WaRMstart data. Warmstart data is information preserved across CP IPLs.
			SYSCKP	Stores spool system ChecKPoint data. Checkpoint data is key information periodically saved during CP operation for restart in case a normal SHUTDOWN is not possible.
			SYSPAG	In VM/HPO, reserves PAGE areas for swapping (block paging), preferred paging, etc.
		DMKSNT	NAMESYS NAMENCP NAME3800 NAMELANG	Various types of saved systems. NAMESYS is used for virtual machine shared systems. The others are used by CP.

Issues in VM DASD Management

What types of system software tools are available to manage DASD? VM DASD *can* be well-managed, but the base VM operating system as distributed by IBM does not provide the necessary tools. This is not a criticism of VM, since almost all operating systems require additional DASD management system software. Fortunately, there is excellent system software currently available from vendors.

Since VM DASD management encompasses many issues, there is a great deal of overlap in our discussion. Some issues can be handled with the proper software, while others require establishing administrative procedures with the user community. In any case, a comprehensive solution is required.

The following issues are discussed:

• Defining and allocating user minidisks
• DASD volume defragmentation
• Hierarchical storage management
• Establishing user accountability
• Planning for capacity
• VM spool space management
• DASD I/O subsystem load balancing
• Access controls for minidisks
• VM DASD allocation mapping
• Managing shared DASD
• Installing new hardware
• End-user VM DASD management

Defining and Allocating User Minidisks

During VM/CMS userid enrollment, a 191 minidisk is normally defined and allocated for the person's use. Since defining a minidisk means allocating a portion of real DASD hardware, this task is usually restricted to one administrator for coordination, often a VM system programmer.

What VM Provides: Under native VM, a DASD administrator defines a minidisk by adding an MDISK control statement to the userid's virtual machine directory entry. To find the right spot, the DASD administrator looks at a map of the DASD subsystem to find available, or "free," DASD space. Once the space is found and the minidisk defined, the directory (a CMS file often called "VMUSER DIRECT") is loaded by running the DIRECT command. Then, the administrator must LOGON to the new userid and issue the CMS FORMAT command to make the space usable. This method of defining minidisks is problematic for two reasons:

1. It requires too much manual intervention by an experienced, costly, VM system administrator.
2. Any minidisk change, addition, or deletion requires re-loading the entire VM user directory, a costly process.

Common Solutions: Most VM shops use VM directory management software to help automate minidisk definition and allocation. This software allows minidisks to be easily created, modified, or deleted. The tools typically:

- Automatically select free space for minidisk allocations. The software locates the space and performs the calculations needed to define, delete, or re-allocate minidisks. The software also automatically updates the CP directory and the changes take effect immediately. This eliminates the possibility of human error and the disastrous results of inadvertently allocating the same space to two users.
- Eliminate the need for the DASD administrator to think in terms of device units. For example, the administrator can request that a 5 megabyte minidisk be created, rather than an 8-cylinder 3380 minidisk.
- Format the disk space automatically. This can be done either on the administrator's userid or as a background task. This frees the DASD administrator and his virtual machine for other, more productive, work.
- Allow real DASD volumes to be carved up into logical *pools* of space. These pools can span real DASD volumes or only part of one DASD volume.
- Allow DASD allocation management to be *decentralized*. Some directory management system software is so powerful and easy to use that large VM shops authorize personnel with virtually no data processing experience to manage minidisk allocations for a particular group of VM userids. This person is often referred to as the *user group manager*. The user group manager allocates minidisks from a DASD pool until the pool is empty. At that time, the user group manager requests more space from the central DASD administrator or administratively works with the end-users in the department to help them better manage their space, perhaps by erasing or archiving old files. Distributing routine minidisk

maintenance to end-user managers removes this task from the trained DASD administrator and also improves service to end-users since the user group manager is normally able to fulfill requests for minidisks faster than a central DASD administrator.

Volume Defragmentation

CMS dynamically manages the DASD space on each end-user minidisk. Within a CMS minidisk, files are not pre-allocated. This is a key distinction between VM and other operating systems where the entire file system is one DASD pool managed by the operating system. The distinction is easy to see if we keep in mind that a minidisk is the virtual equivalent of a real DASD volume. Each minidisk is private and totally controlled by its owner, has its own file directory, and files are written to blocks scattered over the minidisk. There are two types of DASD *fragmentation* in VM:

- Fragmentation of files within a minidisk. This is not normally a problem since CMS automatically reuses space. There may be performance issues if files get too far spread out; and there is a capacity issue if the user does not need all of the space defined on his minidisk.
- Fragmentation of minidisks on a real DASD volume. This is unique to VM because of the minidisk concept.

The second type of fragmentation—volume fragmentation— is important in VM DASD management. The problem occurs because, as minidisks are allocated, re-sized, and/or deleted, small blocks of unallocated space develop on the volume. Since a minidisk must be defined on contiguous real DASD space, these unallocated blocks are wasted space because they are too small to be used for new minidisks.

What Native VM Provides: There are no utilities in native VM to defragment DASD volumes. This problem is handled manually by the DASD administrator by dumping files to tape, changing the directory MDISK allocations, reformatting each minidisk space, and reloading the files from tape. This is an error-prone process that often results in lost data even when done by an expert. Most shops simply accept the cost of the wasted space rather than invest the time or take the risks.

Common Solutions: There are a few solutions to the volume fragmentation problem. For example, some sites set a minimum size for a minidisk, such as five 3380 cylinders, so that the minimum size of a fragment that normally develops is also five cylinders. This wastes space in a different way since many users are allocated DASD space in excess of what they need. It also does not handle the case where a minidisk of the minimum set size is increased or decreased creating fragments.

Some directory management products provide a volume *compression* utility. This tool automates the above procedure by creating new minidisks, formatting them, moving the files, and updating the directory so that all the fragments on a volume are accumulated into one large block of contiguous space. Since volume compression must modify the MDISK statements in the VM directory, it is necessarily a component of VM directory management software.

Many sites run the volume compression on an "as needed" basis whenever contiguous space for a new minidisk cannot be found. Other sites take it a step further and totally automate the process by scheduling the volume compression utility to run periodically. A REXX EXEC can be used, for example, to compress one DASD volume each week, so that over a period of time every volume is compressed and fragmentation never gets out of hand.

Hierarchical Storage Management

Research shows that as many as 25% to 40% of the CMS files on a typical VM system could be archived to more economical media, such as tape (cartridge) or specially reserved DASD in compressed format. Today, a megabyte of tape storage costs about $2 to $3 and online archival storage about $9 to $13 (depending on the amount of data compression achieved).

In *hierarchical storage management*, sophisticated system software uses site-defined *migration rules* to automatically move data files to more economical media. Typically, unused files are migrated to cheaper and cheaper storage and erased from more expensive media based on file naming conventions and how long it's been since they've been used. As data sets are migrated to a cheaper storage medium, the cost of recalling them to online storage for use increases. Hierarchical storage management makes economic sense because, in practice, only a very small percentage of files are ever recalled from the archives. In addition, storage technology improvements are constantly reducing the cost of recalling archived data.

What VM Provides: A major requirement for hierarchical storage management is maintaining the last *reference* (read OR write) date for files. The last reference date allows the hierarchical storage system to keep files online even if they are only being read. An example of this might be an application program which is only changed once a year but read into memory and run almost every day by almost every user.

CMS file directories are stored on the minidisk with the files. CMS maintains the last write date and time for files in the directory, but does not maintain the last read date. The inability to maintain the last read date is a CMS architectural limitation. The CMS file system was designed to be very fast and reliable for a single user and his own files. The design allows the minidisk owner to give unlimited read-only access by other users to his files, but unfortunately has no mechanism for allowing multiple users simultaneous write access. In practice, many minidisks and files are shared read-only by one or more users. It is obviously impossible for CMS to write the last reference date on a read-only minidisk.

However, the new Shared File System, introduced with VM Release 6 (and discussed briefly in the final section of this chapter) provides a possible opportunity to implement hierarchical storage management. Since a service virtual machine controls all access to files stored in the Shared File System, it is technically possible to maintain a true last reference date and exit points could be supplied to interface with hierarchical storage management software.

Common Solutions: Today, very popular and effective CMS *file archiving* software is commonly used. Archiving differs from hierarchical storage management in that files are placed in the archives at the end-user's discretion instead of automatically. File archiving is typically implemented via a service virtual machine that manages a database of archived files. Files can be archived to permanent online DASD areas, to intermediate DASD "staging" areas, or directly to tape or cassette. When archived to the staging area, archived files are migrated quickly to tape, but a copy of the file remains on an online archival area for a specified period of time (commonly 14 days). After that, the online copy is automatically erased. This allows users to immediately recall archived files for up to 14 days after they have archived them. Studies have shown that if a user does not need an archived file within 14 days after archiving it, chances are the user will not need it for several months, years, and probably never.

File archiving must be clearly distinguished from *system backups* and hierarchical storage management. Unlike system backups, which regularly create copies of all files on the system for disaster recovery, file archiving is *user-initiated*. Users request files to be archived by typing a simple command such as:

```
ARCHIVE REPORT01 SCRIPT A (STAGE RETPD 500
```

This command requests that the file "REPORT01 SCRIPT A" be archived to an intermediate "staging" area (where it is later automatically migrated to archival tape storage) and retained by the archival system for 500 days.

File archiving is important for VM DASD management for several reasons:

- It helps avoid the cost of re-allocating minidisks. Users can archive files they are not using instead of immediately asking for more minidisk space when their minidisk fills up.
- It helps make programs more reliable. Many VM applications require work disk space. If this space is not available, the application can fail. File archiving can help users avoid disk full conditions.
- It eliminates the need to maintain multiple versions of files (such as text documents) on minidisks. Instead, the archival system manages multiple versions of files and allows users to set *expiration dates* for archived files, after which the files are automatically deleted. Some VM archival systems also allow users to tag files with comments.
- Online storage requirements are reduced since archived files are typically compressed and moved to economical tape or cartridge storage. VM file archival systems also typically compress archived files by rates of 30% to 60% depending on the content of the archived file. This allows a VM shop to save considerable DASD even when files are stored in the archives using permanent DASD.

To compute the expected savings from file archiving, a DASD administrator calculates the costs of various types of archival storage. For example, the following media have these costs (on a per megabyte basis):

Minidisk space	$18
Online archival storage	$13
Tape storage	$ 3
Archival Storage	
Average Cost	$ 8
Relative Cost	44%

Note two things about these estimates:

1. The "$13" for the online archive storage cost assumes an average file compression ratio of 28%—a conservative estimate. It is derived by calculating the amount of DASD space taken up by files when they have been archived relative to the equivalent space they took up when residing on user minidisks in uncompressed form.
2. The above estimated average cost of a megabyte of archival storage assumes an equal weighting for tape and online archival storage. In practice, about 70% to 80% of archived files are archived to tape and only 20% to 30% remain online, so that the weighted average cost of a megabyte of archival storage is really about $6, bringing the relative cost to less than 33% ($6/$18).

Establishing User Accountability

Because DASD is a scarce resource (in the economic sense) and, therefore, has an economic cost, it cannot be effectively managed without implementing accountability for use. This is perhaps the most misunderstood issue in VM DASD management. By *accountability*, we mean formalizing DASD allocation criteria to establish what economists call *effective demand*. One type of accountability is the price system. This is found in traditional time-sharing shops that actually charge users for their resources each month. Users are thus entitled to DASD simply on the basis of their ability to pay.

But many VM data centers do not actually charge users for the resources they use. They treat data center use as fixed overhead. Yet these data centers typically use one of three methods for establishing accountability:

1. They distribute accounting reports each month, but solely for the purpose of making users aware of the costs of the resources they use. Commonly referred to as *funny money*, this technique can be more or less effective. It works when the reports are actually reviewed by management and have some impact of how overall DASD resources are allocated.
2. They base DASD allocations on some business performance criteria, such as division or department profit performance. Departments that perform well are given favored treatment when requesting additional online storage. This method can work

very well since the allocation mechanism is based on quantitative, well-understood criteria.

3. They establish some non-economic based quota system, such as defining a corporate-wide standard DASD allocation regardless of any specific application requirements. This method is normally not effective since it has no basis in economics and typically results in large amounts of wasted DASD.

Some VM shops have *no* accountability for DASD, which means users receive whatever DASD allocations they think they need with almost no checks and balances. This method is not effective, since it also has no basis in economics. The practical effect is that needy users are often neglected and other users often have unnecessarily large amounts of DASD. This lack of formal allocation criteria limits the shop's ability to manage DASD.

What Native VM Provides: An inherent problem in VM DASD accountability is that a minidisk cannot be seen or touched, so end-users tend to take it for granted and lose sight of the fact that it has a cost. This perception is promoted by CMS commands—such as QUERY DISK—which allow users to query the status of their minidisks, but not the costs of it. Since it's convenient, most users keep every file they've ever created without regard for which files are really needed.

Under native VM, there are no tools for implementing DASD chargeback. Sites that do some sort of minidisk accounting have either written their own software or licensed a third-party package.

Common Solutions: As VM becomes strategic to many organizations, the concept of *service levels*—which formalize service to the end-user community—are becoming more popular. Service levels are key to establishing accountability. In setting up service levels, a VM DASD administrator typically:

- Gains management commitment. There should be a conscious decision to actively manage DASD and an acceptance by management of accountability.
- Conveys the benefits of DASD management to the user community including quicker turn-around for online storage requests and well-defined allocation criteria.
- Introduces file archiving tools to the user community. Users are asked to consider archiving files when their minidisks become full. If a "disk full" condition is repeatedly reached, the user is expected to estimate requirements and request increased DASD space.

- Considers decentralizing DASD allocation management. This gives user group managers responsibility for allocating minidisks to their users. This can be very effective since a user group manager can typically respond to requests for DASD much faster than a central DASD administrator.
- Regularly collects minidisk utilization statistics so that service levels can be evaluated.
- Implements systems software that automatically distributes accountability information. This ranges from automatically distributing real invoices to distributing "funny money" CMS notes to users about the costs of their resource usage.

Planning for Capacity

In managing any scarce resource, an administrator plans for capacity to meet demand. This is a very complex issue. In one sense, planning for capacity encompasses almost all the tasks performed by a VM DASD administrator. For example, capacity planning requires:

- Establishing user service levels and accountability for DASD storage.
- Implementing hierarchical storage management to ensure data sets are placed on the most cost-effective media; that is, migrated to cheaper media when infrequently referenced. A subset of hierarchical storage management is file archiving.
- Monitoring the current installed base to predict when capacity will be reached. This includes regularly collecting minidisk utilization statistics.
- Regularly re-sizing minidisks that are not optimally allocated. This requires efficient tools that make it very easy to move minidisks, delete minidisks, and change their size.
- Planning for the purchase or lease of new hardware.
- Installing new hardware.

The goal of many of these tasks is to make capacity estimates legitimate. Many VM shops that do not effectively manage VM DASD mistakenly evaluate capacity based on how much DASD has been allocated. This is only appropriate when full minidisk charge-back is in place and where end-users are actually invoiced for their allocated DASD each month. Since the data center fully recovers its cost, utilization of DASD is of little interest.

But when users are not charged for their use of DASD, *utilization* statistics must be analyzed. By utilization, we mean how much of the space allocated to a user is actually being used. For example, a user may be allocated a five-megabyte minidisk but only really requires three megabytes, including work disk space requirements. The two megabytes of space not in use is commonly referred to as *wasted space* since it is truly unproductive.

What VM Provides: Native VM provides very little to help manage DASD capacity. End-users can use the CMS QUERY DISK command to query the status of their minidisks, but VM does not have a command for querying the global utilization of CMS space. Standard minidisk mapping reports show the amount of DASD space allocated to minidisks, but not the amount of space actually used. There are no tools to identify under- or over-utilized minidisks, for example. This can force a VM shop to mistakenly base its capacity planning estimates on the amount of *allocated* DASD rather than a more sophisticated estimate based on DASD *utilization*.

Typically, VM sites should try to maintain 60%-70% of their allocated DASD space in use during normal operations. This is significantly higher than most VM sites which do not have an effective VM DASD management program in place today. Further, research of the DASD usage of more than 50 VM data centers shows that a typical VM shop has between 50% to 60% of all minidisks operating between 0% to 30% utilization. (This statistic does not include one cylinder minidisks which cannot be reduced in size.) This suggests that in the absence of effective tools for optimizing the size of minidisks, VM DASD administrators opt for *padding* their allocations to minimize the chance of ever having to resize the disks.

Common Solutions: DASD capacity planning software for VM is well-developed. Tools are available to gather minidisk utilization statistics for the entire DASD subsystem or for particular DASD volumes. Reports show minidisks meeting one or more of the following exception conditions:

- Minidisks not updated in a long time, such as six months. Last update is often a good predictor of when a minidisk was last used.
- "191" minidisks that have not been updated for six months. It is almost impossible for an active CMS user to not update his 191 minidisk. In the vast majority of cases, 191 minidisks that have not been updated in a while belong to virtual machines that are no longer in use. Usually, the person who owns the virtual machine has left the company. A VM system administrator can take a list of such minidisks and corroborate it against the "last LOGON"

information for the userid (normally maintained by the directory management or security system software), delete the inactive userids, and reclaim the DASD space.

- Minidisks greater than 98% full. These minidisks may be in danger of becoming full. Identifying these minidisks allows a system administrator to investigate whether the minidisk needs to be re-sized.
- Minidisks less than 30% full. In the typical VM shop, the majority of these minidisks are probably over-allocated. Normally at least 30% of the space allocated to these minidisks can be recovered by re-sizing the minidisks and then defragmenting the DASD volumes where the minidisks reside.
- Minidisks with zero CMS files that have not been updated in awhile, perhaps one month. Since these minidisks have no files, it logically follows they have not been used since they were created. In most cases, a userid has been set up for someone who will never use it. Many of these minidisks can be simply deleted from the system and the space recovered for productive use.

These minidisk utilization exception reports are not useful unless it is possible to efficiently recover the wasted DASD. Fortunately, VM directory management system software offers two key tools: computer-assisted minidisk allocation and volume defragmentation. These tools make it economical to regularly identify misallocated minidisks, reallocate them, and then recover the wasted space by defragmenting the DASD volume.

Equally important, global minidisk utilization reports clearly distinguish overall space allocated from overall CMS space currently in use. This helps make capacity planning estimates legitimate. If a VM data center can assess its capacity based on utilization and operate at a higher overall space utilization, it can delay additional hardware purchases.

VM Spool Space Management

The VM spooling system has two primary purposes:

1. For sending output to the real printer or real card punch.
2. For transferring files between userids either on the same machine or on different VM machines.

However, sophisticated end-users can store files in the VM spooling system by sending them to themselves when they run out of minidisk space. Generally, this practice should be discouraged because the spooling system is intended for data in transit and is somewhat less reliable than minidisk storage. Nevertheless, the spooling area is freely available to users.

Because there are no allocation limits placed on use of spool space, a virtual machine can actually fill up the entire spooling system, which, in turn, causes CP to *disable* virtual devices that use the spool system. These devices are the virtual printer, reader, and punch. This process is analogous to a real printer running out of paper. Unfortunately, the error messages end-users receive are very cryptic and most users perceive a spool space full condition as "the system is down" or "PROFS isn't working."

While rare, most VM shops encounter a spool space full-condition about once a year and it normally occurs because an application is in a loop writing to a virtual printer. However, because a "spool full" condition can affect the entire VM system rather than a single virtual machine, it can be very costly.

What Native VM Provides: Spool space management tools are weak in native VM. There are commands to manipulate spool files and query individual file status, but no commands to analyze overall spool space utilization or exceptional cases, such as the largest spool files on the system. The CP QUERY command displays lists of spool files on the system. The CP PURGE command allows an administrator to purge specified spool files. The CMS RDRLIST command is the typical end-user tool for manipulating spool files. The SPTAPE command dumps spool files to tape *en masse*.

When spool space utilization reaches 90%, CP sends a warning message to the OPERATOR userid. Normally, this message is too late. If an application is in a loop writing to a virtual printer, spool space can reach 100% utilization in a matter of several seconds.

VM's weak handling of spool space management is understandable. Over the years the VM spooling has grown from a staging area for job control files (the card reader) and printer output to a key application service. But native VM spool space management tools have not kept pace with this expansion. For example, the PROFS office automation program product uses the spooling system to store electronic mail. The CMS NOTE command sends electronic mail to other users in the form of virtual reader spool files. Though not widely promoted as such, the VM spooling system acts as a *de facto undifferentiated* (completely dynamic allocation), virtually unlimited pool of DASD with no accountability.

Common Solutions: Third-party spool space management tools fill most holes in native VM's handling of spool space. Today, a VM site has extensive spool management tools for:

- Querying the overall utilization of spool space at any point in time. Spool space management products allow a system administrator to quickly identify the largest spool files on the system and/or the largest users of spool space.
- Identifying and browsing *open* spool files. This is significant because the most common cause of spool space full is an application in a loop writing to a virtual printer. While the writing is occurring, the printer spool file is "open." There are no native VM commands to view open spool files or identify the user in a loop. The file is closed when the spool system becomes full and CP disables all virtual machine use of spool.
- Monitoring spool space utilization. Spool space management products have built-in scheduling mechanisms to monitor spool space utilization. For example, every two minutes they can sample and give the system administrator advance warning of a developing "spool full" condition.
- Automatically purging selected groups' spool files, for example, PROFs notes more than 20 days old.
- Accounting for spool space use. Some spool management products watch the spooling system and create VM accounting records for spool space *occupancy*. This is analogous to minidisk accounting where a user can be charged for using a specified block of spool space over a specified period of time.
- Backing up and recovering spool files. As IBM eliminates restrictions in the maximum number of spool files on a VM system (the practical limit is now about 100,000), sophisticated spool space backup and recovery software is becoming available. This software allows selected backups of the spool system and individual spool files to be recalled, similar to VM file backup software which allows users to restore individual CMS files from system backup tape volumes.

DASD I/O Subsystem Load Balancing

Seeks analysis, a common DASD I/O performance analysis, gathers statistics about arm movements for each DASD volume over time. Each sample records when the arm is positioned at each cylinder on the volume. The data is then mapped back to the corresponding minidisk definitions, allowing a VM DASD administrator to identify minidisks being infrequently and frequently referenced. By identifying these minidisks, a DASD administrator can move minidisks to minimize arm movement, thereby improving performance. If the site has the appropriate hardware, frequently referenced minidisks can be redefined on special high-performance cache devices.

What Native VM Provides: The native CP MONITOR command starts the collection of extensive statistics about the DASD I/O subsystem. The data collected includes "seeks" information. Unfortunately, the MONITOR command creates one record every time the DASD arm moves on every DASD on the system, rather than using a statistical sampling technique. This generates so much overhead and data that seeks data collection can only be run for very short periods of time. Also, additional software is needed to format the raw data into usable reports.

Common Solutions: To properly implement DASD I/O balancing, most VM shops use systems software which:

- Collects seeks data using statistical sampling techniques during pre-determined time periods and at a specified sampling rate. This normally requires scheduling software to automatically enable and disable the data collection. Using statistical techniques allows seeks data to be collected during all high-use time, creating an accurate picture of DASD usage and allowing more precise fine tuning.
- Resolves the frequency counts of cylinder arm movements to their minidisk counterparts. The result is a frequency count for each minidisk rather than real DASD cylinders.
- Identifies frequently and infrequently referenced minidisks and makes recommendations to a DASD administrator to either leave the minidisks alone or re-allocate them to a different DASD volume to potentially improve overall DASD I/O subsystem performance.
- Interfaces with VM directory management to automatically reallocate certain minidisks based on recommendations of the seeks analysis.

Access Controls for Minidisks

In VM, minidisks are often shared—normally read-only—among many users and groups of users. Common examples of shared minidisks are:

- The CMS "S" and "Y" disks, which contain many common native CMS programs.
- Language compilers stored on minidisk accessible only to certain application programmers who use those languages.
- An accounting application and associated financial data accessible only to staff accountant userids.

What Native VM Provides: Under native VM, passwords can be assigned to minidisks. A program can supply the necessary password as a parameter of the CP LINK command. Normally an interactive user must respond to a password prompt from CP when linking to a minidisk that requires a password. Alternatively, the password can be hard coded into the EXEC which:

- Defeats the purpose of the password by exposing it to anyone who examines the EXEC.
- Creates maintenance problems when the password is changed.

Three types of minidisk passwords are supported:

1. *Read-only passwords.* This allows users to link to the minidisk and read information but not write information to the disk.
2. *Read/write passwords.* This allows only one user at a time to link to the minidisk and write, but allows an unlimited number of users to link to the minidisk and read information.
3. *Multi-write passwords.* This allows many users to have read/write access to a minidisk at the same time other users have read-only access to the minidisk. This is dangerous for CMS minidisks since the CMS file system is not designed to support many users writing to a minidisk at one time. The multi-write facility is provided by CP for other, non-CMS operating systems. If more than one CMS user accidentally gets write access to the same minidisk, the typical result is the loss of one or more of the files on the disk. Native VM does not manage multi-write access to minidisks at all. Thus, CMS applications are responsible for controlling multi-write access "under the covers." Multi-write passwords should rarely be used and only with extreme care and controls.

Common Solutions: A very popular, superior method of defining access controls for minidisks is called *discretionary access control.* Here, passwords are not required, eliminating the need for a DASD administrator and users to manage passwords. It also eliminates the inevitable security breaches that occur when users keep lists of passwords in their desks or on notes taped to their terminals. Instead, a database of resource access rules is managed by a resource control service virtual machine. Access rules specify whether a user can access a specified minidisk and what type of access is allowed (read-only vs. read/write for example). Access rules are simple action statements that begin with a verb such as "ALLOW" or "REJECT." Rules also specify:

- What is being accessed, commonly referred to as the *object*, in our case a minidisk.
- The *owner* of the object. This is sometimes part of the definition of the object itself. For example, a minidisk is completely defined by its owner userid and virtual address such as "BOB 191," which references userid BOB's 191 minidisk.
- A requested type of access, in our case read-only or read/write.
- The conditions under which access should be granted. For example, a user may have to supply a minidisk link password to be allowed to gain access to the minidisk, or may need to supply his own logon password, or may not need to supply a password at all.

A hypothetical access rule for a minidisk might look like this:

```
ALLOW BERT LINK BOB 191 (NOPASS
```

This rule allows user BERT to link to BOB's 191 minidisk without supplying a password. In most sites, the owner, BOB, creates the rule to allow BERT access. In some sites, however, the access rules are created either by a group manager or by a central security administrator.

Discretionary access control software also typically allows access control rules to be defined for specified security groups of userids and for the system as a whole. This allows a VM DASD administrator to set up one simple rule for all allowed users rather than requiring individual user rules and the attendant maintenance.

VM DASD Allocation Mapping

As we have seen, VM uses DASD for a variety of things. Since CP does not prevent overlapping allocations, a system administrator can accidentally misallocate a DASD area. While rare, the effect of problems caused by overlapping DASD allocations range from immediately catastrophic and obvious, to intermittent and obscure. For example, if a user minidisk overlaps a CP virtual memory paging area, CP can abend with no warning and no diagnostic information. In this case, CP tries to use the paging area (which overlaps the user's minidisk), finds that the area is not formatted as expected (via the DMKFMT program), and a paging error results. Of course, the contents of the user's minidisk may be lost too.

What's needed is a tool to map all DASD allocations and clearly identify overlaps. Such a program has to present the various allocation methods in a cohesive fashion. For example, minidisks are always defined in device dependent units (cylinder for CKD devices and 512-byte blocks for FBA devices), while most CP areas are defined in units of 4K-pages.

What Native VM Provides: In native VM, the *minidisk mapping program* maps only the MDISK statements in the VM user directory. There is no single utility to map all CMS and CP DASD allocations and/or validate the allocations to prevent unintended overlaps. Normally, this problem is handled by manually maintaining pseudo-userid minidisk definitions in the VM directory (as discussed previously), but as we have seen this requires a system administrator to keep manual records of the actual CP allocations and make sure they are correctly converted into corresponding fake MDISK statements for userids such as $ALLOC$, $PAGE$, $SYSNUC$, etc.

Common Solutions: Some third-party systems software supply a comprehensive DASD mapping tool, which organizes DASD allocation information from various sources and presents a consistent mapping. The tool clearly segregates CP DASD areas from minidisks. Overlaps are also clearly identified. The software collects data from the following sources:

- MDISK allocations from the VM directory.
- Shared system allocations from DMKSNT (System Name Table).
- CP System Generation allocations from DMKSYS.
- CP FORMAT/ALLOCATE allocations from the volume label record found on real cylinder 0 of each DASD volume.

The software then inspects the allocations for overlaps, flags the overlaps, and creates a volume-by-volume mapping of all DASD allocations.

The software also checks for potential allocation problems. For example, all shared system allocations must be defined on DASD areas formatted as "PERM" space on CP-owned volumes. The software checks any shared system allocations to see if they really do fit with PERM space boundaries on CP-owned volumes.

Medium-to-large VM sites commonly run such mapping programs once a month and store the reports with their off-site disaster recovery tapes and procedures. The mapping program is also useful before or after a DASD migration, where CP FORMAT/ALLOCATE DASD areas may need to be re-allocated.

Managing Shared DASD

In large multi-CPU VM shops, some DASD hardware may also be shared. By "shared" we do not mean file sharing but rather the sharing of real DASD volumes across multiple systems. For example, cylinders 100-400 of a particular volume may be reserved for one processor, while cylinders 401-884 may be reserved for another.

Today, managing shared VM DASD requires considerable manual record keeping and personal knowledge, since VM does nothing to prevent unintended overlapping allocations from occurring across processors. However, eventually the handling of shared files between VM processors will be simplified by the new Shared File System introduced with VM/SP Release 6.

Installing New DASD Hardware

Installing new DASD hardware may or may not be a task of a VM DASD administrator. It is beyond the scope of this article to discuss in detail the installation of physical equipment. However, we can mention the following basic tasks:

- Purchasing or leasing a DASD device and related equipment such as cables and controllers.
- Securing adequate floor space (or rack space in the case of the 9370 minicomputer) and air conditioning.
- Securing a hardware maintenance contract.
- Running DMKFMT to format each DASD volume.
- Adding the real device addresses to the DMKRIO CP system generation control file.
- Identifying in the DMKSYS CP system generation control file volumes on the device that are to be reserved for one or more CP DASD areas.
- Identifying the volume to any system management software that may need to know about it, such as a resource accounting, security, or directory management system.

End-User VM DASD Management

Does the VM/CMS end-user have any DASD management responsibilities? Fortunately, there are only a few; and they are generally analogous to those of a PC user with one or two hard disks. One of the virtues of VM is that the CMS file system transparently manages the allocation of DASD space within the user's minidisk. Applications generally do not need to be concerned with the physical addresses of space allocated for files. The user simply creates files until the minidisk becomes "full." Then the user receives a message indicating that the disk is full. At this time, to make space available, the user must either erase or archive some files that are not needed anymore or get a system administrator to increase the size of the minidisk.

End-users have typical PC-like commands for manipulating files, such as COPYFILE, RENAME, ERASE, and LISTFILE. End-users can use the following CMS and CP commands to manage their own DASD:

Command Name	An Example
CMS FORMAT formats a specified minidisk.	"FORMAT 291 E" formats a minidisk defined at virtual address 291 and assigns the minidisk a CMS access mode of "E."
CMS ERASE erases a specified CMS file or group of files.	"ERASE OLDPROG EXEC A" erases the CMS file called "OLDPROG EXEC" from the user's minidisk currently accessed at filemode "A" (normally the user's 191 minidisk).
CMS LISTFILE displays a list (in line mode) of files on a specified minidisk and/or the characteristics of a specified group of files.	"LISTFILE * EXEC A" displays a line-mode list of CMS files on the user's "A" minidisk, whose filetype is "EXEC."
CMS FILELIST displays a full-screen list of files with a command input area so the user can manipulate files with CMS commands directly from the screen.	"FILELIST * EXEC B" displays a full-screen list of CMS files with filetype "EXEC" residing on the user's "B" minidisk.
CMS RENAME changes the file identification of a specified file or group of files.	"RENAME * SCRIPT A = OLDSCR =" changes all files with filetype "SCRIPT" on the user's "A" minidisk to the filetype "OLDSCR."
CMS COPYFILE copies a specified file or group of files.	"COPYFILE * SCRIPT A = = B" copies all CMS files with filetype "SCRIPT" from the user's "A" minidisk to his "B" minidisk.
CMS QUERY DISK displays a list of currently accessed minidisks and various statistics about those minidisks such as number of files and percent utilization of the disk.	"QUERY DISK A" displays statistics for the minidisk currently accessed at disk mode "A."
CP LINK makes a specified minidisk available to the issuing user's virtual machine.	"CP LINK BERT 191 291 RR" defines a read-only link to user BERT's 191 disk as virtual address 291.

Command Name	An Example
CMS ACCESS makes a specified (already LINKed minidisk) available for CMS use. The specified minidisk can be accessed read-only or read/write mode depending on what type of link the user has established to the minidisk.	"ACCESS 291 E" assigns the minidisk currently defined at virtual 291 an access mode of "E."
CP DEFINE defines a temporary minidisk from a pool of space defined during the CP SYSGEN and via the FORMAT/ALLOCATE program. The user must use the CMS FORMAT command to format the temporary disk after it has been defined.	"CP DEFINE T3380 291 5" defines a temporary minidisk of 5 cylinders at virtual address 291 on a 3380 DASD device.

Enhanced VM End-User DASD Management Tools In addition to the above basic user DASD management tools, VM system software includes commands that accomplish the following:

Command Name	An Example
RESTORE restores a specified file from a system backup tape.	"RESTORE JANSTAT SCRIPT A" restores the specified SCRIPT file to the userid's virtual reader.
ARCHIVE archives the specified CMS file or group of files.	"ARCHIVE JANSTAT SCRIPT A (STAGE" archives this CMS file on an archival staging minidisk, where it remains in compressed format for a site-defined time period and is then automatically migrated to archival tape storage.
RECALL recalls a specified file or group of files from an archival area to the user's virtual machine.	"RECALL JAN* SCRIPT A" restores all archived SCRIPT files with the prefix "JAN" to the user's virtual machine.

New Developments

What does the future hold for VM DASD management? There appear to be two significant trends. First, an effort to simplify and automate CP DASD management. Second, the new VM Shared File System (SFS), introduced with VM/SP Release 6, extends CMS DASD use considerably. The following compares some major SFS features with their minidisk system counterparts. Note, this comparison is not exhaustive. It merely highlights some features of SFS relevant to our discussion of VM DASD management.

Minidisks	Shared File System
End-user is assigned a physical allocation of a real DASD called a minidisk. DASD resource limits are physical and controlled by CP.	End-user is assigned a logical rather than physical file space allocation. Limits are controlled by the SFS file server.
With native VM/SP, there is no DASD pooling concept. The closest analogy is DASD volume naming conventions. With certain third-party directory management products, minidisks can be allocated from DASD space pools.	Specially reserved minidisks are organized into an SFS *file pool*. An SFS service machine manages space allocations for the file pool.
Space allocated to users (via minidisks) but not in use is unavailable to other users on the system.	Since file spaces are logical allocations, space not in use is available to other users on the system.
Minidisk space is allocated in physical device dependent units. For example, minidisks on FBA devices are allocated in units of 512-byte blocks. Minidisks on CKD devices are allocated in cylinders.	File spaces are allocated in units of 4K blocks regardless of the physical device containing the SFS file pool.
Accessing CMS files stored on minidisks on another VM system is a manual process requiring either logging on to the remote system or having the two machines physically close and having shared DASD.	With SFS, files can be shared across VM systems in a TSAF (Transparent Services Access Facility) collection. Eventually files will be shareable when the CPUs are connected via SNA.
CMS minidisks and files cannot span a real DASD volume.	Files can be as large as necessary and span DASD volumes.
I/O via minidisks is done directly through CP interfaces, so performance is high.	I/O is done via an SFS service virtual machine which uses CP interfaces, so performance is reduced.
Access controls are through passwords or discretionary control via a security system software product.	There is built-in discretionary access control via the GRANT and REVOKE commands and exits and interfaces for access control by an *External Access Control Facility*.

Will the Shared File System eliminate the need to manage VM DASD? No. Rather, it introduces a new set of issues that require enhanced VM DASD management system software. At heart, the Shared File System trades minidisk management issues for database management issues. For example, there will be the need for optimally placing data sets; reorganizing SFS databases; backing up and restoring SFS file pools; and tools for easily creating, modifying, and deleting SFS file pools. While the minidisk has its drawbacks— mainly because the unused space on a minidisk is not available to other users on the system—it has high performance and a certain simplicity, neither of which are present in SFS. In practice, VM shops will probably use both file systems.

VM/XA System Product System Data Files

From our discussion of native VM/SP CP DASD management, it should be apparent that CP's use of DASD has several "implicit" file systems. By "file system" we mean that CP DASD areas are composed of "objects" that have names, directories, and allocation mechanisms. For example, saved systems have names (as specified on the SYSNAME macro in DMKSNT), allocations, and are completely specified in a source file during SYSGEN (DMKSNT ASSEMBLE). CP FORMAT/ALLOCATE areas are allocated via the DMKFMT program and the objects—TEMP, DRCT, PERM, etc.—are stored in a directory which is the volume's allocation map.

The latest release of VM, VM/XA SP, automates some portions of CP DASD management. VM/XA SP introduces the concept of System Data Files (SDF), special spool files used for storing saved systems and CP class command override data. This appears to be an effort to begin consolidating certain types of CP DASD allocations into a common file system. Saved system management is now dynamic and simplified. Since there is no longer a DMKSNT ASSEMBLE file to manually define shared storage segments, CP automatically allocates DASD for the blocks that make up a saved system when the SAVESYS command is executed. A new CP DEFSEG command generates saved segments and creates segment spaces. Changes to saved systems can be made without shutting down VM, re-assembling DMKSNT, and regenerating the CP nucleus. This is important since saved systems have evolved into a key VM application service.

Another significant trend is reduced need to define the same allocation in multiple places. For example, in current versions of VM/HPO (the High Performance Option version of VM), a system programmer must allocate PAGE space using the CP FORMAT/ALLOCATE program and then further define how CP should use specific portions of the allocated PAGE space in the DMKSYS SYSPAG macro. In VM/XA SP, there is no longer a SYSPAG macro; the CPFORMAT command simply allocates the space. Part of the reason for this is that VM/XA SP does not distinguish primary and general paging and there is no page migration area. With VM/HPO these different types of PAGE space must be manually defined in the SYSPAG macro.

Conclusion

We have seen that VM uses DASD in a variety of ways. Its popularity as a high-performance interactive operating system coupled with declining costs of DASD storage also means CMS DASD use will likely continue to grow quickly unless managed properly.

Like any operating system, VM's handling of DASD has certain virtues and certain drawbacks. A few of the drawbacks are being addressed in VM/XA SP and the new Shared File System. With these improvements, VM arguably will be more advanced than other multi-user operating systems. The Shared File System will co-exist with the VM minidisk, giving the user the choice of a simple single-user file directory structure giving the user and application programmer the choice of minidisk high performance, or a more sophisticated hierarchical directory with improved file sharing.

With the introduction of the Shared File System, the debate over *differentiated* vs. *undifferentiated* will also continue as new technologies parading as "total automated solutions" enter the marketplace. It is important to recognize in all of this that some sort of administration and accountability will continue to be required as long as DASD is a scarce resource. For all practical purposes, the VM spooling system has already demonstrated the effects of limitless and costless undifferentiated storage. Spool space still "fills up," ultimately requiring some sort of accountability, management, and limits on unbridled use. SFS has features which assign logical allocation limits to users of a file pool. This still creates the requirement for well-defined allocation criteria to distribute limited DASD resources among users.

However, with the use of VM systems software, many DASD management tasks can be effectively automated, making it economical to proactively manage DASD rather than simply purchase more hardware when capacity is reached. This software reduces or eliminates the need for expert human intervention in many areas. Administrative costs are further reduced by installing tools that distribute some DASD management responsibilities down to the end-user. The oft heard cry "Users shouldn't have to think about DASD" neglects the economics of the situation. As long as DASD is a scarce resource, users should play a part in managing its use. The goal of a DASD administrator is to install tools that help users do this without requiring them to know the internals of VM use of DASD.

About the Authors

Todd Margo is the senior member of the National Accounts Sales Support team at Systems Center, Inc. (formerly VM Software, Inc.) in Reston, Virginia. He is currently working as principal designer of an advanced version of Systems Center's VMCENTER II product called "VMCENTER II Pre-configured." The goal of this product is to use the sophisticated features of VMCENTER II to automate key aspects of VM systems management. Todd authored several of the DASD management tools supplied with Systems Center's VMCENTER product and has served as product development manager. He also has experience as an end-user in VM.

Ronald P. Kral is vice-president and chief technical officer at Systems Center, based in the Reston, Virginia, headquarters. Ron joined VM Software in 1982 and has held the positions of senior vice-president for strategic marketing, vice-president of development, and director of development. Previously, Ron was director of systems software at Informatics General, Inc.

Systems Center, Inc. develops, markets, and supports systems software products for use with IBM's VM operating system. The company also markets Network DataMover products for data movement between processors running like and unlike operating systems, network administration products for SNA networks, and relational database products for IBM's SQL/DS.

VM Accounting and Chargeback

by Julie Tray

Introduction

Resource accounting and chargeback in the VM environment provide both a means of monitoring the utilization of resources as well as making users aware of the cost of these resources. VM provides information about resource use through CP accounting records, which may serve as the basis for a sophisticated accounting and chargeback system.

Accounting in VM

The concept of charging for computer resources was probably invented by the timesharing industry, whose very livelihood depended upon the ability to ascertain an accurate record of what resources customers were using and how they were being used. As the term implies, accounting is the ability to identify the utilization of hardware and software resources including CPU time, devices such as DASD and tape drives, and software application packages.

Aside from the issue of charging users for their computer resource utilization, the accounting data provides many other types of valuable information. Accounting data provides valuable input for efforts aimed at balancing system load. With the information you can identify which areas of the organization have the greatest need for computer resources. You can establish required service levels and monitor your performance in terms of providing the desired service levels. Accounting information can also be used as a basis for influencing users to make more efficient use of the times of the day the computer system is in least demand. By identifying your peak utilization periods, you can negotiate realistic service levels with your users and promise improved service levels if the users take advantage of nonpeak times. Accounting data can be used in trend analysis and aid in forecasting the need for additional resources, such as another or a faster CPU or more disk drives.

Someone is paying for computer resources; they do not "grow on trees." Whether the organization subsequently charges users for their use of these resources is a matter of organizational policy. If the data center is also designated as a profit center, or is at least required to break even, then chargeback will be necessary to regain the costs involved in facilitating the delivery of these resource. Even if money is not involved, chargeback is a way of enforcing budget limits and of making users aware of what these resources cost. Other organizations view chargeback as unnecessary, with computer resources considered overhead the same as electricity and telephones.

A system of accounting and chargeback does help the owner of the data, more than it does the user, because those responsible for providing computer resources are more concerned with cost and availability. However, if limits and charges are being imposed on users, a comprehensive and easily understood system provides a means of keeping everyone informed as to what has been used and what is available. Users can only be expected to monitor their use of computer resources if they are given the information they need to control resource usage in an easily understood format.

CP Accounting

The Control Program (CP) generates many records that may be used as a basis for accounting. In fact, there are eight major types of records that may be generated during an average user session. A session is defined as the period of time between when a user logs on to the system and when they log off. Records are based not only on the session itself, but the use of real devices and links to other users. For many of these record types, more than one may be generated during the course of a session. In addition to CP records, software package usage may cause accounting records of their own to be generated at various times. The result is a number of accounting records being generated as a result of system use.

Most CP accounting records are generated automatically. However, five records: unsuccessful LINK attempts, successful LINKs, unsuccessful AUTOLOG and LOGON attempts, VTAM Service Machine usage, and terminal usage, are not generated unless chosen by the system programmer as a system generation option. In the DMKSYS module there is a macro called SYSJRL. To activate the production of CP accounting records the programmer indicates:

```
JOURNAL=YES
```

This, in effect, turns on the production of accounting records that detect and record unsuccessful access attempts by unauthorized users and all successful links. In addition, VTAM service machine usage and terminal usage can be recorded. When journaling is turned on, the system programmer controls when unsuccessful link attempt records, and unsuccessful logon or autolog attempt records, are generated, by specifying the limit of unsuccessful attempts to be reached before a record is generated. This is also specified in the SYSJRL macro. The limit takes into account cases when a user, who is authorized, mistakenly enters an incorrect password. A description of each of the journal records is included in the section that provides a detailed description of the CP accounting records.

With the exception of the journaling records, CP accounting records are generated when the user logs off the system or detaches a device. A site can cause accounting records to be generated at other times by issuing the CP ACNT CLOSE command. This command can be issued for a specific userid, or for all users on the system. It closes out accounting for the current session and a new accounting record is started. Automating the execution of the command ensures consistency and is easy to accomplish through an EXEC.

Sites often use the CP ACNT command to cut accounting records at the end of a shift and at the end of the day. This allows them to associate resource utilization with site defined shifts. This is especially important if the site is using chargeback and uses different rates depending on what shift the work was done. For sites not using chargeback, it is still important to identify resource utilization in each shift. This can be very helpful in balancing system load and trend analysis. In addition, it can help preserve accounting data by minimizing data loss if the system should crash. This is because the data collection begins when a user logs on or attaches a device; but the accounting record is not generated until the user logs off or detaches the device.

The best way to think of a CP accounting record is to envision the "old-fashioned" punch card. CP generates the accounting record in an 80-column format; it has a length of 80 bytes. The records are a combination of character and hexadecimal data format. The first 28 bytes are the same for most accounting records. They contain the virtual machine identification (userid), account number, and the date and time the accounting record was generated. The last 2 bytes indicate the type of accounting record, which is 01–08. The account number is limited to eight characters and is assigned in the user's CP directory entry based on whatever system the organization uses. Generally, VM sites indicate user account numbers through a combination of numbers and letters. The remaining 50 bytes contain resource information specific to the type of accounting record.

In addition to the standard CP accounting records, VM provides a facility for generating site defined records. Like standard CP records, site defined records (often referred to as user defined records), have a record length of 80 bytes. Site defined records must contain a userid in positions 1 through 8 and a record type in positions 79 through 80. The record type is usually "Cn" where "n" is one character or number. The remaining 70 bytes are available for site defined information.

User accounting records are commonly used for tracking operating system virtual machines. For example, if a site runs a DOS system under VM, they can account for DOS usage and associate that usage with a standard VM userid. Other uses include tracking service virtual machine usage, such as data base service virtual machines, and batch job processing service virtual machines. Some routines are available with VM for generating user accounting records. For SNA sites, the VTAM Service Machine produces user accounting records. Users of the Transparent Services Access Facility can generate user

Figure 8-1 CP accounting record layout.

accounting records with these routines and users of the the Remote Spooling Communications Subsystem (RSCS) can, as well.

After accounting records are generated, they are placed in a spool file that is subsequently sent to the reader of a virtual machine. The virtual machine that receives the accounting records is specified in the SYSACNT macro of the DMKSYS module when the VM system is generated. The default userid if a site does not specify one is DIS-KACNT. The system programmer also specifies the number of accounting records to be accumulated in the spool file before it is closed and sent to the specified userid. The ACNT CLOSE command causes the spool file to be closed and sent regardless of the number of records in it.

When determining the number of records to accumulate before closing the spool file, it is important to recognize the potential data loss if a spool file is open when the system crashes. For this reason sites often set the record limit at about 40 to 80 records.

A detailed description of each of the eight types of standard CP accounting records follows.

Type 01—Session Record

Only one session record is created for each user session. A session is the period of time on which a user's virtual machine is logged on. The single record is generated regardless of how long the user is actually logged on (one hour or ten hours) unless the site forces a record to be generated by issuing the CP ACNT CLOSE command. The record is actually generated when the user logs off the system. Some accounting system software packages cause multiple session records to be generated, but this is not part of native VM. The format of the Session Record is shown below:

Column Position	Data
1–8	Virtual Machine Identification
9–16	Virtual Machine Accounting Number
17–22	Date of Accounting
23–28	Time of Accounting
29–32	Connect Time
33–36	Total CPU Time
37–40	Virtual CPU Time
41–44	Page Reads

45–48	Page Writes
49–52	SIOs
53–56	Spooled I/Os—Punch
57–60	Spooled I/Os—Print
61–64	Spooled I/O's—Reader
65–78	Reserved
79–80	Record Type Code (01)

The following describes each of the fields in the session accounting record:

Virtual Machine Identification—this is the userid of the virtual machine that logged onto the system and is a character field.

Virtual Machine Accounting Number—this is the accounting number associated with the virtual machine in the VM user directory and is a character field.

Date of Accounting—this is the date the user logged off the system; it is a character field in the format "mmddyy."

Time of Accounting—this is the time the user logged off the system; it is a character field in the format "hhmmss."

Connect Time—this is the number of seconds the user was logged on (connected) to the system. It is a hexadecimal field.

Total CPU Time—this is the number of milliseconds of CPU time the user used. It is a hexadecimal field.

Virtual CPU Time—this is the number of seconds of virtual CPU time the user used. It is a hexadecimal field.

Virtual CPU time represents the actual CPU usage required to perform the user's work. Total CPU time includes virtual CPU time and the CPU time required by the Control Program to service the user's requests. The CPU time consumed servicing the user's request is referred to as overhead CPU time. Overhead CPU time is not within the user's control; it is dependent on system load. An example of this is "swapping." When the system is heavily loaded, the user is swapped in and out of memory and the resources used to perform the swapping are included in Overhead CPU time.

Total Page Reads—this represents the number of page reads performed during the session and is a hexadecimal field.

Total Page Writes—this represents the number of page writes performed during the session and is a hexadecimal field.

SIOs—this is the number of real I/Os performed during the session. This field records I/O instructions to devices such as tape drives and disk drives and is a hexadecimal field.

Spooled I/Os, Punch—this field represents the number of records spooled to the device that is defined as the user's punch (virtual punch). It is a hexadecimal field.

Spooled I/Os, Print—this field represents the number of lines spooled to the virtual printer. Note that it represents the lines spooled to the printer and not the actual number of lines that were printed. In standard VM the number of lines actually printed is not available in the accounting record. This is a hexadecimal field.

Spooled I/Os, Reader—this represents the number of records in the spool file that the user opened to read. It is a hexadecimal field.

Reserved—this area is unused.

Record Type Code—this specifies the type of accounting record and is a character field.

The data in the session accounting records can be used in many ways to provide the information the organization (specifically the data center) needs. Some information, not specifically available in the accounting records, can be calculated from the available information. For example, you can determine when a user logged on to the system by using the following formula:

```
Time of Accounting - Connect Time = Time of Logon
```

The time of logon is useful in calculating the shift the user was working in.

Similarly, you can calculate the amount of overhead CPU time used in servicing a user by using the following formula:

```
Total CPU Time - Virtual CPU Time = Overhead CPU Time
```

Overhead CPU time is useful in evaluating the efficiency of a user's session.

Type 02—Dedicated Device Usage

A dedicated device is available for a virtual machine's exclusive use. Although many users may share a dedicated device, only one user can use it at any one time. Dedicated device records are generated when the user releases a device that was attached to his userid. The device is attached, either when the user issues a CP ATTACH command or when the user logs on, if there is a device dedicated to the user in the VM user directory. In some instances the CP DIAL command attaches a dedicated device. An example of a device that is dedicated to the user by the ATTACH command is a tape drive. An example of a device that is attached to a user in their directory entry is a special terminal or print device. Multiple dedicated device records can be generated during a single session. Each time the device is attached and subsequently detached a record is generated. The device can be released either when the user issues the CP DETACH command or when they log off.

Following is the format of the Dedicated Device Record:

Column Position	Data
1–8	Virtual Machine Identification
9–16	Virtual Machine Accounting Number
17–22	Date of Accounting
23–28	Time of Accounting
29–32	Connect Time
33	Device Class
34	Device Type
35	Model
36	Feature
37–64	Unused
65–72	Terminal Identification
73–78	Unused
79–80	Record Type Code (02)

Virtual Machine Identification—this is the userid of the virtual machine that the dedicated device was attached to; it is a character field.

Virtual Machine Accounting Number—this is the accounting number associated with the virtual machine in the VM user directory. It is a character field.

Date of Accounting—this is the date the user detached the device. It is a character field in the format "mmddyy."

Time of Accounting—this is the time the user detached the device. It is a character field in the format "hhmmss."

Connect Time—this is the number of seconds the dedicated device was attached to the user. It is a hexadecimal field.

Device Class—this is the class code for the dedicated device. Class codes include terminals, graphics devices, unit record devices such as printers, tape drives, and DASD. It is a hexadecimal field.

Device Type—this is the device type within the class code of the dedicated device. Device types include 3420 and 3480 tape drives and 3350, 3375, and 3380 disk drives. It is a hexadecimal field.

Model—this is the model of the dedicated device that was specified when the VM system was generated. It is a hexadecimal field. This field can be blank.

Feature—this is the feature of the dedicated device. It is a hexadecimal field and can be blank.

Terminal Identification—this is the terminal identification for devices dedicated with the CP DIAL command. It is a character field.

When evaluating dedicated device utilization, connect time is very important. In order to ensure the availability of dedicated devices, a site discourages users from keeping a device attached although they are not using it.

Type 03—TDISK Usage

A TDISK usage record represents the temporary disk space a virtual machine used. Although the user may not have actually used the amount of disk space recorded in the accounting record, they had that amount of disk space dedicated to their virtual machine and not available to other users on the system. Like the dedicated device record, a temporary disk space record is generated when the user releases the TDISK or logs off. Temporary disk space is assigned to a virtual machine with the CP DEFINE command.

Following is the format of the Temporary Disk Space Record:

Column Position	Data
1–8	Virtual Machine Identification
9–16	Virtual Machine Accounting Number
17–22	Date of Accounting
23–28	Time of Accounting
29–32	Connect Time
33	Device Class
34	Device Type
35	Model
36	Feature
37–38	Cylinders of Disk Space Used
or	
37–40	Blocks of Disk Space Used
39–78	Unused
or	
41–78	Unused
79–80	Record Type Code (03)

Virtual Machine Identification—this is the userid of the virtual machine that used the temporary disk space. It is a character field.

Virtual Machine Accounting Number—this is the accounting number associated with the virtual machine in the VM user directory. It is a character field.

Date of Accounting—this is the date the user released the TDISK; it is a character field in the format "mmddyy."

Time of Accounting—this is the time the user released the TDISK; it is a character field in the format "hhmmss."

Connect Time—this is the number of seconds the user had the temporary disk space defined. It is a hexadecimal field.

Device Class—this is the class code for the disk drive where the temporary disk space was defined. For example, the class code can reflect direct access storage devices or fixed-block storage devices. This is a hexadecimal field.

Device Type—within the class of DASD, this is the type of device the temporary disk space is defined on. For example, 3350 and 3380 are device types for the direct access storage device class. This is a hexadecimal field.

Model—this is the model of the device that the TDISK is defined on. Model is specified when the VM system is generated. This is a hexadecimal field and can be blank.

Feature—this is the feature of the device the TDISK is defined on. This is a hexadecimal field and can be blank.

Cylinders of Disk Space—this is the number of cylinders of temporary disk space the user had defined for CKD devices. It is a hexadecimal field and the data is located in positions 37-38.

Blocks of Disk Space—this is the number of blocks of temporary disk space the user had defined for FBA (fixed-block) devices. It is a hexadecimal field and the data is located in positions 37-40.

When FBA devices are used, positions 39-40 of the accounting record contain valid data as described above. For CKD devices that area of the accounting record is unused.

Sites that are concerned with DASD costs often encourage users to use temporary disk space instead of having large quantities of permanent disk space assigned to their userids in the VM directory. It is important that the data center monitor temporary disk space utilization so that they can ensure its availability when their users need it. The temporary disk space utilization records provide data to help do that. On the other hand, this data is useful to identify users that attach and tie up temporary disk space in large quantities when they do not need it.

The amount of temporary disk space utilized is only meaningful when evaluated in terms of the connect time. This gives a true picture of utilization, since it shows the amount of space used and how long it was used.

Type 04—Invalid Logon and Autolog Attempts

This record is generated when a threshold of attempts to autolog or logon a userid unsuccessfully is reached. As discussed earlier, the threshold is defined in the SYSACT macro. This record is useful in identifying particular userids that someone who is not authorized tried to autolog, or a particular terminal address that someone was working from and unsuccessfully attempted to logon a virtual machine.

Following is the format of the Invalid Autolog and Logon Attempt Record:

Column Position	Data
1–8	Target Userid
9–16	Reserved
17–22	Date of Accounting
23–28	Time of Accounting
29–32	Terminal Address
33–40	Invalid Password
41–48	Userid Issuing Command
49–51	Reserved
52–53	Invalid Password Count
54–55	Accounting Record Limit
56–70	Reserved
71–78	LUNAME
79–80	Record Type Code (04)

Target Userid—this is the userid that the attempt was made to logon or autolog. It is a character field.

Date of Accounting—this is the date the attempt was made to logon or autolog the target userid. It is a character field in the format "mmddyy."

Time of Accounting—this is the time the attempt was made to logon or autolog the target userid. It is a character field in the format "hhmmss."

Terminal Address—this field contains the resource-id if the attempt was made from a remote bisynchronous terminal, a real device address, or NONE (if no terminal was identified). This is a character field.

Invalid Password—this field contains the invalid password used: "TOO LONG" if a password greater than 8 characters was entered or "TERM/ERR" if the line dropped during password entry. It is a character field.

Userid Issuing Command—in the case of an invalid autolog attempt, the userid that issued the CP AUTOLOG command is captured. For invalid logon attempts this data is not available. It is a character field.

Invalid Password Count—this is the current count of invalid passwords used. It is a hexadecimal field.

Accounting Record Limit—this is the threshold count of invalid passwords that caused the record to be generated. It is a hexadecimal field.

LUNAME—this is the logical unit name for an SNA terminal that the autolog or logon attempt was made from. It is a character field.

Type 05—Successful Links

This record is generated every time a virtual machine successfully links to another virtual machine's minidisk. By analyzing these records, you may identify minidisk users that are gaining access to what they should not and subsequently identify a security problem. Changing the link password should prevent that, but you should continue to monitor the situation. This record is also useful in identifying minidisks that many users link to. It may be advisable to place the data or programs they are accessing on a public disk, after determining the reason, so all users have access to it when they logon. On the other hand, if you have minidisks that contain shared data that users are not linking to, you may, after determining the reason the shared data is not being used, remove the minidisk, thus freeing up disk space. Link records are generated when a user either issues the CP LINK command or they log on if they have links to other minidisks defined in their VM user directory entry.

Following is the format of the Successful Links Record:

Column Position	Data
1–8	Userid
9–16	Virtual Machine Accounting Number
17–22	Date of Accounting
23–28	Time of Accounting
29–32	Terminal Address
33–40	Reserved
41–48	Target Userid
49–51	Target Minidisk
52–70	Reserved
71–78	LUNAME
79–80	Record Type Code (05)

Userid—this is the userid that issued the link command. It is a character field.

Virtual Machine Accounting Number—this is the accounting number associated with the virtual machine in the VM user directory. It is a character field.

Date of Accounting—this is the date the link occurred; it is a character field in the format "mmddyy."

Time of Accounting—this is the time the link occurred; it is a character field in the format "hhmmss."

Terminal Address—this field contains the resource-id if the link was made from a remote bisynchronous terminal, a real device address, or NONE (if no terminal was identified). It is a character field.

Target Userid—this is the userid of the user that owns the minidisk that was linked. It is a character field.

Target Minidisk—this is the minidisk address that was linked. It is a character field.

LUNAME—this is the logical unit name for an SNA terminal the link was issued from. It is a character field.

Type 06—Unsuccessful Link Attempts

This record is generated when a predefined threshold is reached for a user trying unsuccessfully to link to another user's minidisk. The user that attempted the link can be identified, since the attempt was made from a logged on userid. The information in this record can be used to identify users who are trying to gain access to data that they should not have access to.

Following is the format of the Unsuccessful Link Attempts Record:

Column Position	Data
1–8	Userid
9–16	Virtual Machine Accounting Number
17–22	Date of Accounting
23–28	Time of Accounting
29–32	Terminal Address
33–40	Invalid Password
41–48	Target Userid
49–51	Target Minidisk
52–53	Invalid Password Count
54–55	Invalid Password Limit
56–70	Reserved
71–78	LUNAME
79–80	Record Type Code (06)

Userid—this is the userid that issued the link command. It is a character field.

Virtual Machine Accounting Number—this is the accounting number associated with the virtual machine in the VM user directory. It is a character field.

Date of Accounting—this is the date the link attempt occurred. It is a character field in the format "mmddyy."

Time of Accounting—this is the time the link attempt occurred. It is a character field in the format "hhmmss."

Terminal Address—this field contains the resource-id if the attempt was made from a remote bisynchronous terminal, a real device address, or NONE (if no terminal was identified). This is a character field.

Invalid Password—this field contains the invalid password used: "TOO LONG" if a password greater than 8 characters was entered or "TERM/ERR" if the line dropped during password entry. It is a character field.

Target Userid—this is the userid of the user that owns the minidisk that the attempt was made to link. It is a character field.

Target Minidisk—this is the minidisk address that the attempt was made to link. It is a character field.

Invalid Password Count—this is the current count of invalid passwords used and is a hexadecimal field.

Invalid Password Limit—this is the threshold count of invalid passwords that caused the record to be generated. It is a hexadecimal field.

LUNAME—this is the logical unit name for an SNA terminal the link attempt was made from. It is a character field.

Type 07—VCNA Usage

The VCNA record indicates usage of the VTAM Communications Network Application. It identifies the amount of data that is transmitted across the network. The information recorded for a userid includes data that was both transmitted and received across the network. VCNA records are generated when the user logs off.

Following is the format of the VCNA Record:

Column Position	Data
1–8	Userid or Terminal Identification
9–16	Account Number or 0000
17–20	Overflow Counters
21–24	Counter 1
25–28	Counter 2
29–32	Counter 3
33–36	Counter 4
37–40	Counter 5
41–44	Counter 6
45–48	Logon Time
49–52	Logon Date
53–56	Logoff Time
57–60	Logoff Date
61–78	Unused
79–80	Record Type Code (07)

Note that the order of the date and time fields in the VCNA accounting record may be reversed.

Userid or Terminal Identification—this is the userid that was logged on to the system or the terminal address that was connected through the VM/VTAM network. It is a character field.

Account Number or 0000—if a userid is logged on to the system, their account number is saved. If a terminal was connected to the system but no user is logged on from it, 0000 is placed in the account field. This is a character field.

Overflow Counters—these fields contain four half word fields for holding overflow indicators; each count is equivalent to approximately 2.1 billion. The overflow counters correspond to the following counters, in hexadecimal format:

    Overflow counter 1: Input request units
    Overflow counter 2: Input bytes
    Overflow counter 3: Output request units
    Overflow counter 4: Output bytes

Counter 1—this field contains the number of input request units. If is a hexadecimal field.

Counter 2—this field contains the number of input bytes. It is a hexadecimal field.

Counter 3—this field contains the number of output request units. It is a hexadecimal field.

Counter 4—this field contains the number of output bytes. It is a hexadecimal field.

Counter 5—this field contains the number of console output lines. It is a hexadecimal field.

Counter 6—this field contains the number of copy requests. It is a hexadecimal field.

Logon Time—this is the time the user logged on through the VTAM network. It is in packed format.

Logon Date—this is the date the user logged on. It is in packed Julian format.

Logoff Time—this is the time the user logged off. It is in packed format.

Logoff Date—this is the date the user logged off. It is in packed Julian format.

Type 08—Terminal Record

The terminal record is generated when a user logs off or disconnects from the system. The record identifies the terminal logged on and the userid. This record does not identify the amount of time the terminal was logged on, and is more useful as a security record (like the type 04, 05, and 06) than for tracking resource utilization.

Following is the format of the Terminal Record:

Column Position	Data
1–8	Userid
9–16	Virtual Machine Accounting Number
17–22	Date of Accounting
23–28	Time of Accounting

29–64   Reserved
65–72   Terminal Identification
73–78   Reserved
79–80   Record Type Code (08)

Userid—this is the userid that was logged on to the system. It is a character field.

Virtual Machine Accounting Number—this is the accounting number associated with the virtual machine in the VM user directory. It is a character field.

Date of Accounting—this is the date the user logged off the system. It is a character field in the format "mmddyy."

Time of Accounting—this is the time the user logged off the system. It is a character field in the format "hhmmss."

Terminal Identification—this is the terminal address and can be either a real address or a logical address. This is a character field.

Additional Accounting Records

Depending on the system configuration, additional accounting record types may be available that account for such things as RSCS (the Remote Spooling Communications Subsystem), TSAF (the Transparent Services Access Facility), and SQL/DS usage. In each of these cases the applications must be configured by the site to produce accounting data.

CP accounting records provide an excellent basis for an accounting system, with records covering the major user activities that affect resource consumption. It is the subsequent use of this information, however, that constitutes an accounting system.

Using the CP Records

When accounting records are created they are routed to the userid specified in the DMKSYS Macro via the spooling system. VM has no standard mechanism for periodically copying the records from spool space to a minidisk. Unless the organization provides a means of receiving the records, they miss the opportunity to take advantage of the information provided in the records.

Although the CP records capture valuable information, use is limited if it remains raw information. The records do not provide actual costs, which is really site-determined, nor is there an algorithm provided to determine costs. Capabilities such as these must either be purchased as system software or designed by the installation.

An organization using the standard VM accounting facilities with no added provisions for resource accounting will most likely spool CP-generated accounting records to a CMS minidisk. These can later be recorded on tape to be kept as historical information. Most likely an organization that does not take the time to account for resources is charging this use to overhead, rather than allocating it to users. Even if there is no desire to change this policy, this information is a basis for estimating the future needs of the organization for increased computing resources, based on past use. Resource accounting information can also indicate which system resources are being used most efficiently.

Through the use of resource accounting packages, either purchased or developed in-house, the CP accounting records can be the basis of a comprehensive system for both tracking the allocation of resources and subsequently charging for them.

There are many computer resources that can potentially be included in the tracking for resource accounting. Those that are reported in CP accounting records include the records identified above, as well as site-defined records that can be included in the CP accounting record stream.

Whether implemented in-house or through system software, there are some basic considerations involved in developing a resource accounting system which protects the needs of the VM environment. It is important that the resource usage be tracked at the level needed for the organization to meet its objectives. It should not interfere with the capabilities that users need to perform their online tasks as efficiently as possible. The accounting system needs to be as transparent, performing this service without extensive user involvement. At the departmental level, this transparency, with the lack of onsite technical support, is even more important.

There are many computer system resources that can potentially be included in the tracking for resource accounting. Information that is not obtained from the CP records, but could potentially be accountable expenses, include the following:

• Technical support from central MIS or the data center.

- System programmer time used installing and maintaining end-user application programs, operating systems, system software, and utility software.
- Operations staff assistance for end-users.
- Permanent DASD assigned to users in their VM user directory entries.
- Printed output.
- Tape mounts required by end-users.
- Storage of user data off-line on tapes.
- Storage of user data on-line.
- Application software required by end-users.
- Supplies used supporting end-users including magnetic tapes and paper used for printed output.
- Data entry services.
- Standard system maintenance costs such as system backups and remote site storage of magnetic tapes.
- General data center overhead incurred for office space and utilities.

In each of the above examples, the site must make provisions for collecting the data. It is not available in standard CP accounting data.

If the organization chooses to chargeback the cost of computer resources, they will need to make provisions for crediting users for incorrect charges or for jobs that did not finish successfully.

When setting up an accounting system, planning is critical— a site needs to identify the type of information they need and the detail level that is most meaningful. Also, critical to the success of the accounting is support from management in all areas of the organization.

A rather simple scheme can be implemented using some of the standard CP accounting records. This can be done quickly and provides feedback to the data center to help identify long-term requirements of the resource accounting system. The system can evolve into a comprehensive resource accounting system with the proper planning. A comprehensive system need not be a complicated system. It all depends on the needs of the organization. Although a myriad of accounting data is available, all data types are not meaningful for all organizations to track.

Commercially available resource accounting packages may save time and money, in the long run, if they meet the needs of an organization. In order to evaluate the alternatives, the organization's needs will have to be clearly defined. This is another area where planning pays off.

Chapter Summary

The following information was discussed in this chapter:

- The VM operating system provides a basis for comprehensive accounting through CP accounting records.
- A detailed description of the standard CP accounting records was presented.
- An explanation of additional types of accounting records was discussed.
- Other data center resources that should be considered when designing a comprehensive resource accounting system were identified.
- A comprehensive resource accounting system is very site-specific.

About the Author

Julie Tray has worked extensively in computer resource accounting for the past seven years. She first worked in an MVS environment and for the past five years the VM operating system. Julie currently is employed by Systems Center, Inc., in Reston, Virginia. Systems Center develops system software for the VM operating system environment. Julie has participated in developmental efforts that resulted in bringing two third-party VM accounting system software products to market. Before joining a system software vendor, she worked in the timesharing industry and was involved in the development of a resource accounting system that her employer used for billing customers.

9

VM Audit and Security

by Michael Lude

Introduction

The VM operating system was developed in a university environment in the early 1960s. Since then VM has undergone an evolution of change to make it IBM's premier interactive operating system. Since VM is now used at over 16,000 installations, the issues of security and integrity are much more important now than they were in 1967.

This chapter expresses a system programmer's perspective on the issue of VM security and integrity. This perspective is appropriate since the system programmer is responsible for maintaining VM security as well as reporting the status of VM security to EDP auditors.

This chapter offers a general discussion of security concepts, followed by an overview of how VM implements a security scheme based on the emulation of System/370 architecture, the user directory, and passwords. Potential security breaches are pointed out throughout the chapter and a brief but effective audit checklist has been included at the end of the chapter.

General Security Concepts and Overview

Security Concepts

Computer security concepts are based on traditional techniques long known from the science of defense. Defense has been studied for millenia and security specialists have applied what is known about protecting military positions to computer systems.

The primary objective in defending anything is to make it "expensive" for an attack to succeed. If the cost of taking an objective exceeds that of duplicating it, then it is unlikely that an attack will be pressed to a successful conclusion. Of course, the *perceived* strength of a defense may differ from the *actual* strength, so a defender must count upon his defense being tested occasionally. In addition, an "impregnable" defense invites a certain class of attackers to demonstrate their skill, as an "unclimbable" peak attracts mountaineers. This is a particular problem in defending computer systems.

The relative strength of a defense can be measured as the ratio of the cost of a successful attack to the rewards accruing from the attack, or *work factor*. Thus, a high work factor discourages deliberate attack; subject to the limitations discussed above.

There are three main methods employed in defending systems. The first is *dispersion*, which is an attempt to minimize losses suffered by an attack. The second is *duplication*, which allows the system to survive damage to any individual part. Finally, *defense in depth* requires the attacker to overcome a series of barriers, each more difficult than the last, before damage can occur.

Dispersion can be an effective defense, requiring an attacker to mount several nearly simultaneous assaults, all of which must be successful for the general attack to succeed. However, it is much more difficult to defend multiple sites from attack in the first place. In the past, dispersion was much too expensive a technique to apply to multi-million dollar computer systems, but with the advent of inexpensive mid-range processors, distributed processing has become a valid defense strategy.

Duplication is the method most commonly applied to computer systems' hardware reliability requirements. With the steady drop in the price of hardware components, manufacturers can feasibly duplicate critical hardware components; in some cases being able to automatically switch to the backup in event of failure. With soft-

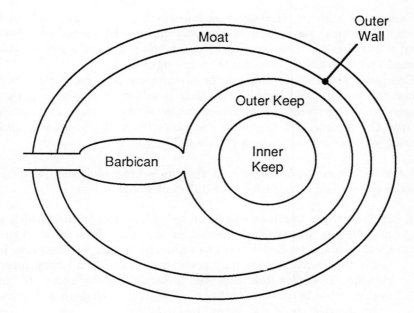

Figure 9-1 Schematic diagram of defense in depth: showing the analogy between computer defense and a castle.

ware, the principle of duplication is demonstrated by the very commonly performed disk to tape backups.

Defense in depth is the principle behind medieval castles, where an attacker must get across a moat, through the barbican, the outer keep, and finally the inner keep. Computer defenses follow this same strategy with the telecommunications software, the applications software, the operating system, and the hardware protecting the database in the "inner keep" (see Figure 9-1). Defense in depth may be applied to the main system or to each of several dispersed systems individually.

Computer Security and How It Can Fail

Before analyzing computer security failure, it is useful to invent a taxonomy of security breaches. We can then examine each genus of failure for methods of prevention. Classification has the further advantage of allowing rigorous risk management analysis. Without a strong statistical treatment of security lapses, the security officer may waste limited resources protecting against highly improbable dangers while leaving the main threats unguarded.

Computer security failures can be divided into six major classifications: the variety and type of *loss* that is suffered; the *hazard* that imperiled the system; the ultimate *target* of the attack; the *motive* behind the attack (if deliberate); the *perpetrator* of the attack; and, finally, who the *victim* is. (see Figure 9-2.)

Loss — When the security of a system is breached, the owner or user of the system may suffer four different kinds of loss:

1. If the system becomes unavailable for use, the service which it provided is interrupted (denial of service). This could result from damage or destruction to either hardware or software. In addition, unavailability may occur because of temporary interruption of service due to power failures, etc., or access to the system may be prevented because of nearby disasters that require evacuation of the computer facilities.

2. If the system is damaged, destroyed, or stolen, then money or material assets are lost. This category includes hardware and software, and computer systems often control monetary assets which might be stolen. In fact, this is the most common target of computer-related crime (as it is with any type of crime).

3. Even if nothing is discovered to be missing, when proprietary secrets are read by unauthorized personnel, then exclusive use of a property is lost. In fact, some information, such as patent applications or exclusive mailing lists, lose most or all of their value when disclosed.

Loss

Hazard

Target

Motive

Perpetrator

Victim

Figure 9-2 Classifications of computer security breaches.

4. Lastly, the computer system can be used to deny human or civil rights such as privacy or to illegally discriminate.

Hazard — Computer system hazards may be subdivided into accidental and deliberate acts, although the dividing line is not always so clear (as in the case of negligence).

An accident is an unexpected and unwanted event that cannot be prevented by its victim and may be caused by acts of God, other people, or by the victim him or herself. A risk manager can only attempt to reduce the damage from such events, since in many cases they cannot be prevented.

Deliberate attacks on a system can attempt to mimic accidents; in addition there are a myriad of ways to steal or damage a system: from an employee stealing computer time for a private project to a professional thief tapping communication lines to steal passwords and ultimately system-controlled assets.

Target — In order to secure a system, it is necessary to define the assets to be protected. It is tempting to consider the computer as a single large target; in fact, it consists of three separate targets: the computer complex itself, including the hardware and operating systems; any assets that can be attacked by using the computer as an instrument or tool; and those assets actually residing in the computer system, such as a database or proprietary programs.

Motive — Financial gain is the motive in the overwhelming majority of attacks on computer systems, as might be imagined. A significant minority are caused by negligence, although this is not properly a motive, but rather a lack of proper motivation. The popular public perception of a computer criminal, and the one that gets newspaper headlines, is the computer hacker, who is motivated by mischief and is challenged by elaborate security measures. In addition, systems have been attacked as a means of political protest or as a route to increased power and/or authority for the criminal.

Perpetrators — Categorizing computer criminals is as futile as categorizing baseball fans: There is an astonishing range of people involved. Employees and staff probably commit the majority of computer crime, if only because of proximity to the machines and the requisite opportunity. With employee loyalties shifting from their employers to their professions, it is unwise to rely solely on the integrity of the staff to defend a computer system.

Victims — When a business handles money by computer, it may possibly lose it through fraud, embezzlement, or other theft. Merchandise may be misdirected from a warehouse; false accounts payables may be set up; or unauthorized increases in authorized payments may be programmed. These scenarios are all too familiar; and could have been prevented by better security precautions beforehand.

Many victims of computer crime do not own a computer or have control over one. These are the millions of customers of firms that carry accounts on computers.

VM Security

Because of its unique method of simulating IBM System/370 architecture, while simultaneously using that same architecture, VM is both an efficient and remarkably secure system. Most VM security breaches are the result of carelessness of systems or operations staff, or even users. A VM system that is installed with add-on security software, as well as attention to operational procedures, should be as secure as necessary for most business applications. Of course, a regularly scheduled and rigorous audit program should be put in place to ensure compliance with security standards as the system evolves.

System/370 Architecture   It is important to view VM security from the perspective of IBM's System/370 architecture, since this is the design-point of the operating system. The original developers were interested only in simulating hardware; VM was, at first, an experimental system written at Cambridge University with no thought of it being a commercially viable product. VM's basic security features come as a serendipitous result of the basic architecture design. What follows, then, is an overview of that architecture, with parallels drawn between the hardware and software whenever necessary. Keep in mind that the following discussion applies equally to MVS or VSE systems in addition to VM; in fact, System/370 architecture is operating system independent.

We start with the basic System/370 components (please refer to Figure 9-3). The central processing unit (CPU) executes programs residing in real storage and may examine or alter real storage. The channel is a kind of auxiliary processor that executes *channel programs*. Channel programs transfer data to real storage from various devices and vice versa. The CPU may execute an instruction that causes a channel program to begin execution and the channel may interrupt the CPU (explained below).

The basic status of any running program is reflected in the Program Status Word (*PSW*), a component of the CPU.

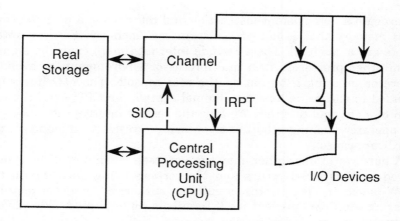

Figure 9-3 System/370 components.

Two features of the PSW embody most of the hardware security facilities available: the problem/supervisor state bit and the storage protect key. All System/370 instructions are segregated into two classes: *problem state* instructions and *supervisor state* instructions. In general, problem state instructions are "safe"; supervisor state instructions allow a program to change its state, start channel programs, and other insecure operations. The storage protect key is really just that: a key that must exactly match a similar key associated with each block of real memory (storage). If the key in the PSW does not match the key of the block of storage currently being referenced, then a type of program interruption occurs. There is a special key of 0 which matches all other keys. In general, all operating systems (VM included) execute in supervisor state with key 0; they dispatch user tasks or programs in problem state with an appropriate non-zero key. By saving the PSW (and possibly one or more registers), the complete running status of any program may be saved; conversely, restoring the PSW is equivalent to restarting the program at the point it was saved.

The six types of *interrupts* are listed in Figure 9-4. A hardware interruption occurs when the indicated condition arises. A *machine check* is a hardware error condition and is not usually encountered by programmers. A *supervisor call* is a machine language instruction. This is the mechanism that allows programs with limited privilege to request services from the operating system or other controlling program. A *program check* occurs whenever a program issues an invalid instruction. Examples of program checks include attempting to execute a non-existent instruction and referencing a portion of virtual memory that is not presently in real memory. *External* interrupts are a catch-all. These include internal timers expiring, signals from other processors in a multiprocessor environment, or even an operator pressing a button on the real console. The *I/O* interrupt, alluded to earlier, is how the channel signals the CPU upon completion of a channel program. Finally, the restart interrupt is caused by an operator pushing a button or entering a restart command on the hardware console.

A hardware interruption may present itself when one of the events listed in Figure 9-4 occurs and the corresponding mask bit in the PSW is set. In other words, a suitably authorized program may (by altering the PSW) prevent itself from being interrupted. A hardware interruption causes the current running PSW to be stored in a fixed location in the first several hundred bytes of real memory and a new PSW to be loaded from another fixed location in memory. This effectively causes the execution of the routine pointed to by the new PSW, which then handles the interrupt. After this first level interrupt handler (FLIH) completes, it reloads the original PSW to return control. Note that this scheme implies that there are "old" and "new" PSW locations defined in low memory for each of the six interrupt types.

System/370 Architecture and VM   Now that the underlying architecture has been explained, it is possible to explain VM operation in terms of that architecture. Remember that VM was designed to simulate this architecture; a program running on the real machine should execute identically to the same program running on a virtual machine (VM).

VM is a common term for what is actually several system components in one. The two primary components of VM are:

Machine Check

Supervisor Call (SVC)

Program Check

External

I/O

Restart

Figure 9-4 System/370 interrupt types: Multiple interrupts are reflected in the order shown.

- **CP** *(Control Program)*, which is actually the VM operating system
- **CMS** *(Conversational Monitor System)*, provides users with the interactive interface for VM applications

One particular subroutine within CP is responsible for running users: DMKDSP, the dispatcher. When the dispatcher is ready to run a user, it selects the first runable user and performs the following operations:

1. The user's *virtual* PSW is retrieved from an internal control block in memory.
2. A "fixed up" PSW is built to protect the VM operating system. VM modifies the virtual PSW to put it in problem state with all interrupts enabled. In addition, the proper storage key is set.
3. An internal timer is set to expire a short while later.
4. CP's registers are saved and the user's are loaded.
5. The "fixed up" PSW is loaded to the real hardware PSW.

At this point, the user is running on the real hardware. Note that this user is running fully enabled for interrupts in problem state and will certainly be interrupted eventually. There are several ways this can happen:

- The user may execute a supervisor state instruction. This will generate a privileged operation program check interrupt.
- The user may execute an SVC instruction and get a supervisor call interrupt.
- The user may get an external interrupt from the interval timer expiring (this is what will happen if the user's program goes into a loop).

Example 1: Let's follow what happens when the user executes an SVC instruction:

1. The interruption occurs and CP's SVC interrupt handler gets control.
2. The user's virtual PSW is stored in the user's "SVC Old PSW" area in virtual storage.
3. The user's SVC New PSW is retrieved and "fixed up" as before.
4. Registers, etc., are restored and this new "fixed up" PSW is loaded.

This is referred to as "reflecting an interrupt," since CP needed to take no action other than handing it back to the user.

Example 2: The user executes a Load PSW (LPSW) instruction. Since this is a privileged instruction, a program check interrupt will occur. The program check interrupt handler then examines the user's virtual PSW. There are two possible cases:

1. The user is in virtual problem state. In this case, it really was an "illegal" instruction, so CP will reflect the program check back to the user.
2. The user was is virtual supervisor state. This is not an error as far as the user is concerned; CP takes the PSW that the user was trying to load, performs the "fix up" on it, and loads it.

From the above discussion it is clear that VM takes full advantage of all hardware features to effect its hardware simulation. User programs may do anything they like, but are still being restrained by a combination of CP and the hardware from doing anything destructive to another user.

The VM Directory

The directory is the heart of a VM system. It contains userid definitions, disk area allocations, user authority classes, and system passwords. The directory should be designed and coded with care and audited regularly for appropriateness.

The directory (also called *source directory*) is a regular CMS file (with filetype of DIRECT) that may reside virtually anywhere on the system. In practice, however, it usually resides on one of MAINT's disks unless some directory management software is installed. All passwords in the directory can be plainly read, although some add-on security packages support password encryption.

The source directory is subsequently processed by the CMS DIRECT command in order to compile it into a more efficient *object directory*. The DIRECT command requires privilege class "C" to execute. The source directory is read and syntax-checked and then written out to a CP-owned disk volume. It is the object directory that is actually referenced by the operating system when validating userids or passwords.

In addition to reading and syntax-checking the source directory, the DIRECT command also reads a file called RPWLIST DATA (if it exists), and uses this file as a list of "illegal" logon passwords. If a logon password is found in RPWLIST DATA, then the object directory is updated so that that user can no longer logon. This feature was added by IBM as a means of forcing VM installers to change the default passwords shipped with the VM system.

Control Statement Overview

What follows is a discussion of security and audit concerns associated with various directory control statements. This is by no means a thorough treatment of each statement. Please refer to the *VM/SP Planning Guide* for more complete information about any of the following control statements.

USER — A USER statement begins the definition of each userid in the directory and defines at minimum the actual userid and logon password. In addition, here is where the *privilege class(es)* for the user are indicated, either by stating them directly or by indicating the existence of a CLASS record (see below). Privilege classes define CP commands into functional types (for example, operations, system programming, IBM customer engineer, etc.).

A userid name is from one to eight characters long and can be almost anything. Defining userid naming standards can separate privileged from non-privileged users and make attempted security breaches easier to spot. The password is also one to eight characters long. A special-case password of NOLOG prevents the user from ever logging on.

ACCOUNT— The ACCOUNT statement defines a userid's account number. The account number is simply a one to eight character alphanumeric string that is carried along with the userid and placed in the accounting records. VM never actually uses the account number; it is provided solely for customer use. If an installation does not have useful userid standards in place, it may be able to choose an account number standard to identify users.

CLASS — The existence of a CLASS statement is indicated by coding the privilege class on the USER statement as an asterisk (*). This is necessary if more that eight classes need be defined for a user. The CLASS statement should immediately follow the USER statement and defines up to 32 privilege classes associated with the user.

CONSOLE — This statement primarily defines the virtual address and device type of the user's virtual console. It also allows specification of a *secondary user*. The secondary user, if logged on, will receive all console messages directed to the primary user if the primary user is running *disconnected* (i.e., without a physical monitor). The secondary user may cause the primary user to issue commands by means of the SEND command. Note that if the primary user has different privilege classes from the secondary user, the privilege class is essentially transferred.

OPTION — The OPTION control statement is sort of a catch-all: It allows specification of many unrelated virtual machine options. The one particular option with auditing ramifications is the ACCT option. Users with ACCT specified may generate accounting records to charge for resource consumption. Unscrupulous users with the ACCT option specified in their directory could generate accounting cards with negative amounts in them, thus crediting their computing account at an installation charging for computer time.

MDISK — The MDISK (minidisk) statement defines an extent on disk that is "owned" by a user. Extents are defined by specifying the first cylinder or block and the length of the minidisk on a particular real volume. In addition, the default access mode (read-only or writable) and up to three optional passwords allowing access to other users may be specified.

Figure 9-5 is a list of minidisk mode definitions. Note that these modes define the *default* access to a user's own disk at logon time; the user may define a different mode any time after logon. The most useful mode for minidisk definitions is "MR"; it guarantees at least a read-only link and gives write access if another user hasn't already linked it in write mode.

The passwords on the minidisk are for use by users other than the owner requesting a link to the disk.[1] The *read* password will be requested for an R or RR link request; the *write* password for a W or

R — Read only, unless already linked in any mode
RR — Read only in any case

---

1. Minidisk passwords may be unnecessary (and in fact undesirable) if add-on access control software is installed. See the section on the Access Control Interface (ACI) for more information.

WR request; and the *multiple* password for an M, MR, or MW request.

The passwords are positional: To specify a write password, a read password must be chosen; to specify a multiple password, both a read and a write password must be chosen. As a special case, a password of ALL indicates that the particular link is to be granted unconditionally (system minidisks meant to be shared by all users, such as the CMS system, or "190," disk, usually have a read link password of "ALL"). Not supplying any password makes the minidisk unlinkable in any case.

Directory Standards and Techniques

The DIRECT Statement The first non-comment control statement in the directory must be the DIRECT statement. It specifies where the object directory resides. The addresses supplied on the DIRECT statement are usually virtual; it is a good idea to code, instead the *real* address of the directory disk volume. This allows use of the source directory with the standalone directory utility (important for disaster recovery purposes) and also makes the system easier to audit.

Placeholder Userids Some system data areas, such as paging or temporary disk space, are defined by the standalone allocation of the volume rather than by minidisk statements in the directory. Since remembering the allocation of a volume is inconvenient, a common technique used to protect these system areas is to define "dummy" userids with minidisks overlaying all system areas. IBM's standard for naming these users is to have a dollar sign ($) as the first and last characters of the userid: Thus $PAGE$ and $SAVSYS$ have minidisks overlaying the paging area and saved system areas, respectively.

These placeholder userids *must* have a logon password of NOLOG and absolutely no link passwords; any user writing on these areas could be disastrous.

Minidisk Overlaps Before the advent of add-on directory maintenance program products, such as DIRMAINT, the inadvertent overlapping of minidisks was a major integrity problem for VM installations. The DIRECT command does absolutely no checking other than for the syntax of the various statements; overlapped minidisks allow users to destroy each other's data. So, from VM's beginning system programmers have written directory mapping utilities that flag overlaying or overlapped minidisks.[2]

IBM provides a directory mapping utility called "DISKMAP." DISKMAP is a REXX EXEC provided as part of the VM/SP base system. It produces a CMS output file listing all disk allocations defined in the VM directory. See Figure 9-6 for a sample DISKMAP output listing.

If placeholder userids have been set up, the resultant listing completely maps all disk volumes, which is a useful report to have. This report is also the only practical way to detect minidisk overlays and overlaps if no additional directory maintenance software has been installed.

In general, any minidisk overlaps detected by these utilities indicates an error. There are some cases, however, where an *overlay* is intentionally defined because it is a useful technique for referring to the same data area via two (or more) different minidisk definitions. For example, most VM installations perform disaster recovery disk to tape backups by defining, then backing up, what is known as a *full-pack minidisk*. The full-pack minidisk is a minidisk defined to start at the lowest end of a real disk volume and extend to the highest end. This minidisk will overlay all other defined minidisks on the volume, but it won't matter since it will only be read by the backup program.

The User Class Restructure

Function Type and Classes CP commands are subdivided into several separate privilege classes, each identified by a letter ("A" through "G"), and a special class not identified by a letter, commonly called "any." A command may belong to more than one class. Userids are assigned the authority to issue commands belonging to one or more privilege classes by putting the corresponding privilege class letters in the userid's DIRECT CLASS directory statement. Any userid in the directory can issue class "any" commands..

---

2. Two disks *overlay* each other if they have exactly the same starting cylinder or block and the same length. They *overlap* if they do not overlay each other yet still share at least one cylinder or block.

```
VOLUME  USERID   ~CUU  DEVTYPE   START      END      SIZE

VMSRES  $ALLOC$   B0A  FB-512   000000   000015   000016

        $SAVSYS$  B0A  FB-512   000016   041015   041000

        MAINT     294  FB-512   041016   066015   025000

                                 66016    91015    25000    GAP

        $TDISK$   B0A  FB-512   091016   109207   018192

        $PAGE$    B0A  FB-512   109208   149207   040000

        DEMO3     191  FB-512   149208   155207   006000

        VMUSER07  191  FB-512   155208   158207   003000

        VMUSER08  191  FB-512   155208   161207   006000   **OVERLAP**
```

Figure 9-6 Sample DISKMAP output.

Before VM/SP Release 4 the command classes were hard-coded in the system; starting in Release 4 the number of classes (not counting "any") was expanded to 32 (A through Z and 1 through 6), and a facility was provided to allow the system programmer to change the class of any or all commands.

Figure 9-7 tabulates the current command class structure. Note that privilege classes are not hierarchical. For example, class "B" is not better or more powerful than class "F"; those class authorities just allow the user to execute different commands. As you can see in the figure, authority classes were structured along functional areas.

Each command has a particular *type* associated with it, which defines the type of analyst, operator, or user that the command is designed for. The type of the command does not change, but only serves to identify the command. The *class*, on the other hand, may be changed by means of the *override directory*.

Override Directory and Command Format The override directory is very much like the user directory. It is a CMS file that may reside anywhere and has a corresponding object format. The override directory object code is usually placed on the VM system residence volume, although it may be on any CP-owned volume. The OVERRIDE command is used to read and syntax-check the override directory, and to optionally write it out. After the override command is issued, the changes take effect upon the next system IPL.

IBM'S Suggestions for GCS Users GCS (the Group Control System) is an operating system which runs under VM. It is a corequisite for products such as VTAM and RSCS.

A - System Operator

B - Resource Operator

C - Systems Programmer

D - Spooling Operator

E - Systems Analyst

F - Customer Engineer

G - General User

Figure 9-7 Command types and classes.

IBM suggests that the classes of several commands be changed if
GCS is installed on the system, because several class "G" commands
can cause corruption of storage and loss of integrity to the GCS
shared storage area. In particular, the ADSTOP and TRACE commands should never be issued from a GCS machine. The STORE,
DISPLAY, BEGIN, DUMP, PER, and VMDUMP commands should
be issued only with great care. As an exercise, the reader may wish
to construct an override directory that fulfills these conditions; IBM
has a sample in the *VM / SP Planning Guide.*

VM System Generation

Some VM system generation parameters have a direct result in the
security of the resulting system. A thorough understanding of the
design and interaction of the various choices available is essential to
the well-being of the system.

Standalone Utilities

A standalone utility is a special-purpose operating system designed
to perform one specific task. Several such utilities are distributed
with VM and are normally installed on the public CMS system disk
as IPLable card-image files and some in readily executable CMS
MODULE format. (An IPLable card-image file must be placed into a
VM userid's virtual card reader and loaded via the VM "IPL" com-

mand. A CMS module has a filetype of "MODULE" and can be invoked merely by entering the module's CMS filename.) There are separate utilities to do disk backup and copy, disk format, and disk hardware analysis. In addition, there is a standalone version of the DIRECT command, and a standalone VM system dump routine.

It is important to note that any of these routines can be executed on even a class "G" userid, since all that is required is System/370 hardware which is simulated by VM. Therefore, remove these utilities from the CMS system (190) disk if you do not want them executed by non-authorized personnel. Listed below is a table of the standalone utilities and their CMS filename(s).

Description	CMS Filename(s)
DASD Copy	IPL DDR
	DDR MODULE
DASD Format	IPL FMT
	CPFMT MODULE
DASD Analysis	IPL DSF
	DSF MODULE
Directory Generation	IPL DIR
	DIRECT MODULE
Memory Dump	user-created

DDR Security Concerns The DASD dump restore utility is used for dumping data in image format from disk to tape, tape to disk, or disk to disk. In particular, it can be used to circumvent CMS-based security since DDR is not CMS-based. One of the most common uses of DDR, to bypass CMS security, is to use DDR to copy a read-only disk to a writable temporary disk. This will allow access to mode 0 files, normally inaccessible to CMS users with read/only access to the target disk on which the file resides. This example illustrates the wisdom of removing public access to DDR, as well as the folly of relying on CMS-level security.

Standalone Directory The standalone directory program does not have any direct security concerns since it requires class "C" and a write link to the directory volume in order to execute.

Tailorable Control Files

A minimal VM system installation requires building a directory, tailoring three CP modules, and rebuilding the nucleus. These three CP modules (DMKRIO, DMKSYS, and DMKSNT) comprise the bulk of VM security and audit concerns outside of the actual user directory.

DMKRIO   This is a table of all real devices available to a VM system. A device is unusable by VM if it has not been generated correctly in DMKRIO. There are occasions when devices listed in DMKRIO do not exist. The cost of these extra devices in real storage is small, but for general purposes no device should be defined in DMKRIO unless there is a good reason for it being there. If this rule is adhered to, DMKRIO can then be used as a good starting point for taking a physical inventory of a VM system.

The greatest security concern with DMKRIO lies with the last macro to be coded, RIOGEN, which lists the primary and all alternate operator consoles. Before explaining RIOGEN in detail, some background explanation is in order.

The *VM system operator* is simply the first userid to logon with class A privileges. This is usually userid "OPERATOR," but does not have to be! The *operator console* is the terminal he is logged on to. If the VM system operator logs off, then the next class "A" user to logon becomes the operator. During VM IPL, the system logs a specified class "A" user on to a specified terminal. The operator userid specification is covered under DMKSYS below; the terminal is generated with DMKRIO's RIOGEN macro.

During VM initialization, the terminal that is listed as the primary operator console is used if available. If it is turned off or otherwise dysfunctional, the first alternate console is tried. If that does not work, then the second, third, and so on are tried. If none work, then VM loads a disabled wait code of "5" into the CPU's PSW and ceases operation.

Keeping all this in mind, several points should be addressed.

- The list of primary and alternate consoles should contain terminals on as many different control units as possible. This way the failure of one terminal controller will not cause a system IPL failure.
- The physical location of *every* terminal in the RIOGEN console list should be in a secure location and should be verified on a regular basis. The physical location of the primary and every alternate console should be documented for the operations staff as well. There is nothing more disconcerting than having the operations and sys-

tems staff running around the building trying to figure out where the operator console is!

It is valid to have consoles generated that do not exist, or exist only in virtual configurations (VM under VM); however, the above security considerations still apply.

DMKSYS There are more than a dozen macros in DMKSYS that control a wide variety of configuration options, including several with wide-ranging security concerns: SYSMON, SYSACNT, SYSJRL, SYSPCLAS, and SYSFCN.

The SYSMON macro of DMKSYS sets the default parameters for the collection of monitor data used for performance tuning and capacity planning. There are no MONITOR security concerns except for RESPONSE class records. These records contain the entire terminal buffer of every user terminal response, which may therefore contain passwords. If RESPONSE class records are being collected, the data should remain secure.

The SYSACNT macro of DMKSYS specifies the disposition of CP-generated accounting records; SYSACNT cannot be entirely disabled. Accounting records are collected in the virtual reader queue of the user, specified in the SYSACNT macro.

The SYSACNT macro of DMKSYS enables logon and link journaling, which is disabled by default. The LOGLMT and LNKLMT parameters specify how many incorrect passwords may be entered before an accounting record is generated, a message is sent, and/or further use of the command is suspended. Messages are sent to the userids coded in the LOGUID and LNKUID parameters, respectively. The PSUPRS option forces users to type in their passwords under a mask to avoid display. Finally, the JOURNAL parameter, when set to YES, allows the system operator to temporarily disable the journaling function. This should not be allowed unless other system security software duplicates this function.

The SYSPCLAS macro of DMKSYS allows an installation to designate one or more printer output classes to have a classification or description printed at either the top or bottom of every page. Class "X" output might, for example, generate "TOP SECRET" across the top of each page.

The SYSFCN macro of DMKSYS need only be coded if extensive changes are made to the command class structure via an override directory. One parameter of general interest, however, is DFLT, which specifies the default directory privilege class when none is coded. This defaults to "G" so that if no authority class is specified for a userid, then "G" will take effect. If DFLT is set to something other than "G" that authority class should then be investigated for correctness.

DMKSNT   There is only one security concern with DMKSNT: the PROTECT option of the NAMESYS macro. When PROTECT is OFF, the storage protection for the shared segment is disabled, allowing users' alterations to the shared storage to be reflected in other users' virtual machines. By default, PROTECT is ON, so it is not likely that it will be turned off inadvertently. Some program products (and GCS, for example) require use of the shared writable storage feature. Any segments with PROTECT-OFF should be investigated and justified.

VM Modifications

VM systems have historically been modified fairly heavily, although not as much now as in years past. The reasons for this are twofold. First, VM has always been distributed with source code; indeed, all IBM-supplied fixes are sent as updates to the source, so that source code is a requirement to applying maintenance. Second, until recently VM did not have as much function as most users desired.

The solution to the latter situation was to modify VM and hundreds of modifications were written and exchanged. Not surprisingly, many of these modifications were quite useful and, in fact, were later incorporated into the product by IBM. Thus, VM is mostly a user-designed product, which helps explain its huge popularity, as well as the code-modifying culture of VM system programmers.

How to Audit   Before a VM modification audit can be attempted, the auditor must have a thorough understanding of how VM maintenance is performed.

Local modifications should be applied to a VM system in the same manner that IBM supplied fixes are—via the IBM-supplied CMS Update Facility. (For more information on the CMS Update Facility refer to the IBM manual entitled "CMS Command and Macro Reference.")

To actually perform a VM modifications audit, it is necessary to first compile a table of all authorized modifications. This list should include, for each modification, its unique identification number (which happens to be the filetype of the associated CMS update files), a list of modules and macros changed by the modification, a description of what the modification does, an approximate number of lines of code, and who wrote the mode, when, and why.

This should be done for each program product and component installed that has modifications, because many products designed to run under VM are also distributed with source code (such as RSCS and IPCS).

A quick audit first checks the current system load map against this list of authorized modifications. Any discrepancy will be immediately apparent. A more thorough job involves actually reading and understanding each modification to make sure that the given description is accurate. A tutorial on VM internals is beyond the scope of this discussion.

Popular Modifications   As an aid to the reader performing a first modifications audit, listed below are the half dozen or so VM modifications that seem to be most popular:

- **Adding a new diagnose code.** Diagnose instructions are the main virtual-machine-to-CP interface available to programmers. IBM has actually left codes 100-1FC available for customer use and a wide variety have been written. Some non-IBM products even require the addition of a vendor-supplied diagnose instruction.
- **Secret global passwords for logging on to the system or linking to other user's minidisks.** This modification will also bypass the journaling exit, as well, so no record is kept of the logon or link events. If this modification was implemented because of a business requirement, it would be better to effect the same function via an additional VM security product.
- **Modification of CP command privilege classes.** Before VM Release 4, this had to be done with a modification. Any installation with modified privilege classes should have removed the modifications and installed an override directory.
- **Changing the VM logon logo.** IBM encourages installations to do this (it's in module DMKBOX) and is rather harmless fun. Anyway, the default IBM-supplied logo has never won points for creativity, originality, or beauty!
- **Adding or modifying CP accounting records.** Here again IBM has left a place in the code where customer written modifications may be inserted to add information to the accounting records. This is done mostly in shops that chargeback for computer resources.

• **Fixing bugs that IBM won't or hasn't gotten to.** Most commonly, the customer writes a local fix for a problem while waiting for the "official" fix from IBM to be generated and distributed.

Overview of Native VM Security Features

Most native VM (i.e., without any program products or modifications) security features result from the simulation of VM System/370 architecture. Aside from the directory, which has already been discussed, IBM has supplied an interface available to add-on security program products.

The Access Control Interface (ACI)

In order to support additional access control software IBM provides an Access Control Interface (ACI) in VM. This interface consists of three CP modules (DMKRPI, DMKRPD, and DMKRPW) which control access to the seven CP commands tabulated in Figure 9-8.

After command class validation, when any of these commands are issued by a user, one of the three ACI routines is called to validate the command. There are three possible results to the validation call: The request is either granted, deferred (meaning that a password is required), or denied. The versions of the ACI routines shipped with VM base grant all requests except for LOGON and LINK, which are given deferred status.

Add-on access control software may replace these three routines with versions supplied by the vendor. These versions then use rules, userids, time-of-day, or other criteria to grant or deny access. Thus, a LOGON or LINK command will be granted or denied without prompting for a password, but rather by checking an ACI control statement (sometimes called a *rule*) that was generated by a security administrator (or sometimes by the user himself).

Two things are important to note about the ACI:

1.   If a product uses the ACI, it can validate only these seven commands and no more. Don't assume, however, that just because a product uses the ACI that all seven commands will be validated (most security packages, for instance, have no provision for disallowing the LOGOFF command).

LOGON/AUTOLOG

LOGOFF/FORCE

STCP

TAG

LINK

SPOOL

TRANSFER (Type "G" TRANSFER only)

Figure 9-8 Commands trapped by the ACI.

2. Some products can do a much more thorough command validation without using the ACI because they require extensive VM
modifications.

Accounting Records

CP generates accounting records, the disposition of which is controlled by the SYSACNT macro of DMKSYS. There are eight different types of accounting records. Every accounting record is an 80-
byte card image; the record type is stored in columns 79 and 80 (see
Figure 9-9).

Record types 01, 02, 03, 07, and 08 are designed for resource accounting and chargeback. Types 04, 05, and 06 result from coding
JOURNAL-YES on the SYSJRL macro in DMKSYS.

There are no native facilities for generating reports from accounting records; installations must purchase a commercial package or
write their own. Journaling should be enabled at all times, and the
resulting records should be analyzed on a daily basis. Care should be
taken, however, with the disposition of the actual records, because
they contain (among other things) incorrect passwords supplied by
users. This is useful information when trying to identify password-
generating programs assaulting a system, but may also give clues to
the correct password of a user with poor typing or spelling skills.

Note that while type 04 and 06 records are generated in response
to the limit specified on the SYSJRL macro being exceeded, type 05
records are generated for *every* successful link for which a password

01 — Connect Time, CPU Seconds, I/O, Paging

02 — Dedicated or Attached Devices

03 — Temporary Disk Space

04 — Logon Journaling (incorrect password count exceeded)

05 — Successful Link (password required)

06 — Unsuccessful Link (password limit exceeded)

07 — SNA Accounting

08 — User Disconnect

Figure 9-9 Accounting record definitions.

was required. This means that links done in the directory or for minidisks with a password of ALL are not recorded.

VM Security and Auditing Concerns

IBM'S Statement of Integrity

IBM issued a VM statement of integrity a few years ago that defines what non-authorized users will *not* be allowed to do on a VM system. In particular, non-authorized users may not:

1. Circumvent or disable the control program main or secondary storage protection.
2. Access a control program (CP) password protected resource.
3. Obtain control in real supervisor state, or with privilege class authority or directory capabilities greater than those it was assigned.
4. Circumvent the system integrity of any guest operating system, which itself has system integrity (i.e., MVS or VSE) as a result of an operation by any VM/SP control program facility.

Note that in the above statements, nothing is mentioned about a user being able to circumvent CMS-level security (e.g., mode 0 files) or even about a user crashing the system. In fact, because of the design of VM, it is very difficult to stop one user from denying the use of the computer system to other users. Some ways this might be done, for example, are by raising response time by going into a loop, forcing an IPL by filling the system spool with thousands of print files, or crashing the system by sending thousands of messages.

Because this is not mentioned in the statement of integrity, IBM is not required to fix this problem, although it is generally very easy to later determine the culprit.

Access Control Standards

It is a good idea to implement some sort of userid and password standards, as well as procedures for handling routine directory changes. Some suggestions for password and userid management are listed below.

- A password should contain a minimum of five or six characters.
- Users should be forced to change their passwords every thirty days or so. There should also be a *minimum* time limit (perhaps one day) between password changes so that people won't just change their password as required and then change it back again.
- It should be forbidden to re-use passwords.
- Certain passwords should be disallowed (for example, the word "PASSWORD," and the names of the months of the year).
- The practice of assigning random passwords is generally a bad idea since it usually leads to having them written down someplace, often right next to the user's terminal.
- A name should be associated with every userid on the system; a phone number is also desirable. Keep these as a comment in the directory entry of each userid.
- Make sure that the personnel department notifies the security administrator whenever an employee terminates employment or is transferred within the company. That employee's userid should then be removed from the directory or at least disabled.

VM Tape Handling

Magnetic tape use and control is one glaring weakness in VM security. In early versions of VM, tape label support was non-existent; even today unlabeled tapes are the default and label processing is a poorly understood option.

On a native VM system (i.e, without any tape management software or modifications) the user requests a tape to be mounted by sending a message to the system operator. The operator then removes the tape from the library, mounts it on a drive, and allocates the drive to the requesting user. At no time is there any automated verification to ensure that the correct tape is being mounted, if it has a write ring or not, or even if it's being allocated to the user that requested it.

Some installations have very little tape use by the general user community and these may be able to operate without any tape controls. When more than one or two tapes are mounted per day, however, some sort of tape management software is desirable if significant tape integrity is to be expected.

With no tape management software, it is pretty much "caveat user," although there are a few things that can be done to minimize risk:

1. Warn all users repeatedly that files left on tape are not secure either from being read or being written over. Establish tape check-in and check-out procedures so that user tapes are in the machine room for a minimum amount of time and are thus exposed for minimum time.

2. Purchase different colored self-loading tape straps for different types of tape-resident data, such as general user tapes, VM backup tapes, and any MVS or other operating system tapes. At the beginning of each shift, dedicate one or more tape drives to VM, and distinguish them with a sign placed on top of the drive. Then, if VM user tapes are orange, for instance, only orange tapes are allowed on the VM drives. Violation of this rule should cause severe censure of the operator at fault. If an MVS tape needs to be mounted on VM, first have the user run an MVS job to copy from the desired tape to a VM scratch, then mount the VM tape.

    This scheme does not work with 3480 cartridge drives or 9347 drives because the tape reel cannot be seen when mounted. It is always best, of course, to buy tape management software.

3. Encourage users to use label processing. This may mean education or writing utility programs and/or menus. Tape labels will prevent most accidental tape errors, although they do nothing to prevent willful misuse.

VM Backup Systems

At a minimum, the IBM-supplied DDR (DASD Dump Restore) utility may be used to do system backups. Although it is a no-extra-charge item, it is slow and cumbersome and requires a lot of manual intervention. Keeping track of what data is backed up on which tapes must be done by hand and is error-prone, to say the least. In addition, it is difficult to restore just a single file; DDR is better suited to restoring entire minidisks (or even entire volumes).

It is highly recommended that a commercial backup system be purchased; there are several on the market. When shopping for a backup product, the following items should be considered:

- **Integrity**
  - The system should maintain a complete catalog of all backups run and all files backed up.
  - Tape labels should be supported.
  - Multiple output volumes should be created simultaneously so a set of backup tapes can be sent to an off-site storage location.
  - Only authorized users should be able to restore others' files.
  - It should perform disk-image backups, like DDR, when necessary.
  - Since the backup system reads every bit of data on the system, it should perform data file integrity checking.

- **Performance**
  - The backup system should be capable of incremental backups, where the only files backed up are those that have been changed since the last full backup.
  - The system should be able to write different backup datastreams to multiple tapes concurrently. This will reduce the time it takes to complete the backup.

- **Usability**
  - Individual files, as well as full minidisks, should be able to be backed up and restored.
  - Users should be able to restore their own files.
  - The entire product should be optionally menu-driven (user-friendly interface).

VM Disaster Recovery

Much has been written about data processing disaster recovery that need not be reported here. Nevertheless, there are some concerns specific to VM that should be addressed. Mainly, it should be noted what data must be kept off-site to ensure that the production VM system may be re-built from scratch. It is not enough to have a backup of the running system nucleus since after restoring the current system changes it will most likely need to be made to the system. Thus, a complete set of IBM-supplied tapes, as well as all system modifications, should be stored in a way that the production-level system may be regenerated (not just restored) where and/or whenever needed.

To rebuild a VM system, tape copies of the following items should be kept on-site, as well as in an off-site vault:

• Standalone version of CP Format/Allocate
• Standalone version of DDR
• Standalone directory utility and directory source code
• A DDR backup of the system residence volume
• The IOCP source code if the processor requires it

In addition, to rebuild VM to the current maintenance level, you need the VM product tapes, the PUT at the installed level, possibly a level-set PUT, the IBM-supplied error bucket for the installed PUT, and copies of all authorized modifications.

CMS Security

By CMS security, we mean file-level and application security. CP stops users from unauthorized access to other users, but a user can still corrupt or destroy their *own* environment. For instance, a user's own private copy of CMS can be corrupted or multi-write links can destroy minidisks unintentionally.

A more subtle violation occurs when a user with a read-only link to a minidisk has the data changed while it is being read. This condition can cause applications to use inconsistent data or even to abend. It is best to use multi-read and multi-write links cautiously, if at all.

Systems personnel may wish to set up a "padded cell" environment for CMS end-users, restricting access to commands that can change the environment, such as STORE, DEFINE, and IPL, and disabling functions such as the PA1 key. This is not necessarily easy to do, but a fairly secure environment may be built with a fair amount of planning and without any system modifications.

As a final warning, beware of unsupported programs that have been received from public domain resources. Well-known and respected IBM-user organizations such as SHARE and GUIDE have been a clearing house for utilities and programs for years, many of which were later adopted by IBM. It is only prudent to require information on the background of any program installed as a system-wide utility and to urge caution on the part of users who wish to bring in programs from non-vendor sources.

Guest Operating System Security

Security of a guest operating system running under VM is best left to security software running on that operating system. However, there are some security concerns that must be addressed in the area of *accessing* the operating system running as a virtual machine under VM's control.

For performance, as well as security reasons, it is best to dedicate DASD to a guest operating system. (This can be done via the CP "ATTACH" command or "DEDICATE" directory control statement.) A dedicated volume may never be accessed by more than the one dedicated user. On the other hand, defining a volume as a full-pack minidisk is a much more versatile solution, allowing several users access to the data simultaneously.

A point to remember is that CMS commands exist which allow a user to read and/or write OS- or VSE-formatted disk files; there is no such facility in any other operating system to read CMS-formatted disks.

Job Submission to a Guest Operating System
Many installations run an MVS or VSE guest and do development work by submitting JCL to the guest from CMS users. Although this is an extremely productive system, there arises a security quandary: If no passwords are required to submit a job, then *anybody* can gain access to the guest. If passwords *are* required, then users will probably have the plainly-typed passwords in their JCL files.

Some installations have disallowed all job submission to guest operating systems from CMS users. A less severe solution is to write a "submit" EXEC which prompts users for the correct MVS or VSE password, then adds the card to the job stream being submitted. Of course, this last scheme can be circumvented by users familiar with EXECs and is in any case worthless for automatically submitted jobs.

Security Breach Examples

As a final and somewhat lighthearted look at VM security, a smorgasbord of VM security breach examples have been collected and documented below. Some are serious breaches, some not; but all illustrate points covered above and all have actually occurred.

Security Breach #1: A user names several files with mode A0, attempting to make them private. He allows read access to other files. A villain links to the disk, defines a temp disk, and then uses DDR to copy disk-to-disk. Since the villain has write access to the temp disk, the A0 files appear.

Security Breach #2: The same villain modifies the ACCESS command to always show A0 files. Now, the villain doesn't have to bother with messy temp disk and DDR to look at mode 0 files.

Security Breach #3: An ambitious young programmer browses EXECs on public disks and finds an EXEC with the following statement:

CP LINK MAINT 501 300 RR KETCHUP

He now has the read password for the minidisk owned by MAINT .
. . interesting.

He wonders if (just possibly) the write password might be MUSTARD. He guesses correctly and he now has write access to the MVS system residence volume. (Keep in mind that incorrect guesses could have resulted in the creation of accounting records.)

Security Breach #4: An ambitious young programmer gets his own copy of the VM installation guide and decides to try out all the default userids and passwords. He finds that the password to MAINT is still "CPCMS"; elated, he spends several hours practicing his system programming skill, with the result that the system is unusable for the next three days.

Security Breach #5: A user requests class "C" privileges because a product that he is installing requires it. He is granted (temporary) class "C" privileges. Two days later, the user accidentally shuts the system down in the middle of the work day. How did he get class "A" authority?

1. "LOCATE userid"
2. add offset to the user class definition
3. "STCP offset FFFFFFFF"

Two simple commands, a little hexadecimal arithmetic, and presto! A new super-user!

Security Breach #6: A system programmer modifies the CP password validation routines, adding two instructions to let her use a "super-password" for any logon or link attempt. She then leaves the company and forgets to remove the modification.

Security Breach #7: A third shift operator is responsible for performing the nightly backups. The installation-written backup system obtains a list of minidisks to be backed up from the VM source directory. The operator finds the directory and prints out a copy of her own.

Security Breach #8: An EDP auditor prints a copy of the directory (complete with passwords) for an impending audit. An operator realizes what is being printed and makes himself a copy via the class "D" REPEAT command.

Security Breach #9: A resourceful programmer who is over budget on her computer usage for the month gets hold of CP's accounting record layouts in the System Programmer's Guide. She then uses XEDIT to create several "accounting records" with a negative number of CPU seconds, then punches these records to DISKACNT, and receives a credit on her next month's bill.

Security Breach #10: A young man aspiring to be a system programmer writes a program that displays what looks like a VM logo on a neighboring terminal. An unsuspecting user attempts to logon. The spy program saves his userid and password for later retrieval by the aspiring sysprog. It then goes away quietly. The unsuspecting user's second attempt at logon is successful and he thinks no more of it.

Security Breach #11: An unscrupulous system programmer amuses himself by TRANSFERing spool files to himself, PEEKing them, then TRANSFERing them back. No one who has had his spool file browsed is any wiser.

Note 1: All PROFS unread mail is kept in the spool

Note 2: The ACI does not trap the type "D" TRANSFER command.

Security Breach #12: Widgets Unlimited has installed expensive and thorough access control software on their VM system. A system programmer builds a single-pack test VM system *without* the access control package installed. During scheduled down time, on a Sunday morning, he brings up his test system on the real machine and sees (and copies) whatever he wants.

Security Breach #13: A company employee is trying to debug a problem with a port on a 3274 terminal controller. He exchanges two coaxial cables to see if the problem moves with the port. He failed to check if there was anyone logged on to either of the terminals . . . as it turns out, he just moved the operator console to the desk of a junior programmer on the eleventh floor.

Audit Checklist and Summary

In summary, we include a checklist of items that should be investigated during an audit of a VM system. This list is not meant to serve as a thorough auditing methodology for VM, but as a relatively complete list of action items to follow to help ensure that the system is fairly secure.

DMKRIO

• Document the location of all alternate consoles

DMKSYS

• Check the SYSJRL macro
• Check the SYSCLR parameter of the SYSRES macro
• Check the security of all userids specified in DMKSYS

Directory

• Justify all non-class "G" userids
• Remove passwords from comments (mapping programs that mask out passwords won't recognize comments)
• Associate a name with every userid
• Audit directory links
• Check all full-pack minidisks

Override Directory (if present)

• Audit for appropriateness
• Should be implemented if GCS is installed

System Data

• Check accounting records and journaling reports
• Check raw monitor data if RESPONSE class is ever enabled

Change control

- For software changes
- For hardware changes
- For down-time logs

Guest Operating Systems

- Investigate remote job submission procedures
- Check out full-pack minidisks owned by guest
- Restrict access to userid MAINT
- Review tape management system and procedures

Do a system modifications inventory

- Check each modification individually
- Cross-reference with the system nucleus map

Secure the system console area
Eliminate userids never logged on to
Eliminate disks never linked to
Audit userids that AUTOLOG others; e.g., AUTOLOG1, VMUTIL, and SMART
Monitor userids used by vendors and consultants. Make sure they are given appropriate authority and that they are removed from the directory when the userids' usefulness has expired.

Review the disaster recovery plan

- Make sure that standalone backups are available
- Back up all necessary service programs
- Archive all service tapes

Assign the least powerful privilege class necessary

- An override directory may be helpful

The backup system

- Who can restore?
- Restore files one day old, one week old, one month old
- Check backup frequency and retention period

Tape management

- Tape management software installed?
- Separate VM tapes from MVS and/or VSE tapes
- Investigate operator training

CMS security

- Audit "freeware"; know what public-domain software has been loaded to the system and why
- Check M, MR, and MW links and passwords on production disks

  Make sure old extents are formatted when moving minidisks.

Bibliography

Norman, Adrian R. D., *Computer Insecurity*, New York: Chapman and Hall

About the Author

Michael Lude is manager of technical support with VM Assist Inc. in San Francisco.   He is currently responsible for the central VM the installation and maintenance services offered by VM Assist to clients in the San Francisco Bay area. In addition, Mr. Lude has developed and presented several VM end-user, operator, and technical courses. He has worked with VM since 1977 and holds an A.B. degree in mathematics and computer science from U.C. Berkeley.

VM Assist Inc. provides system programming, administrative, and educational services nationwide. System programming and administrative services are provided in a highly efficient manner using centralized system installation and maintenance techniques. Educational services are provided in areas not fully addressed by other vendors, including VM system security and auditing, capacity planning and management, as well as for certain vendor program products available in the VM marketplace.

VM and Development
Considerations

During VM's early days, it gained acceptance as an operating system because of its capabilities in the development center. VM serves as an ideal development environment. Versions of code, for example, can be developed and tested in different virtual machines and moved to the production environment when the testing is completed. Development center considerations are discussed in Part D.

Michael Seadle's "VM in the Development Center" (Chapter 10) provides an overview of how the development center can get the most from the unique capabilities of VM. Seadle discusses the use of VM in relation to the major aspects of system development; from the requirements definition to the final signoff and production turnover. Seadle includes XEDIT and REXX examples.

In "REXX" (Chapter 11), Bebo White provides an in-depth look at VM's multi-faceted REXX language. He begins by discussing the history of REXX, then breaks REXX down into its components. White presents a practical discussion of the use of REXX supplemented by numerous examples.

The C language is rapidly growing in popularity and John Donaldson discusses C from a VM perspective in "C in the VM Environment" (Chapter 12). He begins with a perspective on the C language itself followed by a practical discussion, with examples, of the advantages of C development under VM.

Multiple IBM mainframe operating systems often coexist within the same organization and the technical staff is in the position of bringing VM into a previously MVS-based environment. Because the design of these two systems differs substantially, erroneous assumptions can be made. Janet Gobeille's "MVS to VM: Avoiding the Pitfalls" (Chapter 13) discusses the differences between MVS and VM from design and functional perspectives, with practical guidelines for making transitions between the two environments.

10

VM in the Development Center

by Michael Seadle, Ph.D.

Introduction

This chapter describes how a development center can take advantage of VM's procedural language, its electronic mail, and its interactive environment. The term development center refers to those teams of programmers and users who create new application systems, generally for MVS or VSE systems.

As the local VM expert, management will ask you to explain why the development center should work in VM and how to configure it. We will discuss the answers for each of the major aspects of system development listed:

- The requirements definition.
- Design and prototyping.
- Coding and testing.
- Documentation.
- Signoff and production turnover.

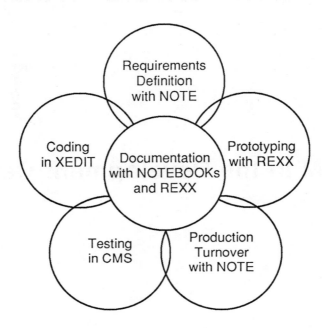

Figure 10-1 The flowering of VM Applications Development.

The main issue is how to improve productivity for system development. VM offers three ways to do this. The first is through the use of tools like REXX, which help automate the development process much as traditional systems have automated the way companies do business. The second is to involve users in design and testing as part of the project team in a VM information center environment. And the third is to generate project documentation from electronic mail records.

Technical virtuosity alone builds no new systems. Productivity packages, which focus on how to improve coding speed, touch only one narrow aspect of the development process. VM provides a complete environment in which project teams can work from the initial requirements study to the final production turnover.

This chapter makes extensive use of REXX EXECs. It assumes a basic knowledge of such REXX functions as PARSE, EXECIO, and indexed variables. The various examples are not meant to represent complete EXECs. They are only illustrations with no special interfaces or error checking.

Requirements Definition

Electronic Discussions

The first stage of new system development is a study to define the system's requirements. This study involves broad discussion between programming staff and one or more groups of users. The result is a document describing specific features of the new system, with supporting material on each point. VM facilitates this process by providing an electronic mail system to speed communication and the means for turning that communication into a draft document.

Traditionally, the first stages of the requirements study are verbal, either meetings or phone calls. Minutes reflect only a small portion of the discussions at meetings and nothing at all of the phone calls. The authors of the final document must rely heavily on memory and must prepare draft after draft until one emerges which satisfies all parties. The normal medium of these drafts is paper. The turnaround time rarely allows more than one per week, depending on the internal mail system. Many project teams tolerate incomplete work because the process seems too slow.

The process need not, however, be slow. VM's electronic mail allows the exchange of several messages per day. For this to work effectively, both users and programmers must have easy access to VM and be prepared to use it. The whole project team must use the same tools to gain the productivity advantage.

A new project team should begin by using the NAMES command to set up an "address book." The main purposes are:

1. To establish group names (NICKNAMEs) for the project team and simple entries for individual team members.
2. To designate a project NOTEBOOK for all project related correspondence—otherwise notes will automatically go into the default ALL NOTEBOOK file. Using the correct NOTEBOOK is important because the information in them will become part of the final requirements definition.

After setting up an address book, team members can send electronic mail by typing NOTE and the appropriate NICKNAME. NOTE sets up a full screen XEDIT session in memo form and automatically enters the Date, To, and From information. These entries appear in the middle of the screen, not at the top as most people expect. You can change the appearance if you wish.

NOTE is nothing more than a program written in the old EXEC2 command language. It resides on the CMS system "S" disk, as does PROFNOTE XEDIT, the XEDIT profile which NOTE uses. This ready access may tempt you to make substantial revisions, but remember that IBM provides ongoing fixes and updates for the original version of NOTE. Major changes could mean debugging updates later on.

The safest modifications affect only PROFNOTE XEDIT. You can change the default location of the Date, To, and From lines by adding the following to a copy of PROFNOTE XEDIT:

```
COMMAND SET CURLINE 5
```

The CURLINE is normally 12 lines from the top of the screen. This XEDIT command moves the "current line" (CURLINE) down only five lines from the top. The Date, To, and From display shifts upwards as a result.

This solution creates a new problem. If you use the PF2 command to add lines, all previous text moves upwards, and only a few lines remain visible. You need another change, one which also improves the ease of editing. Find the line in PROFNOTE XEDIT which reads:

```
COMMAND SET PREFIX OFF
```

And replace it with:

```
COMMAND SET PREFIX ON
```

The PREFIX command turns the leftmost 5 bytes on the screen into a command area. Now you have available all of XEDIT's line commands for adding (A), copying (C or CC), moving (M or MM), and deleting (D or DD) text. The reformatting capabilities still fall below the norm for professional word processing packages, but the prefix commands and the PF11 split/join command let you manipulate words and phrases without retyping. Ragged margins mean little compared to the clarity of the message.

In addition to configuring the software, your company needs to train the users. Beginners in electronic mail often make the mistake of writing the same memo on the screen as they would on paper. Paper memos tend to fill one or more pages and frequently cover several aspects of a topic or even several topics. Their relatively slow transit time encourages including as much as possible.

Long memos in electronic mail are difficult to read. One screen holds less than half of what is on a page, so that readers must change screens, on a long memo, two or three times as often as they flip pages in the paper form. Also, a memo with multiple topics makes them go though it several times to answer each part. The problem is that one topic may have an immediate answer, while another requires research. With paper memos, they may well wait until a complete answer is ready. For electronic mail, the wait is self-defeating.

Project teams should follow three basic rules when using electronic mail:

Rule 1:   A memo that fills more than two screens should be more than one memo.

Rule 2:   A memo which has more than one topic should be more than one memo.

Rule 3:   Electronic mail deserves rapid response.

The idea of the first two rules is to make the third possible. If team members answer even just half the questions they get immediately, the lag should be only a couple of hours on the average, instead of a couple of days via departmental mail. Timeliness is important. Unanswered questions can lead to false assumptions and a slow response may arrive too late to alter a line of thinking. A person who has spent two days working on an idea may not abandon it willingly.

Notebooks

A project team which uses VM's electronic mail will have a machine readable record of the discussion. The NOTE command automatically saves every memo into a NOTEBOOK file which, with proper editing, can become part of the final, formal requirements definition.

Keeping the project related NOTEBOOKs clean of extraneous memos is important. Each NICKNAME entry has only one NOTEBOOK associated with it. If project team member Joan writes to project team member Michael, every memo will go automatically to the PROJECT NOTEBOOK she assigned to his NICKNAME. This includes any collegial gossip or invitations to lunch. She can segregate such private memos by specifying a keyword qualifier. Instead of a simple:

```
NOTE MICHAEL
```

she could enter:

```
NOTE MICHAEL (NOTEBOOK LUNCHES
```

If Joan and Michael serve jointly on two project teams, she can either make up two NICKNAMEs for him in the "address book," or use a shell EXEC called MICHAEL:

```
/* REXX EXEC to send notes to Michael */
ARG PROJECT /* Specify which project notebook.*/
/* Establish "FINREC" as the default. */
IF PROJECT = '' THEN PROJECT = FINREC
EXEC NOTE MICHAEL '(' NOTEBOOK PROJECT
EXIT
```

Then if she wants to write to him about the financial records project (FINREC), she need only enter:

```
MICHAEL
```

Or if she is responding to a question about the PAYROLL project, she would add:

```
MICHAEL PAYROLL
```

Likewise, if she is asking him to lunch (on business, of course), she can also save keystrokes:

```
MICHAEL LUNCHES
```

The overhead of such a shell EXEC is minimal compared to the convenience. IBM uses the technique frequently in its own code.

Joan will want to save notes that come to her reader queue. Again VM makes this simple. When she reads her mail, she can use the PF9 key in PEEK or from the RDRLIST display to RECEIVE the message. It will go into whichever NOTEBOOK she specified for the sender in her "address book." Again, this may be a problem if she and Michael are working on two projects at once. Another shell

EXEC could be useful for receiving notes into the PAYROLL NOTE-BOOK.

```
/* REXX EXEC
```

The filename of this EXEC should be PAYROLL */.

```
ARG FILENUM
RECEIVE FILENUM '(' NOTEBOOK PAYROLL
EXIT
```

To save a note correctly now, she need only type PAYROLL over the desired entry on the RDRLIST display.

Joan can examine her project notebook while writing a reply. VM provides two ways to do this. First, she could go to the command line of her current XEDIT session and enter:

```
X FINREC NOTEBOOK
```

This will replace her note with a full-screen display of the financial records project notebook. When she has seen everything she wants, she could QUIT using PF3 and VM would return to what she had been writing. She can also keep the FINREC NOTEBOOK open by entering:

```
SCREEN 2
```

to split the screen. If at some point she wants a single screen again, SCREEN 1 will change it back. She can also define any of her PF keys to split and un-split screens:

```
SET PF19 SCREEN 2
SET PF20 SCREEN 1
```

These settings are useful enough that you should consider including them in an updated PROFNOTE XEDIT on the Y disk.

These techniques for using NOTEBOOKs let project team members keep a paperless "paper trail" of all questions and decisions, filed chronologically and backed up on a regular schedule. Later in the chapter, you will learn how to turn these NOTEBOOKs into project documentation. Good record-keeping cannot substitute for a well-researched requirements study, but it can help the team avoid re-working issues already resolved.

Prototyping in VM

The Advantage of VM and REXX

First drafts are frequently wrong. This is a rule of writing which applies equally to literary compositions and computer systems. Using VM to prototype the prospective system gives project teams a chance to test their initial design at a modest cost in time and resources.

VM creates a prototyping environment with the robustness of a micro and the power of a mainframe. Team members can use a VM prototype from any terminal. If an individual CMS session fails, it will not interrupt others. The team member can IPL CMS and be back to work in 30 seconds.

One way to control prototyping costs is to choose the right tools. COBOL still represents the mainstream of DP development, but third generation languages like COBOL are among the worst prototyping tools, in part because of the temptation to patch the prototype and make it a production system. The ideal tool is an interpreted language like REXX which is easily coded, easily debugged, and easily structured. Processing efficiency does not matter compared to the ease of writing.

REXX compensates for its less efficient use of computer cycles by saving human cycles in coding and debugging. It has called routines, do-loops, and the functional equivalent of an END-IF clause. A staunchly antediluvian programmer could write unstructured REXX, but he would have to struggle against its natural biases. Another important feature of REXX for prototyping is that it requires no pre-definition of variables. Any unreserved word becomes a variable the moment you use it as one.

REXX's parsing ability is one of its greatest assets. It can strip out any portion of a record based on position, delimiter, or any variety of delimiters. This allows for an enormously flexible record structure. Fields can vary in length as the system needs evolve during the prototyping process. For example, Michael might design a simple name record which looks like this:

```
Last name 20 bytes
First name 20 bytes
Middle initial 1 byte
```

Joan then finds real names for testing which do not fit: Alexander Hohenlohe-Schillingsfurst and Pierre DuPont IV. The first is too long and the second has a suffix which should go into a separate field (for editing). In COBOL accommodating this would require a change to the record layout and a re-compiling of all programs which used it. In REXX, if team members choose a record structure with delimiters, for instance a "$," the length increase would require no change and the new field can come into existence by adding an extra delimiter and field name ("SUFFIX") to the parsing statement:

```
PARSE VAR RECORD,
    LASTNAME '$',
FIRSTNAME '$',
MIDDLE '$',
SUFFIX
```

SUFFIX could go after LASTNAME. The advantage of putting it at the end is that, if other test records already exist, no one needs to convert them to the new format. REXX will just set SUFFIX = " (null) if it finds no final delimiter and field.

REXX normally uses the CMS file structure via the EXECIO command for its record handling. The disadvantage of using CMS files is a lack of indexing within files. You could help team members turn the CMS minidisk directory into an indexing system with keyword filenames and filetypes; but that kind of trick defeats the goal of simplicity in a prototyping tool. The easier alternative is a do-loop that simply reads through the file to find a match. A prototype system ought to have few enough records that this is feasible and it keeps control over the index search in the REXX program, where team members can easily change it.

REXX's debugging tools are another asset in prototyping. The issue is not syntax, but errors in logic. In a structured language, team members generally have some idea which routine contains the error. The TRACE ALL command shows each line on the screen as it executes, complete with the values of all variables, and it will stop the display when it encounters a TRACE OFF. Team members can also display data independently using SAY. Nothing is unseeable inside of REXX, not even core.

Errors which cause CMS to abend are rare in REXX prototyping, but inevitably some occur. Team members may solve such problems simply by re-ipling CMS and TRACEing the REXX program to its point of abend. The CP DISPLAY command will show any portion of core online. Those in love with paper can spool their console to print, but six-inch dumps should never be necessary.

What REXX will not do alone is manage full-screen displays. To have the prototype of an online system, you must couple REXX with another product.

The REXX Interface

Several products work well with REXX for full-screen management, including two from IBM. XEDIT comes with the base system product as the full-screen editor. It allows team members to define fields and their attributes and will return data in REXX variables. XEDIT's problem for prototyping is that building each screen is a laborious process with no quick, user-friendly way to see the result.

DMS/CMS is IBM's alternative. DMS has a series of panels through which team members can build screens with minimal help. It allows a wide range of field definitions and attributes, including color. The DMS panel generator builds its own execution code and it handles all modifications through the same interactive process. DMS has some interface limitations, but offers exceptional value as a low-cost system extra.

One of the reasons DMS is little used with REXX is that its documentation does not describe the REXX interface. In fact that interface is very simple. DMS will map directly to REXX variable names, as in the following example:

```
Line  1.  DO FOREVER
Line  2.  MAKEBUF
Line  3.  EUDEXEX2
Line  4.  ADDRESS DISPLAY
Line  5.  USE PANEL SAMPLE1
Line  6.  MAP DATA 1 'FIRSTNAME'
Line  7.  MAP DATA 2 'MIDDLE'
Line  8.  MAP DATA 3 'LASTNAME'
Line  9.  DISPLAY
Line 10.  ADDRESS CMS
Line 11.  IF RSTATUS = 'PF3' THEN LEAVE
Line 12.  IF RSTATUS = ... /*Include other PF keys as needed.*/
Line 13.  DROPBUF
Line 14.  END
```

Line 1 establishes a loop which will always return the screen, unless the operator requests some other function, with a PF key (see lines 11 and 12). Line 2 creates a separate buffer for the display.

Line 3 calls the EXEC2 interface module EUDEXEC2, which REXX also uses. Line 4 allows REXX to address the DMS command "DISPLAY." Line 5 tells DMS to use a pre-designed panel called "SAMPLE1." The next 3 lines tell DMS to map the three open fields in the panel to the three REXX variables in that order. Line 9 tells DMS to display the panel SAMPLE1 and it fills the fields with whatever values the variables contain. Line 10 restores addressability to CMS commands. Lines 11 and 12 examine the REXX variable RSTATUS for PF key values and lines 13 and 14 drop the special buffer and end the loop.

There are two features of CICS which REXX does not emulate with any of these screen handlers. The first is pseudoconversational technique and the second is the XCTL unconditional transfer of control to another program. In both cases the original REXX program never loses control. This may seem like an alarming divergence, but it need not be. Team members can simulate pseudoconversational interaction by returning control to the display loop. And they can create a pseudo-XCTL by coding an EXIT command immediately after the call to another REXX program.

A REXX prototype should foster a more hierarchical and more structured design than in a conventional COBOL/CICS system. This is partly because of the ease with which REXX uses shared utility programs. Each REXX program can run on its own with no special linkage or library requirements. Logical processes separate easily into semi-autonomous units, which several members of a design team can work on simultaneously in separate virtual machines.

REXX prototyping will not solve all applications development problems. REXX's facility in skirting database management questions in particular leaves open that realm for further analysis. REXX's tolerance for bad data can also mislead team members into underestimating the need for edits. REXX gives a detailed outline, but not the final finished version. No prototyping tool will.

The Cost of Prototyping

Prototyping has short-term costs which project managers must plan for. In VM shops, the budgetary impact is negligible. The real expense comes from additional man-hours in the development cycle. The question is, how many?

The number of hours should be a function of complexity. For small projects of three to nine months, a project manager might set a rough rule of one day of prototyping per month of projected effort.

This is less compressed than it seems. In a four-month project, for example, one month might be for the requirements definition, one for design and coding, and two for testing and turnover. Each month has roughly 20 working days. Thus, four days to build the prototype equals one-fifth (20%) of the design and coding period, but only one-twentieth (5%) of the project time.

Project teams can reasonably expect to build a prototype in one-fifth the coding time. REXX is two or three times faster to code than a production language like COBOL and half the production coding time is ordinarily spent on issues the prototype may bypass in accomplishing its goals.

For systems that take over nine months, more than a simple arithmetical increase in days is necessary. Project teams need to decompose the prototyping process into smaller units before coding begins. They will also have to spend more time to link the prototype system together. The latter process in particular is vulnerable to unanticipated complications—complications which mirror what happens when a production system comes together for the first time. Unfortunately, any simple formula for time estimation is likely to be inaccurate. The time will probably be more than 5%, but should remain a modest fraction of the project total. Your shop might wish to set a 15% maximum and scale its goals accordingly.

The justification of these short-term costs is the long-term savings prototyping provides. Design errors push up maintenance costs throughout the life of a system and they offer the user less than originally desired. VM prototyping cannot eliminate all problems, but it gives the project team a way to catch mistakes and correct them.

Coding and Testing

Program Writing in XEDIT

Both prototyping and program writing require a full-screen editor: XEDIT. You should configure XEDIT so that the full-screen display begins just below the lines showing file name, line number, and cursor position. You may also want to move the scale line with its column numbers from mid-screen to the top. To do this, you need to create a PROFILE XEDIT:

```
/* REXX profile for XEDIT */
SET SCALE ON 3
SET CURLINE ON 4
```

If you FILE at this point, your next edit session will use these new commands.

Typing errors for common commands occur frequently. You can anticipate certain transpositions and tell XEDIT to treat them as synonyms. For example:

```
SET SYNONYM FILE 4 FILE
```

This command tells XEDIT to treat the four character string FILE as if it were FILE. You can include any number of synonyms, but you should be careful not to transform one command accidentally into another.

XEDIT has an option which saves your file at regular intervals during each session. Shops where the system crashes with appalling frequency need to set this option on. More stable installations may prefer not to. All editing in XEDIT takes place in memory. XEDIT normally updates a file only when told to do so. This has some advantages. Michael might have a bright idea about moving code around, get halfway through, and realize it will not work. With AUTOSAVE on, he must either move all the code back, or have had the foresight to make a prior copy. In normal XEDIT mode, without AUTOSAVE, a simple QQUIT command leaves his original unaltered.

Effective use of this option requires some common sense. If Michael spends eight hours editing a file without SAVEing it, he leaves himself seriously vulnerable if the system crashes. Likewise when he does feel a bright idea coming on, he would do well to SAVE before starting and not to SAVE again until he is sure he wants to keep what he has done.

XEDIT allows inserting forgotten words or letters into a line using the INSERT key. This is easiest if you include:

```
SET NULLS ON
```

in the PROFILE. If you set NULLS OFF, Michael must move the cursor to the end of the line, hit ERASE-EOF, then move back to where the insert belongs. The disadvantage of NULLS ON is that anything he puts at the righthand edge (such as comments) will fall to the left unless he explicitly enters spaces.

You can avoid this disadvantage by adding

```
SET FULLREAD ON
```

to the PROFILE. Then XEDIT will read every position on the screen, including nulls which it converts automatically into the missing blanks. FULLREAD has higher overhead, because it causes more data transmission. It may cause a performance problem, particularly for remote terminals. You should monitor how well your system performs with FULLREAD ON. Instead of including it automatically in a system PROFILE XEDIT, you might want to train team members to activate it only as needed from the command line.

You will probably want to define the PF keys to fit familiar conventions, perhaps some from prior edit environments. XEDIT allows you to set as many PF keys as the terminals have and to override any defaults. You should, however, observe some exceptions to this freedom. PF3 is one. VM uses PF3 again and again to QUIT a process. Moving QUIT to another PF key may ultimately slow the project team's adaptation to VM. Also, you should never set a PF key to QQUIT, even if you think they will use that command frequently. QQUIT exits an edit session immediately, without saving the file, and with no user-friendly "are you sure" message. The extra effort of typing the command (or its abbreviation, QQ) is worthwhile to avoid serious loss from hitting the wrong PF key accidentally.

You should define the PF keys so that team members can easily examine more than one file at once in split-screen mode. These are the same commands as you used with NOTE. Just add them to the PROFILE:

```
SET PF21 SCREEN 2
SET PF22 SCREEN 1
```

You can, of course, use any PF key, not just 21 and 22. The first command splits the screen horizontally, the second unsplits it. The horizontal splits are the most common because they show a full 72 columns, but team members may also want a vertical split for comparing, possibly, two versions of the same program:

```
SET PF23 SCREEN 2 V
```

You can let them move the cursor manually from one split-screen area to another with the arrow or tab keys or you can set up another PF key to speed the process:

```
SET PF24 SOS TABCMDB
```

TAABCMDB jumps the cursor from command line to command line.

Some uses of XEDIT require all uppercase—coding COBOL, for example. Others, such as documentation, must have mixed case to be readable. You may also wish to write your REXX EXECs in upper case and put the comments in mixed case to make them easier to distinguish. Defining two more PF keys simplifies switching from mixed to upper case and back:

```
SET PF16 CASE U
SET PF17 CASE M
```

Team members may want to look at data files whose line length exceeds the screen width. XEDIT's default lets the extra data wrap around onto the following lines. Most people find this difficult to read. You could have them type a VERIFY command. Or you can define another PF key:

```
SET PF18 VERIFY 1 72
```

You may even want to implement this command automatically every time they XEDIT a file. In that case you add to the PROFILE:

```
SET VERIFY 1 72
```

XEDIT's default settings include PF keys for paging through a file one screen at a time. This will suffice for very small files, but not for anything over 60 lines (3 screens). Team members will need to be able to move to one end of a file or the other quickly. A PF key for the TOP command is simple:

```
SET PF13 TOP
```

BOTTOM, however, puts the last line of the file at the current line, which is often so high that only one line displays. A multiple command solves this situation:

```
SET LINEND OFF
SET PF13 BOTTOM# '-17'
SET LINEND ON #
```

By temporarily turning off the normal end of line character (#), XEDIT equates PF13 to a string which includes the #. PF14 then treats BOTTOM and -17 as two commands and it executes -17 after

BOTTOM as if they were on separate lines. The result is that they see a full-screen display of the final 18 lines of data.

From the command line team members can move any distance up and down a file by typing + or - the number of lines. To repeat the action, they can use the default setting for PF9, ",", which automatically reexecutes the last command. Or if they wish to recall the command to change it, they can use the default setting for PF6, "?." Moving through a file this way requires several keystrokes. You can, instead, define extra PF keys for commonly used screen shifts. A half screen shift, forward and backward, would be:

```
SET PF19 '+10'
SET PF20 '-10'
```

VM allows several PROFILE XEDITs. You may put a standard edition on the public access Y disk and also set up one specifically for the project team on another shared minidisk. Individual team members can ignore both of these and keep a unique PROFILE XEDIT on their own A disks. VM will use whichever PROFILE XEDIT it finds first in the search chain, beginning with the A disk and proceeding down the alphabet. A shop can have as many different PROFILEs as staff members. Remember, however, that such a PF key Tower of Babel makes training and trouble-shooting decidedly more difficult.

XEDIT Macros

XEDIT allows you to write additional commands called macros. Two of the most popular macros simplify the process of copying lines from one file to another in split-screen mode. The first copies either one line (XC) or a group of lines (XCC . . . XCC). The second (G) inserts whatever XC or XCC copied. Both are available on public VM Workshop tapes. The versions below offer a more visibly structured format:

```
/* XEDIT prefix area copy macro */
PARSE ARG PREFIX CALLTYPE PLINE OPERANDS
100.MAINLINE:
      PARSE SOURCE . . . . . MACNAME .
      /*    Error checking    */
      IF PREFIX NOT = 'PREFIX' THEN SIGNAL 200.NOTPREFIX
      IF CALLTYPE = 'CLEAR' THEN EXIT
```

```
IF CALLTYPE = 'SHADOW' THEN SIGNAL 210.SHADOW
IF CALLTYPE NOT = 'SET' THEN SIGNAL 200.NOTPREFIX
/*    Is the command XC or XCC?    */
SELECT
WHEN MACNAME = 'XC' THEN DO
 IF OPERANDS = '' | DATATYPE(OPERANDS,'W') THEN
  'COMMAND : 'PLINE 'PUT' OPERANDS
 ELSE SIGNAL 330.INVALIDOP
 END
/*   For XCC, determine whether it is the first or
     last of the pair. If first, set up the start of
     a block. If last, close and save the block.   */
WHEN MACNAME = 'XCC' THEN DO
IF OPERANDS NOT = '' THEN 220.INVALIDOP
'COMMAND EXTRACT /PENDING BLOCK' MACNAME '/'
 /* Was there a prior XCC? */
IF PENDING.0 = 0 THEN       /* No prior XCC */
 'COMMAND : 'PLINE 'SET PENDING BLOCK' MACNAME
ELSE DO               /* There was a prior XCC */
 'COMMAND : ' PENDING.1 'SET PENDING OFF'
 'COMMAND : 'MIN(PENDING.1, PLINE) 'PUT',
   ABS(PLINE - PENDING.1) +1
 END
END
/* Something went wrong if the command is neither
     XC or XCC                        */
OTHERWISE 'COMMAND EMSG INVALID SYNONYM -' MACNAME
END
EXIT
 /*    Various error message routines    */
200.NOTPREFIX:
   'COMMAND EMSG USE ' MACNAME ' AS A PREFIX COMMAND'
EXIT
210.SHADOW:
   'COMMAND EMSG DO NOT USE' MACNAME 'ON A SHADOW LINE'
EXIT
220.INVALIDOP:
   'COMMAND EMSG INVALID OPERAND -' OPERANDS
EXIT
```

XEDIT supplies the values for PREFIX, CALLTYPE, and PLINE. The macro itself checks to make sure the command was used in the prefix area, and not on a shadow line (one which the X or XX . . . XX function made invisible). With XC, it does an immediate write to storage (PUT) for the number of lines indicated by the operand. For example:

```
XC3== FIRST LINE TO COPY...
===== SECOND LINE TO COPY...
===== THIRD LINE TO COPY...
```

will hold all three lines for copying. If Joan used XCC instead, the macro determines whether a pending block exists or should be started. It simply does the counting for her. This form:

```
XCC== FIRST LINE TO COPY...
===== SECOND LINE TO COPY...
XCC== THIRD LINE TO COPY...
```

has the same result as above.

The PUT command loads the block she copied into a temporary file, which lasts the length of her XEDIT session. To retrieve the block, you need another XEDIT macro called G:

```
/* XEDIT macro for inserting stored blocks */
PARSE ARG PREFIX CALLTYPE PLINE OPERANDS
100.MAINLINE:
       /*      Error checking       */
     IF PREFIX NOT = 'PREFIX' THEN SIGNAL 200.NOTPREFIX
     IF CALLTYPE = 'CLEAR' THEN EXIT
     IF CALLTYPE = 'SHADOW' THAN SIGNAL 210.SHADOW
     IF CALLTYPE NOT = 'SET' THEN SIGNAL 200.NOTPREFIX
       /*      Get the stored block and forget any operands */
     'COMMAND :' PLINE 'GET'
     IF OPERANDS NOT = '' THEN,
     'COMMAND EMSG OPERANDS IGNORED'
EXIT
       /*      Various error message routines      */
     200.NOTPREFIX:
          'COMMAND EMSG USE G AS A PREFIX COMMAND'
EXIT
210.SHADOW:
     'COMMAND EMSG DO NOT USE G ON THE SHADOW LINE'
     EXIT
```

This macro reads the same XEDIT values and does the same error checking as XC, then simply inserts the stored text. For example, if Joan used G here:

```
G==== LAST LINE BEFORE THE COPIED BLOCK
===== FIRST LINE AFTER THE COPIED BLOCK
```

the result is:

```
===== LAST LINE BEFORE THE COPIED BLOCK
===== FIRST LINE TO COPY...
===== SECOND LINE TO COPY...
===== THIRD LINE TO COPY...
===== FIRST LINE AFTER THE COPIED BLOCK
```

You should put the G macro in a file called G XEDIT and the XC macro in a file called XC XEDIT. It is important that you include a synonym command for XCC in the PROFILE XEDIT so that XCC commands find the macro under its XC name:

```
SET PREFIX SYNONYM XCC XC
```

You could instead also separate XC and XCC into two macros.

XEDIT macros are nothing more than REXX programs which use XEDIT facilities and run during an XEDIT session. Team members might want to write macros that enhance existing commands, such as the search and replace. If, for example, they want to replace a variable name only under certain conditions, a macro can check for that condition before executing the replacement. Macros can run either from the prefix area, as in the examples above, or from the command line. They can be as long and elaborate as the writer chooses.

Source Library Maintenance

Auditors concern themselves increasingly with source code integrity. The question is whether your development center can match source and object code. Failure to match creates a difficult maintenance situation at best and an opening for fraud at worst.

Source maintenance packages provide one level of security. They offer password protection for source code and generally they insert a tag into the source which you can read in the executable module.

That tag identifies the update level and which source library it came from. Maintenance programmers should check that tag to make sure they are modifying the most current version of production code. A good package generally has options to restrict programmers from using more than one copy of the source. This prevents two people from altering the same code at the same time and then overlaying each other's changes.

Some development centers write their own source library systems. Such home-made systems can work well enough, but they lack the variety of features available in commercial packages. Also, auditors often hate such home-made systems. One reason is that they cannot be sure that it works as reliably as a commercial product. Another reason is that home-made systems require local maintenance, which allows for error and opens greater potential for fraud.

A VM development center has a variety of options for commercial library packages, including those running in a guest operating system. With guest system packages, you make use of their batch interfaces.

Project team members often keep code they are working on in private libraries and update the source library only after finishing the modifications. In VM they can use XEDIT to write or modify the source, then store it on their minidisks. When finished, they submit a batch job into the guest machine to update the source library. This procedure works equally well for shops which maintain several levels of source code security. They can update a test library first and production control can update the production library after testing is complete.

You can automate this batch update process with a simple REXX EXEC. It should prompt for the program name and library password, then generate an update job stream which it submits to the guest. You can even set up a full-screen menu using DMS/CMS and include all the names and options your shop uses. Such an EXEC makes batch updating more friendly than the online interfaces of some packages.

Another alternative is to buy a VM source maintenance system. Most major MVS and VSE source library packages now have VM versions. Frequently these have been retrofitted to VM and still use MVS type routines and file structures. You may instead wish to look at VM-only products which use the CMS file structure for data storage. These CMS-oriented packages have advantages for your system backups. Commercial VM backup products handle CMS files efficiently and allow selective restoration, but for non-CMS formatted space, such as the retrofitted MVS packages use, they can only backup the data on a slow cylinder-by-cylinder basis.

Testing in VM

VM offers two alternatives for testing non-CMS programs: emulation or transfer to a guest operating system. Final testing should always take place in the environment the production version will use. Not doing so might give some unpleasant surprises. Nonetheless emulating OS or DOS as a first phase of testing lets team members take advantage of VM's debugging facilities.

Programs they assemble or compile in CMS result in a TEXT deck, which is unlinked object code. They must LOAD any other programs necessary for execution, then BUILD the module. The process mirrors what they do when they link a module in VSE or MVS. They just LOAD the main component of the module, INCLUDE any subprograms, then generate the module with a GENMOD. You can build a simple EXEC that can automate the process for them. IBM's AS-MGEND EXEC provides an example to work from. If the programs are using OS macros, you should also access the disk the MACLIB is on, point to the MACLIB with a FILEDEF, and issue a GLOBAL command to make the macros available.

VM offers a good environment for testing batch programs, but team members may need help setting up their test files. Programs using a database management system require the VM version; without it, they cannot test. Ordinary VSAM files cause less trouble. A duplicate VSAM license costs little and installs relatively quickly. You should note, however, that VM uses VSE VSAM, which means you must invoke DOS emulation routines before starting.

You can put a VM VSAM catalog on any minidisk, even TDISK, but it cannot share the minidisk with CMS files. The reason is that the disk must have CP—not CMS—formatting. You can use IPL FMT from the S disk to reformat the minidisk, but remember that it will erase any files you have there. You have probably used IPL FMT to configure disk packs or to allocate the bit-map which specifies cylinder usage, but non-system programmers may not be familiar with it. To help them, you should set up an EXEC that uses IPL FMT's batch control option. If, for example, you need to format a five-cylinder minidisk called TMP01 at virtual address 19F on an IBM 3380, the batch command is:

```
FORMAT,19F,3380,TMP01,000,004
```

You put this command in a file called FORMAT DATA, then stack
FORMAT DATA behind IPL FMT in the reader queue, and IPL the
reader:

```
/* REXX EXEC to format a disk for a VSAM catalog */
100.MAINLINE:
/* Direct your PUNCH to an unused RDR class */
SPOOL PUNCH '*' CLASS P CONT
/* Put IPL FMT and its batch commands into your RDR */
'PUNCH IPL FMT * (NOH'
'PUNCH FORMAT DATA A (NOH'
SPOOL PUNCH '*' CLASS P CLOSE
/* Make sure IPL FMT heads the RDR queue */
'ORDER RDR CLASS P'
/* Invoke IPL FMT by IPLing your RDR
'IPL 00C'
EXIT
```

After formatting the minidisk, they can set up a VSAM catalog
using standard Access Method Services commands.

To use files in the catalog, team members must establish DOS labels by doing a SET DOS ON and coding DLBLs. VM VSAM does
not use FILEDEFs. They will need a DLBL for the master catalog,
as well as ones for any user catalogs. VM allows any number of master catalogs, as long as each virtual machine uses only one. Some
team members may prefer to let their master catalog serve as a user
catalog too. In a test environment, this causes no problems. After the
DLBLs are ready, they should SET DOS OFF unless the program
requires DOS emulation.

Joan can begin the test by entering the name of the module. Testing in an interactive environment will not degrade VM the way it
does CICS or TSO. This is because the VM scheduler automatically
treats a virtual machine which exhausts its interactive Q1 timeslices
as a batch Q2 user.

If Joan encounters an abend, she can examine the dump online
with the DISPLAY command. DISPLAY shows any portion of virtual
memory in hexadecimal format and translates the hexadecimal code
exactly as would a paper dump. DISPLAY G will also show the general registers. If she wishes to save the information for later reference, she should first:

```
SPOOL CONSOLE * START
```

Then everything displayed on the screen will go into a reader file. To stop the recording, she enters:

```
SPOOL CONSOLE STOP
```

And to close the spool file and send it to your reader:

```
SPOOL CONSOLE CLOSE
```

She can either print the results or RECEIVE them onto her minidisk. The latter is better because it lets her use REXX and XEDIT to help find the problem.

She can also take advantage of other VM debugging tools such as PER and TRACE. PER will trace assembler instructions, branches, or register changes for particular ranges of program addresses. TRACE displays all virtual machine activity, including supervisor calls and I/O. She can use these commands with COBOL or any other high-level language, as long as the compiler's assembler listing is available as a guide.

At present, VM has no test environment for CICS programs. IBM has announced plans for a VM version of CICS at the earliest. At least one third-party company has announced a VM implementation of CICS. Others will probably follow. But until these products have more public use, it is difficult to say whether they provide a sufficiently standard CICS environment to rely on them for testing.

Program development in VM does not require testing in VM. Joan can easily submit batch jobs into MVS or VSE guest machines. Both JES and POWER can route the output back to her VM reader queue. They handle job streams the same way, regardless of whether they came from internal or external sources. The biggest difference is that in VM Joan has only her own listings in the queue. She need not search for them.

You can write REXX EXECs to build JCL for batch submission. A compile job, for example, generally needs only a few pieces of variable information: the program name, account numbers, and other modules for the linkage editor. The EXEC can prompt for these variables, build the job stream in a temporary file (using EXECIO), and COPY the program to it. Then it can submit the job and delete the temporary file.

The most common problem your submit EXEC will encounter is a lack of file space. You can build in a simple routine to check for space:

```
300.SPACE.CHECK:
    MKBUF               /* Get separate buffer */
    QUERY DISK A '(STACK'
    PARSE PULL LINE  /* Discard headings line */
    PARSE PULL LINE  /* This is the line you want */
    PARSE VAR LINE . . . . . . BLKSIZE . . BLKLEFT .
    /* Blocksize makes a big difference. Check that before
     deciding on space availability. */
    IF BLKSIZE = 4096 & BLKLEFT <50 THEN DO
     SAY 'TOO LITTLE SPACE AVAILABLE --' BLKLEFT 'BLOCKS'
     EXIT 50  /* Return Code 50 = have <50 blocks */
    END
    IF BLKSIZE = 1024 & BLKLEFT <200 THEN DO
     SAY 'TOO LITTLE SPACE AVAILABLE --' BLKLEFT 'BLOCKS'
     EXIT 200 /* Return Code 200 = have <200 blocks */
    END
    DROPBUF             /* Drop separate buffer */
RETURN
```

Of course, you will have to decide how many blocks the temporary file is likely to need. This will depend on your disk type and blocking, as well as the maximum size of the programs. If you have chronically limited disk space, you can build the EXEC to define TDISK, format it (just stack the format commands), and use that space to build your job stream. Remember, however, that the heavy I/O involved in formatting your TDISK can make job submission rather slow.

VM does lack one popular feature present in both MVS or VSE. Team members cannot easily monitor the input queues to discover the relative position and priority of their jobs. Some people check constantly. They set up the commands on a PF key, which they hit constantly for long periods to watch their job run. Any programmer who is not a saint has undoubtedly done this. Few will argue that such monitoring does any good. VM removes temptation, which saves time and perhaps a few ulcers.

Online testing almost always requires changing from one interactive environment to another. Anyone working in TSO must sign onto CICS and those already in CICS usually need to switch to a different CICS. Likewise in VM team members must switch—in their case—to a guest system. VM VTAM should connect them directly to the right region or partition in the guest. Or, if your shop has no VM VTAM, they can DIAL to the guest. You may need to give them a specific address to get the right CICS.

Documentation

Written Descriptions

Team members need to produce documentation for any new system. Often this is one of the least automated parts of the development process. In VM that need not be the case, as long as the team members have planned how and what they want to document well in advance.

The narrative portion of the documentation represents a summary of project team decisions and discussions on topics ranging from initial requirements to final testing. When such discussions take place via electronic mail, a record exists in each team members' NOTEBOOK. The difficulty is to extract that information in a meaningful way.

Each NOTEBOOK contains a record of one person's notes, both sent and received, and thus also includes some entries in other NOTEBOOKs. The team members could avoid duplication by discarding replies rather than receiving them, but that would undo the ability to look back over conversations without actually imposing any intelligible sequence. What the documentation needs is a structure, one which team members devised and began using during the earliest phases of the project.

They need to establish an outline, based on the form they wish the final project documentation to take. The structure should allow for growth, as team members add unforeseen aspects to the project. Some may want to bypass these aspects of planning to get on with what they call real work. If that happens, everyone will eventually face the harder task of organizing huge amounts of detailed information without machine help.

Once they have the outline, they can develop a code for each level. Traditional outline formats (e.g., III.A.4.f) add unnecessary complexity to a machine-readable structure, particularly because of the variable length of Roman numerals. Instead, they can set up a simple structure of alternating letters and numbers. For example, III.B.4.f in the traditional system could become C2D6. This new code could then later become a CMS filename and the documentation can ultimately reside on a minidisk for easy access. This makes more and more sense as disk prices drop and the cost of maintaining printed documentation grows.

To use the outline for creating documentation, team members should code the relevant level number each time they send a project-related note. The level number should appear in a consistent position, probably on the line following the heading information, and should have a tag associated with it. For example:

```
Date: July 14, 1988 ...
From: MICHAEL
To: JOAN
Code: C2D6
```

The code is both the subject of Michael's note and a built-in pointer for organizing system documentation.

The technical task of building documentation from the NOTEBOOKs now becomes relatively simple. You can write a REXX EXEC to read each NOTEBOOK and write the note to a file for that code. The EXEC should also create an index to make sure you do not write the same note from two different NOTEBOOKs. You might write a simple form of the EXEC this way:

```
100.MAINLINE:
      /* Set variables to initial values */
      MAX = 0
      MTCH = 'NOMATCH'
      DROP = 'NO'
      CODEFILE = 'FIRST-TIME'
      /* The names of the notebooks are in a file. E.G.
            MICHAEL (Notebook from userid MICHAEL)
            JOAN (Notebook from userid JOAN) */
      DO FOREVER
            EXECIO 1 DISKR NOTENAME DATA A
            IF RC > 0 THEN LEAVE /* End of file. */
            PARSE PULL LINE
            PARSE VAR LINE FN . /* Discard any comments */
            CALL 200.READALL
      END
EXIT
200.READALL:
      /* Read the whole notebook */
      DO FOREVER
            EXECIO 1 DISKR FN NOTEBOOK A
            IF RC > 0 THEN LEAVE /* End of file. */
            PARSE PULL LINE
            PARSE VAR LINE FLAG INDX
            IF FLAG = 'Date:' THEN DO
```

```
            TIMEDATE = INDX /* Save the time stamp */
            CALL 300.INDEX
            DROP = 'YES' /* Save no heading lines */
         END
         IF FLAG = 'Code:' THEN DO
            CODEFILE = INDX /* Use the code as filename */
            DROP = 'NO' /* Body of the note begins */
         END
         /* The first entry in Notebooks is always a line.
            Get rid of it. */
         IF CODEFILE = 'FIRST-TIME' THEN DROP = 'YES'
         IF MTCH = 'NOMATCH' & DROP = 'NO' THEN DO
         /* Substitute the timestamp for the code.
            All entries in the file are for that code. */
         IF FLAG = 'Code:' THEN LINE = 'Date:' timedate
            EXECIO 1 DISKW CODEFILE DOC A '(STRING' LINE
         END
      END
RETURN
300.INDEX:
      /* Reset the switch. */
      MTCH = 'NOMATCH' /* Reset the default */
      /* Test whether the new index (INDX) matches an
         old one.
         MAX = total entries thus far. */
      DO N = 1 TO MAX
         IF INDX = INDX.N THEN DO
            MTCH = 'MATCH' /* Indicate a match. */
            LEAVE
         END
      END
      /* When no match occurs, you have a unique note */
      IF MTCH = 'NOMATCH' THEN DO
         MAX = MAX + 1 /* Increase the index counter */
         INDX.MAX = INDX /* Enter the new index value */
      END
RETURN
```

This example does not use a particularly efficient search routine. For large systems you might want to break up the search by the first letter of the code or some similar algorithm. The principles, however, remain the same and it will run relatively quickly as long as your index remains small enough to stay in memory.

Your REXX EXEC should run against all project NOTEBOOKs. Team members can SENDFILE their NOTEBOOKs to one person for processing, or even send them to a batch machine that has a front end RECEIVE routine. Allowing read-only links to team members' minidisks will work only if each team member changes the NOTEBOOK's default filemode from A0 to A1. A0 files remain invisible in read-only links.

After your EXEC has written each note to the correct file for its reference code, the project team may want to combine the files in order by the code number and insert chapter headings, page breaks, and other print control information. They can do this manually, or use REXX to combine files (sorting the LISTFILE output will give them the correct order with no hardcoding). Chapter and section headings should come from a table.

The result is a compilation of all issues and answers. Instead of too little documentation, the project team may end up with too much. In any case they should edit the output before making it permanent. They will want the final product to be both smooth and grammatical. Combining the NOTEBOOKs does not eliminate all the work of making good documentation, but it facilitates the process by creating a rough draft.

This process is cost effective in two ways. First, the need for coded pointers forces the project team to adopt some semblance of structured techniques for its analytical process. Although structured analysis is no panacea, any orderly process for examining a problem will save time in the long run. Second, the automatic compilation saves days of work on a task which project teams too often ignore or give minimal attention to in their rush to get done. Such detailed and accurate documentation saves maintenance teams time later on and may spare your shop from replacing a viable system simply because no one understands the logic by which it was built.

Flowcharts

One other critical element of documentation is diagraming the system flow. Ordinary 3270 type terminals do not lend themselves well to graphics and CMS itself has no built-in graphics capabilities. You can buy a computer-aided design package, but the cost would exceed the benefit if your shop used it only for flow charts. REXX offers a cheaper, though less elegant, alternative.

You can write a REXX EXEC that puts flowchart symbols into a file and adds a program or file name for each item. For example:

```
/* REXX EXEC to write flowchart symbols and their labels */
PARSE ARG FN FT FM SYMBOL LABEL1 LABEL2 LABEL3 LABEL4
100.MAINLINE:
      /* Create a process box */
      IF SYMBOL = '1PROCESS' CALL 301.1PROCESS
      /* Create a decision box */
      IF SYMBOL = '1DECIDE' CALL 311.1DECIDE
      /* Create a single DASD symbol */
      IF SYMBOL = '1DASD' CALL 321.1DASD
      /* Create two DASD symbols */
      IF SYMBOL = '2DASD' CALL 322.2DASD
      /* Create a single tape symbol */
      IF SYMBOL = '1TAPE' CALL 331.1TAPE
      /* Create one DASD and one tape symbol */
      IF SYMBOL = '1T1D' CALL 341.1TAPE1DISK
      /* You can create any other symbols or combinations
         that you want... */
EXIT
301.1PROCESS:
      LINE.1 = '                    ********        '
      LINE.2 = '                    *      *        '
      LINE.3 = '                    *      *        '
      LINE.4 = '                    ********        '
      LINE.5 = '                       *  '||LABEL1
      LINE.6 = '                       *            '
      DO N = 1 TO 5
            EXECIO 1 DISKW FN FT FM '(STRING' LINE.N
      END
EXIT
/* The drawing process repeats for each symbol or set of
   symbols. */
```

This EXEC creates one symbol at a time. Team members should execute it from a second REXX EXEC which describes the actual flow of logic. For example:

```
/* This sample REXX EXEC diagrams a job with a tape and
/* disk input, and a single disk file as output. */
PARSE ARG FN FT FM
/* You tell it which file (FN FT FM) to write to. */
100.MAINLINE:
```

```
EXEC FLOWCHRT FN FT FM 1T1D TIMECARD PERSONNEL
EXEC FLOWCHRT FN FT FM 1PROCESS BHOGCOM2
EXEC FLOWCHRT FN FT FM 1DISK PAYCHECKS
EXIT
```

The result looks like this:

```
        **                          * * * * *
     *     *                      *           *
     *     *                      *           *
     * * * * * *                  *           *
     *  TIMECARD                  * * * * *  PERSONNEL
     *                                  *
     * * * * * * * * * * * * * * * * * * * * * * * * * *
                          *
                          *
                     * * * * * * * * *
                     *             *
                     *             *
                     * * * * * * * * *
                          *     BHOGCOM2
                          *
                     * * * * *
                     *         *
                     *         *
                     *         *
              * * * * *  PAYCHECKS
```

Such drawings lack elegance; and some standard shapes, such as the DASD symbol with its curved top and bottom, reproduce poorly. Nonetheless this form of diagraming has several advantages.

First, it imposes some structure on the team's system diagraming, because the EXEC limits the shapes and connections available. Second, team members can change their diagrams easily by recoding the second EXEC. Traditional hand-drawn diagrams cannot change without much erasing and the result may look so messy that the person has to redraw it completely anyway. Third, all project team members can get copies of the diagrams electronically via NOTEs. This means of distribution ensures that the documentation will include these diagrams automatically.

The limitation of REXX flowcharting depends on your imagination. You can include any symbol or combination of symbols that fit in XEDIT—not just 80 columns by 20 rows, but 256 columns by virtually any number of rows. The larger format would, however, require special print control if the project team wanted hard copy and it is harder to read on an ordinary CRT.

Program Documentation

The final form of documentation is a compact description of the project's programs. Program documentation is especially important in prolonging the useful life of a system. Those doing maintenance need some reliable guide to help them find where to make a change. In-program comments are essential, but too often they follow no standard format. Some are no more than a line or two of general description at the front, others are cryptic notes about abstruse routines. A project team must first establish standards about the kind of comments and how to use them. Then VM can perform the same collecting and organizing role for program documentation as with the NOTEBOOKs.

Team members can also extract useful documentation from the code itself, though the extent varies from language to language. In COBOL, for example, each paragraph name can be 30 characters long. Even documentation-resistant programmers might cooperate to the extent of using descriptive paragraph names. An EXEC can strip out these paragraph names and write them to a file. Such documentation offers no more than a rough outline, but it is still more useful than flipping pages of heavy volumes of source code.

VM can produce better documentation if team members agree to write a few lines of description immediately after starting each new routine. An EXEC can then recognize the paragraph name and copy any comment lines which immediately follow, but still ignore other comment lines embedded in the code to explain obscure tricks of processing.

This procedure will work for COBOL, PL1, and most other higher level languages. Assembler presents a different problem because of its short labels and tendency toward linear logic. If team members establish strict conventions for commenting their assembler programs, a REXX EXEC can strip out useful documentation. Otherwise, old-style assembler programmers may find themselves trapped forever maintaining their own aging systems.

The most important feature of using REXX EXECs is that it does not limit your shop to traditional static forms of documentation. Printed documentation requires expensive maintenance. Even

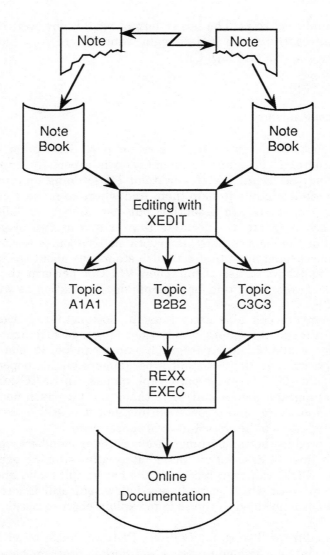

Figure 10-2 Documentation with REXX and XEDIT.

ordinary online documentation requires human intervention to re-write it after each maintenance update. But an EXEC can search the source code of any program at any time. You need only keep the EXECs available. Team members can rebuild the documentation whenever they want and have complete confidence that what they are reading is the latest version.

Even the best documentation does not always tell team members what they need to know. For example, Michael might need to find out how a series of programs use a particular variable from a copybook statement. In VM he can create a modified documentation EXEC of his own, which searches each program to extract the lines where that variable is used. Such EXECs automate the analytical process much as programs have automated record keeping and accounting.

Signoff and Production Turnover

Test Verification

Verifying test results is one of the most tedious, but important parts of system development. The fact that a series of programs work without abending does not guarantee the validity of their answers. Yet people often fail to check results carefully, or neglect to recheck them only to discover that changing an unrelated routine has altered the results. VM can help automate a project team's verification process.

Once team members have a test plan, they need to establish a test database. This can be either a random sample of production records, if available, or manufactured data designed to cover all known conditions and errors. The latter makes a good first-stage test, but is no substitute for the unpredictable variety of live data. Team members should keep two copies of this test database, one in files owned by the guest operating system, and another in VM, in the format used for the system prototype. That prototype can calculate answers to check against the test system reports.

For online applications, they can check screen prints from the prototype against the same queries in CICS. Some results may differ because of errors in the prototype, or because of last-minute changes in the design which no one incorporated into the prototype. But most results should agree. This procedure helps guard against any psychological predisposition to accept unthinkingly what appears on the screen.

Batch reports may take more effort to verify because they tend to be longer and more complex. If the prototype produces identical reports, team members can COMPARE them on a minidisk. Normally, however, the prototype would not include all headings, footings, and other formatting specifications. One way to deal with this problem is to use XEDIT's "search all" capability ("ALL /") to display and delete heading and footing lines so that the COMPARE will work. Another is to write an EXEC which parses each line to look for and compare valid data elements. Or, at a minimum, they can write an EXEC which searches through the reports for critical results. An EXEC will catch unexpected changes a person might not notice when glancing through the output.

The cost-effectiveness of writing such EXECs depends on the importance of accurate results. For simple jobs like internal mailing labels, it may suffice to look for the names of a few senior vice-presidents. For customer account summaries, however, each failure of quality control can have a significant dollar price, not only in good will and lost business, but in the man-hours required to identify and correct errors. The EXECs will vary somewhat from report to report, but the project team's effort in writing them will be less than the time needed to correct the first production error.

Production Turnover

User sign-off is the next step after testing. Some troubles inevitably occur during the test phase. Even a well-prototyped, well-designed system will have omissions. If team members communicate these in NOTEs, they will have a machine readable record of each problem and its resolution. During testing the users can use NOTEs to sign off on each part of the system in turn. At final sign-off time a slight modification to the EXEC that organized their requirements definition can put together the notes about each part and each problem. The managers involved in the sign-off can examine that record and assure themselves that no major issues remain outstanding.

In the real world, a project team rarely has time to fix every minor problem before a system enters production. The sign-off document should describe any remaining problems, and assign a maintenance priority to them. This accomplishes more than a grudging signature on a form letter and if the sign-off is a NOTE, it too can become part of the machine-generated documentation.

The next step is for operations staff to review job and program documentation. If they also work in VM, they can read the documentation by accessing its minidisk. Any questions should go in electronic notes, so that this interchange, like all others, can become part of the ongoing record. Operations sign-off should come in NOTE form and it should include the new schedule of production jobs.

The final step is project cleanup. All members of the project team will have minidisks bulging with NOTEBOOKs, programs, data, and JCL specific to the project. You should not allow members haphazardly to save and delete pieces of the system. Some artifacts, such as the EXECs for building documentation, can be modified for future systems. Such reuse is clearly cost-effective, but it also prevents reconstructing a project in the unhappy event that a senior vice-president demands revisions.

You should back up all project related files onto a special tape before a project ends. If your normal backup tool is DDR (Dynamic Dump and Restore), you must do this for each cylinder of each project minidisk. But DDR is not an ideal tool for such archiving, because it cannot restore individual CMS files and will not restore to different device types.

Most VM shops purchase more sophisticated and user-friendly backup systems than DDR. These systems use the CMS file structure to do their backups and can restore individual files as well as whole minidisks. They can also restore to CMS formatted minidisks regardless of the device type. No backup system, however, is ideal for archiving individual project files. One reason is that these systems have their own directory structures to keep track of when to recycle tapes. Long-term archiving means establishing an exception. A better alternative is to acquire a CMS-based archiving system. It can pay for itself by conserving DASD and it facilitates restoring project records whenever someone needs them.

Conclusions

The real issue for a VM development center is whether its cost effectiveness justifies abandoning more traditional development centers in MVS or VSE. Many companies believe it does. Four common reasons are: VM's responsiveness, its portability among IBM processors, its tools, and its information center capabilities.

Productivity today for users and programmers depends on their having quick response time. Each lag reduces the amount of work a person can do. Even occasional slowdowns hurt long-term productivity as frustrated staff members begin to avoid online tools. VM is one means of keeping response time short. Applications programmers began moving to VM in the late 1970s because CMS offered a better interactive environment than TSO. VM's scheduling algorithm automatically favors interactive users over longer batch processes. Other IBM systems do not.

Portability from one model to another is another reason why development centers have migrated to VM. VM runs on all systems from the smallest 9370 to the largest 3090. A VSE shop contemplating growth into a high-end processor can migrate its development center staff into VM well before switching to MVS. At one time MVS shops discounted the reverse prospect of having to support smaller processors, but departmentally based 9370s have begun to change that, as have software products which link small and medium sized models into powerful clusters.

VM's productivity tools are widely considered the most user-friendly of any IBM system. Chief among these tools is REXX, with its full range of programming capabilities. REXX allows development center staff of all sorts to write short ad-hoc programs for almost any purpose, including prototyping. Similar capabilities exist in theory in MVS CLISTs, but CLISTs are much less friendly and efficient. Proof of this is IBM's strategic decision to introduce REXX into MVS.

The savings such tools offer is equivalent to automating a business function. Development center staff rely on many precomputer techniques. They might, for example, read a program page after page to find certain variables, instead of scanning the code in a tenth of the time with an edit macro. Of course the availability of tools like REXX or XEDIT does not guarantee their use. Many staff members will persist with old habits. But if the tools are there, some will adopt them, gain from them, and teach them to others. Just as businesses began to use computers increasingly two decades ago, data center managers today must concern themselves with automating their own system development procedures.

The way VM most helps automate development is through the regular presence of users in a VM information center. This sets VM apart from other interactive environments. Communication among members of a project team has always been a key element in developing systems. In MVS and VSE shops this communication often takes place with the same tools as were available before computers: meetings, memos, and telephone calls. In a VM shop the team members can use the power of the mainframe to make communication faster and more effective.

VM turns the machine-readable record of these electronic discussions into useful documentation. Team members may spend hours in meetings discussing detailed questions and find the minute taker (if there is one) produced no more than a page or two of notes. The result is that the same questions reappear again and again. If team members hold the same discussions electronically in VM, the answers are there for anyone who cares to look.

Automating the development process through VM will require changing the way people work. For users this means learning how to do simple programming tasks in REXX and using electronic facilities like NOTE. For programmers it means learning to write clearly and succinctly. Frequently they have excellent literary skills in COBOL or PL1, but lack training and confidence in ordinary English. Without changing work methods, VM still offers a solid platform for development center work. But it is like driving a sports car and never going over thirty.

A VM development center is no panacea, but it is the best environment currently available for automating the way project teams do their work.

About the Author

Michael Seadle has worked on MVS, VSE, and VM systems. He began his data processing career in 1981 as an applications programmer for Assembler Language Actuarial Systems in the insurance industry, became an SQL database administrator, and then a VM systems programmer. He is currently head of User Support Services at Eastern Michigan University.

Michael received his Ph.D. in history from the University of Chicago in 1977. During the past decade he has lectured, written, and taught history and computer-related subjects. In 1987 he helped found the VM Enthusiasts of Michigan, a VM system programmers' user group, based in the Detroit area.

You can reach him at:

University Computing
Eastern Michigan University
Ypsilanti, MI 48197
  Telephone 313-487-3141

11

REXX

by Bebo White

Introduction

One of the great strengths of VM/CMS is its facility for the creation of user-defined commands. The two processing environments in which this facility can be most useful are the CMS command environment and XEDIT. In CMS, these commands are called CMS EXECs. EXEC files are very useful to add commands to the system which perform functions that were not foreseen by CMS; or to simplify a collection of frequently used commands, thus hiding complicated features; and to create a user-tailored computing environment.

User-written XEDIT subcommands are called XEDIT macros. XEDIT macros are used for much the same reasons as REXX EXEC files: to create new editor commands, to eliminate repetitive tasks and, in general, to tailor XEDIT to a user's applications.

This chapter contains a description of the REXX macro language for writing CMS EXECs and XEDIT macros. Hopefully it will illustrate how useful this facility can be. REXX can also be a fun language in which to write programs, so the reader should always expect the unexpected.

This chapter cannot be viewed as complete coverage of REXX and any serious user should also refer to the "de facto" standard REXX language reference documents from M. F. Cowlishaw and IBM. The program examples in these references should fully complement the material in this chapter.

The approach used in this chapter to describe REXX is quite different from that of other texts. It was developed by the chapter's author as a result of his extensive use of REXX and has proven effective in teaching the language to a variety of audiences.

Why REXX?

In the beginning days of VM/CMS there were basically two macro languages, EXEC and EXEC-2. Both of these languages are based upon the common principle that program variables and controls (i.e., language keywords) should be distinguishable (in these languages by a "&") and that literal values should exist in plain text.

When EXECs consisted mainly of sequential "scripts" of commands, with very little logic in between, this design was a fair and sensible choice. However, later examination of the style utilized in most CMS EXECs written in EXEC and EXEC-2 indicates that the majority of words used are symbolic (i.e., they begin with "&"). This observation has led to a re-examination of this syntactical form.

As the use of VM/CMS became more widespread, CMS EXECs were expected to interface with a wider variety of products and environments. Additional concerns arose involving the use of "complicated" strings in EXECs (e.g., in Editor macros, full-screen applications, etc.). EXEC-2 can handle such strings moderately well, whereas EXEC cannot manipulate them at all.

The necessity of using uppercase characters exclusively throughout the EXEC languages makes programs in these languages awkward to type and difficult to read. Continuing research in computer human factors has consistently indicated that mixed case programs are easier to read, comprehend, and actually contain fewer errors.

Finally, the underlying syntax of the EXEC languages makes the efficient interpretation of the recognized "modern" control structures (If-Then-Else, Do-Until, While-Do) extremely difficult, if not impossible to implement. However, these facilities became more in demand by EXEC and macro developers who found them easier to use when writing, modifying, and maintaining programs.

The following program written in EXEC-2 illustrates some of the concerns expressed about the structure and design of that language:

```
&TRACE OFF
&LOOP -BIGLOOP 100
TEST
-BIGLOOP
&EXIT &RC
```

The following is the same operation expressed in the REXX macro language. It clearly demonstrates how specific concerns in EXEC-2 have been addressed in REXX. Its readability, even to someone not familiar with the language, illustrates a minimal emphasis on language structure and syntax:

```
/* */
do 100
"TEST"
end
exit Rc
```

A Short History of REXX

In 1983, REXX (named as the System Product Interpreter) was announced as the third of the series (following EXEC and EXEC-2) of macro languages supported by VM/CMS. REXX is an interpretive language that provides very powerful features to the writers and users of CMS EXECs and XEDIT macros. Unlike EXEC and EXEC-2, REXX has most of the capabilities of a procedural/macro language. It permits a full "structured programming" style and offers high precision arithmetic.

REXX (or the Restructured Extended Executor Language) was developed by M. F. (Mike) Cowlishaw of the IBM United Kingdom Laboratory, Hursley Park, during the period between 1979 and 1982. It is probably accurate to say that REXX is the first language developed by an international, electronic committee. Cowlishaw distributed the language description and specifications and early versions of the interpreter over the IBM internal network, VNET. The response was overwhelming and hundreds of users contributed to the development and refinement of the language.

The contributors to Cowlishaw's REXX language definition created a formidable wish list which provided the basis for the conceptual foundation of the language. To these users, an ideal macro language for writing EXECs and macros should have the following features:

1. Readability—EXECs and/or macros should be highly readable, both for the benefit of the author/programmer and for that of any reader/user/maintainer. Human factors research in language design has indicated that readability is improved with the use of:
   a. mixed case
   b. free formatting
   c. use of punctuation only to avoid ambiguity
   Simple EXECs which consist of only a sequential series of CP and CMS commands should be "readable" as such with a minimal addition of confusing macro language syntax or semantics.
2. Natural Data Typing—While strong data typing is a desirable feature in high-level programming languages, it may not be desirable considering the environments in which CMS EXECs and XEDIT macros are written and designed. An ideal macro language should be weakly typed or place maximum emphasis on symbolic manipulation, where data types are defined within the context of the data usage. No data type or variable definitions or declarations should be necessary.
3. Structured Design—The desirable features of a "structured programming language" are also desirable in the definition of a language for CMS EXECs and XEDIT macros.
4. Hardware/System Independence—An ideal macro language should operate independently of the hardware and the operating system within which it functions. This concept allows the programmer the maximum degree of independence and permits the greater functionality allowed by the portability of macros. For vendors such as IBM, who support multiple operating systems, this independence provides the potential for a common interface. (This concept became a reality later with the announcement of the Systems Application Architecture— SAA.)

Cowlishaw incorporated these concepts into REXX and produced a language that:

- Can be used to produce CMS EXECs and XEDIT macros of unprecedented simplicity or complexity.
- Can be used as a personal programming language instead of alternatives such as BASIC.
- Can be easily used as a "prototyping or pseudo-code language."

"If REXX were just another language, it would be interesting because of its conscious design to emphasize ease of use. But since

REXX also encompasses a set of standard interfaces, it represents something more—a tool for fully exploiting the facilities of an operating system; a portable, standard macro language for multiple applications; and a facility for constructing applications out of available building blocks." [8]

General Properties of the REXX Language

Above all, REXX is a complete high-level programming language with powerful facilities for handling text strings. It has logical constructs and many other properties of a structured language.

As mentioned previously, REXX programs are processed by an interpreter. This means that they are executed word for word and line by line. It also implies that when an error occurs, the program immediately halts and the exact position of the error is known. Another language which is often interpretive is BASIC. This language is quite unlike FORTRAN, where a program is first translated into machine code by a compiler, then subsequently loaded into memory, and executed. When an error occurs in compiled programs, it is not easy to trace the mistake that caused it. The primary disadvantage of interpreted programs is that they use far more system resources and execute more slowly than compiled programs.

Components of the REXX language

All REXX programs are constructed from the following basic components:

- **Clauses or statements**—each program line will usually contain at least one statement (unless it is empty). REXX deals with one clause at a time.
- **Tokens**—each clause can be divided into tokens which are separated by blanks.
- **Expressions**—tokens may form expressions in a clause.
- **Instructions**—a clause or set of clauses containing special REXX keywords performing a task.
- **Assignments**—a clause defining a variable to contain a given value.
- **Separators**—semicolons (;) separate clauses on a line, a comma (,) continues a clause on the following line.

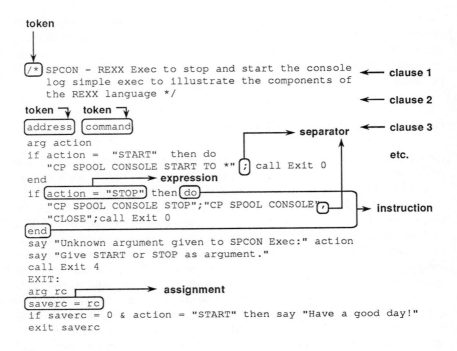

token

```
/* SPCON - REXX Exec to stop and start the console     ← clause 1
   log simple exec to illustrate the components of
   the REXX language */                                 ← clause 2
token ↴  token ↴
address  command                            → separator ← clause 3
arg action
if action =  "START"  then do                           etc.
   "CP SPOOL CONSOLE START TO *" ; call Exit 0
end                      → expression
if action = "STOP" then do
   "CP SPOOL CONSOLE STOP";"CP SPOOL CONSOLE ,          → instruction
   "CLOSE";call Exit 0
end
say "Unknown argument given to SPCON Exec:" action
say "Give START or STOP as argument."
call Exit 4
EXIT:
arg rc          → assignment
saverc = rc
if saverc = 0 & action = "START" then say "Have a good day!"
exit saverc
```

Figure 11-1 The elements of REXX are illustrated.

Examples of these elements are displayed in the SPCON program in Figure 11-1. The following is a more detailed description of each of these elements:

Clauses

One may distinguish five different varieties of clauses in a REXX program (see Figure 11-2):

1. Null Clauses—These are blank lines which are ignored by the REXX interpreter. They are generally used to improve the readability of a program.
2. Labels—They are defined by a token (e.g., EXIT in Figure 11-2), followed by a colon (:), and indicate the start of a subprogram or a branch point (reachable by the REXX Call or Signal instructions).

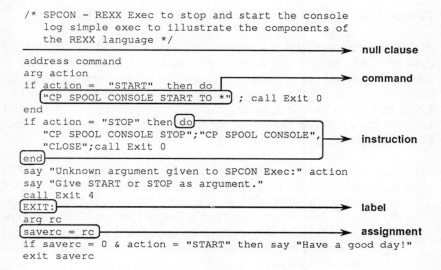

```
/* SPCON - REXX Exec to stop and start the console
   log simple exec to illustrate the components of
   the REXX language */
```
──➤ **null clause**
```
address command
arg action
if action =  "START"  then do
```
───➤ **command**
```
    "CP SPOOL CONSOLE START TO *" ; call Exit 0
end
if action = "STOP" then do
    "CP SPOOL CONSOLE STOP";"CP SPOOL CONSOLE",
    "CLOSE";call Exit 0
end
```
───➤ **instruction**
```
say "Unknown argument given to SPCON Exec:" action
say "Give START or STOP as argument."
call Exit 4
EXIT:
```
───➤ **label**
```
arg rc
saverc = rc
```
───➤ **assignment**
```
if saverc = 0 & action = "START" then say "Have a good day!"
exit saverc
```

Figure 11-2 Labels indicate the start of a subprogram or a branch point and are defined by a token followed by a colon.

3. Assignments—These are of the general form

   ```
   variable = value
   ```

   ```
   e.g.
   saverc = rc
   ```

4. Instructions—These are of the general form

   ```
   REXX keyword action [keyword]
   ```

   ```
   e.g.
   if xyz then do
       ...
   end
   ```

5. Commands—These are clauses possibly containing an expression that is evaluated and passed to an external environment such as CP, CMS, or XEDIT for execution (e.g., "CP SPOOL CONSOLE START TO *").

Tokens

A clause consists of tokens, which may be described as "islands of data in a sea of spaces." Every item delimited by blanks inside a clause is defined as a token. The special characters—comma (,), semicolon (;), and colon (:)—are also used as token delimiters; i.e., EXIT in Figure 11-2 is a token since it is preceded by a blank and followed by a ":." The five most commonly occurring different varieties of tokens are (see Figure 11-3):

1. Comments—Any text between an opening (/*) and a closing (*/) is a comment and is ignored by the REXX interpreter. A REXX program must start with a comment. (This is the mechanism by which CMS determines that a file of filetype EXEC is written in REXX.) The two characters composing the comment delimiters should not be separated, otherwise they would become two different tokens.

2. Strings—Any text delimited by single (') or double (") quotes (e.g., "START") is a string. An empty string, e.g., " " is called the null string. In order to include quotes inside a string which

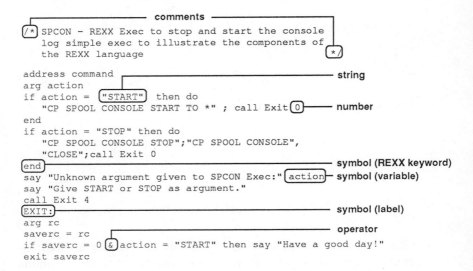

Figure 11-3 The most commonly occurring varieties of tokens are illustrated.

uses them as a delimiter, simply repeat them. A string may not contain more than 250 characters.

3. Symbols—These have the following properties:
   - They are composed from any combination of EBCDIC characters (A-z,0-9,$.!?); e.g., "freD is a valid symbol.
   - Lowercase letters are translated to uppercase (unless placed inside quotes); i.e., "freD = "FRED.
   - If a symbol does not start with a period (.) or a digit (0-9), it may be used as a variable and it may be assigned a value (e.g., saverc = rc).
   - It may be a label (EXIT:) or a REXX keyword (arg, if, do, etc.).

4. Numbers—Valid numbers consist of one or more digits preceded by the plus (+) or minus (-) sign, optionally including a decimal point. Symbols may be defined to be numbers, but a number cannot be the name of a variable (otherwise it would be possible to redefine numbers; e.g., 0=-1). REXX is a typeless language; i.e., there are no integer or real variables. All numbers are considered as character strings.

5. Operators—The characters +,-,/,%,*,|,&,=,~,>, < are operator tokens. Clauses (after removal of redundant blanks and comments) may consist of a combination of tokens no longer than 500 characters.

Expressions

An expression is composed of terms and operators. There are three specific varieties of terms:

1. Strings—These are identified by a pair of delimiting quotes or double quotes; e.g., "START." Such strings are also known as literal constants.

2. Symbols—These may be variables, in which case they are replaced by their value; e.g., in Figure 11-4 the variable "action" will have the value "START" or "STOP." If a symbol does not have a value, it will be translated to uppercase; i.e., the default value of a symbol is its name in uppercase.

3. Function calls—These may be added anywhere in an expression and have the general form:

```
function-name( [expression][,[expression]]... )
```

where function-name is a string or a symbol. The expressions are separated by commas and compose the function argument list. The use of functions and function names in expressions is analogous to that in other high-level programming languages. For example, the ABS function returns the absolute value of a numeric value. Therefore, X = ABS(' -0.414') assigns to the variable X the value 0.414.

Each operator acts on two terms (except for prefix operators, which act on the term following it). There are four varieties of operators/operations:

1. String Concatenation—Concatenation takes place between any two strings, combining them to form a single string. One may concatenate two strings with a blank or without a blank (using abuttal or the symbol | |). For example, if a variable named Action contains the value "START," then Action "1" (Action concatenated with the literal constant "1" with an intervening blank) contains the value START 1; Action"1" (Action concatenated with the literal constant "1" with no intervening blank) contains the value START1; Action| |"1" (Action, "1" and the | | operator) contains the value START1.

2. Arithmetic Operators—REXX has seven arithmetic operators that may be used between numeric strings. The majority of these operators are similar to those of other programming languages.

+	Add
-	Subtract
*	Multiply
/	Divide
%	Integer Division
//	Modulo Division
**	Exponentiation

3. Comparative Operators—Comparisons may be made between any two strings. If the result of the comparison is true, the value 1 is returned; otherwise 0 is returned. The results of comparative operations are quite sensitive to the string characteristics of REXX and can lead to erroneous results. There are nine comparative operators/operations in REXX. For example, given the variable Action = "START," the following comparisons can be defined:

==	True if the terms are exactly equal including blanks and leading zeros; e.g., Action == " START " is False.
=	True if the terms are equal after removing leading and trailing blanks and leading zeros; e.g., Action = " START " is True.
~== or /==	True if the terms are not exactly equal (the inverse of ==); e.g., Action /== " START " is True.
~= or /=	not equal (the inverse of =); e.g., Action /= " START " is False.
>	greater than; e.g., 5 > 3 is True.
<	less than; e.g., 5 < 3 is False.
<> or ><	greater than or less than (but not equal); e.g., 5 >< is True.
>= or /<	greater than or equal to, but not less than; e.g., 5 >= 3 is True.
<or />	less than or equal to, but not greater than; e.g., 5 <= 3 is False.

4. Logical (Boolean) Operators—These act between two logical terms; i.e., variables or strings with the value 1 ("True") or 0 ("False"). The result of a logical operation is always 1 or 0. There are four logical operators in REXX:

&	AND. The result is "1" if both terms are True; e.g., SaveRC = 0 & Action = "START" is True.
|	Inclusive OR. The result is "1" if either term is True; e.g., SaveRC = 0 | Action = "START" is True.
&&	Exclusive OR. The result is "1" if either (but not both) of the terms is True; e.g., Action = "START" && SaveRC = 0 is False.

Expression evaluation is from left to right, evaluating first expressions in parentheses and following the usual algebraic precedence rules for operators:

~,/,-,+	Unary prefix operators
**	Exponentiation
*,/,%,//	Multiplication and Division
" ",||	Concatenation, with or without an intervening blank
=,<,>,/=, etc.	Comparison operators
&	And
|,&&	Or and exclusive or

Instructions

Instructions are identified by a REXX keyword, or a group of REXX keywords, specifying a particular task. For example:

```
if A = B then do
     call subroutine
     XX = function(Y)

end
```

"if", "then", "do", "call" and "end" are REXX keywords.

Assignments

A variable is a symbol that may change its value during the course of the execution of a REXX program. For example, it may be useful to make a variable assignment at the beginning of an EXEC file (i.e., initialization) and then allow the value to be changed multiple times during processing. If another execution is required using a different value, the variable needs to be changed in only one place (i.e., where it was initialized). This process is called assigning a value to a variable. An assignment has the following general form:

```
symbol = expression
```

This statement in interpreted as follows: Replace the current value of the symbol with the value resulting from the evaluation of the expression.

An expression may be any operation which results in a value that can be associated with a symbol. Note that the occurrence of an assignment operator (=) indicates to REXX that the clause which follows is an expression. There are four types of symbols which occur in expressions:

1. Constant symbols—A constant symbol is a symbol that starts with a digit (0-9) or a period. For example, 165&$7 is a valid constant symbol. Constant symbols may not be used as variables.
2. Simple symbols—A simple symbol does not start with a period or a digit. For example, in the preceding examples Action is a valid simple symbol. Simple symbols may be used as variables.
3. Compound symbols—A compound symbol does not start with a period or digit and has at least one period in it with characters on either side. Before the symbol is used in an expression, the values of the simple symbols on either side of the period are substituted. For example, if i=2 and Action = "START," then Action.i will contain the value START.2. Compound symbols may be used as variables.
4. Stems—A stem contains one period, which is the last character. It may not start with a digit or period. For example, Action. is a valid stem; Action. = " " would set all variables that start with the stem Action. to the null string. Stems may be used as variables.

Assignments are very common and flexible clauses. The assigned value is substituted for any symbols when REXX interprets a clause.

A symbol without any assigned value is unchanged and is translated to uppercase.

Separators

Separators are defined as special characters which indicate the ending or continuation of a clause. It should be noted that:

• Normally each clause occupies one physical program line;
• Multiple clauses on one line are separated by a ";" (semi-colon);

• One clause spanning more than one line is continued with a "," (comma) at the end of each line to be continued. The continuation "," is not interpreted as a meaningful part of the clause.

Interpretation of a REXX Program

When a REXX program is being interpreted, each clause is subjected to two processes.

1. Translation—In general all components, except strings, are automatically translated to uppercase. Subsequently,

   a. Comments are ignored;
   b. Substitution occurs; each token is checked to see if it is a variable, in which case it is replaced by its value. Variables which have not been previously referenced are dynamically defined.

2. Execution—There remain only three types of clauses that require some action:
   a. Instructions recognizable by REXX keywords are executed;
   b. Assignments are made. These are identified by the "=" operator; all variables occurring in assignments change their value.
   c. System commands are executed. Any string that is not recognized as any of the other clause types is passed on to the calling environment for execution (i.e., CMS or XEDIT).

Very few programming languages include the concept of recursive interpretation. In REXX, this is accomplished by the Interpret instruction. This instruction can be used to initiate additional scanning of a clause, thereby treating what had been perfectly innocent data as a program fragment. For example:

```
Data="NewValue"
interpret Data "= 5"
```

will build the string "NewValue = 5" and execute NewValue = 5; the result being that the variable "NewValue" is assigned the value "5."

The REXX Environment Model

REXX is usable as a command or macro language for any application which has internal commands. It is also an extremely effective programming language due to the fact that it can utilize separately compiled program packages as REXX subprograms. These capabilities are possible due to what is referred to as the REXX Environment Model.

The recognition and the understanding of this model can be of great use to the author of a REXX program and/or to anyone who wishes to understand a REXX program.

The elements of the Environment Model are:

- There are essentially no illegal commands or statement forms in REXX (there may, however, be expressions which are illegal syntactically).
- Commands and statement forms can be categorized into those which are meaningful to the REXX interpreter and those which are not.
- Commands or statement forms which REXX does not understand are passed to the underlying environment in which REXX is executing. This "passing" uses the command interface defined for this environment.

When a REXX program is called from a certain environment, e.g., CMS or XEDIT, this will be the default environment in which commands will be executed. Notice that an EXEC file executed from the XEDIT environment will have been passed on to CMS by XEDIT, thus making CMS the calling environment.

This is called the addressed environment. Executing commands inside REXX programs may be achieved via a clause of the form

```
expression;
```

Expression will be evaluated, resulting in a character string which does not represent a legitimate REXX operation and is, therefore, submitted for execution in the addressed environment; for example, "CP SPOOL CONSOLE START TO *" in Figure 11-4.

After execution of the command, control is returned to the interpreter after setting a return code appropriate for the addressed environment. This return code is assigned to a special REXX variable, RC. EXECs should check the value of this variable in the event

expression   instruction

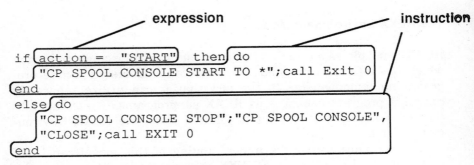

```
if action = "START"  then do
    "CP SPOOL CONSOLE START TO *";call Exit 0
end
else do
    "CP SPOOL CONSOLE STOP";"CP SPOOL CONSOLE",
    "CLOSE";call EXIT 0
end
```

Figure 11-4 An example of an expression.

alternative action is required. For example, the following EXEC issues the STATE command and displays a message when RC=28 was
returned (i.e., a file was not found). In this example, the calling environment is CMS; for XEDIT macros the procedure is similar.

```
/* RCTEST EXEC to show the use of the RC variable */
arg Fn Ft Fm
"STATE" Fn Ft Fm
if Rc = 0 then do
    say "File" Fn Ft Fm "exists."
    call Exit 0
end
if Rc = 28 then do
    say "File" Fn Ft Fm "not found."
    call Exit 28
end
say "Return code" Rc "from the STATE command."
call Exit Rc

Exit:
arg Rc
exit Rc
```

The previous explanation of CMS processing is actually over-sim-
plified. For example, in the case of the clause "STATE" Fn Ft Fm,
additional processing does occur at the CMS level. After substitution
of the variables Fn, Ft, and Fm, the complete string is passed to
CMS for execution. At this time CMS analyzes "STATE" with respect
to the CMS command resolution:

1. If an EXEC file named STATE EXEC is found, it is executed.

2. If STATE is defined as a synonym for an EXEC file, that EXEC is executed.
3. If STATE is a resident CMS command, it is executed.
4. If STATE is a MODULE (compiled program), it is executed.
5. If none of the above actions occur, STATE is passed to CP for resolution and possible execution.

Thus, if an EXEC named STATE EXEC is found on any minidisk accessed by the virtual machine in which CMS is running, this EXEC is executed. In order to avoid this, the command environment should be used. This environment may be defined by adding the clause address command at the beginning of the program. In this way, the entire program is placed in the command environment. The command environment is strongly recommended for all EXEC files in order to make them more efficient and more predictable. It implies that all strings go directly to CMS for execution and are processed according to the VM command form:

```
        Processor CommandName ArgumentList ( OptionList
   e.g., EXEC FILELIST * * B ( APPEND
```

Therefore, EXEC invocations must be prefaced by the processor name EXEC, e.g., "EXEC STATE" Fn Ft Fm; and CP commands must be prefaced by the processor name CP. For example, in Figure 11-3, due to "address command" if the CP were omitted from the SPOOL command, that command would fail.

The Environment Model is indicative of why REXX is potentially system and hardware dependent. It is, in this way, capable of passing commands to any system which is capable of supporting its execution (i.e., "running it").

Critical to the success of this model is REXX's emphasis on symbolic processing. The analysis of clauses, statements, and commands within this model depends on the ability to parse, interpret, and make substitutions symbolically.

REXX Data Typing and Data Structures

As has been mentioned, data values are typeless symbols, and if a symbol looks like a number it can be used in calculations (with rules about maximum integer size, fuzz, and rounding set by the user or defaulted). However, Cowlishaw makes the point that data typing is not excluded from future implementations, "though at present there seems to be little call for this. . . . Strong typing, in which the values a variable may take are tightly constrained, has become a fashionable attribute for languages over the last ten years. In this author's opinion, the greatest advantage of strong typing is for the interfaces between program modules. Errors within modules that would be detected by strong typing (and would not be detected from context) are much rarer and in most cases do not justify the added program complexity." ([3], p. 331)

Cowlishaw's concept of how type checking would be implemented is interesting. He envisions "ASSERT-like instructions that assign data type checking to variables during execution flow" (ibid.). This implies that checking could be controlled and only that which was desired would be used. It also implies that types could still change dynamically and the checking facilities could be made to anticipate that change.

Considering their "typelessness," REXX variables are fundamentally scalar (one name, one value) in nature. It would, therefore, appear impossible to define any type of data structure using such variables.

In lieu of well-defined data structures, REXX allows the user to define "families" of variables using compound symbols and stems. The definition of such families (i.e., data structures) is quite simple, but can be extremely effective.

Compound symbols in REXX are symbols containing a period (.) or periods. That portion of the symbol to the left of the period defines a stem. That portion to the right of the period identifies a value specifying an element within the family of symbols identified by the stem (like a subscript, but actually far more). For example, "Line." indicates the presence of a stem variable named Line. "Line.Current" is a member of the family of variables defined by "Line." The stem variable is basically dimensionless in that any declaration of its size, shape, or permissible element values is not required. "Line.Current" would seem to imply that "Line." is a one-dimensional data structure. This is inaccurate in that "Line." could also have a member named "Line.Old.1." Given a conventional interpretation of data structures in programming languages, such a definition would be ambiguous in that it implies that one element of "Line.," namely "Line.Current" is scalar (one-dimensional) and another element, "Line.Old" is structured. In REXX, however, this is possible, due primarily to the fact that REXX variables are dynamically allocated upon their first reference. Therefore, "Line.Old.1" has no logical relationship to "Line.Current" other than reference via their common stem.

In the analysis of compound symbols, value substitutions occur as with scalar variables except that the periods operate as symbol delimiters. Therefore, the single symbol "Line.Old" will be analyzed in terms of the two symbols "Line" and "Old."

Despite the possible convoluted data structures, compound variables in REXX are generally used in a way consistent with that of simple array data structures in other languages (e.g., Line.1, Line.2, Line.3, etc.). Many of the examples which will follow in this chapter illustrate use in this manner.

REXX Control Abstractions and Keyword Instructions

The REXX programming language is oriented to a "single-entry, single-exit" programming methodology. The language control structures represent carefully designed structured programming concepts embodied in a syntax which completely forbids the unconditional transfer (i.e., GO TO statement) and makes the user like it. The need for a GO TO instruction has been completely eliminated by providing unique instructions for accomplishing particular "acceptable" operations which would otherwise justify its inclusion. Certain keyword strings provide the syntactical basis as a programming language. These keywords provide the capability for compound statement construction, selection (conditional) processes, and repetition processes. These operations are similar in form and function to those of other programming languages which emphasize a structured program approach (e.g., Pascal, FORTRAN 77, etc.).

Conditional processing is accomplished in REXX by use of the If instruction, optionally accompanied by Else:

```
If expression [;] Then instruction
[Else [;] instruction]
```

where the following rules apply:

- The "expression" must have a value 1 ("true") or 0 ("false").
- The Then is obligatory, followed by the instruction to be carried out if the expression is true.
- Else may optionally be given, followed by the instruction to be carried out if the expression is false.

The NOP instruction (NO-Operation) is useful when no operation should occur when a certain condition is met. For example,

```
if Action ~= START then NOP
```

This instruction is necessary as null clauses following Then are not allowed. Any valid comparative operators can be used in the expressions governing an If condition.

Loops are used to group instructions and optionally execute them repetitively. This is done with the Do ... End instruction. It may appear in several different forms depending upon its function. For example,

Simple Do Group:

```
Do
   instruction1
   instruction2
   ...
End
```

The instructions in the loop will be executed once only.

Simple Repetitive Do Group:

```
Do n|Forever [Until expru] | [While exprw]
   instruction1
   instruction2
End
```

Where n is any non-negative integer (or an expression resulting in this), the instructions in the loop will be executed n times, or Forever. If While or Until was given, these keywords must be followed by a logical expression (having the value 0 or 1). The loop is then executed Until a condition is true, or While a condition is true.

Controlled repetitive loops:

```
Do Name=expri [To exprt] [For exprf] [By exprb] [Until
expru]|[While exprw]
   instruction1
   instruction2
End [Name]
```

The controlled repetitive loop at least contains a control variable, given by Name, which is assigned an initial value by expri.

If no other keywords are given, the control variable is incremented by 1 and the loop is executed forever.

Execution may be halted by giving a value following the To, For, Until, or While keywords. The values following To and For are numbers indicating the value of the control variable when the loop is to terminate (To) and the number of times the loop should be executed (For) respectively.

If the name of the control variable is given on the End statement, REXX will check whether there is a matching Do statement. This is very useful inside nested loops.

The Leave instruction is used to end a (repetitive) loop regardless of any condition controlling the loop being met. Control passes to the next clause after end. Leave is the acceptable manner for exiting from a Do Forever loop.

The Iterate instruction is used to interrupt the current iteration through a loop. Control is returned to the top of the Do loop.

There is no Go To instruction since leaving a loop in that manner would mean the loop would never terminate. This is due to the fact that scoping is entirely dynamic and not lexical. Likewise, once a loop has been exited, it cannot be reentered.

The Signal instruction can also be used to exit from active loop constructs. This instruction is designed to be used with REXX subprograms and is discussed later in this chapter.

The Exit instruction terminates an EXEC immediately when it is encountered. The format is:

```
Exit [expression]
```

The string in "expression" is passed back to the calling environment. This allows a return code to be set; e.g., Exit 4 would result in the variable Rc being set to 4 in the calling EXEC file or XEDIT macro.

Exit instructions are necessary to allow termination before the last line of a program. Otherwise the execution will continue to the last line of the program.

The REXX Input/Output Model

The REXX input/output model incorporates the use of simplistic, device-independent input and output data streams in a manner very similar to that of Pascal. Application of this model presents a system-independent view of how REXX programs acquire input data

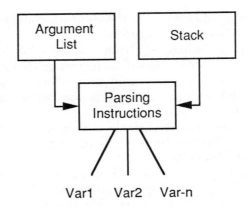

Figure 11-5 The elements of the REXX input model.

and output program values. Figure 11-5 is a graphical representation of the elements of the REXX Input Model.

The Program Argument List

The first element of the REXX input model is the argument list. The argument list is a special form of input consistent with the expected form of many REXX applications (i.e., REXX EXECs are supposed to operate like system commands which generally have arguments, options, etc.).

Values in the argument list are provided to the REXX program when it is executed (invoked). Program statements are used to capture and parse values included within the argument list.

The REXX Arg and Parse Arg instructions take an argument list (i.e., the string following the EXEC name on the command line) and parse that list according to a specified template. These instructions are non-destructive in that the original argument list is retained. The specified template can be as simple as a list of program variable names for which a one-to-one mapping between argument values and template variables is accomplished. More sophisticated parsing may be accomplished using pattern matching, absolute and relative column matching, and parsing after the evaluation of an expression. Provisions are also made for the "capturing" of extraneous argument list elements and the "skipping" of elements. All of these parsing operations in REXX emphasize its fundamental reliance on string and character manipulation procedures.

Using the Stack for Input

The second element of the REXX input model is the stack. One of the fundamental elements of CMS is a two-part storage area called the console stack (or more simply "the stack"). Many CMS operations rely upon the stack as a processing area. The console stack itself is sub-divided into two buffers:

• the Terminal Input Buffer
• the Program Stack

The function of the Terminal Input Buffer is to retain lines keyed in from the virtual console (i.e., the user's terminal) until CMS has the opportunity to process them. Line processing operates in a FIFO (First-In-First-Out) fashion.

The Program Stack serves as temporary storage for lines (or files) being exchanged by programs executing in CMS. CMS commands and EXEC control statements are used to manage the Program Stack and data flow through it.

The order or sequence in which CMS normally reads and processes input lines within the stack is well-defined:

• sequential processing of lines within the buffer areas within the Program Stack
• sequential processing of lines from the Terminal Input Buffer
• processing of lines keyed directly from the virtual console/user terminal

Figure 11-6 is a pictorial representation of the Console Stack. This picture illustrates from the "top-down" how the processing of lines within the stack occurs. The curved lines represent the REXX instructions which perform operations on the stack.

CMS also allows the Program Stack to be partitioned into dedicated working buffers. In this manner stack operations may be directed only at a particular portion (buffer) of the stack. This capability may be used to affect the processing sequence of lines within the Program Stack.

Such partitioning is accomplished using the CMS commands MAKEBUF and DROPBUF. MAKEBUF is used to create a new buffer within the Program Stack. Subsequent stack operations will be localized to that buffer independent of the status of the remainder of the Program Stack. DROPBUF is used to discard a particular buffer or range of buffers from the Program Stack. As before, it is

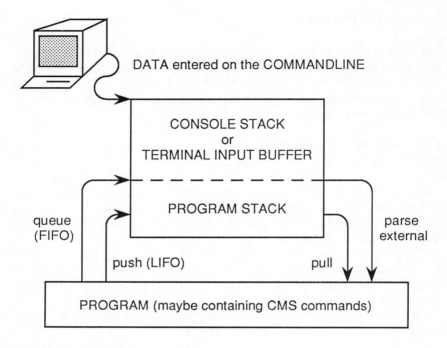

Figure 11-6 The console stack.

important to emphasize that MAKEBUF and DROPBUF are CMS operations and not REXX instructions. Their use clearly illustrates how REXX can take advantage of operations native to the environment within which it operates. An example of the effect of partitioning of the Program Stack resulting from the use of MAKEBUF is illustrated in Figure 11-7.

Use of the Program Stack permits REXX programs to receive input from the terminal or from any other facility (CMS, other EXECs, etc.) which has access to the Program Stack and is capable of inserting values on it.

The REXX Pull and Parse Pull instructions read a line of data from the Program Stack. If the Program Stack is empty, then according to the stack processing sequence, a terminal read will be invoked. The line of data acquired by either of the Pull instructions is processed with respect to a specified template in the same manner as the Arg and Parse Arg instructions.

In the following example, the values of file_mode and file_type are read from the terminal when the Program Stack is empty. The

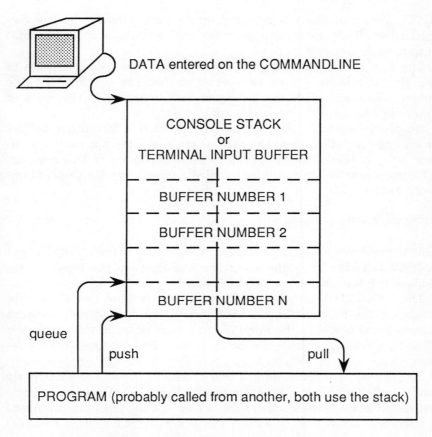

Figure 11-7 The effect of partitioning of the Program Stack.

apparent effect of this operation is simple terminal input or input via a standard input data stream.

```
/* SAMPLE EXEC */
pull file_mode file_type
"ACCESS 194 " file_mode
"LISTFILE * " file_type file_mode
exit
```

Virtual Console/Terminal Output

The first element of the REXX Output model involves interactive output to the virtual console/terminal. In the CMS implementation of

REXX, this operation in provided, quite simplistically, by the Say instruction. This instruction provides access to a standard terminal output stream.

The Say instruction, when followed by an expression, outputs to the virtual console a scanned version of that expression. All value substitutions are made in the expression according to the rules of scanning and analysis of statements and clauses.

No provisions are made via the Say instruction for output to files or any devices other than the virtual console. This apparent limitation actually reinforces REXX's device-independence. In this manner, all device-dependent output is handled through the REXX Environment Model.

Using the Stack for Output

The second element of the REXX Output model is the stack. Output operations to the Program Stack are analogous to the input operations which have been described previously.

The REXX Push and Queue instructions are used to output data strings to the Program Stack. Each instruction is used to implement a conceptual model in the mind of the programmer of the stack as a First-In-First-Out (FIFO) device or a Last-In-First-Out (LIFO) device.

The Queue instruction adds a line of data to the end of a currently active buffer within the Program Stack. This is FIFO queuing. Comparably, the Push instruction adds a line of data to the beginning of a currently active buffer within the Program Stack. This is LIFO queuing.

Stack Status

While the Program Stack is an important part of the REXX Input/Output Model, it must again be emphasized that it is a component of CMS and not peculiar to REXX. Therefore, operations in REXX programs utilizing the stack can have effects external to those programs. A simple case in point involves any data which remains in the stack upon completion of a REXX program. Inasmuch as CMS examines the stack contents prior to input from the terminal, these contents will be interpreted by CMS. In most cases these stacked lines are not legitimate CMS or CP commands, thereby leading to a series of CMS error messages (e.g., UNKNOWN CP/CMS COMMAND).

It is, therefore, often of interest during the execution of a REXX program to know the status of (i.e., the current number of lines) the Program Stack. A simple case in point is the fact that this number represents the maximum number of Pull instructions which can be executed without terminal input.

Two facilities are available to REXX programmers for obtaining such information: SENTRIES and QUEUED().

SENTRIES is a CMS command which determines the number of lines currently in the Program Stack. When the SENTRIES command is issued, CMS returns the number of lines in the Program Stack (but not the Terminal Input Buffer) as a return code. QUEUED() is a REXX function which will also return the number of lines in the Program Stack at the time that the function is invoked. The number is returned as the value of the function name.

Additional applications and examples using the stack are presented later in this chapter.

Broader Applications of the Parse Instruction

The Parse instruction, in general, is used to assign data (from various sources) to one or more variables:

```
Parse [Upper] Operand [template]
```

The Arg and Pull operands of the Parse instruction have already been described as elements of the REXX Input Model. Other useful operands of Parse are:

- Parse External—The next string from the terminal input buffer is parsed while the program stack is left unaltered. If the console stack is empty, a console read results. This operation is useful for forcing input to come from the terminal.
- Parse Source—The data parsed contains the information on the source of the program being executed. It contains, in order, the environment (CMS), the function (EXEC, COMMAND, SUBROUTINE, FUNCTION), the filename, the filetype, the filemode and the calling program. This is very useful for writing execname independent code, as the name may always be put in the same variable.
- Parse Value [expression] With [template]—The expression is evaluated and the result is parsed according to the template following the With. For example,

```
Parse Value "" With A B C
```

initializes the variables A, B, and C to a null string.
* Parse Var Name—The value of the variable "Name" is parsed; it may also occur in the template, providing a very useful trick to remove words from a string one by one:

```
Parse Var options option options
```

will parse the value of "Options" with the template "Option Options"; i.e., remove the first word of Options and place it in Option.

Other Input/Output Models

The Input/Output model described in *The REXX Language, A Practical Approach to Programming* is not completely implemented in the CMS version of REXX. This model includes facilities for:

* a character input stream (CHARIN)
* a character output stream (CHAROUT)
* a line input stream (LINEIN)
* a line output stream (LINEOUT)
* a facility for counting the number of characters currently remaining in a character input stream (CHARS)

REXX Subprograms

Subprograms (functions, subroutines/procedures) can be used in REXX programs to:

* accomplish modular program design;
* isolate program fragments which are used multiple times in order to avoid code duplication;
* build a user-defined function and/or procedure library to complement the intrinsic REXX function library;
* define special function routines (e.g., for escape, error-trapping, etc.)

User Defined Internal and External Subprograms

The Call instruction allows control to be passed from the main program to a subprogram. When this program has terminated, control will be returned to the next clause after the call

```
call Name [expression [, expression [,...]]]
```

where "Name" is the name of the subroutine. They may be:

• Internal routines, where "Name" is the label indicating the beginning of the subroutine.
• Built-in functions or functions from the REXX local function package.
• External programs; if "Name" is not found as an internal routine function, REXX will search for any EXEC or module of that name.

Expression is an argument for the subroutine. Each string, separated by commas, is passed as a different argument to the subroutine.

A call is ended by the first Return or Exit instruction found or, if it is an external program, by the end of that program.

```
Return [expression]
```

The string defined by expression is placed in the special variable Result. All variables are shared when the subroutine is internal.

The following EXEC illustrates how the Call instruction should be used:

```
/* Callex—example of how CALL should be used */
address "COMMAND"
arg Operand "(" Option
if Operand = "" then do
   call GetArg 'OPERAND'
   Number = Result
end
else Number = Operand
if Option = "" then do
   call GetArg 'OPTION'
   Letter = Result
end
else Letter = Option
```

```
say Number Letter
call Exit 0

GetArg:
arg Type
Answer = " "
if Type = "OPERAND" then do while Answer = " "
   say "Please give a number (Q To QUIT) =>"
   pull Answer
end
if Type = "OPTION" then do while Answer = " "
   say "Please give a letter (Q To QUIT) =>"
   pull Answer
end
if Answer = "Q" then call Exit 4
return Answer
Exit:
arg Rc
exit Rc
```

A procedure is a special internal subroutine which does not share variables with the main exec. The first REXX keyword following the label is the Procedure instruction:

```
Name_of_Subroutine: procedure [ expose Name [Name ...]]]
```

The expose operand allows one or more variables to be selected which should be shared with the main program. The subroutine Get-Arg in the previous example is an ideal candidate for a procedure since the EXEC arguments and options could be protected from undesirable side effects.

Sometimes it is necessary to call a subprogram or procedure without returning to the clause immediately following the call. This may be done with the Signal instruction:

```
signal Name
signal on condition
```

Where Name is the label value where the program should branch. This form of the Signal instruction should only be used if a return from this routine is not required. A very useful form of the Signal instruction is the Signal on condition form. Condition is the name of a special label to which control is passed when a certain condition has been met. The four possible conditions are:

- Error—Control is passed to the label Error if any command has a non-zero return code.
- Halt—Control is passed to the label Halt if the user types HI during the execution of the EXEC file.
- NoValue—Control is passed to the label NoValue if an uninitialized variable is encountered.
- Syntax—Control is passed to the label Syntax if a REXX error is detected.

These four conditions become particularly useful when they are used in conjunction with the special REXX variable Sigl, which will contain the number of the line where the Signal instruction was invoked.

EXEC files should normally contain at least the Halt and NoValue Signal on conditions with appropriate subroutines. Sample EXECs which illustrate such use are presented later in this chapter.

When a variable has a certain number of different values, it may be tedious to select the desired one by using If statements as follows:

```
if Number = 1 then call Routine1
if Number = 2 then call Routine2
if Number = 3 then call Routine3
```

A more elegant way of doing this is with the Select instruction:

```
select
     when Number = 1 then call Routine1
     when Number = 2 then call Routine2
     when Number = 3 then call Routine3
     ...
     otherwise NOP
end
```

A similar technique can be used to write a "driver routine" within a REXX program. Such a routine would call a sequence of other subprograms under the appropriate conditions.

After executing any of the instructions following a When, control is passed to the next clause after the End. Each Select instruction needs at least one When and End and possibly an Otherwise clause. The following example could be part of a PROFILE XEDIT:

```
        "COMMAND EXTRACT /FTYPE"
        type = ftype.1
        Select
            When type = "EXEC" | type = "XEDIT" Then "SET CASE MIXED IG-
    NORE"
            When type = "MEMO" | type = "SCRIPT" Then Do
            "COMMAND SET VARBLANK ON"
        End
        When type = "SGML" Then Do
            "COMMAND SET VARBLANK ON"
            "COMMAND SET SPILL WORD"
            "COMMAND SET CASE MIXED"
        End
        Otherwise Do
            "COMMAND SET TRUNC *"
            "COMMAND SET SERIAL OFF"
        End
    End
End
```

REXX Functions

A symbol immediately followed by a bracketed expression is defined as a function (there must be no blank between function name and bracket):

```
function( [expression] [, [expression]] ...)
```

The expressions (separated by commas) between parentheses are called the arguments to the function. A function call may be included anywhere in an expression by simply including its name followed by parentheses as shown above. For example:

```
Log="DATE"('O')||" & "||"XNAME"('USERID')
```

Internal functions may be used instead of subroutines; the only difference is that a value must be returned (as an expression on the Return instruction). For example:

```
/* factor EXEC */
arg X
/* either (a): */
say X "! =" "FACTORIAL"(X)
```

```
/* or   (b): */
call "FACTORIAL"(X)
Say X "! =" Result
exit


Factorial: procedure
arg N
if N = 0 then return 1
return "FACTORIAL"(N-1)*N
```

The REXX Function Library

A large measure of REXX's flexibility is due to its built-in function library. The functions in this library primarily perform three types of operations of particular use to a command and macro language. They also provide the variety of operations expected within a language which has a strong emphasis on string and character processing. These operations can be categorized as:

• Character Manipulation—example, "FIND" (string, phrase) returns the word number of the first word of the phrase in the string; otherwise it returns 0.
• Data Conversion—example, "D2X" (whole-number [,n]) converts a decimal value to the corresponding hexadecimal value.
• System Information—example, "QUEUED" () returns the number of lines remaining on the Program Stack.

The quotes around the function names in the above examples are included as a part of a REXX programming style discussed later in this chapter. The semantics of the language do not require their use.

For complete descriptions of each of the functions in this library, the REXX Reference Manual should be consulted.

External Subprograms

The power of the REXX function library and the extensibility of the language through subprograms provides a high level of flexibility for the REXX user. However, if the Call instruction invokes a routine with a name that does not appear among the labels in a program, nor is found in the built-in function library, REXX assumes it to be external routine and searches for it elsewhere. External routines may be written in any language, including REXX, which supports the system dependent interfaces used by the interpreter and must return data to the calling routine.

The following guidelines should be considered when using the Call instruction in this manner:

- Call is best used for passing control to logically independent parts of REXX programs (i.e., subprograms).
- Call may be confusing when used with the REXX built-in function library.
- Call should not be used with system modules.
- For external REXX programs, it is better to invoke them directly (i.e., by name) rather than using Call.

For external routines, all variables are local. For internal routines all variables are global unless otherwise specifically designated. Data hiding is only tangentially addressed in the REXX definition. The problem is recognized and the Expose mechanism in routines for showing the variables of a called routine to the caller is the only solution. Because the language is truly dynamically scoped, the problem of dealing with the variables of another, still active, block not in the execution stack above the current position does not arise. The caller's variables will be shadowed by the local ones if there is a name conflict.

The TRACE Instruction

There is a powerful tracing facility specified as part of the REXX language. Commands can be issued from the console for interactive debugging and intermediate results of computations can be traced if needed. These actions are controlled by the REXX Trace instruction.

To the beginning REXX programmer, Trace offers an excellent facility for reinforcing the rules by which REXX scans and analyses statement lines. The following options are available using the Trace instruction:

- N(ormal)—any environment command resulting in a negative return code is traced after execution (i.e., the commands that are rejected).
- E—any environment command resulting in a non-zero return code is traced after execution.

- C—any environment commands are traced before execution and any non-zero return code is shown.
- A(ll)—all statements are traced before execution.
- R(esults)—all statements are traced before execution together with the final result.
- I(ntermediate)—same as R; but all terms and intermediate results are traced.
- L(abels)—trace only labels during execution.
- S—all remaining statements are traced without being executed.
- O(ff)—nothing is traced.
- !—toggle environment command execution.
- ?—toggle interactive tracing.

Many of these options are for sophisticated program analysis and may, therefore, present little useful information to the beginning REXX user.

REXX statements are traced and results displayed during program execution using the following format:

Every statement traced is displayed with indentation indicative of its logical nested depth within the program. Any control codes (defined as EBCDIC values less than X"40") are replaced by a question mark (?) in order to avoid any interference they might initiate at the console. Results (if requested) are indented an extra two spaces and are enclosed in double quotes so that leading and trailing blanks are apparent.

The first statement traced on any line is preceded by its line number. If the line number is greater than 99999, it is truncated on the left and the truncation is indicated by a prefix of ?.

All lines displayed during tracing have a three-character prefix to identify the type of data being traced. These prefixes are defined as follows:

-   identifies the source of a single clause

++   identifies a trace message; this may be the non-zero return code from a command, the prompt message when interactive debug is entered, an indication of a syntax error when in interactive debug, or the traceback clauses after a syntax error in the program

>>>   identifies the Result of an expression (for trace result), or the value assigned to a variable during parsing, or the value returned from a subroutine call

>.>   identifies the value "assigned" to a placeholder during parsing

The following prefixes are used only if Intermediates (trace intermediate) are being traced:

>C>   the data traced is the name of a compound variable, traced after substitution and before use, provided that the name had the value of a variable substituted into it

>F>   the data traced is the result of a function call

>L>   the data traced is a literal (string or uninitialized variable)

>O>   the data traced is the result of an operation on two terms

>P>   the data traced is the result of a prefix operation

>V>   the data traced is the contents of a variable

The following is an interesting example of the effects of the Address command as detected using the Trace instruction. The REXX program:

```
/* */
Trace All
"CP QUERY time"
"CP query time"
"cp query time"
Address "COMMAND"
"CP QUERY time"
"CP query time"
"cp query time"
```

yields the following results when traced:

```
        3 *-* "CP QUERY time"
          >>>    "CP QUERY time"
TIME IS 19:40:58 PST FRIDAY 08/28/87
CONNECT= 34:22:02 VIRTCPU= 001:05.75 TOTCPU= 002:04.51
        4 *-* "CP query time"
          >>> "CP query time"
TIME IS 19:40:58 PST FRIDAY 08/28/87
CONNECT= 34:22:02 VIRTCPU= 001:05.75 TOTCPU= 002:04.51
```

```
    5 *-* "cp query time"
      >>> "cp query time"
TIME IS 19:40:58 PST FRIDAY 08/28/87
CONNECT= 34:22:02 VIRTCPU= 001:05.75 TOTCPU= 002:04.51
    6 *-* Address "COMMAND"
    7 *-* "CP QUERY time"
      >>>   "CP QUERY time"
time NOT LOGGED ON
    +++ RC(45) ++       8 *-* "CP query time"
    >>>   "CP query time"
    +++ RC(1) ++        9 *-* "cp query time"
    >>> "cp query time"
    +++ RC(-3) ++
```

It will be left as an exercise to the reader to interpret these results.

CMS Facilities Useful in REXX

As the REXX Environment Model indicates, REXX programs are
able to utilize facilities native to the environment in which they execute. This section discusses two extremely powerful CMS facilities
which can be used to supplement REXX EXECs and XEDIT macros,
EXECIO, and GLOBALV.

The EXECIO Command

The CMS EXECIO facility is an extremely powerful (and often confusing) stack manipulation tool which can be used in REXX programs. The "CMS Reference Guide" should be consulted for a comprehensive discussion of EXECIO and all allowable parameters and
options.
  EXECIO is used primarily to accomplish three operations:

1. read CMS files from disk or the virtual reader to the Program
   Stack.
2. write lines from the Program Stack to a CMS disk file or to a
   virtual spool device (i.e., the virtual reader, punch, or printer).
   In some cases output data to be written can be supplied directly within the EXECIO option list.
3. initiate execution of CP commands and capture the results.

The following are examples of simple applications using EXECIO and brief explanations of their operation:

Example 1:

```
/* READIO EXEC to demonstrate the use of DISKR with EXECIO */
/* to read a file on disk              */
address "COMMAND"
"EXECIO * DISKR PROFILE EXEC A (STEM LINE. LOCATE /SET/"
do I = 1 to Line.0
   say Line.I
end
exit
```

This instruction uses EXECIO to locate the first occurrence of the string "SET" in the file PROFILE EXEC A. The LOCATE option would, under normal circumstances, stack two lines of information. The first would be the contents of the first line containing the string "SET" and the second the relative line number of that line. However, the STEM option instructs EXECIO to place these two lines in a structured variable with the stem Line. By definition, the "zeroth" element of this variable (Line.0) will contain the number of elements of Line. not containing their default values. In this case Line.0 will be equal to 2, Line.1 will be equal to the first line containing "SET" and Line.2 will be equal to the relative line number of that line.

Example 2:

```
/* FIO EXEC—to illustrate the EXECIO pointer */
address "COMMAND"
"EXECIO * DISKR PROFILE EXEC A (STEM LINE. LOCATE /SET/"
do I = 1 to Line.0
    say Line.I
end
"EXECIO * DISKR PROFILE EXEC A (STEM ALINE. LOCATE /SET/"
do I = 1 to Aline.0
    say Aline.I
end
exit
```

This example is identical with that of Example 1 except that it illustrates the use of the EXECIO pointer. The second use of

EXECIO in this EXEC (using stem Aline.) will locate the second occurrence of the string "SET" in the file PROFILE EXEC A.

Example 3:

```
/* READIO EXEC to demonstrate the use of DISKR with EXECIO */
/* to read from a file on disk */
address "COMMAND"
"EXECIO * DISKR PROFILE EXEC A (LIFO LOCATE /BREAKIN/"
do I=1 to "QUEUED"()
      pull Line.I
      say Line.I
end
```

The operation of this EXEC is similar to that of Example 1. Its function is to locate the first occurrence of the string "BREAKIN" in PROFILE EXEC A. However, the absence of the EXECIO option STEM specifies that the two lines resulting from the LOCATE will be placed in the Program Stack. The LIFO option will specify that the lines be placed Last-In-First-Out. The "QUEUED"() function will return the number of lines in the Program Stack (in this case two) and use that value for a range of subscripts of the variable Line. As a result, Line.1 will contain the relative line number of the first line containing "BREAKIN" (due to the LIFO) and Line.2 will contain the contents of that line.

Example 4:

```
/* WRITEIO—simple EXEC to illustrate writing to disk files */
/* using EXECIO    */
address "COMMAND"
"QUERY DISK (FIFO"
queue ""
"EXECIO * DISKW RANDOM FILE A"
"TYPE RANDOM FILE A"
exit
```

This example illustrates the use of EXECIO to write to files. The FIFO option to the CMS QUERY DISK command instructs that the results of that command be placed in the Program Stack First-In-First-Out. The Queue " " instruction places a null line on the stack FIFO. The EXECIO instruction reads these lines from the stack until the null line is encountered and writes them to the file RAN-

DOM FILE A. The execution of this EXEC yields the same results as the CMS command QUERY DISK with the addition that the results of that command are also placed in RANDOM FILE A. If the Queue " " instruction were omitted from this exec, a terminal read would result and a null line entry would be required in order to terminate the EXECIO write operation.

Example 5:

```
/* VARIO EXEC to illustrate writing the contents of a */
/* variable directly to a disk file          */
address "COMMAND"
Line = "A line of text"
"EXECIO 1 DISKW RANDOM FILE A (VAR LINE"
exit
```

In VARIO EXEC the current value of the variable Line is written directly to the file RANDOM FILE A. This is a result of the VAR option of EXECIO. There is no obvious use of the stack in this example as in the previous example.

Example 6:

```
/* ERRORIO EXEC to show how to use EXECIO to display EMSG */
/* messages */
address "COMMAND"
"ESTATE PROFILE EXEC"
if Rc = 28 then do
     "EXECIO 1 EMSG ( STRING BEBERR001E PROFILE EXEC not found."
     exit 28
end
```

ERRORIO EXEC illustrates how the EMSG parameter and the STRING option of EXECIO can be used to generate error messages during EXEC execution.

Example 7:

```
/* CPIO EXEC to show how to use EXECIO to capture the */
/* results of CP commands */
address "COMMAND"
"EXECIO 1 CP (VAR TIME STRING QUERY TIME"
exit
```

CPIO assigns to the variable Time the results of the CP command "QUERY TIME." The CP command is specified to EXECIO using the STRING option. If the VAR option were omitted in this example, the result would be placed in the Program Stack. This particular application is extremely useful since CP commands do not have stack options.

The GLOBALV Command

The GLOBALV (GLOBAL Variables) command addresses two primary needs:

* the need for several EXECs to share a common set of values.
* the need to retain those values, either temporarily or permanently, for subsequent use.

Values are often given names, describing what they represent, for easy reference. Although the values often vary, their names usually do not. The GLOBALV command processor builds and maintains group(s) of named, variable values in free storage for shared use by EXECs. EXECs "share" a value by referring to it by a common name. When requested, GLOBALV retrieves a variable(s) from the group(s) and places it in the Program Stack or in REXX variables for subsequent use by the requesting exec.

GLOBALV supports the use of more than one group. This allows for grouping distinct variables, that are either related or often used together, facilitating more efficient retrieval and more selective use. The "global variable group(s)," built by GLOBALV from a set of CMS GLOBALV-type files, exist throughout an IPL, unless explicitly purged or re-initialized.

When variables are defined or changed, the user decides whether the variables or changes are to:

* last for the current IPL only—variables are stored in virtual memory.
* last throughout an entire session (the duration of which is defined by the user)—variables are stored in a CMS file named SESSION GLOBALV.
* last permanently (i.e., across sessions)—variables are stored in a CMS file named LASTING GLOBALV.

The IBM documentation on GLOBALV suggests that SESSION GLOBALV is active under normal conditions within a session defined between LOGON and LOGOFF. This documentation is misleading in that such action implies the presence of a LOGOFF EXEC and a synonym (either System or User) for LOGOFF so that CMS will execute that EXEC instead of the CP LOGOFF command. Such EXEC would also contain a statement to erase the current SESSION GLOBALV file.

The following example illustrates the usefulness of GLOBALV in the definition of command parameter defaults.

```
/* TESTDEF EXEC to show how to retrieve and set globalv vari-
ables */
/* for use with the DEFAULTS command */
/* DEFAULTS SUPPORTED */
address "COMMAND"
/* get hold of the source name to make it name independent */
parse source . . Execname .
parse value "" with A B C
Set = 0
/* override exec's own defaults with GLOBALV defaults if they
exist */
"GLOBALV SELECT *EXEC GET" Execname
Execdef = "VALUE"(Execname)
if Execdef ~= " " & Execdef ~= "" then do
     parse var Execdef " " A " " B " " C " "
end
/* parse arguments that were given with the call         */
arg Operands   "(" Options
/* here the operands given on the commandline should be checked
*/
/* they override the defaults found in globalv or from the EXEC
*/
/* itself */
if operands ~= "" then parse var Operands A B C
/* first check the options - this EXEC only accepts */
/* the set and list options    */
do while Options ~= ""
     parse var Options Option Options
     if Options = "SET" then Set = "1"
     if Option = "LIST" then do
          if Execdef ~= " " & Execdef ~= "" then do
          /* re-retrieve for safety */
          parse var Execdef " " A " " B " " C " "
```

```
            if A ~= "" then say "Default for A=" A
            if B ~= "" then say "Default for B=" B
            if C ~= "" then say "Default for C=" C
          end
          else say "No defaults in effect for " Execname
          call Exit 0
      end
end
/* end of parsing of variables given on the command line  */
/* here the EXEC gives some prompts if info is needed  */
if A = "" | Set then do
    say "Enter value for A=>"
    pull A
end
if B = "" | Set then do
    say "Enter value for B=>"
    pull B
end
if C = ""| Set then do
    say "Enter value for C=>"
    pull C
end
/* set the GLOBALV defaults if required - now all variables have
*/
/* been gathered */
if Set then do
    Variables = " "||A||" "||B||" "||C||" "
     "GLOBALV SELECT *EXEC SETPL" Execname Variables
      call Exit 0
end
/* now the EXEC does what it is supposed to do          */
say "A=" A "B=" B "C= " C
call Exit 0

Exit:
arg Rc
exit Rc
```

For complete information about the features and use of GLOBALV, the "CMS Reference Guide" should be consulted.

XEDIT Macro Applications

The majority of applications discussed at this point involve the use of REXX programs as CMS EXEC files. The power of REXX to build XEDIT macros (subcommands) should not be overlooked.

All of the REXX features previously covered are also available in the writing of macros. This should be expected in that CMS EXECs should operate equivalently in XEDIT since XEDIT is a sub-environment of CMS.

There are, however, additional capabilities available to the authors of XEDIT macros that are not available in CMS EXECs.

Command, Extract, Macro, Read, Stack, and Transfer are XEDIT subcommands (not REXX instructions) that may be used to supplement the REXX Input Model in the XEDIT command environment. The complete details on their usage are available in the XEDIT reference materials. The following are examples of XEDIT macros utilizing these subcommands:

```
/* Sample XEDIT macro demonstrating use of the */
/* STACK subcommand. It examines the first two */
/* characters in the first line of a file. */
"COMMAND :1"
"COMMAND STACK 1"
pull Line
if "SUBSTR"(Line,1,2) = "/*" then
     say "This is beginning to look like REXX"
exit


/* Sample XEDIT macro demonstrating use of the */
/* READ subcommand. It reads a line from the */
/* stack (or terminal) and inserts it in a file.*/
"MAKEBUF"
"COMMAND READ"
pull Line
":1"
"INPUT" Line
"DROPBUF"
exit
```

Developing a REXX Programming Technique

It has been emphasized that one of the important features of REXX is environment independence. However, if the REXX applications being developed are CMS EXECs and XEDIT macros (as are most often the case), the interaction of REXX and the constituents of those environments cannot be overlooked. The elements of such interactions can be summarized as REXX programming techniques and are specifically directed toward minimizing translation errors within the REXX Environment Model.

It is important that a command name invocation (call) is consistent independent of the environment from which it is made. Therefore, the same filename for a CMS MODULE, EXEC, or XEDIT macro should not be used unless each performs the same operation or is part of the same facility. Failure to follow such consistency in naming can often result in different results in different environments.

The order of CMS command resolution should always be considered. Since CMS EXECs are executed before CMS MODULES in command resolution, EXECs may be used to "set up" the proper conditions for command execution.

Using lowercase or line editing characters in file identifiers should be avoided. While such practice may appear to be a secure way to avoid naming conflicts, problems may easily arise in a default CMS environment.

The filenames and command names of CP, CMS, XEDIT, and REXX should be avoided unless the intention with respect to CMS command resolution is clear. Certain instances such as the "set up" of procedures can be useful if implemented with care.

REXX Programming Style

Of comparable importance to a REXX programming technique is the development of a programming style to be followed. While REXX contains many of the elements of other high-level programming languages such as Pascal or PL/1, the programming styles peculiar to those languages are quite different. The flexibility of REXX can be deceiving with respect to the implementation of operations. A well-defined and adhered-to style is also extremely important from the perspective of documentation and maintenance. The readability of REXX programs should be extended from the program author to anyone else who may read the program.

Examples of Style Conventions

The following is an example of a REXX programming style. It is apparent that many of the elements of such a style are empirical and/or arbitrary. This is the style that has been used in the examples throughout this chapter. The most important element of such a style is consistency of use.

1. **Element:** All commands passed to CMS or XEDIT are capitalized and contained within double quotes (e.g., "MAKEBUF").

   Rationale: Capitalization of environmental commands is used for emphasis. Since REXX allows mixed mode expressions, all capital strings stand out for any reader. Enclosing such commands in quotes (the use of double quotes is arbitrary) insures that no accidental value substitution will occur for the command string in the analysis of the clause containing it.

2. **Element:** A consistent standard for the use of upper- and lowercase should be established. For example:

   • Environment commands in uppercase (as previously discussed)
   • REXX keywords in lowercase
   • REXX token names (variables and constants) in mixed case.

   Rationale: Once again, the key in this style is readability. Standardization of the use of case allows the reader to use case in order to obtain information about the program elements. The choice of mixed case for token names is to increase the flexibility of naming; for example, FirstVar relays more information and is more readable than FIRSTVAR or firstvar.

3. **Element:** Use structured indentation conventions as with compound statements in Do blocks, If statements, etc. (One of the XEDIT macro examples given in this can be used to do this automatically.)

   Rationale: A common programming technique in free-formatted structured languages (such as Pascal) is to use indentation in order to visually identify embedded program components. This practice increases the readability of programs and can be very useful in maintenance and debugging.

4. **Element:** Use internal program documentation (i.e., comments).

    Rationale: All rationales applicable to the commenting of programs (readability, maintainability, etc., are applicable to REXX programs. However, it must be remembered that REXX is an interpreted language, so comments do impact speed of execution. For example, comments contained within loops should be kept to a minimum.

5.   **Element:** Do not use command and option abbreviations in EXECs and macros.

    Rationale: For example, use "XEDIT," not "X." Command and option abbreviations are useful in interactive operations. However, in EXECs and macros, the advantages for their use (e.g., convenience, entry speed) is lost. Their use actually adds to program processing time in the underlying environment. In addition, such abbreviations may also be mistaken for program variables (such as the "X" above) unless the commands which contain them are exempt from substitution (i.e., enclosed in quotes).

6.   **Element:** A REXX EXEC or XEDIT macro should leave its calling environment unchanged unless its function was specifically to do otherwise. Example 1—The user environment, accessed disks, SET operations, GLOBALed operations, etc., should be restored. Example 2—The status of the Program Stack and its contents should be undisturbed.

    Rationale: User environment modifications made during the execution of an EXEC or macro should not be imposed on the user after execution of the process. Doing so may present the user with an unfamiliar and potentially disturbing working environment. Two EXECs which may be used to retain and restore user environments are given in the Examples.

7.   **Element:** EXECs should use appropriate CP/CMS return codes if possible. The following return codes are defined for CP/CMS commands: It is likely that many of them would not be applicable to CMS EXECs.

-0001:   No CP command with this name was found.

-0002:   An attempt was made to execute a CMS command while in CMS subset mode which would have caused the module to be loaded in the user area.

-0003:   No CMS command issued from EXEC was found with this name, or an invalid function occurred when issuing the SET or QUERY command from EXEC with IMPCP active.

-0004:   The LOADMOD failed.

-0005:   A LOADMOD was attempted in the wrong environment.

4:   The user did not specify all the conditions to execute the command as intended. Execution of the command continues, but the result may or may not be as the user intended.

8:   Device errors occurred for which a Warning message was issued, or errors were introduced into the output file.

12:   Errors were found in the input file.

20:   There is an invalid character in the fileid. Valid characters are 0-9, A-Z, $, <, #, and a-z.

24:   The user did not correctly specify the command line.

28:   An error occurred while trying to access, or manipulate, a user's files; for example, file not found.

32:   The user's file is not in the expected format, or the user's file does not contain the expected information, or an attempt was made to execute a LOADMOD command while in CMS subset mode. This would cause the module to be loaded in the user area.

36:   An error occurred in the user's devices; for example, a disk is in read-only status and needs to be in write status in order to write out a file.

40:   A functional error by the user occurred during execution of the command, or the user failed to supply all the necessary conditions for executing the command, or an end of file or end of tape was reached (where applicable).

41:   Insufficient storage was available to execute the command.

88: A CMS system restriction prevented execution of the command, or the function requested is an unsupported feature, or the device requested is an unsupported device.

100: Input/output device errors.

104: A functional error for which the system is responsible occurred during execution of the command.

256: An unexpected error for which the system is responsible (Terminal Error) occurred during execution of the command.

Rationale: It is the function of CMS EXECs to operate in a manner consistent with that of CMS commands. Therefore, CMS return codes should be used. Such return codes also provide a useful mechanism enabling EXECs to successfully invoke other EXECs.

8. **Element:** XEDIT macros should use appropriate XEDIT return codes if possible. The following return codes are defined for XEDIT subcommands. It is likely that many of them would not be applicable to XEDIT macros.

0 Normal

6 Subcommand rejected in the profile due to LOAD error or QUIT subcommand has been issued in macro called from the last file in the ring

20 Invalid character in filename or filetype

24 Invalid parameters or options

28 Source file not found (UPDATE MODE), library not found (MEMBER option), or file XEDTEMP CMSUT1 already exists

32 Error during updating process; file is not a library, library has no entries, or file is not fixed 80-char. records

36 Corresponding disk not accessed

88   File is too large and does not fit into storage, or previous MACLIB function was not finished, or Maclib limit exceeded

100   Error reading the file into storage

104   Insufficient storage available to read library map

Rationale: It is the function of XEDIT macros to operate in a manner consistent with that of XEDIT subcommands. Therefore, XEDIT return codes should be used. Such return codes also provide a useful mechanism enabling macros to successfully invoke other macros.

9. **Element:** If the "stack" is used, data lines should be stacked LIFO so as not to interfere with terminal input which is FIFO.

    Rationale: This technique reduces the possibility of confusion and allows operations using the stack to proceed more smoothly.

10. **Element:** Consider starting an EXEC or macro with "MAKEBUF" and ending it with "DROPBUF."

    Rationale: Beginning an EXEC or macro with "MAKEBUF" creates a buffer within the Program Stack exclusively for the use of that REXX program. This insures that stack operations within the program should not interfere with the existing contents of the stack. Ending the program with "DROPBUF" purges the contents of the buffer associated with the program.

11. **Element:** Use the Address instruction for repeatability and integrity.

    Rationale: Incorrect environment address can easily occur within EXECs and macros which are shared between multiple users. Likewise, problems with the resolution of command names can possibly occur. The Address instruction, by requiring the full VM command resolution, can be used to prevent such problems in many circumstances.

12. **Element:** Consider if the EXEC should be able to function properly in CMS Subset.

    Rationale: The author of a CMS EXEC should be aware of whether his/her EXEC contains any elements/commands which are inoperable in CMS subset. Such restrictions should be documented in an attempt to avoid sudden user failure which may occur during the exec's use.

Use of a Standard EXEC/Macro Program Outline

The following is an example of a program outline which can be followed in the development of CMS EXECs and XEDIT macros. The use of comments at the beginning of this program to provide name, description, author, revision and date information is self-explanatory. The numbered statements in this program are explained following the outline.

```
      /* Program Name                        */
      /* Program Description                 */
      /* Program Author                      */
      /* Current Revision Number and Date    */
1)    address "COMMAND"
2)    signal on error
3)    signal on halt
4)    signal on novalue
5)    signal on syntax
6)    arg ArgList "(" OptionList ")"
7)    ArgList = "STRIP"(ArgList)
8)    OptionList = "STRIP"(OptionList)
9)    if ArgList = "?" then signal Help
         < Program Body >
10)   call Exit 0

      Help:
      < Program Description, Parameters, Options >
      call Exit 0

      Halt:
      call Exit 4
      return

      Novalue:
      "EXECIO 1 EMSG ( STRING xxx900E Uninitialized variable ",
      "encountered on line" Sigl "."
      call Exit 8
      return

       Exit:
       arg Rc
       exit Rc
```

1) address "COMMAND"—indicates that system commands in the program will use the full VM command form (i.e., processor command parameters options);

2) signal on error, 3) signal on halt, 4) signal on novalue, 5) signal on syntax—indicate that the program will use the REXX facilities for error trapping and interrupts; Procedures Halt and NoValue are examples of operations which may be used in such cases;

6) arg ArgList "(" OptionList ")"—provides a program argument interface directly analogous to that of CMS commands and XEDIT subcommands;

7) ArgList = "STRIP"(ArgList) and

8) OptionList = "STRIP"(OptionList) — insure that argument and option parsing will be done correctly even if extraneous blanks are included in the argument and option lists; for example, A(B, A (B, A(B, and A (B will all be equivalent;

9) if ArgList = "?" then signal Help—provides interactive help information if the program is invoked with "?" as the argument; this help information is independent of the CMS Help system;

10) call Exit n—provides all program exits through a single Exit procedure; the argument to that procedure is the return code indicative of the exiting condition; the use of a single exit subprogram is consistent with the single-exit design feature of structured programs.

REXX Pitfalls and Traps

Despite its many positive features and capabilities, REXX does contain a number of pitfalls to which an unwary user may fall prey. Many of such problems are related to the character processing features of the language and to specific syntactical characteristics. The following are examples of some potential problems:

1. Some characters which have special meaning in CMS and/or XEDIT, but may have different meanings or connotation when used in REXX clauses.

   - "*" is the REXX multiplication operator, but also means "all" in CMS.
   - "/" is the REXX division operator, but also means LOCATE to XEDIT.
   - "(" and ")" are used to group expressions in REXX, but also act as CMS option delimiters (e.g., if a single "(" is given as an option but is not enclosed within quotes, REXX interprets as a mismatch error).

2.   Avoid using variable names that:

   • are host commands (CMS or otherwise)
   • may be used in the parameter lists of CMS commands (such as filemode letters)

3.   If variable naming ambiguities are unavoidable, remember:

   • quotes in a REXX statement prevent substitution and interpretation
   • "undefined variables" retain their name as their value

4.   Beware of the ";" that lies in the middle of the If statement syntax.

The Future of REXX

REXX and Personal Computers

In 1985, IBM announced a modified subset of REXX known as REXX/PC as part of the PC/VM Bond product. This product does not contain a full implementation of the REXX function library.

   In September 1985, a full implementation for IBM PCs and clones, Personal REXX, was announced by Mansfield Software Group (Storrs, CT). Personal REXX also includes emulations of the CMS Program Stack and the CMS operations LISTFILE, EXECIO, GLOBALV, MAKEBUF, DROPBUF, SENTRIES, and CONWAIT.

Systems Application Architecture (SAA)

In March 1987, IBM announced Systems Application Architecture (SAA). SAA does not represent a product, but rather a long-term strategic direction, analogous to System Network Architecture (SNA), which was announced fifteen years ago.

   The objectives of SAA are to provide a framework across the three major IBM computing environments:

• System /370 (TSO/E under MVS/XA and CMS under VM)
• System /3X
• Personal Computer (Operating System/2)

These objectives define:

- a common programming interface with which customers, independent software vendors, and IBM can productively develop applications that can be integrated with each other and ported to run in multiple environments
- common communications support that will provide interconnection of systems and programs and cross-system data access
- a common user access, including screen layout, menu presentation and selection techniques, keyboard layout, and use and display options.

Figure 11-8 illustrates how SAA is supposed to work.

At the Programming Interface level, IBM has identified REXX as SAA's procedures language, a language for issuing commands that

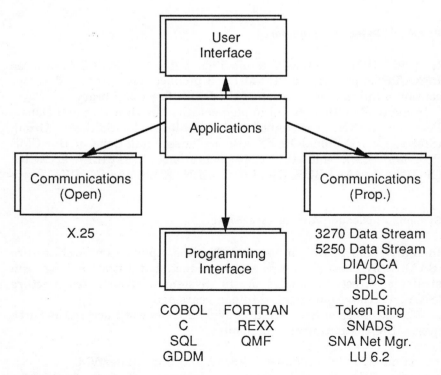

Figure 11-8 An overview of Systems Application Architecture.

invoke programs and system facilities, a function most notably identified in the past with MVS/TSO. In addition to its availability on
VM, IBM is rumored to have an internal version of REXX that provides an alternative to CLIST commands under TSO. A version for
the S/3X line is implied in the SAA announcement and would make
sense as a way of easing portability between that line and the 937X,
which provides REXX under VM/CMS.

IBM released the specifications for all components of SAA in the
third quarter of 1987. The actual availability of implementations of
the various components will, of course, be much later. At the time of
this writing, the only generally available implementations of the
complete REXX language are IBM's original version for System/370
under the VM/CMS operating system and Mansfield Software's Personal REXX for the IBM PC and compatibles, which was introduced
in 1985.

Bibliography

1. Abacus, Alexander, *REXX: A Beginner's Alternative*, Computer
   Language, June 1986
2. Cowlishaw, M. F.,*Design of the Restructured Extended Executor
   Language*, TR12.223, IBM U.K., October 1983
3. Cowlishaw, M. F., *The Design of the REXX Language*, IBM
   Systems Journal 23[4], 1984, 326-335; reprint order no. G321-
   5228. Also reprinted in SIGPLAN Notices, V22 #2, February
   1987
4. Cowlishaw, M. F., *The REXX Language, A Practical Approach
   to Programming*, Prentice-Hall, Inc., Englewood Cliffs, NJ
   07632, 1985
5. Gomberg, David, and O'Hara, Robert, *Modern Programming
   using REXX*, Prentice-Hall, Inc., Englewood Cliffs, NJ 07632,
   1985
6. Jeffries, Ron, *Hello REXX—Goodbye, .BAT*, in PC, 2/25/86
7. *Personal REXX Manual* v. 1.50, Mansfield Software Group,
   Inc., P.O. Box 532, Storrs, CT 06268
8. *REXX Language Overview*, Mansfield Software Group, Inc.,
   P.O. Box 532, Storrs, CT 06268, September 1986
9. *Virtual Machine/System Product Release 3: System Product Interpreter Reference*, IBM Publication SC24-5239-0 (1983)
10. *Virtual Machine/System Product Release 3: System Product In-
    terpreter Users' Guide*, IBM Publication SC24-5238-0 (1983)

11. Fosdick, Howard, *VM / CMS Handbook for Programmers, Users and Managers*, Hayden Books, Indianapolis, IN 46268, 1987

As a guide, [1], [6], and [8] are short overviews. Their technical content may be correctly inferred from their sources. [2], [3], and the first chapter of [4] are essentially the same: insight into the design decisions resulting in REXX. The rest of [4] is the definitive language specification, but in very clear and easy-to-read English. [5] is a guide to structured and top-down programming for the neophyte, using REXX as the vehicle. [7] is an installation and use guide for the Personal REXX implementation, telling of features peculiar to that version and of its surprisingly full emulation of the salient features of the CMS environment, such as the console stack and the LISTFILE command. (They provide a copy of [4] with their product.) [9] and [10] are, of course, the complete reference and tutorial manuals, respectively, for the original implementation as it now exists under VM/SP CMS.

About the Author

Bebo White is a member of the technical staff of the Stanford Linear Accelerator Center (SLAC), a major VM/CMS installation. SLAC was a beta-test site for REXX and had the opportunity to develop thousands of lines of REXX programs even before it became an IBM product. Mr. White has developed and taught classes on VM/CMS and REXX for various academic and private institutions in the United States and Europe. He is currently (1988–1989) on sabbatical as a scientific associate at the European Organization for Nuclear Research (CERN) in Geneva, Switzerland.

Mr. White is the author of two books (*Programming BASIC,* Cushen-White Publications, 1983; and *Programming Techniques for Software Development,* Van-Nostrand Reinhold, 1989) and numerous articles on programming languages and techniques.

His mailing address is:

Stanford Linear Accelerator Center
P.O. Box 4349, Bin 97
Stanford, CA 94309

Mr. White is always interested in learning of new REXX applications, including interesting EXECs and XEDIT macros, REXX tricks and techniques, and teaching and learning aids and tips.

The author would like to acknowledge the contributions of the following persons in the preparation of this material:

- Ed Brink (IBM)
- Ginger Brower (Stanford Linear Accelerator Center – SLAC)
- Cathie Dager (SLAC)
- Charles Daney (Mansfield Software)
- Eric van Herwijnen (CERN)

C in the VM Environment

by John L. Donaldson

The C Language

The C programming language, developed at Bell Laboratories by Dennis Ritchie, has gained great popularity for a variety of applications in recent years. C has become the "language of choice" for systems programmers, particularly in UNIX environments on minicomputers and workstations. Although it has not yet become prevalent at IBM mainframe installations (and VM installations in particular), there are several good compilers available (for example, from Waterloo, SAS Institute, and IBM itself). The availability of the language and its proven record of usefulness at non-IBM shops makes it worthy of consideration for development of systems in the VM environment.

While ostensibly a general-purpose programming language, C has a number of characteristics which have made it especially attractive for systems programming. C is a compact and portable language. It is "low-level" in the sense that it provides for direct manipulation of the simple data types implemented at the machine language level: numbers, characters, and addresses. This means that the programmer can directly access specific machine locations, such as the interrupt PSWs on the IBM 370 architecture. The simplicity of the language allows efficient code to be generated.

At the same time, C is unquestionably a modern programming language which is based on the ideas of "structured programming." The conventional selection (if, switch) and iteration (while, for) control-flow structures are provided, as is recursion. Modularization and regularity of structure are encouraged by the fact that every C routine (including main programs) is written in the form of a function with arguments and a single return value. Extensive data structuring capabilities are provided through pointers, arrays, and record structures.

All these features have made C popular among programmers. As a result, C has a combination of characteristics which makes it quite suitable for systems programming: It combines the efficiency and machine-level power of assembly language with the structure and ease of use of a high-level language.

C on VM Systems

C has been used successfully as a systems programming language primarily in non-IBM environments. However, in many of these environments, it has almost completely replaced assembly language for systems programming. It is reasonable to ask whether C can be used as successfully for systems-level projects on VM systems. This chapter is based mainly on the experiences of the author in the development of an operating system kernel for a virtual machine under VM, written using the IBM C compiler. Rather than a tutorial on C, which can be found in a number of texts, the chapter details the important features of the language which are critical to the systems programmer. Also described are some of the aspects of the language which distinguish it from other high-level languages such as FOR-TRAN or Pascal. These features are illustrated with program examples taken from the code written for the kernel. Some of the features discussed are header files and modularization, direct memory addressing, data types, the C run-time environment, interrupt handling, bit fields, and privileged machine instructions.

Header Files and Modularization

One of the important advantages of using a high-level language such as C is the convenience of dividing a large program into (for the most part) independent modules. C compilers typically allow the code for a single program to be divided among several source files which can be compiled separately. Inevitably, this division cannot be complete; there is always some need for shared information between modules. Sharing at run time is handled through the passing of arguments; sharing at compile time is done through header files. A header file collects a group of related declarations into a single file which can then be utilized at compile time by several modules. Thus, the header files are used primarily to define global constants and declarations and the interfaces between modules. A header file typically contains definitions and declarations of data types and structures, global variables, and function headers rather than executable code. That is, the header file for a particular module contains the declarations especially associated with that module, which are to be shared with other modules. Header files are included at compile time (by an "include" statement) by the source files of all related modules.

For example, a typical header file used in the VM environment might consist of the definitions of C macros for all the 370-architecture-defined addresses (external old PSW, SVC new PSW, etc.) in low memory. Another example would be a file containing a set of declarations associated with a file handling module. The file handler might contain functions to open and close CMS format files and read and write records to those files. Appendix B contains an example of a header file which could be used by such a file handling module. The header file contains structures corresponding to CMS-defined data blocks such as the CMS volume label and the CMS directory entry. It also contains application-specific structures such as the file control block, as well as function prototypes for all external functions which comprise the module (open, close, read, write, etc.). Thus, the header file brings together related data structure definitions into a single file accessible at compile time from several C functions. It would be included by the file handling module itself, as well as other modules which interface with it.

Header files can also be used for the external declaration of global variables. For example, the actual declaration of a variable called std_in, defined as a pointer to an FCB (file control block) structure, would appear in a source file as:

```
FCB *std_in;
```

The header file would contain the following declaration:

```
extern FCB *std_in;
```

In this way, storage is allocated to the variable only once, but any source program using the header file can refer to it.

Any C source file which wishes to make use of the declarations in a header file may do so through the use of an "include" statement, as follows:

```
#include file.h
```

In this way, interfaces between modules are clearly and uniformly defined. Of course, a change in a header file may require the recompiling of several source files.

Data Types

C is a typed language—less strongly typed than Pascal but more strongly typed than FORTRAN. Each variable must be declared. C is rather flexible, however, when it comes to compatibility between types.

C has separate types for character and integer data, but the types can be mixed freely. Assigning a "char" value to an integer variable gives the EBCDIC code representation of the character. This is convenient for the programmer, but can lead to some rather cryptic code, such as:

```
digit = getchar(); sum += digit - '0';
```

which adds to sum the value of an input digit.

Pointer types (addresses) are heavily used in C, for example in dynamic memory allocation, accessing arrays, and passing parameters to functions. Dynamic memory allocation routines return pointers. An array name actually represents a pointer to the first element of the array. Because all function arguments are passed by value, the only way to modify a variable in a calling program within a function is to pass a pointer to the variable.

The basic rule for type compatibility for pointers is that pointers are only compatible if they point to the same type of object. This is rather restrictive since, after all, at the machine level, all pointers are simply memory addresses. There are, however, three ways in which this restriction can be circumvented:

1. Type casting. The type casting operator makes it possible to change the type of a value. In particular, a pointer can be cast

to an integer, an integer can be cast to a pointer, and a pointer to one type of object can be cast to a pointer to another type of object. For example, if x is a pointer variable and y is an integer variable, the value of x can be moved to y by the statement

```
y = (int) x;
```

2. Pointer to void. "Void" is a special data type used for functions which do not return a value. But a function can be declared to return a "pointer to void" (*void), which is then compatible with any type of pointer. This is particularly useful for generalized routines which must return a pointer, where it is not known what type of structure the pointer is being used to address. For example, a general table search routine can be written to handle tables of any type of structure, by passing as arguments the address of the table, the length of a table entry, and the offset and length of the key field. The value returned by the function is a pointer to an entry in the table where the key is found. By declaring the function to return a pointer to void, the return value can be assigned to the appropriate type of pointer variable. This technique could also be applied to a dynamic memory allocation routine. The routine would search for a block of memory from a pool of free space and return the address of the block. Again, the routine returns a pointer, but it does not know what data type the pointer addresses, so it returns a pointer to void.

3. A third way to mix incompatible pointers is to take advantage of the fact that unless parameter types are explicitly declared in a function prototype, the C compiler cannot check the compatibility of parameters to external functions. As a result, the programmer is not bound by any restrictions on type compatibility. This approach, however, is less desirable because it hides the implicit type conversion across module boundaries, leading to potential debugging problems. It is preferable to put prototypes for external functions in header files so that the compiler can check for compatibility, but use method (1) or (2) to explicitly override types when necessary. Making type conversions explicit makes it much less likely to have errors caused by accidental mismatching of parameters.

An additional remark about types: C compilers vary as to the degree to which they enforce type compatibility. In particular, the Waterloo compiler is less stringent than the IBM compiler in its type checking. Although it may result in more compile-time type incompatibility errors, the more careful checking does have an important advantage. Errors detected at compile time are usually easier to detect and correct than run-time errors. Without strict type-checking, there is more of a tendency to produce code which will compile properly, but not execute properly.

Addressing Absolute Memory Locations

The ability to address absolute memory locations from within a C program is extremely important to the systems programmer, yet it is really a simple operation. Locations can be given names through the use of C "macros." It is then convenient to place macros defining important memory locations and other constants in a header file. For example, macros defining addresses and constants pertaining to the IBM 370 architecture can be placed in a header file called ibm370 h. This file can then be included by any C source file that needs access to these macros. A portion of such a header file is shown below. In it, for example, the identifier EXTOLDPSW is defined to be equivalent to the hexadecimal constant 18. (The names PSWBLKPTR, WORDPTR, etc., in parentheses are type cast operators which refer to data types defined elsewhere in the header file. The complete text of the header file is in Appendix A.)

```
/*-----------------------------------------------*/
/* IBM/370 Reserved Memory Locations             */
/*-----------------------------------------------*/

#define EXTOLDPSW (PSWBLKPTR) 0x18        /* Location of External Old PSW     */
#define EXTNEWPSW (PSWBLKPTR) 0x58        /* Location of External New PSW     */
#define PRGOLDPSW (PSWBLKPTR) 0x28        /* Location of Program Old PSW      */
#define PRGNEWPSW (PSWBLKPTR) 0x68        /* Location of Program New PSW      */
#define SVCOLDPSW (PSWBLKPTR) 0x20        /* Location of Supervisor Old PSW   */
#define SVCNEWPSW (PSWBLKPTR) 0x60        /* Location of Supervisor New PSW   */
#define MCKOLDPSW (PSWBLKPTR) 0x30        /* Location Machine-Check Old PSW   */
#define MCKNEWPSW (PSWBLKPTR) 0x70        /* Location Machine-Check New PSW   */
#define IOOLDPSW (PSWBLKPTR) 0x38         /* Location of I/O Old PSW          */
#define IONEWPSW (PSWBLKPTR) 0x78         /* Location of I/O New PSW          */
#define INTERVAL_TIMER (WORDPTR) 0x50     /* Location of Interval Timer       */
#define CAW (CAWBLKPTR) 0X48              /* Location of Channel Address Word*/
#define CSW (CSWBLKPTR) 0X40              /* Location of Channel Status Word  */
```

The following C statements illustrate the use of these definitions:

- To assign a value of 100 (hexadecimal) to the interval timer:

```
(*INTERVAL_TIMER) = 0x100;
```

- To extract the interrupt code from the Program Old PSW and store it in a variable called i_code:

```
i_code = PRGOLDPSW->format.intr_code;
```

- To move the address of a CCW from a variable called ccwptr to the Channel Address Word:

```
(*CAW).word = (int) ccwptr;
```

- To store the address of the SVC interrupt handler function in the second word of the SVC New PSW:

```
extern svchandl();
SVCNEWPSW->word[1] = (int) svchandl;
```

- To copy the Channel Status Word to a local variable called status:

```
status = *CSW;
```

Bit Fields and Bit Operations

Record structures as they appear in programming languages (DSECTs in Assembler, records in Pascal, structures in C, etc.), provide a way to place a template on an area of memory, defining data fields within that area. This language feature is of great importance in creating tables of data. In systems programming, structures are used to define various system control blocks. These blocks may be defined by an application or may be set up to conform to an underlying system block. For example, the header file given in the previous section includes one structure used to access CMS directory records and another for an application-defined file control block. Generally, structures allow the programmer to divide a block of memory into fields, each containing a fixed number of bytes.

C takes the notion of a structure one step further by allowing fields to be specified with a length in bits as well as bytes. This is particularly useful in accessing IBM-defined structures such as PSW, CSW, etc., which include many fields defined at the bit level. The following structure (taken from the IBM370.h header file in Appendix A) is defined to conform to the IBM CSW structure. Bit fields are designated as "unsigned" with the number of bits given after the field name.

```
typedef struct {               /* CSW has the following format    */
unsigned key : 4;              /* Key mask field                  */
unsigned suspended : 1;        /* Suspended mask (only by PSI)    */
unsigned log_pend : 1;         /* Logout pending mask             */
unsigned defer_cc : 2;         /* Deferred Condition Code         */
unsigned chprg_addr : 24;      /* Address of channel program      */
unsigned attention : 1;        /* Attention mask, see ATTENTION   */
unsigned stat_mod : 1;         /* Status modifier, see STAT_MOD   */
unsigned ctrlun_end : 1;       /* Control-unit end , see CU_END   */
unsigned busy : 1;             /* Channel Busy, see CHNL_BUSY     */
unsigned chnl_end : 1;         /* Channel End, see CHNL_END       */
unsigned device_end : 1;       /* Device End, see DEVICE_END      */
unsigned unit_check : 1;       /* Unit check , see UNIT_CHECK     */
unsigned unit_excp : 1;        /* Unit exception, see UNIT_EXCP   */
unsigned prog_int : 1;         /* Program-controlled interruption */
unsigned len_err : 1;          /* Incorrect leng th flag          */
unsigned prog_check : 1;       /* Program check flag              */
unsigned protection : 1;       /* Protection check flag           */
unsigned chnl_data : 1;        /* Channel-data check flag         */
unsigned chnl_ctrl : 1;        /* Channel-control check flag      */
unsigned inter_ctrl : 1;       /* Interface-control check flag    */
unsigned chain_chck : 1;       /* Chaining check                  */
unsigned byte_count : 16;      /* Incorrect length flag           */
} CSW;
```

The structure can be used easily. If "cswptr" is a variable containing the address of a csw, the statement

```
cswptr->key = 6;
```

will store the value 6 in the "key" field of the structure. Any necessary shift or masking instructions are generated automatically by the compiler.

C also provides explicit bit manipulation operators. They are: & (bitwise AND), | (bitwise inclusive OR), ^ (bitwise exclusive OR), >> (right shift), << (left shift), and ~ (one's complement).

The Stack Environment

For more advanced work in C, such as interfacing with assembly language or writing interrupt handlers, it is necessary to become familiar with the C run-time environment. Like other modern recursive languages such as PL/I and Pascal, the implementation of C is usually based on a run-time stack. The stack is used for subroutine linkage, parameter passing, register save areas, and allocation of local storage. When one function calls another, arguments and a return address are placed on the stack. Within the called function, register contents are saved on the stack and space for local variables is allocated on the stack. The set of data placed on the stack for each function call is called a "stack frame." This stack frame provides the local environment in which the function is executed. Thus, as the main program calls a function, which calls another function, which calls another, etc., a series of stack frames is constructed. When a function is completed, the frame at the top of the stack always contains the information needed to return to the calling routine. The top stack frame is deleted, thereby restoring the environment (local variables, register contents) of the caller. In addition to providing an elegant implementation of the language, this method of implementation allows functions to be recursive.

The stack-based approach, however, leads to two problems on IBM systems: The IBM 370 architecture does not support the notion of a memory stack and the standard OS subroutine linkage conventions are not stack-oriented. These problems have, however, been successfully addressed by C compiler designers. Although it does not explicitly contain a stack implementation, the 370 architecture provides enough registers for a stack to be implemented in memory, by reserving several of the general purpose registers as stack pointers. This reduces the number of registers available for code generation, but is necessary for a correct implementation of C.

The limitations of the OS linkage conventions are typically handled by simply adopting a new set of conventions. Generally, registers are reserved for various functions (return address, base register, parameter addressing, stack frame addressing, etc.), but there is no standard usage from compiler to compiler. Some, like the IBM compiler, attempt to use as much of the OS conventions as possible, allowing some compatibility with non-C code; others, like Waterloo's compiler, have entirely scrapped the OS conventions and developed their own.

In any case, each C compiler does adopt its own set of register usage conventions and uses a standard code sequence for both subroutine entry and exit. The C programmer should become familiar with the conventions employed by the compiler he is using.

The remainder of this section will describe the stack environment as implemented by the IBM C compiler. The following diagram shows a snapshot of the stack before and after the entry to function g from function f.

Note that registers 9, 10, and 13 are used to address various parts of the stack. At any point in time, two consecutive stack frames are accessible to a program: The current stack frame (addressed by registers 9 and 10) contains local variables and the previous stack frame (addressed by register 13) contains incoming arguments. The following table is a complete list of the register assignments used by the compiler:

Register	Function
15	Subroutine address (as in OS).
14	Return address (as in OS).
13	Previous stack frame pointer.
12	Return code from functions. Every C subroutine is, in fact, written as a function and may return a function value. If a value is returned, it is always an integer or pointer value and passed back to the calling routine in register 12.
11	Base register. Equal to the entry point of the function, copied from register 15.
10	Current stack frame pointer. Each stack frame contains storage for function arguments, local (automatic) variables, and a register save area.
9	Used in allocation of stack frames. Used to address local storage.
8	Points to special global storage area. This area is set up by C$START (described later) and contains the following:

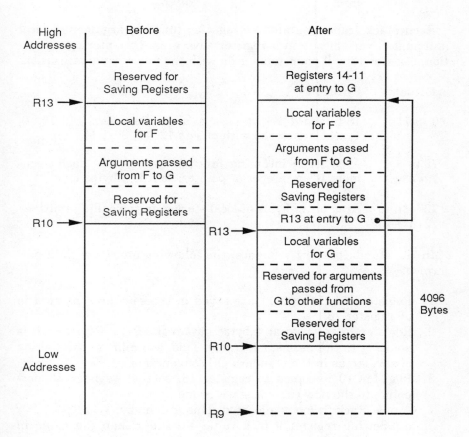

Figure 12-1 An illustration of the stack environment.

Offset	Contents
4	low stack boundary
8	address of routine to branch to if stack overflow occurs (i.e., if register 10 becomes less than the low stack boundary address).
12	x"1000," used in step 4b of the stack allocation routine below

Each stack frame contains storage for function arguments, local (automatic) variables, and a register save area. On entering a function, register 13 will point to an area with the following organization:

Offset	Contents
0 to 71	18-fullword register save area. Registers 14, 15, 0, 1,...,11 are stored with offsets 12, 16, 20,...64.
72 to 72+4*n	Area for n incoming function arguments. Each argument is an integer or pointer, so it is 4 bytes long.
72+4*n to 72+4*n+m	Area for m bytes of local storage in the calling routine.

In the standard entry sequence, the following steps are then performed:

1. Registers 14 through 11 are saved in the save area pointed to by register 13.
2. Register 13 is saved at 4 bytes past register 10. Register 10 is pointing to the next stack frame. This is similar to the linking of save areas in the standard OS conventions.
3. Register 10 is copied to register 13, so that register 13 now points to the new current stack frame.
4. A new stack frame is allocated. This is done by:
   a. Setting register 9 to a value 4096 less than the value in register 10.
   b. Setting register 10 to a value greater than register 9 by an amount sufficient to leave space between registers 10 and 13 for the stack frame. The result is that register 10 is less than register 13 by m+4*n+72, where m is the number of bytes of local storage needed by this function and n is the greatest number of arguments passed to any called function.

After this is done, the main body of the function uses registers 9, 10, and 13 to address data on the stack. Register 9 is used to access local storage; register 10 is used to place arguments to called functions on the stack; and register 13 is used to address incoming arguments.

Entry sequence:

```
FUNCTION       EQU     *
               USING   FUNCTION,15
               STM     14,11,12(13)      SAVE CALLER'S REGISTERS
               ST      13,4(10)          SAVE OLD FRAME POINTER
               LR      13,10             R13 --> CURRENT FRAME
               LR      9,10
               S       9,12(8)      R9 IS 4096 BELOW CURRENT FRAME
               LA      10,4096-m-4*n-72(9)      ALLOCATE NEW FRAME
               LR      11,15             ESTABLISH BASE REGISTER 11
               DROP    15
               USING   FUNCTION,11
               CL      10,4(8)           TEST FOR STACK OVERFLOW
               BNL     ###               IF NOT LOW, NO OVERFLOW
               L       15,8(8)           ELSE BRANCH TO ERROR ROUTINE
               BR      15
               DS      0F
###            EQU     *                 BEGIN BODY OF FUNCTION
```

(This sequence is altered slightly in unusual cases where the amount of local storage for a function exceeds 4096 bytes. The LA 10,... instruction is replaced by subtraction of a literal.)

Within the function body, incoming arguments are addressed as 72(13), 76(13), 80(13), etc. Arguments to called routines are addressed as 72(10), 76(10), 80(10), etc. Local storage is addressed as 4096-m(9), 4096-m+4(9), 4096-m+8(9), etc., depending on the value of m above.

Exit sequence:

```
               L       13,4(13)          RESTORE PRIOR FRAME POINTER
               LM      14,11,12(13)      RESTORE CALLER'S OTHER REGS
*                                        (EXCEPT 12 AND 13)
               BR      14                RETURN TO CALLER
```

Assembly language routines following these conventions can be called by C routines. (Assembly language routines without local variables which do not call other routines can get by with a much simpler entry sequence. See the assembly language routines SVC@, DIAG@, SIO@, and LPSW1@, for example.) The called routine may assume that register 13 points to a register save area; register 14 contains the return address; register 15 contains the entry address, just as in the OS conventions. And that register 10 (plus an offset of 72) points to any incoming arguments. The following example shows a C routine called searchtab and the compiled version of the program. Note that names must be truncated to eight characters at the assembly language level and that names are converted to all capitals. Another naming convention is that the underscore character is replaced by "@" in names at the assembly language level.

```
/*------------------------------------------------------------*/
/*     searchtab(table,key,keyoffset,keywid,hght,rowwid)       */
/*                                                             */
/*     This function searches a table of records for the       */
/*     record containing a specified key value. If a          */
/*     record containing the matching key value is located,    */
/*     a pointer to that record is passed back as the          */
/*     function value. If no match is found, a value           */
/*     of 0 is returned.                                       */
/*------------------------------------------------------------*/
void *searchtab(table,key,keyoffset,keywid,hght,rowwid)
    char    *table;     /*  pointer to the table               */
    char    *key;       /*  pointer to the key                 */
    int     keyoffset;  /*  offset of key within the record    */
    int     keywid;     /*  number of bytes in the key         */
    int     hght;       /*  number of records in the table     */
    int     rowwid;     /*  number of bytes per record         */
    {

    /* Local Variables */
      char *recptr;
      int i;

    /* Begin searchtab */
      recptr = table;
      for (i = 0; i < hght; ++i) {
        if (memcmp(key,recptr+keyoffset,keywid) == 0)
          return(recptr);
        recptr += rowwid;
        }
    return(NIL); } /* End searchtab */
```

The assembly language version of searchtab, as produced by the C compiler:

```
SEARCHTA EQU    *
##1      EQU    *
         USING  ##1,15
         STM    14,11,12(13)      SAVE REGISTERS
         ST     13,4(10)          SAVE CURRENT FRAME POINTER
         LR     13,10             COPY NEW FRAME POINTER TO REG 13
         LR     9,10              AND TO REG 9
         S      9,12(8)           SUBTRACT X'1000' FROM REG 9
         LA     10,3992(9)        POSITION REG 10 TO NEXT FRAME
         LR     11,15             USE REG 11 AS BASE REGISTER
         DROP   15
         USING  ##1,11
         CL     10,4(8)           TEST FOR STACK OVERFLOW
         BNL    #6
         L      15,8(8)
         BR     15
         DS     0F
###1     EQU    *
         DC     A(##1)
#6       EQU    *                 START OF SEARCHTAB BODY
         MVC    4092(4,9),72(13)     RECPTR = TABLE
         XC     4088(4,9),4088(9)    I = 0
#1       EQU    *
         L      12,4088(9)        R12 <-- I
         C      12,88(13)         COMPARE R12 WITH HGHT
         BNL    #11               IF NOT LOW, EXIT FROM FOR LOOP
         MVC    80(4,10),84(13)   PUSH KEYWID (3RD ARG TO MEMCMP)
         L      12,4092(9)        R12 <-- RECPTR
         AL     12,80(13)         ADD KEYOFFSET TO R12
         ST     12,76(10)         PUSH R12 (2ND ARG TO MEMCMP)
         MVC    72(4,10),76(13)   PUSH KEY (1ST ARG TO MEMCMP)
         L      15,=A(MEMCMP)
         BALR   14,15             CALL MEMCMP
         LTR    12,12             TEST RETURN CODE
         BNE    #14               IF RET CODE = 0 (KEYS MATCH!)
         L      12,4092(9)        SET R12 TO POINT TO MATCHING RECORD
         L      13,4(0,13)        AND RETURN
         LM     14,11,12(13)
         BR     14
```

```
#14      EQU    *                      ELSE
         L      12,4092(9)
         AL     12,92(13)              INCREMENT RECPTR BY ROWWID
         ST     12,4092(9)
         L      12,4088(9)
         AL     12,=F'1'               INCREMENT I BY 1
         ST     12,4088(9)
         B      #1                     BRANCH TO TOP OF FOR LOOP
#11      EQU    *                      IF NO MATCH,
         XR     12,12                    SET R12 TO 0
         L      13,4(0,13)               AND RETURN
         LM     14,11,12(13)
         BR     14
         LTORG
         DROP   11
```

The C library (CLIB TXTLIB) contains a routine called C$START which initializes the stack. A call to C$START is generated by the compiler to be performed at the beginning of the main program. In some situations it may be necessary to replace the library C$START function. In particular, C$START makes calls to CMS functions. If C is used to write a program which runs in a non-CMS virtual machine, it will be necessary to write a C$START routine to initialize the stack registers.

Interrupt Handlers

The compiler-generated entry and exit sequences are not suitable for use in interrupt handlers. They assume that register 13 is pointing to a save area on the stack. However, this may not be the case if an interrupt occurs at an inopportune moment (that is, during a subroutine entry), so special entry and exit sequences must be used for interrupt handlers. It is possible, however, to write all of the interrupt handler, except the entry and exit code, in C by writing an assembler shell which saves current status information, makes a call to a C routine to do the work, restores the saved status, and returns to the interrupted program. This is illustrated in the examples in Appendix C.

The alternate entry and exit sequences are based on the observation that at all times in the standard entry and exit, register 10 points to an as yet unused save area. (Values are only stored in one save area after register 10 has been used to allocate another one.) The only exception to this is that the word at 4(10) may be occupied by a saved frame pointer. At any rate, there are 17 full words available for saving registers. The code in Appendix C shows how it is used. At 0(10), register 9 is saved. 4(10) is skipped. Between 8(10) and 63(10), registers 11 through 8 are saved. The old PSW is saved at 64(10). Register 10 itself need not be saved, because its value is recovered in the exit code by calculation.

Because it is possible that an interrupt could occur while a stack frame is being allocated, the interrupt handler cannot make any assumption about the value of register 13. So the entry code actually allocates two stack frames: one to act as the old frame and one as the current frame when the C subroutine is called.

Two examples of the use of this technique (I/O and EXTERNAL interrupt handlers) are found in Appendix C. Note that in both cases, the entry and exit code is the same. In fact, the only difference between the two routines in the name of the external C routine that they call.

The first-level SVC handler (Appendix D) uses a slightly different approach. The save area used is again the one pointed to by register 10, but with some differences. Since SVC interrupts do not occur at unpredictable times, the word at 4(10) need not be avoided. Register 12 is used to pass back a return code and is neither saved nor restored. The SVC handler was written entirely in assembler to take advantage of the multi-way branching capability of the BALR instruction. All the SVC service routines, however, are written in C.

Access to Special Machine Instructions

A critical concern of the systems programmer is the capability of using the full instruction set of the machine. This is ordinarily not possible in a high-level language. Instructions such as SVC, SIO, LPSW, SSK, DIAGNOSE, etc., are never generated by the compiler. It is, however, a relatively simple task to write short assembly language driver routines to execute these instructions. The following example shows a driver routine to execute the SVC instruction:

```
*-----------------------------------------------------------------*
*    SVC@ -- Execute SVC instruction.                             *
*    Parameter: SVC code number.                                  *
*                                                                 *
*    usage: rc = svc_(202);                                       *
*-----------------------------------------------------------------*
```

```
SVC@         DS    0H
             ENTRY SVC@
             USING SVC@,15
             L     12,72(10)      LOAD SVC CODE NUMBER INTO R12
             LA    10,4(10)       R10 --> ARGUMENTS FOR SERVICE
*                                       ROUTINE
             EX    12,SVCINST     EXECUTE SVC
             BR    14             RETURN
SVCINST      SVC   0
```

The routine is designed to be called as a C function whose first argument is the SVC interrupt code and whose remaining arguments are to be passed to the SVC service routine, which can also be written in C. Register 10 is incremented by 4 in order to point to these remaining arguments.

(The C library contains its own routine for making SVC calls. It is undocumented and used only by some of the other library functions. It passes parameters to the SVCs in registers; the routine above passes parameters on the stack instead, thus making it possible for the service routines also to be written in C.)

SIO is another example of a machine-level instruction not generated by the C compiler. Again, a short interface routine makes this instruction callable by C. The routine's one parameter is the device address (as in the SIO machine instruction). This value is loaded into register 12 and then the SIO is executed. Depending on the resulting condition code, a value of 0, 1, 2, or 3 is returned in register 12.

```
*-------------------------------------------------------------------*
*     SIO@ -- Execute SIO instruction.                              *
*     Parameter: device address.                                    *
*                                                                   *
*     usage: rc = sio_(device_address);                             *
*     if (rc != 0)                                                  *
*     error;                                                        *
*-------------------------------------------------------------------*
```

```
SIO@         DS    0H
             ENTRY SIO@
             L     12,72(10)      R12 <-- DEVICE ADDRESS
             SIO   0(12)          EXECUTE SIO
             LA    12,0           IF CC = 0
```

```
BCR    B'1000',14              RETURN 0
LA     12,1             IF CC = 1
BCR    B'0100',14              RETURN 1
LA     12,2             IF CC = 2
BCR    B'0010',14              RETURN 2
LA     12,3             IF CC = 3
BR     14                      RETURN 3
```

Direct control of the PSW (as with the LPSW machine instruction) in order to set masks, disable interrupts, set protection keys, etc., can be achieved with the following function called LPSW1. It loads a full-word value into the first word of the PSW register, without modifying the second word.

When the LPSW instruction is executed, the first word of DPSW contains the incoming argument value and the second word contains the address of the next instruction, so that flow of control is not interrupted.

```
*-------------------------------------------------------------------*
*    LPSW1@ -- Load first word of PSW.                              *
*    Parameter: full word to be loaded from memory.                *
*                                                                   *
*    usage: lpsw1_(full_word);                                     *
*-------------------------------------------------------------------*

LPSW1@          DS     0H
                ENTRY  LPSW1@
                USING  LPSW1@,15
                MVC    DPSW(4),72(10)   MOVE PARAMETER TO 1ST WORD OF
*                                       DPSW
                LPSW   DPSW             PERFORM LPSW
LBL             BR     14               RETURN
                DS     0D
DPSW            DC     A(0,LBL)
```

The DIAGNOSE function can be called from C by diag_(code,x,y) using the following routine. The first argument is the DIAGNOSE code number and the second and third are values to be passed as parameters to the DIAGNOSE instruction, as specified in the VM Systems Programmers Guide.

```
*--------------------------------------------------------------------*
*    DIAG@ -- Execute DIAGNOSE instruction.                          *
*    Parameters: DIAGNOSE code.                                      *
*    First register operand.                                         *
*    Second register operand.                                        *
*                                                                    *
*    usage: diag_(code,x,y);                                         *
*--------------------------------------------------------------------*
DIAG@ DS 0H
                 ENTRY DIAG@
                 USING DIAG@,15
                 STM   14,11,12(13)      SAVE REGISTERS
                 MVC   DG+2(2),74(10)    MOVE CODE TO DIAGNOSE
*                                        INSTRUCTION
                 L     4,76(10)          MOVE X TO R4
                 L     6,80(10)          MOVE Y TO R6
DG               DC    X'83460000'       EXECUTE DIAGNOSE INSTRUCTION
                 LM    14,11,12(13)      RESTORE REGISTERS
                 BR    14                RETURN
```

Reference to Specific Machine Registers

Another situation in which it may be necessary to revert to assembly language is when access to a specific general purpose register is needed. For example, this occurs in the design of a multi-tasking operating system kernel when a context switch is made from one process to another. Each process is represented in memory by a Process Control Block (PCB). The term "context switch" refers to the operation performed by the operating system to transfer control from one process to another. When this occurs, it is necessary to save the stack pointer (register 13) of the current process into its PCB in memory and load the stack pointer from the new process' PCB. Thus, direct access to register 13 is needed.

The following routine, CSWITCH, callable as a C function, accomplishes this. It has two arguments, the addresses of two memory locations. The first is the address of the location from which the new stack pointer is to be loaded; the second is the address of the location into which the current stack pointer is to be saved. When a running process gives up the CPU, it calls CSWITCH. The return from this call is made in the context of the new process, making a smooth transition undetectable by either process. The system will eventually resume the suspended process from precisely this same point in CSWITCH.

```
*-------------------------------------------------------------*
*    CSWITCH -- CONTEXT SWITCH ROUTINE                        *
*    CURRENT STACK POINTER IS STORED IN RUNNING PCB.          *
*    NEW STACK POINTER IS LOADED FROM NEW RUNNING PCB.        *
*                                                             *
*    usage: cswitch(pcbptr-stkptr,running-stkptr);            *
*                                                             *
*-------------------------------------------------------------*
CSWITCH      DS    0H
             ENTRY CSWITCH
             STM   14,11,12(13)
*
             L     3,76(10)          R3-->RUNNING PCB'S STKPTR
             L     4,72(10)          R4-->NEW RUNNING PCB'S STKPTR
             ST    13,0(3)           SAVE OLD STKPTR
             L     13,0(4)           LOAD NEW STKPTR
*
             LM    14,11,12(13)
             BR    14
*
```

Standard Library Functions

C is a compact language, without built-in facilities for input and output, string manipulation, or other common operations. As a result, C
compilers are normally packaged along with a C library which contains a set of string functions, I/O functions, mathematical functions,
dynamic memory allocation functions, etc. A standard set of such
functions has been developed on UNIX systems and ported to most
other C libraries. Programmers who have used C on UNIX or other
systems will find that the IBM C library contains the usual standard
functions. Supplied also are header files which include the declarations needed to access these functions.

Debugging

VM/CMS is a superior environment for debugging programs. Two
features of the C compiler provide additional support for debugging,
a source-level debugger and an assembly code generator. The source-
level debugger includes the capabilities of displaying variables, executing with breakpoints, and single stepping. It does, however, use

CMS calls, making it unsuitable for use in a non-CMS virtual machine.

In some cases it may be desirable to debug at the machine language level, in order to avail oneself of the TRACE and PER facilities of CP. To do this, it is useful to have an assembly-language level listing available. This is, in fact, very easy to get, because the normal mode of operation for C compilation is to first generate a complete assembly language source file and then feed this to the standard IBM assembler. Thus, an assembly source file and an assembly listing are automatically generated during the compilation process. These are normally deleted after they are used, but certain compiler options make it possible to save them. The "LIST" option directs the compiler to save the complete assembly language listing, complete with source code, machine code, ESD, RLD, etc. This is useful in identifying the locations of variables, addresses for setting breakpoints, etc. The "NOASM" option directs the compiler to generate and save the assembly-language source file, but not to actually assemble it. This is useful in checking if the compiler is really generating code that does what the programmer intends.

Another comment related to debugging is that the C compiler does not generate code to check for out-of-bounds subscripts or pointers, so the programmer must be very careful in the use of subscripts and pointers. The IBM C library does include, however, a function called "assert" which allows the programmer to insert validity tests anywhere within a program. For example, if "pswptr" is a pointer to a PSW block, the statement

```
assert(pswptr != 0);
```

will check that pswptr is not equal to 0. If the assertion is false, an error message is generated and the program is aborted at that point.

Conclusions

Based on the experience gained by writing an operating system kernel in C, it is the judgment of this author that C is indeed an excellent language for system-level program development on VM systems. The language is relatively easy to learn for anyone experienced in using a block-structured language like Pascal. Use of the compiler resulted in all the advantages that working in a high-level language should provide, such as faster program development, easier debugging, better readability of code, and easier modification of code. The stack-based run-time environment is particularly convenient for dynamic allocation of local storage and for recursive programming. The language contains the low-level functions which previously required the use of assembly language. It was possible to write an operating system kernel for a VM (virtual machine) using only about 100 lines of assembly code, with the remainder written in C. For those few functions which cannot be performed directly in C, such as the use of privileged instructions and direct access to machine registers, C can be easily interfaced with assembly language.

The only drawback to the use of C is in speed of execution. In examining the code generated by the compiler, one can easily identify several places where inefficiencies occur:

Addressing — Pointers are normally stored in memory locations, not registers. Thus, to access a variable or record through a pointer, the machine must first load the pointer into a register and then use it to address memory. This problem can be alleviated somewhat by the use of the "register" storage class in C. Variables designated as "register" will be kept in machine registers if possible.

Bit fields — Access to a single bit field often requires use of several machine-level shift or logical instructions. Bit fields are probably best used for access to system-defined structures such as the PSW. For structures defined by the application, the designer must weigh the trade-off between the storage saved by compressing data into bit fields and the additional instructions required to access those fields.

String functions — The C compiler includes a library of standard string functions. The overhead of a function call occurs whenever these are used, whereas the assembly language programmer could make use of machine instructions such as MVC to carry out string operations directly.

Optimization — Compilers vary as to the degree to which they attempt to optimize code. As an example of the inefficient code which is sometimes generated, consider the following two statements which appeared consecutively in a generated program:

```
ST 12,72(10)
L  12,72(10)
```

The compiler apparently made no attempt to keep track of the contents of machine registers from one statement to the next. A manager selecting a C compiler needs to investigate the degree to which each compiler performs routine code optimization.

Despite this drawback, the advantages in using C appear to outweigh the disadvantages. The use of C can lead to improvements in software design and programmer productivity. It is already the systems programmer's language of choice in many non-IBM environments. As compilers become more widely available and their quality improves, it is likely that C will gain acceptance in the IBM world as well.

Bibliography

Kernighan, Brian W., and Ritchie, Dennis M., *The C Programming Language*, Prentice-Hall, Inc.: Englewood Cliffs, NJ, 1978.

Appendix A—the ibm370.h Header File

```
/*-------------------------------------------------------------------*/
/* ibm370.h                                                          */
/*-------------------------------------------------------------------*/


/*---------------------------------------------------------*/
/* Data types defined specifically for 370 architecture */
/*---------------------------------------------------------*/


typedef int          FULLWORD;   /* Signifies fullword storage     */
typedef FULLWORD     *WORDPTR;   /* Pointer to fullword            */
typedef double       DOUBLE;     /* Signifies doubleword storage   */
typedef short int    HALFWORD;   /* Signifies halfword storage     */
typedef unsigned int ADDRESS;    /* Signifies Memory Address       */


/*----------------------------*/
/* Union Data Block : DBLOCK   */
/*----------------------------*/


typedef union {                  /* Define addressing options      */
          FULLWORD word[2]; /* Allow access by fullword       */
          DOUBLE blok;      /* Allow access as doubleword     */
          BYTE byte[8];     /* Allow addressing by byte       */
          HALFWORD half[4]; /* Allow addressing by halfword   */
} DBLOCK;
typedef DBLOCK *DBLOCKPTR;
```

```
/*-------------------------------------------------*/
/* Program Status Word (BC mode) data structure */
/*-------------------------------------------------*/

typedef struct {
    unsigned ch_0_5         : 6;    /* Mask for channels 0 - 5       */
    unsigned ch_6_up        : 1;    /* Mask for channels 6 and up    */
    unsigned external_mask  : 1;    /* External mask                 */
    unsigned pswkey         : 4;    /* PSW storage key               */
    unsigned bctrl_mode     : 1;    /* Basic Control Mode            */
    unsigned machine_check  : 1;    /* Machine-check mask bit         */
    unsigned wait_state     : 1;    /* Wait-state mask bit            */
    unsigned prob_state     : 1;    /* Problem-state mask bit         */
    unsigned intr_code      : 16;   /* Program interruption code     */
    unsigned instr_len      : 2;    /* Instruction Length Code        */
    unsigned cc             : 2;    /* Storage for condition code     */
    unsigned fix_ovflow     : 1;    /* Fixed-point-overflow mask      */
    unsigned dec_ovflow     : 1;    /* Decimal-overflow mask          */
    unsigned exp_ovflow     : 1;    /* Exponent-overflow mask         */
    unsigned significance   : 1;    /* Significance mask              */
    unsigned instrptr       : 24;   /* Instruction Address            */

} PSW;
typedef PSW * PSWPTR;


/*-----------------------------*/
/* Union Data Block : PSWBLOK  */
/*-----------------------------*/

typedef union {                     /* Define PSW protocol options        */
    INTFUNC fptr[2];                /* Allow access as function ptr       */
    FULLWORD word[2];               /* Allow access by fullword           */
    DOUBLE blok;                    /* Allow access as doubleword         */
    BYTE byte[sizeof(DOUBLE)];      /* Allow byte addressing of PSW       */
    PSW format;                     /* Allow access to bit mask fields    */
} PSWBLOK;


typedef PSWBLOK *PSWBLKPTR;


/*----------------------------------------------------------*/
/* Channel-Status Word (CSW) constants and data structure   */
/*----------------------------------------------------------*/
```

```
#define CSW_ADDRESS 0x40 /* CSW is at location hex 40 */

typedef struct {                      /* CSW has the following format  */
    unsigned key          :  4;       /* Key mask field                */
    unsigned suspended    :  1;       /* Suspended mask (only by PSI)   */
    unsigned log_pend     :  1;       /* Logout pending mask            */
    unsigned defer_cc     :  2;       /* Deferred Condition Code        */
    unsigned chprg_addr   : 24;       /* Address of channel program     */
    unsigned attention    :  1;       /* Attention mask, see ATTENTION  */
    unsigned stat_mod     :  1;       /* Status modifier, see STAT_MOD  */
    unsigned ctrlun_end   :  1;       /* Control-unit end, see CU_END   */
    unsigned busy         :  1;       /* Channel Busy, see CHNL_BUSY    */
    unsigned chnl_end     :  1;       /* Channel End, see CHNL_END      */
    unsigned device_end   :  1;       /* Device End, see DEVICE_END     */
    unsigned unit_check   :  1;       /* Unit check, see UNIT_CHECK     */
    unsigned unit_excp    :  1;       /* Unit exception, see UNIT_EXCP  */
    unsigned prog_int     :  1;       /* Program-controlled interruption */
    unsigned len_err      :  1;       /* Incorrect length flag          */
    unsigned prog_check   :  1;       /* Program check flag             */
    unsigned protection   :  1;       /* Protection check flag          */
    unsigned chnl_data    :  1;       /* Channel-data check flag        */
    unsigned chnl_ctrl    :  1;       /* Channel-control check flag     */
    unsigned inter_ctrl   :  1;       /* Interface-control check flag   */
    unsigned chain_chck   :  1;       /* Chaining check                 */
    unsigned byte_count   : 16;       /* Incorrect length flag          */
} CSW;

typedef CSW *CSWPTR;

/*------------------------------*/
/* Union Data Block : CSWBLOK   */
/*------------------------------*/

typedef union {                  /* Define CSW protocol options       */
    DOUBLE blok;                 /* Allow access as doubleword        */
    FULLWORD word[2];            /* Allow access by fullword          */
    BYTE byte[sizeof(DOUBLE)];   /* Allow byte addressing of CSW      */
    CSW format;                  /* Allow access to bit mask fields   */
} CSWBLOK;

typedef CSWBLOK *CSWBLKPTR;
```

```
/*------------------------------------------------------------*/
/* Channel-Command Word (CCW) constants and data structure  */
/*------------------------------------------------------------*/

typedef struct {                    /* CCW has the following format    */
    unsigned cmd_code   :  8;       /* Command Code                    */
    unsigned data       : 24;       /* Address of data buffer          */
    unsigned cd         :  1;       /* Causes use of next CCW's data   */
    unsigned cc         :  1;       /* Uses next cmd code and data      */
    unsigned sli        :  1;       /* Turns off incorrect length test */
    unsigned skip       :  1;       /* Suppresses information transfer  */
    unsigned prog_int   :  1;       /* Causes prog-controlled interrupt */
    unsigned ida        :  1;       /* bits 8-31 of CCW specify 1st IDAW */
    unsigned suspend    :  1;       /* Suspend Channel execution now    */
    unsigned zero       :  1;       /* Bit 39 should always be zero     */
    unsigned unused     :  8;       /* Bits 40-47 are not used          */
    unsigned byte_count : 16;       /* Residual Byte Count              */
} CCW;

typedef CCW *CCWPTR;


/*------------------------------*/
/* Union Data Block : CCWBLOK   */
/*------------------------------*/

typedef union {
                                    /* Define CCW protocol options    */
    DOUBLE blok;                    /* Allow access as doubleword      */
    FULLWORD word[2];               /* Allow access by fullword        */
    BYTE byte[sizeof(DOUBLE)];      /* Allow byte addressing of CCW    */
    CCW format;                     /* Allow access to bit mask fields  */
} CCWBLOK;

typedef CCWBLOK *CCWBLKPTR;


/*-------------------------------------------------------------------*/
/* Standard CCW Command-Codes (bits 0-7) by field -- .cmd_code       */
/*-------------------------------------------------------------------*/
#define WRITECMD     0x01
#define READCMD      0x02
#define RDIPLCMD     0x02
#define TRAN_IN_CHNL 0x08
#define RD_BACKWARD  0x0c
```

```
#define TOP_PAGE      0x8b
#define NEXT_LINE     0x0b
#define PRTADVNC      0x89
#define CONSREAD      0x0a
#define CCWSTOP       0x09


/*-----------------------------------*/
/* Channel-Program related data types */
/*-----------------------------------*/

typedef struct {
    int ccwcount;         /* Number of CCWs in sequence   */
    CCWBLKPTR prog_base;/* Pointer to first CCW           */
} CHNLPROG;
typedef CHNLPROG *CHNLPRPTR;


/*-------------------------------------------------------------*/
/* Channel-Address Word (CAW) related constants and data types */
/*-------------------------------------------------------------*/


#define CAW_ADDRESS 0x48

typedef struct {
    unsigned key       :  4;    /* Protection Key                */
    unsigned suspend   :  1;    /* Suspend-Control bit           */
    unsigned zeros     :  3;    /* Bits 5-7 are always zero      */
    unsigned chnlprog  : 24;    /* Channel-Program Address       */
} CAW;


typedef CAW *CAWPTR;


/*----------------------------*/
/* Union Data Block : CAWBLOK  */
/*----------------------------*/


typedef union {
    FULLWORD word;                  /* Allow access by FULLWORD       */
    BYTE byte[sizeof(FULLWORD)];/* Allow byte addressing of CAW   */
    CAW format;                     /* Access CAW by bit fields       */
}CAWBLOK;


typedef CAWBLOK *CAWBLKPTR;
```

```
/*--------------------------------------------------*/
/* IBM/370 Reserved Memory Locations            */
/*--------------------------------------------------*/


#define EXTOLDPSW (PSWBLKPTR) 0x18 /* Location of External Old PSW     */
#define EXTNEWPSW (PSWBLKPTR) 0x58 /* Location of External New PSW     */
#define PRGOLDPSW (PSWBLKPTR) 0x28 /* Location of Program Old PSW      */
#define PRGNEWPSW (PSWBLKPTR) 0x68 /* Location of Program New PSW      */
#define SVCOLDPSW (PSWBLKPTR) 0x20 /* Location of Supervisor Old PSW */
#define SVCNEWPSW (PSWBLKPTR) 0x60 /* Location of Supervisor New PSW */
#define MCKOLDPSW (PSWBLKPTR) 0x30 /* Location Machine-Check Old PSW */
#define MCKNEWPSW (PSWBLKPTR) 0x70 /* Location Machine-Check New PSW */
#define IOOLDPSW  (PSWBLKPTR) 0x38 /* Location of I/O Old PSW          */
#define IONEWPSW  (PSWBLKPTR) 0x78 /* Location of I/O New PSW          */
#define INTERVAL_TIMER (WORDPTR) 0x50 /* Location of Interval Timer    */
#define CAW (CAWBLKPTR) 0X48        /* Location of Channel Address Word*/
#define CSW (CSWBLKPTR) 0X40        /* Location of Channel Status Word */


/*----------------------------------*/
/* Virtual Device Memory Locations  */
/*----------------------------------*/


#define CARD_READER 0x00c      /* Location of virtual card reader     */
#define CONSOLE 0x009          /* Location of virtual console         */
```

Appendix B—file.h

```
/**************************************************************/
/*                                                          */
/* file.h -- header file for file system                    */
/*                                                          */
/**************************************************************/


typedef struct { /* structure for CMS directory entries      */
    char    filename[8];
    char    filetype[8];
    char    rsrv1[8];
    char    filemode[2];
    char    rsrv2[4];
    char    recfm;
    char    rsrv3;
    int     lrecl;
```

```
    int    rsrv4;
    int    index_ptr;
    int    nblocks;
    int    nrecords;
    char   ndx_level;
    char   ptr_size;
    char   date_mod[3];
    char   time_mod[3];
    int    rsrv5;
    } DIRNODE;
typedef DIRNODE *DIRPTR;

typedef struct {           /* structure for CMS volume label         */
    char   label[10];
    char   rsrvl[2];
    int    blksize;
    int    dir_ptr;
    int    ncyl;
    int    nblocks;
    int    ent_len;
    int    ent_per_blk;
    char   date_form[3];
    char   time_form[3];
    } VLABEL;
typedef VLABEL *VLABELPTR;

struct VRSTR {             /* structure for variable-length records   */
    short  length;
    char   data[2];
    };
typedef struct VRSTR VRECORD,*VRECPTR;

struct VRPTR {             /* structure for index block entries in    */
    int blknum;            /* variable-length record files            */
    int maxrecnum;
    int offset;
    };
typedef struct VRPTR VXPTR,*VXPTRPTR;

struct FCBNODE {           /* structure for internal file control     */
                           /* blocks                                  */
    struct FCBNODE *next;
    char   type[4];
```

```
    int     filenum;
    int     current;
    int     blksize;
    int     blok_ptr;
    int     pin;
    int     vaddr;
    struct IOBLKNODE *iobptr;
    char    devtype[4];
    struct SEMPNODE *semaphore;
    int     dir_offset;
    int     dir_block;
    int     blk_offset;
    DIRPTR dirptr;
    }   ;
typedef struct FCBNODE FCB;
typedef FCB *FCBPTR;


int  fopen_(char *fname,int vaddr);
int  fseek_(int fnum,int recnum);
int  size_(int fnum);
int  fread_(int fnum,char *buffer);
int  fwrite_(int fnum,char *buffer);
int  getblock(FCBPTR fptr,int nlevels,int n,...);
void *findfile(FCBPTR list,int fnum);
int  searchdir(char *fname,int vaddr,DIRPTR dptr);


/**********************************************************/
/*                                                        */
/* end of file.h                                          */
/*                                                        */
/**********************************************************/
```

Appendix C—Interrupt Handlers

```
*----------------------------------------------------*/
* IOHANDLR                                            */
*----------------------------------------------------*/
IOHANDLR DS    0H
         ENTRY IOHANDLR
         ST    9,0(10)
         STM   11,8,8(10)        SAVE REGS AT ENTRY TO IOHANDLER
         MVC   64(8,10),IOOPSW   SAVE OLD PSW ON STACK
```

```
        LR    9,10
        LR    13,10
        S     9,12(8)
        LA    10,3920(9)
        LA    13,104(10)
        BALR  2,0
        USING *,2               SET UP BASE REG FOR INTERRUPT HNDLR
*
        L     15,=V(IOINT)
        BALR  14,15
*
        LA    10,72(13)
        MVC   0(8),64(10)       MOVE SVCOPSW TO LOCATION 0
        LM    11,8,8(10)
        L     9,0(10)
        LPSW  0                 RETURN TO CALLER
*
*--------------------------------------------------*/
* EXTNHNDL                                         */
*--------------------------------------------------*/
EXTNHNDL DS    0H
        ENTRY EXTNHNDL
        ST    9,0(10)
        STM   11,8,8(10)        SAVE REGS AT ENTRY TO EXTHANDLER
        MVC   64(8,10),EXTOPSW  SAVE OLD PSW ON STACK
        LR    9,10
        LR    13,10
        S     9,12(8)
        LA    10,3920(9)
        LA    13,104(10)
        BALR  2,0
        USING *,2               SET UP BASE REG FOR INTERRUPT HNDLR
*
        L     15,=V(DISPATCH)
        BALR  14,15
*
        LA    10,72(13)
        MVC   0(8),64(10)       MOVE SVCOPSW TO LOCATION 0
        LM    11,8,8(10)
        L     9,0(10)
        LPSW  0                 RETURN TO CALLER
*
```

Appendix D—SVC Interrupt Handler

```
*---------------------------------------------------*/
* SVC INTERRUPT HANDLER                             */
*---------------------------------------------------*/
SVCHANDL DS     0H
         ENTRY  SVCHANDL
         STM    13,11,0(10)        SAVE REGS AT ENTRY TO SVCHANDLER
         MVC    64(8,10),SVCOPSW   SAVE OLD PSW ON STACK
         LR     9,10
         LR     13,10
         S      9,12(8)
         LA     10,3920(9)
         MVC    72(32,10),72(13)   MOVE SVC PARAMETERS
         LA     13,104(10)
         BALR   2,0
         USING  *,2                SET UP BASE REG FOR INTERRUPT HNDLR
*
         L 1,   SVCOPSW
         SLL    1,16               CLEAR HIGH BITS OF SVCOPSW
         SRL    1,14               R1 HAS 4*(SVC INTERRUPT CODE)
         L      15,SVCBRANC(1)
         BALR   14,15              CALL SERVICE ROUTINE
*
         LA     10,72(13)
         MVC    0(8),64(10)        MOVE SVCOPSW TO LOCATION 0
         LM     13,11,0(10)
         LPSW   0                  RETURN TO CALLER
*
         DS     0F
SVCBRANC DC     AL4(0)
         DC     AL4(0)
         DC     VL4(FWRITE@)
         DC     VL4(FREAD@)
         DC     VL4(CREATE@)
         DC     VL4(DESTROY@)
         DC     VL4(PIN@)
         DC     VL4(P@)
         DC     VL4(V@)
         DC     VL4(ALSEM@)
         DC     VL4(FRSEM@)
         DC     VL4(AMBOX@)
         DC     VL4(FMBOX@)
```

```
DC      VL4(SEND@)
DC      VL4(RECEIVE@)
DC      VL4(FOPEN@)
DC      VL4(FCLOSE@)
DC      VL4(FSEEK@)
DC      VL4(STDIO@)
DC      VL4(TERM@)
DC      256XL4'00160A9C'
LTORG
```

About the Author

John L. Donaldson is an associate professor of mathematical sciences at the University of Akron. His research into the use of C on VM systems was performed under a grant from VM Software, Inc., Reston, Virginia. His current interests include operating systems, computer graphics, and computer science education.

Donaldson received his B.S. in mathematics from Case Western Reserve University in 1971 and his Ph.D. in Mathematics and M.S. in computer and information sciences from Ohio State University in 1975 and 1977, respectively.

13

MVS to VM: Avoiding the Pitfalls

by Janet Gobeille

Introduction

Because the differences between MVS and VM can be confusing, and because confusion causes time consuming (and embarrassing) errors, this chapter familiarizes you with VM and assists you in becoming a more effective, productive, and valuable VM programmer by discussing areas often misunderstood or omitted when reading the usual manuals.

This will discuss the basic operating system differences that will affect your work, processing environments and how they differ, system control authority, data and file access, and the overall interface to using VM.

Operating System

First, let's define the major terms used in this chapter:

CP — Control Program. This is a basic component of VM.

SCP — System Control Program. This generally refers to an operating system that controls computer hardware and provides an environment in which other programs can run. MVS is an SCP. CP is also an SCP.

Guest SCP — A Guest SCP is a system control program that runs under CP (a "second level system"). Both VM and MVS can be guest SCPs.

CP

The core of VM is the control program: CP. CP controls real hardware resources (I/O devices, CPU memory, and virtual machines.) Each virtual machine generally runs an additional operating system since CP alone doesn't provide basic amenities such as data control. CP controls access to devices such as printers, tape drives, and disk drives (both real and virtual), but doesn't have file or data management commands.

Where MVS actually controls data storage, by intercepting every file OPEN or CLOSE, CP controls devices and leaves data manipulation (including opening and closing files) to the virtual machine. This allows each virtual machine to run individual operating systems and have individual methods of data storage and use. In the CP directory, where each virtual machine is defined to CP, an operating system is also usually specified to be started automatically when the virtual machine is started via LOGON or AUTOLOG.

Running a control program (or operating system) in a virtual machine and actually under control of CP, rather than having to have its own real CPU, is the heart of VM. Running multiple operating systems on the same computer second level (or under VM control) as opposed to first level (or on "bare iron") is often a basic reason for running VM.

Processing Environment

Since the purpose of running a computer is generally to accomplish work, the next consideration is the type of work to be done since operating systems generally have a bias to a specific environment: an area which they do best. For this chapter, let's use the following definitions of processing environments to see how they can be addressed:

Interactive — Interactive work is done by a user sitting at a terminal of some type. The user issues a command to do a task and waits for the computer to signal that the task is complete. So, a major consideration for interactive work is that tasks be completed as soon as possible to minimize the user's idle time.

Batch — Batch work is work that, by using a control language, includes the instructions to tell the computer what to do. However, no person is sitting at a terminal waiting for this one batch task to be accomplished. A major consideration for a system running batch work is that overall throughput be the highest priority.

Those are rather limited definitions. But, for this chapter, they identify major differences between VM and MVS.

MVS is known as the workhorse of IBM's major operating systems and can process massive amounts of data with batch processing. It has a complex job control language so that work (a job) can be pre-defined and run without having a person interactively enter each command or job step from a terminal. For interactive processing, TSO (the Time Sharing Option) runs under MVS and provides interactive access to the computer and to MVS data. Excellent management of batch processing is the primary goal of MVS. Ease of use is a lower priority.

VM provides an excellent interactive operating environment which has a simple operating system called CMS (Conversational Monitor System) for its interactive users to allow computer and data access. For batch processing, MVS or VSE can be run in a virtual machine, or a CMS task can be pre-defined (using a command language such as EXEC or REXX instead of a job control language) and run in a disconnected virtual machine. This disconnected mode provides the capabilities of running an unattended task on VM as a "background" or batch-type task. However, VM's strength is its ease of use with CMS. Setting up a good batch processing capability is generally left up to the system programmer (see the chapter on service virtual machines).

Interactive Processing

Interactive functions of TSO under MVS and CMS under VM are similar to the end-user, but the environment underlying each is quite different.

Simple operating system to control one user: The usual interactive operating system used under CP is CMS. Since it was designed to run in a virtual machine, it is a (relatively) simple operating system designed to provide an easy-to-use interface to data and to CP. Where TSO manages many interactive users, all sharing the same file system and resources, VM provides an isolated environment for each user, each having his own operating system, his own resources, his own data.

Each user has his own copy of operating system: For performance reasons, shared storage segments (DCSS) store a copy of CMS for many users to share. However, effectively each user has his own operating system. If a user wants to modify CMS, he can: CP simply gives the user his own unshared copy. The DCSS does not make CMS into a multi-user operating system, but reduces the amount of storage required when many users run the same code (CMS) at the same time.

This is not at all the same as in TSO. TSO runs under MVS control (as CMS does under CP), but TSO controls all users. When a user logs on under TSO, he is now under the same operating system as all other TSO users. If TSO crashes, all users are affected. The data center must then restart TSO. For VM, if CMS crashes, only the single CMS user is affected; he just has to say "IPL CMS" to restart the program.

Span of Control

The system programmer must clearly comprehend what is controlled by CP and what CMS controls. CP controls real and virtual devices such as tape drives, card readers/punches, printers, and DASD. It also controls the real use of storage, capabilities of virtual machines, and system access controls.

A CMS user can look at and modify his virtual storage, request or examine virtual devices, load an operating system, or request links to disk data owned by other people. These tasks are all done by issuing CP commands. For ease of use, most CMS users don't know they're talking to CP. If CMS doesn't recognize a command, it generally passes it directly to CP to see if it is a CP command. But, knowing which are CP commands and which are CMS can make a system programmer's job much easier. For example, a CP command can be issued while another VM system has been IPLed for testing in his virtual machine. So, you know that you can issue the CP command without having to stop the program, while a CMS command requires that CMS be ready for your command. See the section on "VM User Interface" for more on how to manipulate this.

CP Controls

CP is where system-wide controls are kept because it is the only system that all virtual machines must run under, and the only area that cannot be modified by users without special privileges. Some of the areas that can be controlled and the extent of that control include storage, DASD, and tape volumes.

Storage

Users can modify any part of their virtual memory. If they modify their operating system (such as CMS) to a point where it cannot continue to run, it will abend and they will have to re-load (IPL) a clean copy.

Users cannot access areas outside of their virtual machine since CP controls how much storage they have and where it is located.

Unit Record Devices (Printers, Card Reader/Punches)

CP controls all access to real and virtual system printers, card punches, and card readers. Real devices need not exist to have virtual counterparts. Many VM systems have run for years without ever having had a card reader or card punch. But, virtual readers and punches are a critical component to VM since file transfer between virtual machines is often done by punching a virtual card deck and having it placed it the virtual reader of another machine.

Users can define additional virtual unit record devices. However, whether a file printed on a virtual printer will ever be physically printed on a real printer is controlled by CP and the system operator.

DASD

DASD use is one of the biggest differences between TSO and CMS. TSO users are given access to files and all I/O to files is actually done by MVS (see Figure 13-1).

In contrast, the VM directory tells CP what virtual DASD areas (minidisks) are assigned to each user and where they are located on the real DASD. However, CP has no way to know about the data on those minidisks. If CP gives a user read/write control over a minidisk, the user then has total access to any area on that minidisk. Although most are formatted for CMS files, the user can even destroy the file directory (equivalent to the VTOC) which points to CMS files on that minidisk. The only control CP has over this minidisk is whether to give the user access to it and should that access be

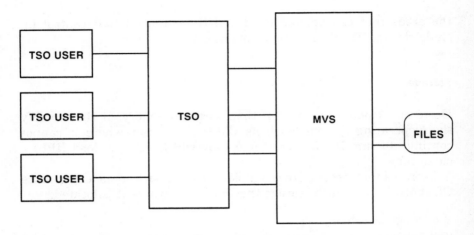

Figure 13-1 MVS data use.

read-only or read/write. From then on, the contents of that minidisk are under control of that virtual machine (see Figure 13-2).

Besides having no control over what a user does to the data on a minidisk, if they have read/write capabilities, CP also cannot control what areas of a minidisk can be read by a user if they have any access to the minidisk. CMS does attempt to control this by allowing users to create files with a filemode number of "0" (for example: "ALL NOTEBOOK A0"). These files are not normally seen by anyone else with a read-only link to that minidisk.

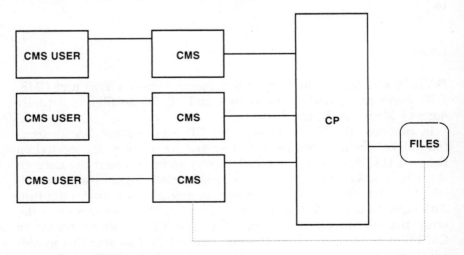

Figure 13-2 VM data use.

However, the restriction against seeing the A0 files is only controlled by some CMS commands and is easily bypassed. Do not depend on filemode "0" to provide security for sensitive data. Any unprivileged user can easily see those files if they know how. I am not going to detail the process of how to do this here but, rest assured, many users and most system programmers can tell you two or more ways to see those files with a single CMS command. The safest way to prevent access to specific files is to place them on their own minidisks. Then, control access to the minidisk.

Tapes

To get access to a tape volume, a privileged user (discussed in the next section) must use the CP ATTACH command to give the tape drive to a virtual machine. After that, the tape drive is under control of that virtual machine until he gives it up (by a DETACH or LOGOFF command).

Tape volumes used on CMS are normally unlabeled. SL (Standard Labeled) tapes can be used by programs using OS simulation data access which does support labels. So, if you do program development under VM, you can easily read MVS SL tapes as program input.

The CMS user has several choices of commands to write data to tape; the most common are TAPE DUMP, DDR, and MOVEFILE. You can also control whether tape data is to be written with or without a tape label. But since writing tape labels is an involved process, requiring knowledge of tape movement for each command, tape labels are generally not written.

Another item on CMS tape use: CMS does not provide a way to write data onto a tape volume that is too short. While MVS will simply provide another tape volume for the rest of the dataset, CMS will stop and give an error. In VM/SP Release 5, the capability to have multiple-volume tape files was added to CMS, but only for tapes written using OS simulation.

Each of the commands mentioned before handles end-of-volume conditions on a tape drive differently:

TAPE DUMP will stop and give the user a device error when the end of tape is reached. This is the most commonly used device to put files out on tape as individual files can be selectively retrieved.

MOVEFILE can be used with LABELDEF and FILEDEF to use the OS-simulation I/O routines and write out tapes with standard labels. When it reaches the end of a volume, CMS is notified, it requests another tape volume, and continues.

DDR provides its own end-of-volume routine to handle its unlabeled tapes. DDR is commonly used to backup DASD onto tape since it can quickly dump large quantities of data. But, DDR handles the data by transferring entire tracks; so, individual files cannot be recovered as with TAPE DUMP and the tapes produced with DDR are device dependent. They can only be restored to the same type of device with the same track size or larger.

Unlike MVS, there is no operating system verification in CP or CMS to check the internal label (SL) of a tape against the user's tape mount request. Also the operating system doesn't send tape mount messages to the operator. Under VM, the user must send a CP MESSAGE to the operator (perhaps repeatedly) to get a tape drive attached and a volume mounted.

There are several reasons on VM for tape access; system programmers need to install or maintain VM and products with tapes from vendors, production systems use tape input and output (these should be done on service machines to minimize user mistakes), and a backup system copies DASD data to tape for disaster protection (again, this should be done using a service machine and pre-defined procedures to reduce errors). But, because it is very easy for a CMS user to destroy the label on an MVS tape (just mount a tape and say "TAPE DUMP"), it may be desirable to keep users from writing on tapes.

If your users frequently bring in tapes or require tape access for other reasons, you might consider:

To automate getting a tape drive attached, or to remind the operator to mount a tape, VMUTIL (provided with VM IPF) offers a MOUNT command. This can simplify the mount process.

If users need access to tape files, make sure that backup tapes and other volumes containing sensitive data are kept separate from the others so that they are not accidentally used. This creates a problem. Making them more prominent and separate adds to the "intrigue" factor and points to tapes most likely to contain data worth stealing or prying into. This is also a reason not to label tapes with their contents. If you have sensitive tape data, a catalog relating a tape serial number to the contents provides more security.

Most of this discussion has been for CP controlling the "G-class" or general user under CMS. However, once a user gets more capabilities in VM, they may be able to manipulate CP or real devices. For this reason, privileges should be limited to what is needed for the job and audited where possible. However, VM is very flexible in providing just the privileges needed.

Control Authority

VM provides several types of privileges and privileged users. The capabilities of these people, as well as the capabilities of an auditor or security officer, to audit and control their activities are very different from MVS.

The end-user can do nothing to the real machine or to CP. He only has access to the limited "world" of his virtual machine. This restricted environment keeps any user from affecting another. The costs of this are discussed later in how data management is affected by this environment.

The VM users, capable of going outside their virtual machine, are the subject of this section. These privileged users include the VM directory manager, the system operator, and the system programmer. There may be more than one of each: This complicates the task of determining who is doing what (or more importantly—who *did* what).

The Directory Manager

If there is a single major control point, it is the VM directory and the person responsible for maintaining it—the directory manager. The VM directory defines every virtual machine to CP so that when a user logs on (or a service virtual machine is AUTOLOGed), CP knows how much memory to give it, which disk areas it manages, what VM commands it can issue, and its passwords. This directory is the single point of control and security on an unmodified VM system with no additional security system.

The VM directory begins as a CMS file where the components of each virtual machine are spelled out in easy to read control records. The directory manager edits this file, makes changes or corrections, and saves the updated file. The DIRECT command converts the CMS file into a form that CP is expecting and puts it on a pre-defined CP disk area. Since the directory is maintained in an easy-to-use CMS file, the exposures here include:

Passwords The simplicity of updating the VM directory (edit the file, correct it, and file it) is also its weakness. The CMS editor does not provide any audit capabilities so there is no way to determine what changes were made and when. Also, all data is kept in clear text. This means that passwords are easily seen.

Data Access Because all DASD areas controlled by a virtual machine are defined in the directory, the directory manager must track who uses which areas of DASD. As this can be error-prone, when done manually, a DASDMAP utility is provided with VM that goes through the CMS directory file and shows areas multiply defined or as yet unassigned.

If the directory manager mistakenly assigns an area to two users, the data will most frequently be destroyed. For example, Figure 13-3 shows a frequent directory manager accident: The directory manager thought the area was free and assigned part of it to someone else.

As a result, two virtual machines both think they have exclusive use of that area. When the second person logs on and formats the area for use by CMS, it destroys any data on the minidisk owned by the first user. If the first user doesn't know why his data was destroyed, he may well re-format his disk to use again, which destroys the data the second user has created. This has been known to bounce back and forth for days before one of the users decides to find out *why* his data is being destroyed. The directory manager then had to redefine one of the minidisks and place it on an area of DASD not being used by someone else.

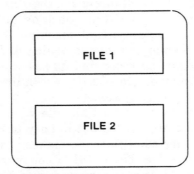

Figure 13-3 MDISK1 overlaying MDISK2.

The major point is that there is no protection against making mistakes with the directory. No audit trail of directory changes means that, if someone has special privileges normally but the directory manager changes that before an audit, there is no way to know that changes were made to avoid the audit exposure.

One of the first products usually added to a VM system is a directory manager. By having an automated process that prevents re-assigning previously assigned areas and providing an audit trail of who is making what directory changes, the VM directory is no longer subject to human error.

Privilege Classes

Commands that can affect areas outside of their own virtual machine are restricted by CP to specific privilege classes. These classes are defined in the directory. The standard classes are:

Class A—System operations authority. A user with Class A can enable system monitoring, force users off the system, and issue the CP SHUTDOWN command to terminate CP on the real machine.

Class B—Device operations authority. A Class B user can vary real devices on- and offline and attach them to users.

Class C—This is generally given to the system programmer. However, Class C provides only one command not allowed by other privilege classes: the command to modify real CP storage (STCP).

Class D—Spool system controller. Class D commands are used to manage real printers and card punches as well as manipulate system spool files such as transferring them to tape or between userids.

Class E—System Programmer. Class E allows the system programmer to examine real storage, turn on system monitoring, and issue commands to query and affect system performance.

Class F—CE. This class is for diagnostic purposes only and should never be given out unnecessarily. This provides no capabilities generally needed by the system programmer.

Class G—General user authority. These are CP commands that control a virtual rather than a real machine.

In the directory, virtual machines are generally defined with a combination of these privilege classes. One does not imply another. For example, if the system operator has Class A, he cannot control the system printer without also having Class D.

Modifying Privileges

There are several ways to control or restrict these privileges further without modifying VM or keeping people from doing their job. First, because these classes are necessarily broad, the capability has been added to VM of allowing directory OVERRIDE files. Override files allow specific CP commands to be assigned to specific classes and removed from others. For example, CP SHUTDOWN can be removed from Class A and assigned to Class S. This way a system operator can still do normal Class A tasks, but still not be able to shut the system down.

System Operator

The system operator generally needs at least privilege Class A and G. He is often given Class B and D as well, since he generally is responsible for managing printers, attaching tape drives to users, and other manual tasks concerning real (not virtual) equipment.

Several system operator tasks can be error-prone or difficult to audit, such as transferring spool files (including electronic notes/mail) between users and deleting (purging) those files. There is no auditing other than a console log that can be turned off by the operator or lost in a system cold start. By giving the operator the authority to transfer the files, he is also given the authority to purge them (more than one person has accidentally purged all system electronic mail). Also, if sensitive data is sent through the spool system, the operator has the authority to transfer the file to himself, read it, and return the file without the user knowing it.

One way to provide the operator with the capability needed, but still audit its use and prevent accidents, is to set up a privileged service virtual machine. It can do many privileged tasks (such as transferring spool files from one user to another). This machine can receive requests from the operator or system programmer, verify if they are allowed to request this (through tables set up on the server), issue the command for the user, and create an audit entry saying what was done and who requested it. This will allow the operator to transfer files between users when requested, but not to himself; or to purge files, but not do a "PURGE SYSTEM RDR ALL." The service machine can be selective.

System Programmer

The system programmer generally has all classes of commands except Class F. Although the Class C STCP (store CP) command is not normally used, most system programmers also have that class.

Unless the use of the STCP command to modify real CP memory is specifically required, the system programmer should avoid giving himself Class C. Most system programmers agree that having more capabilities than needed for a specific task is an invitation to an accident. For example, when installing and testing a new system under VM, only a G-class userid is required since all privileged operations are done second-level with virtual machines given additional privileges only in the second level system. Since these privileges aren't also given first level, commands intended for the test system cannot be accidentally given on the real machine (such as SHUT-DOWN).

When possible, normal system operations commands should be given on the system operator's console since the console spool should show routine operations activity.

Procedures and Privileges

Many people have procedures to prevent accidents and provide an audit trail so that if a problem occurs, they can track back to see what might have contributed to it. For example:

- Use the service machine mentioned before for all Class D purge and transfer of spool files. Then, pull those commands out Class D by using the OVERRIDE file.
- Have only one fully-privileged userid (usually MAINT). For most other purposes, use a G-class machine. Use a machine with only G privileges *especially* for putting up second-level systems, since on a second-level VM, you will need to issue privileged CP commands. This way you can't accidentally issue one on the main system.
- Keep track of all service machines with special privileges and who has the password to logon to it or to issue privileged commands through it. Removing the capability for a user to link to other users does little good when he has the authority to mount any backup tape and look at the data.

These all tie into one primary goal: not to give a virtual machine more privileges than needed.

Data Management

Now to explore an earlier topic in more detail: how the operating system manages your data. A major difference between MVS and VM is the way they manage (or don't manage) data.

DASD Access

As mentioned before, CP controls the minidisks and type of access via the CP LINK command (Read-Only or Read/Write). MVS doesn't do this as it controls access to files, not DASD volumes. A closer equivalent in MVS to a minidisk is the PDS (Partitioned Data Set). This is an MVS library where multiple members are kept in a single data set. MVS controls the dataset, not individual PDS members. VM controls minidisks, not individual files.

The next level down is file control. MVS controls access to files by intercepting every file OPEN, CLOSE, READ, and WRITE. When files are OPENed or initially accessed, MVS can validate access to this file and audit its use. But, because of this central control of files, users cannot create files to be managed by the system without prior authorization and space for the dataset being pre-allocated. The system owns the data, not the user. The system can delete it, if it expires, or restrict access to it.

In CMS, the user owns the data. He can create any file he wants, as long as it will fit in the pre-defined minidisk, and can keep it as long as he wants. It is manipulated using CMS (usually), but a user can access files and data by using the CMS FSOPEN and other CMS file system macros, use OS simulation (such as opening a file from a program written in COBOL or other languages), or request I/O services directly to CP bypassing CMS entirely (done frequently by products that run in service machines and need high I/O performance). Since CMS isn't necessarily used to access the data, and even if it is, CMS can be modified by the user. This is not a good location for security controls over file access.

Data Access: Techniques and Exposures

A minidisk is added to a virtual machine with the CP LINK command. Data on a minidisk is made available to CMS with the CMS ACCESS command. The combination of "CP LINK" and "CMS ACCESS" causes the most grief to users more familiar with other operating systems than with VM.

The LINK command requires you to specify the userid who owns the minidisk, the owner's minidisk address, the virtual address you want it assigned to in your virtual machine, and a linkmode. You will also be asked for a password if one is assigned in the directory.

The link modes used are controlled by minidisk passwords in the CP directory. There are up to three for each minidisk: READ, WRITE, and MULT. These are used to do the following:

Linkmode   Action

Two linkmodes controlled by the READ password:

R   Get a Read-Only link to the minidisk only if no one else is linked to it. Instead of this, use the "RR" linkmode. When you get a Read-Only link, it doesn't matter if anyone else is linked to it. If you are interested, after you link to the disk, type "CP QUERY LINKS" to see who else is linked to it.

RR   Get a Read-Only link to the minidisk. It doesn't matter if anyone has any type of link to it. This is the most common type of link.

Two linkmodes controlled by the WRITE password:

W   Get a Read/Write link to the minidisk only if no one else is linked to it. This isn't very useful. If you need to modify data on a minidisk, you generally don't care if anyone has a Read-Only link. Just because they have the link, does not mean that they are actively looking at any file or data on that minidisk.

WR   Get a Read/Write link to the minidisk only if no one else is linked to it. If one or more others have only a Read-Only link, get a Read-Only link too. This is one of the most useless link modes. If you need to update a minidisk, a Read-Only link doesn't help you.

Three linkmodes controlled by the MULT password:

M   Get a Read/Write link to the minidisk as long as no one else has a Read/Write link to it. This is a valuable linkmode and frequently used to update disks (such as public utility disks) where many people have permanent or frequent Read-Only links. See Figure 13-5 for an example of how to update this without causing errors for the other users.

MR   This is like "M," with the addition that if anyone already has the disk linked Read/Write you will get a Read-Only link to it. This is the safest linkmode to use in the directory when defining minidisks, so that if someone has a Read/Write link to a minidisk, when you logon, you will not also get a Read/Write link.

MW   Get a Read/Write link to the minidisk even if someone else has the minidisk linked Read/Write. **Warning: this is one of the most dangerous things you can do in VM.**

Once CP allows a LINK to a minidisk (or there is a permanent minidisk assignment or LINK in the CP directory), CMS is used to ACCESS the minidisk. This reads a copy of the file directory (or catalog) showing which files are on the minidisk, where they are, and some information about the file. The file directory is re-written when a file is changed or when the user releases the minidisk (via CMS RELEASE command).

This is why the MW link is so dangerous. If you get an MW link and ACCESS a minidisk when another virtual machine also has R/W access to it, you do *not* need to modify anything on the disk to destroy it. All you need to do is RELEASE the minidisk. Because CMS only knows about you and doesn't realize that anyone else may be updating the minidisk, and since it realizes that you no longer want access to that minidisk, it rewrites the file directory which naturally points to where the files *were*. If anyone else had modified any data on that minidisk, your file directory won't reflect their change. This is the most frequent cause of damaged and destroyed data in VM.

Since each user with access to a minidisk has a copy of the file directory in memory, this also means that if you modify a minidisk that others are reading, they may get errors when reading files you have replaced, moved, or erased.

Updating Files without Disturbing Users

There is one simple technique for updating files on a publicly-used minidisk that is used by most system programmers with a few variations:

• Never logon and get MW access to a minidisk. (This is rule 1 of any VM system programmer, so this will be the last time I'll repeat it).
• Avoid disturbing file pointers that users might be using in their file directory.
• Change files on your own minidisk. Only replace files on a public minidisk after they have been tested (to avoid making more changes than necessary).

Here's a simple EXEC that you can use:

```
ADDPUB EXEC
/* update a file on PUBLIC 191 minidisk */
/* to call this exec, say: ADDPUB filename filetype */
parse upper arg fn ft .
/* first, link and access the minidisk */
'CP LINK PUBLIC 191 222 M multpassword'
if rc /= 0 then exit rc
'ACCESS 222 J'
if rc /= 0 then exit rc
'ERASE' fn 'OLD'ft 'J'
'RENAME' fn ft 'J' fn 'OLD'ft 'J'
'COPYFILE' fn ft 'A' fn ft 'J (OLDDATE'
holdrc = rc
'RELEASE J (DET'
exit holdrc
```

In CMS, the RENAME command does not disturb the file directory pointers since only the file name changes, not the file location. By renaming the file, the original file is left undisturbed in case anyone is currently using it. But, when users re-access the minidisk, they will then see only the new file.

The second time the same file is updated, the first file is erased, the second is renamed, and the current file copied to the disk. This keeps the older files from cluttering up the minidisk. This is why you don't want to modify the file too many times in a short period. Since the second update of the same file causes the original file to be erased, the next time you put a file on the disk, it will overlay some of the pointer and data areas used by the original file and cause the user to receive file system errors. If files must be changed more than once, users should switch to the more current version of the file as soon as possible, and send a message to all users (using CP MESSAGE ALL) to request that they re-access the minidisk.

However, that command is likely to confuse some people, especially those not using that minidisk. Another common EXEC (not given here) that system programmers write is one that uses the CP QUERY LINKS command to see which users are linked to the minidisk in question, then sends a message just to those users. This "selective message" command is very useful.

Correcting Minidisks with Damaged Files

Damaged files are generally detected by trying to read a file, either through a program (which abends) or a CMS command (such as XEDIT or TYPE). CMS commands often return a message such as "FILE SYSTEM ERROR" although, because the area of file damage is unpredictable, so is the error message. These files are not normally recoverable. When damaged files are found:

First, determine how they were damaged. If anyone is using MW links to get to those files, that should be stopped. If a program was used that puts out files in error, it should be corrected.

Second, recover your data. Get a new minidisk (either another directory-defined minidisk or a Tdisk [temporary minidisk] so that you have a place to recover data without destroying the damaged disk. This should be the same size as the original.

Do you have a backup of that disk? If so, you should be able to recover a copy of the minidisk to your new minidisk. However, if the backup was taken after the minidisk was damaged and didn't detect it, that copy may also be bad. Still, go back to as many copies of backup data trying to get a good copy of the minidisk.

Next, recover current files from the damaged minidisk. Copy all files from it to the new one. You cannot use the "COPYFILE * * D = = N" command (for this example, I'm using "D" as the damaged disk, "N" as the new one) because a bad file will stop the command progress. Instead, copy them this way:

```
LISTFILE * * D (EX ARGS
EXEC CMS COPYFILE % = = N (OLDDATE
```

The LISTFILE command creates a file called CMS EXEC, which contains a list of all files we can locate on the damaged disk. The next command says to run that EXEC, putting the command "COPYFILE" before the name of each file and putting "= = N (OLDDATE)" after each file. The percent sign (%) is just a place-holder: It's needed here but has no effect. This effectively creates an EXEC which performs a single COPYFILE command for each file on the damaged minidisk. If you encounter a damaged file, it will display that the COPYFILE hit an error and then continue trying to copy the next file. This should allow you to recover all the files you can.

Get rid of the damaged minidisk and replace it with the new one. If you got a permanent minidisk set up in the directory for your new disk, go back into the directory, eliminate the definition for the damaged minidisk, and re-assign this new one to the original userid and address and replace all minidisks passwords (if any).

If the new minidisk is a temporary minidisk, simply use DDR to copy it to the damaged minidisk. Since the damage was in the data and not in the device, DDR will overlay the bad data with the new files.

One note of warning here, that doesn't seem to fit anywhere else in this book: If you look up the LISTFILE (EXEC option in the CP Command and Macro reference, or look up EXECs in general, be aware that VM has three (yes, 3) EXEC languages. All are run from files with a filetype of EXEC. They are only differentiated by the first line in the file.

1. First line contains a comment in the form: /* */ — This is a REXX EXEC and contains REXX code.
2. First line starts with: &TRACE—This is an EXEC 2 exec
3. First line starts with anything else (or &CONTROL)—This is "OLD EXEC": the original CMS EXEC processor. The reason that I'm covering this now is because LISTFILE (EXEC produces EXECs processed by the original EXEC processor. Be-cause of this, some things may not work as you expect. For example, if you try to pass in a variable with more than eight characters, it will truncate everything to eight. There are some other differences, but if you ever work with an EXEC that doesn't seem to behave as you expect, see if it is EXEC2 and the &TRACE has been accidentally removed. I mention this is because the percent sign (%) placeholder I suggested using above will NOT work for EXEC2 execs.

User Interface

VM has several command environments. The environment name is displayed when you press ENTER twice. Generally, when you logon to VM, CMS is automatically loaded and you are placed in the CMS environment. Most general users know only about the CMS and EDIT environments. But knowing how to deliberately move between environments allows you to execute CP commands while others are already executing in CMS and address specific levels of CP when testing new systems.

CP

If your status message on your terminal says CP READ, you are in the CP environment. If you were in CMS, it has been temporarily suspended. At this point, you can only enter CP commands such as QUERY, MESSAGE, or LOGOFF. If you enter the CP environment for any reason, you can re-enter the system you are running under CP (such as CMS) where you left it by issuing the CP command "BEGIN." There is no need to re-load (IPL) your operating system.

One reason that you might LOGON and find yourself in CP is if you did a DISCONNECT instead of LOGOFF the previous time you used CMS.

CMS

For CMS users, normally the status on your screen says "RUN-NING." If you enter the command "CP" or hit PA1, it will say "CP READ." You are now in the CP command environment.

As mentioned before, you can get into CMS by entering "IPL CMS" from CP, entering "BEGIN" if CP was entered after you were in CMS or, automatically, when you logon if "IPL CMS" is in your VM directory entry.

You can issue CP commands directly from CMS. You can also direct a command to be issued immediately in the CP environment. First, find out your terminal "LINEND" character by issuing the CP command "QUERY TERMINAL," normally it is the number sign [#]. Then, put the LINEND character and CP in front of any CP command. Even if a program or command is currently running in CMS, this command will be issued immediately, run in CP mode, and the CMS process will continue. This is a good way to monitor program

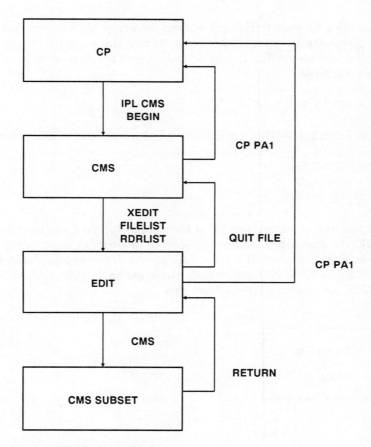

Figure 13-4 Changing environments.

progress (using the CP INDICATE command) or even to send a message during a long-running command. For example:

```
#CP IND
```

This also allows you to communicate with CP from any operating system. If you are planning to IPL a second-level VM system, first set your linend character to something else. for example:

```
TERM LINEND $
```

Then, IPL your system. Once in your second level VM system, you can issue second level CP commands by using "#CP command" and commands to your first-level system by using "$CP command." This also prevents mistakes where you think you've entered your command second-level and it was actually executed first-level.

For example:

```
#CP ENABLE 330
```

(oops, I don't have this device defined to my second-level system.) So:

```
$CP DEFINE GRAF 330
#CP ENABLE 330
#CP VARY ON 330
```

If you are in second level and have forgotten to reset your terminal LINEND character, knowing how to switch environments again comes to the rescue. Hit your PA1 key to force yourself into CP, do the TERM LINEND command, then go back into CMS with the BEGIN command. You're all set now.

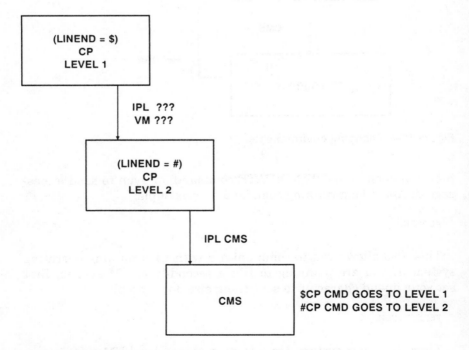

Figure 13-5 Multi-level CP.

Another time when you may have to deliberately transfer between environments is if a program appears to hang up or loop and you can't get out of it. You can get into CP (using PA1) and issue an external interrupt (EXT) command. This generally interrupts the CMS process. On some VM/SP systems, this will enter DEBUG mode. Enter "HX" to get out of this. You should then be ready for another CMS command. If EXT doesn't fix the problem, just IPL CMS while in CP.

EDIT

The next environment down is an editor environment. Several editors are available in CMS, but the most flexible and frequently used is XEDIT. However, the type of edit doesn't matter. You get into an editor by any command that starts up the editor (such as "XEDIT MY FILE"). When you terminate the editing process (through QUIT or FILE), you are returned to CMS. You can issue CMS and CP commands from an EDIT environment, subject to editor limitations.

CMS Subset

One of the more "interesting" things that can happen in an EDIT environment is to find yourself in CMS Subset. This is a remnant of the "old days" where to issue a CMS command, it had to be able to exist without wiping out the editor itself. So, a subset of commands was made available to be issued while in the EDIT environment. This is rarely needed now. However, what DOES happen is that you may accidentally enter CMS subset. To enter subset mode, you enter "CMS." In some cases, pressing the PA2 key will also trigger this.

To return to the editor, the command is "RETURN."

The negative return codes are the most visible evidence that you might be in the wrong environment. A somewhat unofficial interpretation is:

-3—You are in CMS and have entered a command invalid for this mode. You've probably misspelled it or don't have the minidisk that contains the command accessed.

-2—You are in CMS Subset and have entered a command invalid for this mode. You probably got here by accident and don't know how it happened. It's not important. Just enter "RETURN" and continue where you were.

Besides allowing you to switch between command environments, CMS allows you to enter more than one command at a time (unlike TSO which doesn't allow anything more until the command completes).

Under CMS, once a command is entered, the keyboard remains unlocked during processing unless the command specifically locks it (such as going into full-screen processing). The user can enter a long-running command and then type several more commands that are *stacked* for later use. If the commands do not disturb the list of pre-stacked commands, they are executed in sequence.

The status message on the lower right of the screen shows "RUNNING." However, it generally shows this whether or not it is actually running anything. Even if it is idle, it will generally show "RUNNING." These status messages are cryptic at best:

MORE or HOLDING says that more data is waiting to be displayed on the screen and the user is generally expected to take some manual action of clearing the screen before the additional lines will be shown. In the case of MORE, the screen will clear itself after a predefined time, but HOLDING indicates that manual action (CLEAR or PA2) is required.

VM READ states that CMS is temporarily halted waiting for the ENTER key to be hit. Nothing is happening. However, this doesn't mean that a program is waiting for data. VM READ can be entered by simply hitting the ENTER key at the wrong time. In this case, hitting the ENTER key again results in the perfectly normal RUNNING status. If it again results in VM READ and no program is running that could be in a "read loop," enter the command

```
'SET AUTOREAD OFF'.
```

Conclusion/Summary

This chapter is intended to give the new VM user a taste of the areas that VM probably handles in an unfamiliar way. Still, the areas addressed are used in the everyday life of any VM system programmer.

• Use the least privileges needed to get a job done
• Avoid causing data-sharing problems
• Be careful with your directory

About the Author

While writing this chapter, Janet Gobeille was a product manager at Systems Center, Inc., in Reston, Virginia, and was responsible for VMSECURE product. During her five-year tenure at Systems Center, she also managed the company's VMBACKUP, VMARCHIVE, and VMTAPE products and served in various capacities in the Customer Services Department. Prior to Systems Center, Janet spent nine years with AMOCO Corporation in VM systems support and as a VM instructor.

Janet accepted a position with the IBM Corporation during the second half of 1988 and is currently involved in VM support in the Washington, D.C., Systems Center.

An Overview of the Control Program

by James McCreary

What is "CP"?

CP, the Control Program in VM/SP, VM/IS, VM/HPO and VM/XA, is the VM manager between the hardware and the end user. Some of what CP manages are:

- Real Devices
- Real Storage
- Virtual Devices
- Virtual Memory
- Paging Areas
- Temporary disks
- Spool Areas
- CP Commands and Diagnoses
- Guests under VM
- The Object Directory
- Shared Virtual Memory

Through CP's management techniques, the end user in his own virtual machine can emulate the functions of a real machine. For example, the end user has a virtual printer defined to his virtual machine. He can send output to this printer. CP then takes this output and sends it to the real system printer. The result is the appearance that the end user sent output to a real printer.

CP is a program made up of numerous individually assembled modules. It is loaded into the real machine from the SYSRES (SYStem RESidence volume). The name of each module that makes up the CP nucleus is of the form DMKxxx; DMK is the prefix assigned for CP and "xxx" is the three character acronym for each function. For example, DMKRIO is the CP routine that describes the Real I/O configuration for the system. There is also a naming convention for entry points within each module. They are usually eight characters long, the first six characters representing the module name. For example, routine DMKFRE (Free storage management) has an entry point named DMKFREE (allocate free storage).

The CP modules that make up the resident nucleus are loaded into a dedicated area in real storage. They consist of highly used modules, those that affect performance and interrupt level routines. The remainder are pageable modules that are less frequently, or rarely called. These modules fit into a single page of storage (4K) and are loaded into any available real page in the Dynamic Paging Area.

CP uses a variety of control blocks to maintain information about the resources it controls. These control blocks are normally maintained in a fixed area of real storage known as "free storage." There are control blocks for each virtual machine, each virtual device, and each spool file, just to name a few. For example, the VMBLOK (Virtual Machine Control Block) is the primary control block for a virtual machine. It contains information about the current priority assigned to the virtual machine, the last CP command issued by the virtual machine, the name of the Secondary User (if any) assigned, as well as a multitude of other information related to a virtual machine. CP allocates and deallocates blocks as needed. Related control blocks are linked together. Many control block structures are anchored in the commonly addressable low memory area know as the Prefix Storage Area (PSA).

CP Managing Real Devices

Each virtual machine defined in VM usually has its own virtual console at virtual address ("vaddr") 009, a virtual card reader at vaddr 00C, a virtual punch at vaddr 00D and a virtual printer at vaddr 00E. When I/O directed at any of these devices, CP manages the I/O and sends it to the appropriate destination. CP does Real I/O to unit record devices such as printers.

CP allows you to define sections of real DASD devices to be virtual DASD devices owned by virtual machines. These virtual DASD areas are know as minidisks. CP maps your minidisks in your virtual machine to the real DASD devices on which they are located. When you update a file on a minidisk, CP directs the I/O to the real device at the location where the minidisk is defined.

Management of Real Storage

CP partitions Real storage as described in Figure A-1. The first area described is the **Prefix Storage Area (PSA)**. It is the primary control block and resides on page 0 (the first 4K) of real storage. It is the anchor for other control blocks.

```
+----------------------------------+
| Free Storage                     |               |
|----------------------------------|
| CP Trace Table                   |               |
|----------------------------------|
|                                  |               |
|                                  |               |
|                                  |               |
|                                  |               |
|                                  |               |
| Dynamic Paging Area              |               |
|                                  |               |
|                                  |               |
|                                  |               |
|                                  |               |
|                                  |               |
|----------------------------------|
|                                  |               |
| CP Resident Nucleus              |               |
|                                  |               |
|----------------------------------|
| Prefix Storage Area (Page 0)     |               |
+----------------------------------+
```

Figure A-1 Real machine layout.

The **CP Resident Nucleus** contains all the resident CP modules. The last module in the load list that generates the CP Resident Nucleus is DMKCPE. It has the descriptive ending point DMKCPEND.

The **Dynamic Paging Area** is the major portion of real storage. This is where pageable CP modules are written; as well as pages of executing guests, free storage extensions, and virtual machine pages.

The **CP Trace Table** records events that happen in the real machine, that can be used for debugging CP errors.

Free Storage is where control blocks, accounting cards, system log messages, and segment, page, and swap tables are located. The size of of free storage is defined in DMKSYS. If the free storage area is filled, the system will "extend" it by allocating pages from the Dynamic Paging Area.

Management of Virtual Devices

CP allows each virtual machine to act like a real machine. As mentioned earlier, each virtual machine usually has unit record devices, such as printers and card readers. CP manages these devices, as well as minidisks, T-disk, virtual consoles, etc.

For example, one can ask CP for temporary minidisk space (T-disk) for use during your session. CP will find the requested space (if available) on CP-Owned volume containing TDSK, and allocate that space for your virtual machine. It will manage any I/O to or from the temporary minidisk. If you detach the minidisk, it will make that space available for other users.

Management of Virtual Memory

When you logon to a VM userid, you are assigned a minimum amount of virtual memory. Virtual memory is managed by CP so that it appears to a virtual machine as consecutive pages of real memory but is actually mapped to dispersed pages, some in real storage and some in dedicated paging areas on DASD devices. CP can allow portions of your virtual memory to be in the real machine, when the memory is used. If an area of your memory previously unused is referenced, CP can fetch the memory from disk into the real memory. CP may have to move a page of your or another virtual machine's memory, not currently being referenced, out to disk to make room for your memory.

Management of Spool Area

System spool files are built and kept in specified DASD areas (TEMP SPACE) defined on CP-Owned volumes. This spooling area contains spool files for each user on the system. It is also the area where CP will will store pages of virtual memory if the paging space has overflowed.

Each virtual machine in VM usually has a virtual printer, card reader, card punch and console. These simulate real devices that may or may not be on the real system (few systems have a real card reader any more). If you wish to print data to a real printer, you would spool your printer to that device (providing any TAG information that may be needed), then print the data. CP will open the spool file and create a spool file block associated with that file. After the spool file is created, CP reads each 4K page as stored on disk and writes it to the the required printer. The process is very similar to that used for sending output to a real punch.

VM also provides a facility for capturing lines displayed on the virtual console in a spool file. First all 3270 special characters are eliminated or converted to blanks. A spool file is then opened, unless already opened. A line can be no longer than 132 characters. Every 60 lines of output are placed in a spool buffer and written to the spool file. This continues until the file is closed.

Processing CP Commands and Diagnoses

CP provides its own set of commands to communicate with. Not all commands are available to all users on the system. Each command has a privilege class associated with it. The default privilege classes available in VM are:

CLASS DESCRIPTION

A   Primary System Operator (normally OPERATOR) —
        These include commands to shutdown VM, control system
        accounting, lock and unlock pages in real storage, etc.

B   System Resource Operator — These include commands that manage real resources such as DASD, printers, etc.

C   System Programmer — These include commands to change real storage and generate updates to VM/SP.

D   Spool Operator — These include commands to manage system spool files and unit record devices.

E   System Analyst — These commands include commands to examine real storage.

F   Customer Engineer — Used by the CE.

G   General User — These include commands to control a user's own virtual machine.

any   These commands are available to all users and allow you to enter and leave the VM system.

Beginning in VM/SP Release 4, a command class override capability is provided to allow you to change privilege classes of CP commands and diagnoses. This gives you the flexibility to deal with site-specific needs. For example, if several service virtual machines running on your CPU need MSGNOH, LOCATE, DIAGNOSE x'84' and DIAGNOSE x'04', you could give these virtual machines class B and E, or you could define a class V that contains these four privilege commands.

Several CP commands are defined in more than one privilege class. Depending on the CP classes available to your virtual machine, you will get different responses and have different parameters for each. Here are the duplicate class commands:

Command	Class A B C D E F G	Comment
AUTOLOG	x x	Same command for each class
CHANGE	x x	Different command for each class
DCP	x x	Same command for each class
DEFINE	x x x	A,B same command, different than G
DETACH	x x	Different command for each class
DISABLE	x x	Same command for each class
DMCP	x x	Same command for each class
ENABLE	x x	Same command for each class
INDICATE	x x x	Different command for each class

LOCATE	x x	Same command for each class
MESSAGE	x x	A,B same command, different than any
MONITOR	x x	Same command for each class
MSGNOH	x x	Same command for each class
NETWORK	x x	Different command for each class
PER	x x x x x x x	Same command for each class
PURGE	x x	Different command for each class
QUERY	x x x x x x x	Different command for each class
SET	x x x x x	Different command for each class
WARNING	x x	Same command for each class

For example, if you issue CP QUERY DASD in a G privilege machine and in a B privilege machine, you will get different results. The G privilege command deals with a user's own virtual machine, whereas the B privilege command displays information about the real system.

```
query dasd DASD 191 3380 VMPK01 R/W     5 CYL
etc.
```

```
query dasd
DASD 0123 CP OWNED VMSRES 0000
etc.
```

In class B machine, QUERY VIRTUAL DASD would yield the same results as the class G QUERY DASD.

Another way to communicate with CP is via diagnose instructions. This direct communication with CP has a privilege class structure just like CP commands. It can be used by a program running in the virtual machine to issue CP commands, as well as to collect and modify information about the real and virtual machine.

A common diagnose command is DIAGNOSE x'08'. This enables a virtual machine to issue CP commands and return the response to the program running in the virtual machine.

Scheduler

The CP scheduler (DMKSCH) attempts to get minimum response time for users and maximum use of the resources available. CP attempts to control the scheduling to give every user their fair share of CPU time.

Let's first define some terms to be used in this section:

TIME SLICE — The initial time slice is calculated at system IPL time. It is a constant that is CPU model dependent. It is approximately the time it takes to run 10,000 instructions.

RUN LIST — The list of virtual machines currently having access to the processor. The current referenced pages of these virtual machine pages fit into real memory.

ELIGIBLE LIST — The virtual machines not on the RUN list. These virtual machines are runable, but their virtual machine pages will not fit into memory.

Q1 — Interactive virtual machines. They get into the RUN list eight times as often as Q2 virtual machines, however their time slice is 1/8th as long. This is where a user's virtual machine starts when they logon.

Q2 — Non-interactive virtual machines. Q2 virtual machines have not yet completed their time slice.

Q3 — Non-interactive virtual machine with longer transaction. Once a virtual machine completes six consecutive Q2 slices without becoming Q1, it is placed on Q3. They get eight times the time slice of Q2, however, they get on the RUN list 1/8th as often.

DEADLINE PRIORITY — Indicates the delay that the user can encounter until the user can finish its next time slice.

When a virtual machine logs on, it is placed in Q1. If it finishes its time slice, it is dropped from the RUN list and placed on an eligible list. At queue drop, the user is assigned to Q1, if it returned from a long wait, or Q2/Q3 otherwise. CP then calculates the working set size, the amount of storage needed to be paged into real memory during your next time slice. CP then calculates your deadline priority. Your position on the eligible list is based upon your deadline priority. You are moved back to the RUN list when you are at the top of the eligible list and your projected working set size will fit into available page frames of storage. The entire logic is obviously a bit more complicated than described here, but this is basically how the scheduler works.

Dispatcher

The dispatcher in VM does a multitude of tasks, including working closely with the scheduler. It also collects wait time, problem state time and CP time.

Paging and the Dynamic Paging Area (DPA)

To allow virtual machines, running under VM, access to the real storage on the CPU, CP uses the concept of paging. In a real machine, the Dynamic Paging Area is the largest portion of real storage. This is where CP allocates pages of storage for each virtual machine's use.

When a user logs on to VM, a virtual machine is defined with a certain amount of virtual memory. This memory is broken up into 4K page allocations. As you reference areas of your storage, each 4K page will hopefully reside in the Dynamic Paging Area so that the CPU can process your request. Your real machine may have 16 Megabytes of real storage. With many users having virtual machines that in total far exceed the real storage, CP will resort to paging to manage the real storage available to users.

Let's digress a little. When a DASD volume is FORMATTED using DMKFMT, areas on a volume or several volumes was allocated as PAGE and TEMP. These areas are written to hold as many 4K records that each track (CKD) or group of blocks (FBA) can hold. In some cases, filler records are written to the DASD for performance considerations.

In addition to being formatted and allocated, you must tell CP via the SYSOWN macro of DMKSYS, that these volumes are available for CP's use. These are referred to as CP-Owned volumes. CP will first use the PAGE space on these volumes until it is exhausted. At that point it will spill over into TEMP space. Remember, the main purpose of TEMP space is to hold spool files

CP will keep referenced pages of storage in the Dynamic Paging Area. Other pages of storage are then maintained on the CP-Owned DASD devices. If a page of storage on the DASD is reference, CP will find an available page of storage in DPA, and fetch your page from disk. CP may have paged to DASD another virtual machine's inactive page to make room for yours. Each page maintained on DASD has a 4 byte address assigned to it by CP. The address is derived from the locating on a cylinder (or block) and a number assigned from the position of the DASD volume in the SYSOWN list of DMKSYS.

Each page frame in the DPA is already assigned or available. CP maintains two lists; a FREE list containing pages immediately available and a FLUSH list containing pages that are currently assigned, but can be paged out to DASD. CP allocates pages in the DPA from the FREE list. As assigned pages are no longer referenced, they are placed on the FLUSH list. When the page on the FLUSH list is written to DASD, it is placed on the FREE list and is available for assignment. This is a circular maintenance (FREE to ASSIGNED to FLUSH back to FREE) method that CP uses to manage the DPA.

Free Storage

Free storage is the area used for CP control blocks. The size of Free Storage is defined in the SYSCOR macro of DMKSYS. (You should allocate two to three pages for Free Storage for every user, based upon an average number of users simultaneously logged on.) CP routines DMKFRE and DMKFRT manage the free storage area. If insufficient free storage area exists, CP will "extend" into DPA for its control blocks.

The Directory

The directory provides CP with information it requires to allow you to logon and do productive work. When the system was generated, an area on a CP-owned volume was allocated with type "DRCT" to hold the directory. A directory is maintained in this area which defines all virtual machine known to the system. Each user must have an entry in the directory in order to logon to the system. A typical directory entry for a user would contain:

- USERID and LOGON password
- Default and Maximum virtual machine size
- The privilege classes assigned
- An account number and 8-character distribution code
- Definition of the security group the user is associated with
- IPL CMS (or other)
- A definition of the console * A definition of the reader, punch and printer
- LINKs to system and other disks
- Location of and minidisks and Read/Write/Mult passwords for each

A source directory is made up of multiple user directory entries along with profiles common to multiple users, and the definition of the device containing the area where the object directory is written. In a virtual machine, the DIRECT module may be used to "compile" the source directory and update the object directory on disk. After the directory is written to disk, CP is informed to switch to the new object directory using DIAGNOSE x'3C'. Some items in the object directory can be updated in place by a privileged user issuing a DIAGNOSE x'84'. An IPLable form of the DIRECT module (DMKDIR) can be used stand alone or in a virtual machine to update the object directory.

About the Author

James McCreary has been with VM Software, Inc. in Reston, Virginia, since 1985. He has been involved in the support of VM Software's VMBACKUP and VMCENTER II products; and is currently part of a specialized sales support team. Jim previously installed and tested VM applications at Boeing Computer Services, for use by Boeing's customer base. He has also taught mathematics and science to gifted students in a junior high school.

Glossary

31-Bit Addressing — The ability to access memory locations with addresses as large as can be stored in 31 bits.

308x — The 3080 family of IBM computers: 3081, 3083, 3084.

370-XA, XA — 370 Extended Architecture. 370-XA is a set of architectural extensions to the 370 family architecture that provides for greater addressability of real and virtual memory (up to two gigabytes), improved I/O, and microcode assisted virtualization.

90xx — The 9000 family of IBM computers.

ABEND — ABnormal END, a term used to describe the result of a program that has terminated unexpectedly.

Access Mode Letter — The letter of the alphabet assigned to a minidisk by CMS at the time of Initial Program Load or by the user with the ACCESS command, to allow CMS to use the disk.

ACI — Access Control Interface, a feature in VM that provides exits for enhanced CP LOGON and LINK security.

ACI Group — Users designated in the system directory as belonging to the same ACI (Access Control Interface) group, used to grant access to resources by group members rather than individual userids.

ACONS — Refers to address constant, a specific memory reference in a program that is not relocatable. The memory reference will not change as the program is loaded at varying memory addresses.

Addressability — The ability for a processor to reference memory.

Address Space — A set of memory, virtual or real, that can be accessed immediately by instructions at any given time. Some instructions allow applications to select among address spaces.

A-Disk — When users are reading or writing to a minidisk through CMS, it is generally given a filemode of A. Thus, each user's minidisk is often referred to as his A-disk.

ADT — Active Disk Table, a control block built when a CMS minidisk is ACCESSed and Discarded when the minidisk is RELEASEd. The ADT contains data about the disk such as block size, number of files, etc.

A-Flag — A bit flag in a 370-XA processor that determines the current execution mode. If the A-flag is set to zero, most instructions continue to operate as in a 370 processor and only 24 bits are considered for addressability. If the A-flag is set to one, 31 bits are considered for addressability and some instructions perform differently so as not to interfere with the high-order byte of registers.

AFT — Active File Table, a control block built by CMS when a disk file is opened, then discarded when the file is closed.

Alternate Path — When I/O may be done to a device using more than one channel. Used for performance and/or to reduce the effects of hardware failures.

AMODE — Refers to the addressing mode. The AMODE of an application specifies the size of addresses the application is capable of handling.

Analytic Modeling — A scientific method of forecasting, used in capacity planning, providing a means of assessing the impact of various "what if" scenarios.

API — Applications Programming Interface, a defined set of functions provided by an operating system for use by applications.

APPC/VM — The abbreviation for Application Program to Program Communications/VM, APPC/VM is an interface that applications use to communicate with each other via TSAF and, in VM/SP Release 6, via VTAM over SNA networks.

Archive — A user-initiated process that serves to place seldom-used CMS files on tape as a means of conserving DASD.

ATTACH — A command that serves to attach a tape drive to the user's virtual machine.

AUTOLOG — A CP operator command that allows a userid to be logged on in the disconnected state. Normally used to start service virtual machines via the PROFILE EXEC of the AUTOLOG1 userid immediately after CP IPL.

AUX File — A control file that is used when the VM system is being updated, as with PTFs.

Backup — An installation-initiated process in which a copy is made of all information stored on DASD, so that it is available in case of disaster or user error. Information is generally transferred to tape (though backup to DASD is also possible) and stored offsite. Backup may be full, transferring everything on the system to tape, or incremental, which essentially captures only changes that have been made to data since the last backup.

Bimodal CMS — The CMS provided with both VM/XA SP and VM/SP Release 6. Bimodal CMS provides for the execution of applications which take advantage of a 370-XA environment.

BSEPP — The abbreviation for Basic System Extension Program Product, a program product of IBM that removed critical limitations to the usefulness of VM/370 Release 6.

CCS — An abbreviation for Console Communications Service, CCS is an alternative to logical device support and is the basis for VM SNA support.

CCU — Channel Control Unit, an abbreviation used to uniquely define an I/O device. Also known as the virtual or real device address. The three letters represent the three pieces of hardware which comprise the path to the device.

CCW — Channel Command Word, an instruction, eight bytes long, built by a program before an SIO to describe to the channel how to perform an I/O.

Channel — This is essentially a small computer, mediating the transmission of data between the CPU (main memory) and I/O devices. The channel helps in keeping the CPU from becoming burdened, for example, with "stacked up" requests for data from DASD.

Channel Program — One or more Channel Command Words that collectively constitute an I/O operation.

Checkpoint Start — In the event of a hardware failure, due to a power failure or an error, a warmstart may not be possible. A checkpoint start allows for the recovery of closed spool files. This may be a comparatively time-consuming process.

CKD — Count Key Data, one of the two physical formats of IBM and compatible disk drives (the other format is referred to as FBA).

Class — Userids may be assigned a specific class in the CP directory that limits, for example, the CP commands that the user associated with the userid may use.

Client — A virtual machine which invokes or relies on SVM service.

CMS — Interactive services are provided to VM users through this component of the VM operating system. CMS is a single-user operating system, running under CP as an "operating system with an operating system." CMS is the abbreviation for the Conversational Monitor System.

CMS Subset — An environment under CMS where the execution of user area or application programs allow the end-user to enter a limited CMS environment without exiting the application in order to perform commands such as ERASE and RENAME.

CNTRL File — The master file for source code maintenance for an individual component of VM such as CP, CMS, or RSCS.

Cold Start — If the VM system is being recovered, or "brought up" with a cold start, all VM spool files will be discarded.

Compatibility Interface — An API provided by bimodal CMS for use by existing applications to provide compatibility with bimodal CMS.

Console Spooling — A CP function which allows the writing of console input and output to a spool file instead of, or in addition to, having it displayed on the userid's terminal.

Control Block — A precisely defined area in memory used by the operating system to "hold" data about an object.

Control Unit — The control unit is positioned between I/O devices and the channel and serves to manage individual devices, such as tape drives or DASD.

CP — The component of VM which complements CMS. CP is responsible for creating the virtual machine illusion (that each user has a complete 370 processing environment) and managing the real hardware that VM is running on. CP is the abbreviation for Control Program.

CP Command — Commands which are initiated through CP rather than CMS. CP commands, for example, may be used in directory maintenance.

CP Owned Volume — DASD that is specifically for CP, rather than users. This DASD is defined in the DMKSYS program module and includes an area for the directory and the paging process.

CPU — This term is used to refer to the computer itself, including memory and channels. It is an abbreviation for Central Processing Unit.

CTCA — Channel To Channel Adapter, a piece of hardware used to connect two real CPUs. A CTCA looks like an I/O device to each CPU and allows both CPUs to read and write into each other's memory under controlled conditions. CP has the ability to create a virtual CTCA connection between virtual machines or between a virtual machine and another real machine.

DASD — An abbreviation for Direct Access Storage Device, or disk drive, which actually stores data.

DDR — A CP program within VM that allows data to be transferred from DASD to tape, and vice versa. It is an abbreviation for DASD Dump/Restore.

Dedicated Device — An I/O device that is not being shared among VM users. The device may be permanently assigned to a particular virtual machine via the directory or temporarily attached by the CP system operator.

Departmental Computing — An information management strategy in which the specific resources needed by specific work groups are located within each department, through a mid-range CPU, while organization-wide resources are centralized on a large mainframe. The departmental processors are connected to the central mainframe to facilitate user communications and data exchange.

DES — The Data Encryption Standard, according to the National Bureau of Standards. This is used in data security.

DETACH — A CP command which indicates that the user no longer needs a tape drive and that it may be detached from his virtual machine.

Device — A hardware item used in the I/O process, including a DASD, a tape drive, or a printer.

DIAGNOSE — A means for virtual machines to request CP service by executing a particular privileged machine instruction. Subcodes and parameters specify the function to be performed.

DIAL — A CP command that allows a user to connect to an interactive virtual machine instead of logging on to his own virtual machine.

Directory — Similar to an address book, the virtual machines on the VM system are defined in the directory. Directory information includes userids, the amount of DASD associated with each user, as well as his privilege class, and the address of his minidisk.

Disconnected Virtual Machine — A virtual machine that is not associated with a physical terminal. System software products often run as disconnected virtual machines, "lying in wait" until issued a command to perform a task.

Disk Resident — A CMS command that resides on disk as opposed to the CMS IPLable nucleus.

Dispatcher — The program in an operating system that is responsible for giving control to tasks.

DMKRIO — Essentially a program module, an assembler program that is part of the CP nucleus. DMKRIO defines the I/O device configuration of the VM system. RIO refers to Real I/O.

DMKSNT — Also part of the CP nucleus, in which the saved systems are defined, such as CMS. Saved systems are essentially "communal copies" of programs, to which users have access. SNT refers to System Name Table.

DMKSYS — Another assembler program in the CP nucleus. DMKSYS is used in defining options that are critical to the performance of the VM system, including the definition of CP-owned DASD areas. SYS refers to System Definitions.

DOS — DOS is an abbreviation for Disk Operating System, an older, batch-oriented IBM operating system. For the mainframe, it is now referred to as DOS/VSE or simply VSE.

DOS Simulation — DOS application programs may be developed and tested within VM, through this CMS feature.

Doubleword — Eight bytes, usually aligned on a memory location that can be evenly divided by eight.

ECF — Enhanced Connectivity Facilities; a method for sharing resources between PCs and host computers.

Eplist — A means for CMS applications to pass a string of text to other CMS applications or CMS provided functions in a raw or untokenized form.

EREP — Environmental Recording, Editing and Printing; a program that reads and formats for analysis I/O error records written to a special DASD data set by the operating system.

ESA — An enhancement to 370-XA that provides for access to larger memory sets by allowing applications to switch among address spaces; the abbreviation for Enterprise Systems Architecture.

EXEC — The oldest and most limited of three command language interpreters in CMS, providing users with the ability to write their own CMS commands using sequences of CMS commands and control logic.

EXEC2 — A second generation version of EXEC with more capabilities.

FBA — A type of disk drive. FBA is an abbreviation for Fixed Block Architecture and DASD of this format is assigned in blocks, rather than cylinders.

Fence — A doubleword with all bits set to one (having a value of x'FFFFFFFF').

Fileid — A CMS file is identified by a fileid, which consists of a filename, filetype, and filemode.

Filemode — An identifier for a CMS file that essentially helps in identifying the minidisk on which the file is stored. For general use, the filemode is "A" to refer to the A-Disk. It may contain as many as two characters.

Filename — A name given to a file by the user. Up to eight characters in length, the composition of the filename is at the discretion of the user and provides a means of quick reference to the content of the file.

Filetype — A further descriptive term for the file, the filetype may help in grouping files that fall into a specific user-defined category or may identify the file, for example, as an EXEC. The filetype may also be as many as eight characters.

Fix — Software programs, including VM releases, with an error, or a "bug," may be corrected by a fix. The fix is a modification to the program.

FLIH — First-level interrupt handler, a routine in the operating system that detects an interrupt, classifies the interrupt, and invokes a second-level interrupt handler (SLIH).

FORCE Start — An option used during the IPL of CP to recover all the closed spool files when a warmstart or checkpoint start is not possible. A FORCE start will discard invalid spool files.

FST — File Status Table, a CMS control block that describes a CMS disk file. FSTs reside on disk with the data and are read into virtual memory during ACCESS.

GDDM — An IBM program product, Graphics Data Display Manager, that provides graphics capabilities to various operating systems environments.

GENMOD Command — A CMS command that writes the binary image of a program in memory to a disk file.

Guest — The CP component of VM is also capable of serving as an "umbrella" in which other operating systems are managed within the VM environment, executing in the virtual environment provided by CP. MVS, DOS, and UNIX may run as guests under VM.

Handshaking — The performance of DOS may actually improve through this capability of CP which essentially relates to the paging function.

HPO — HPO is an IBM program product that provides for enhanced performance of high-end 370 family processors (especially those that are 370-XA capable). HPO has provisions to support one MVS/SP guest without the overhead normally associated with virtualization. HPO refers to High Performance Option.

IMPL — Initial Micro Program Load, the process by which micro code is loaded during CPU power up. The code is generally loaded from a floppy disk. This process is also referred to as IML.

IPF — Interactive Productivity Facilities, an IBM program product consisting of system function screen panels and utility programs which are useful in building SVMs.

IPL — When the operating system is "brought up," or loaded into memory, the Initial Program Load (IPL) refers to this action.

IUCV — Inter-User Communications Vehicle, a CP interface for exchanging data between virtual machines or between a virtual machine and CP. IUCV allows user programs on a local VM system to communicate among themselves and is the basis for many database systems on VM/SP. IUCV has made VMCF obsolete.

Link — The means by which users grant access to their minidisks to other users, as well as gain access to frequently used applications.

LKED Command — A CMS command that reads text records and creates a binary image of a program in a disk file. The disk file is called a LOADLIB and it is the way programs are usually stored in MVS.

LOAD Command — A CMS command that reads text records and creates, in memory, a binary image of a program.

Load List — An EXEC that lists all the modules comprising a VM subsystem nucleus.

Logical Device Support — Logical device support allows programs to programmatically emulate CRTs. Logical device support makes programs such as IBM's PassThrough (which allows 3270 users on one VM system to communicate with other VM systems) and protocol conversion programs possible.

Macro — An instruction to a language processor that expands into many other instructions. In the case of CMS, there is typically a one-to-one correspondence between a CMS provided assembly language function and a macro that a programmer will code, which will generate instructions to invoke the CMS function.

MAINT — This userid is associated with the maintenance function. IBM recommends that the MAINT userid be used, for example, when installing a new VM release.

Megabyte — 1,048,576 bytes.

Memory Management System — The portion of an operating system that manages the use of memory.

MESSAGE — A CP command used in sending a message to another logged on user.

Minidisk — DASD space is assigned in portions called minidisks. A minidisk is a logical, or virtual, area of the physical DASD. Depending on the type of DASD, minidisks are assigned in either cylinders or blocks. The addresses of minidisks are assigned in the VM directory.

MIPS — A means of measuring the speed of a CPU. MIPS is an abbreviation for Millions of Instructions Per Second.

MIS — An abbreviation for Management Information Systems; this group is the central department in the organization which serves as the focal point of technical decision-making and coordination of information resources.

MOUNT — A command sent from a user to the computer operator requesting that a tape be placed on a tape drive. The mount command is not native to VM; rather, it is defined within the installation.

MS-DOS — A popular operating system for personal computers.

MVS — The abbreviation for Multiple Virtual System. MVS is the generic name for MVS System Product (MVS/SP) and MVS/XA. It is a popular operating system used primarily to support either online transaction-based environments and/or batch processing.

MVT — Multiple Variable Tasks; an operating system that predates MVS. MVS is based on MVT.

Native Performance — The performance of an operating system running on a real machine as opposed to running as a guest under CP.

Native VM — Also referred to as "vanilla" VM; this is the basic VM operating system without modifications and without the enhancements offered through system software.

NOTE — A CMS command, similar to TELL, which is used to send what is generally a more lengthy online message to another user. A note is similar to a memo. The user(s) for whom the note is intended does not need to be logged on at the time the note is sent.

NTO — The abbreviation for Network Terminal Option; an IBM program product designed to provide support for asynchronous ASCII-based terminals and make them appear to the SNA network as asynchronous EBCDIC terminals. NTO runs in IBM teleprocessing attachment devices called front-ends or FEPs.

NUCEXT — A CMS function that provides a means to enhance or modify CMS commands or functions. It also allows the storing of new commands, functions, or applications in the user's virtual storage for improved performance.

Nucleus — The "heart" of VM, the nucleus is loaded into memory during the IPL process. The nucleus contains the basics of CP.

Nucleus Extension — A module may be loaded into memory to be made a logical extension of the CMS nucleus. This is a mechanism under CMS. It is used to improve performance and is used when a program needs to call another user area program. A nucleus extension may also be used to front-end CMS nucleus commands.

Nucleus Resident — A CMS command residing in the CMS IPL-able nucleus rather than on a disk module.

NUCON — Nucleus Constant Area, a control block located from address zero to hexadecimal address x'5000' used by CMS to store data concerning the present CMS session.

N-Way Processor Support — The ability of an operating system to manage multiple processors in a processor complex and make them appear as one operational entity.

Object Code — Source code that has been compiled or assembled is object code and this code is what is actually executed by the CPU.

Offline — An I/O device that is physically attached to the CPU but not logically in use by the operating system.

Operating System — This is software that provides overall management of the environment, as is provided through the VM operating system. The operating system, for example, controls I/O and the allocation of system resources.

OS Environment — An environment that is based on MVS and its predecessors.

Page — A portion of data or instructions that may be swapped between the main memory of the CPU and DASD. A page in VM is 4K in size.

Page Fault — The means by which the micro code notifies the operating system that a page is not in real memory.

Page Zero — Memory storage locations 0-4095, also known as low core.

Paging — The process of swapping (transferring) pages of data or instructions between main memory and DASD. Paging provides a means of more efficient use of the CPU's main memory, enhancing overall throughput.

Parallel Processing — A batch processing option in which tasks are completed simultaneously.

Password — The foundation of security in native VM, the password is a word (generally user defined) that supplements the userid in the logon procedure and is used in granting link privileges to other users.

Performance Monitoring — The monitoring of the operational aspects of a processor complex.

Physical I/O — Using channel programming to read and write data instead of the standard operating system interfaces.

Plist — A sequential list of eight byte entries (doublewords) that serve as parameters passed between CMS applications and other CMS applications or CMS-provided functions.

PMA — Preferred Machine Assist, a micro code performance feature on dyadic and quadratic machines which allows CP to dedicate one of the CPUs to an MVS guest.

Porting — The process of making revisions and changes to a program so that it can run in a different execution environment.

Preferred Interface — An API provided by bimodal CMS that IBM recommends as a means to assure migration from release to release of CMS.

Problem State — A performance concept, Problem State refers to the amount of time devoted exclusively to the execution of user tasks. This can be contrasted to Supervisor State.

Processor Resources — Typically functions performed by or managed by the processor, such as machine cycles to execute instructions, memory, virtual to real memory mapping, and the execution of I/O.

PROFS — An IBM program product, the Professional Office System, that provides for interactive computer-assisted office functions such as electronic mail, document storage and retrieval, and time management.

PROP — Programmable Operator, a facility for automating actions to be taken in response to arriving transactions, often used to automate VM system console operation.

Protocol Converter — A device or software that provides for conversion from one device's protocol to that of another. Protocol conversion is primarily used in IBM environments to make non-IBM terminals appear to operating systems and applications as IBM terminals.

PSA — Prefix Storage Area, the CP control block that maps page zero of real memory and contains pointers and flags for CP operation.

PSW — The abbreviation for Processor Status Word, a register in a 370 family processor that indicates the state of the processor as well as the address of the memory location of the next instruction to be executed by the processor.

PTF — The IBM term given to a fix, an abbreviation for Program Temporary Fix. PTFs are distributed on PUTs (Program Update Tapes).

PUT — An abbreviation for Program Update Tape, the PUT is a tape that is periodically sent by IBM to VM installations. The PUT contains recent fixes to the operating system. PUTs are also sent for other operating systems and application software.

PVM — PassThrough Virtual Machine, written by IBM to allow 3270 terminals to logon to other VM machines that also have PVM available. Runs as a service virtual machine and uses the DIAL command. PVM can also be used with MVS systems that support remote 3270s.

Queue 1 — The schedule in CP maintains three lists of tasks waiting to be executed. The tasks in Queue 1 are associated with users who are currently working interactively.

Queue 2 — This is a list of userids that need processor time to complete their current task, but are not entering more data.

Queue 3 — The Queue 3 list contains userids that will require a large amount of CPU time to complete the current task.

RACF — A program product of IBM, Resource Access Control Facility, that provides for access control of data resources in a processing complex.

RCHBLOKs — A series of control blocks generated by the assembly of DMKRIO that contain the status for each real channel on the real machine.

RCTBLOKs — A series of control blocks generated by the assembly of DMKRIO that contain the status of each real control unit on the real machine.

RDEVBLOKs — A series of control blocks generated by the assembly of DMKRIO that contain the status for each real device on the real machine.

Real Address — The address of a main memory location.

REXX — A CMS command language interpreter similar to EXEC and EXEC2, but much more sophisticated. REXX refers to Restructured Extended Executor. REXX can best be thought of as a cross between EXEC2, PL/1, and BASIC.

RMODE — Refers to the residency mode. The RMODE of an application specifies which locations in memory the program is capable of being executed.

RSCS — A communications facility for VM that enables the transfer of spool files between CPUs. This allows, for example, users to send messages to each other. RSCS is an abbreviation for Remote Spooling Communications Subsystem.

SAA — The abbreviation for Systems Application Architecture, a set of guidelines developed by IBM to allow applications developed on a given IBM processor and given IBM operating system to run on varying IBM processors running various IBM operating systems, without the need for porting.

Scheduler — A program within CP that selects from Queue 1, Queue 2, or Queue 3 in deciding which task to process next. The Scheduler acts as a dispatcher.

S-Disk — Contains the nucleus, disk resident commands, and EXECs, CMS IPLable. Accessed as mode letter "S," usually at address 190.

SENDFILE — A CMS command used in sending a CMS file from one user to another, through RSCS.

Serial Processing — A batch processing option in which tasks are completed one at a time.

SEPP — The abbreviation for System Extension Program Product, a program product of IBM that removed critical limitations to the usefulness of VM/370 Release 6. SEPP was a superset of BSEPP.

SFS — Shared File System, an extension of the CMS file system providing an alternative to personal and shared minidisks for storing CMS files. SFS stores files in "file pools."

Shared Segments — A facility of CP that allows program code and data to be shared (that is, made a part of the virtual memory image) of multiple users.

SIE — A 370-XA instruction that provides for virtualization of an instruction stream residing in memory, the abbreviation for Start Interpretive Execution.

SLIH — Second level interrupt handler, a routine in the operating system that processes specific interrupt conditions.

SMSG — Special Message, a general user CP command to send messages to virtual machines programmed to accept and process such messages.

SNA — SNA, or Systems Network Architecture, defines the way that devices communicate among themselves in an IBM-based teleprocessing environment.

Source Code — Original program code that has not yet been compiled or assembled to become Object Code. Generally, source code must be compiled or assembled before it can be run on a computer, as is true for VM source code.

Spool — An area of DASD that acts as a holding area for files that are being transferred, for example, to a printer or between users. Spool refers to Simultaneous Peripheral Operation On-Line.

SQL — A standard language, originally defined by IBM, that is used with relational database management systems. SQL is an abbreviation for Structured Query Language and is pronounced "Sequel."

SQL/DS — IBM's relational database management system for the VM environment and an IBM program product.

SRPI — Service-Requester Programming Interface, part of ECF, allowing PCs to access host SVMs.

Standalone Restore — Generally used for disaster recovery, a program running on a bare CPU to copy data from tape to disk. Also referred to as SAR.

Starter System — A basic and relatively easily installed VM operating system, on a tape.

Storage Protection Key — A hardware mechanism that requires the current PSW to have an appropriate value before it can access specific blocks of memory that were assigned specific values. Storage protection keys prevent programs from accidentally overwriting memory.

SUBCOM — A CMS function which supports the providing subcommands to applications. By using SUBCOM, other applications can access a given application's subcommands.

Subpools — A mechanism by which memory locations can be managed as a unit, usually by the function the memory locations are serving.

Supervisor State — The amount of time that CP spends in doing work, such as paging and managing I/O, as opposed to specific user tasks.

SVC — Supervisor call, a 370 instruction that causes an operating system function to be invoked. SVCs are one of many ways for an interrupt or direct branch to a specific location in the operating system to occur.

SVM — Service Virtual Machine, a virtual machine running a program that provides service to users or other SVMs.

SVM Owner — An individual responsible for supporting an SVM.

SYSGEN — A means of referring to System Generation, this is the process of creating an operating system nucleus that may be loaded in memory through an IPL. SYSGEN is used when tailoring the operating system to the organization, as well as when applying fixes or enhancements.

SYSRES — SYStem RESidence, an area of DASD on which the nucleus of the operating system resides.

System Product Interpreter — See REXX.

System Software — Though an operating system can be broadly defined as system software, this term generally refers to utilities which enhance the performance of the operating system. System software utility functions include system security, tape management, accounting, and DASD management.

Tag Data — A field used by RSCS in identifying the destination of a spool file. It is a 136-character data field.

T-Disk — An area of DASD that is used as an extended work area and that "disappears" once the user ends the session. This is a means of having a large area of DASD to work in during the user session. T-Disk refers to Temporary Disk.

Teleprocessing — The interconnection of processing equipment in a network to facilitate the exchange of data.

TELL — A CMS command used to send a message to another logged on user, through RSCS.

Text Deck — After source code is compiled or assembled, the object code is contained in a Text Deck, an 80-byte, fixed-length record file.

Text Library — A CMS file that contains one or more text decks.

Text Records — The output of language processors (e.g., compilers or assemblers).

Thrashing — When system load is such that CP is being forced to page heavily as a means of accommodating heavy demand, CP may be using so many resources in the paging process that user tasks are not being completed efficiently. Supervisor State overtakes Problem State and response time suffers. This is referred to as thrashing.

Token — A unit of text within a string of text set apart by characters called delimiters. In CMS, spaces (blanks) and parentheses serve as delimiters. In CMS, tokens are typically thought of as being eight bytes in length.

Tokenization — The process of breaking text up into tokens.

Trace Table — Significant events, for the purpose of debugging, are contained in this area of memory.

Transient Area — An eight kilobyte area in a CMS virtual machine starting at hexadecimal address x'E000' used to load and run commands and applications in support of commands and applications in the user area.

TSAF — TSAF, or Transparent Service Access Facility, is a CP service that provides networking of up to eight processor complexes for the exchange of data between applications. APPC/VM uses TSAF to communicate data among systems.

TSO — An abbreviation for Time Sharing Option, this is the component of MVS that provides a form of interactivity.

Two Channel Switch — A tape or disk control unit which allows the attachment of two channels. The two channels may be from the same CPU for added performance or from two different CPUs to achieve data sharing.

User Area — Memory locations in CMS virtual machines starting with hexadecimal address x'200000' used by most applications to load and run from.

Userid — The identification assigned to each user and contained in the directory.

USERSAVE — A bimodal CMS control block used to pass information to a called program.

V=R — Virtual equals Real, a performance option used with guest operating systems. This CP option allows the guest to run in real memory without causing the CP to page.

V=V — Virtual equals Virtual, applying to any real machine not running V=R.

Vanilla VM — Another term for native VM; VM in its unaided and unadulterated form.

VCNA — VTAM Communications Network Application, an application program, running under VTAM under DOS/VSE or VS1. It allows a VM system to participate in an SNA network.

VCTLBLOK — Virtual Control Unit Block, the control block in CP containing control unit status for each control unit in a virtual machine's configuration.

VDEVBLOK — Virtual Device Block, the control block in CP that contains I/O device status, for each I/O device in a logged on virtual machine's configuration.

Vector Processing — The processing of arrays of numbers. Vector processing instructions provide for the efficient processing of arrays as opposed to the discrete programmatic treatment required when vector processing instructions are not available.

Virtualization — The process of providing an execution environment that emulates a real environment.

VM — An abbreviation for Virtual Machine, this refers to the IBM interactive operating system comprised of CM and CMS. Virtual machine is the concept of each user having privileges and a storage area that simulate being in control of the total CPU, rather than sharing with other users.

VMBLOK — Contains information about a user and his or her present status. VMBLOK is a control block that is built in real memory, by CP, when the user logs on. It disappears when the user discontinues the session and logs off.

VMCF — A communications facility that evolved into IUCV. VMCF is an abbreviation for Virtual Machine Communication Facility and was a CP interface for exchanging data between virtual machines.

VMFASM — A program that transforms source code and PTFs into updated object code that is usable for the VMFLOAD process.

VMFLOAD — The program which creates the CP nucleus.

VM/PC — A VM variation for the PC/370 personal computer.

VM/SP — The standard VM operating system, designed for CPUs at the midrange, including the 9370 and the 43XX series. SP is an abbreviation for System Product.

VM/XA/SF — A VM variation providing Extended Architecture capabilities. Currently this is used as a conversion aid for MVS/XA. IBM is aggressively enhancing VM/XA to include CMS capabilities.

VSAM — Virtual Storage Access Method, a set of services provided by MVS and VSE and partially provided by CMS to programs for the organization, storage, and access of disk-based data files.

VSE — Originally referred to as DOS on the mainframe, VSE is an abbreviation for Virtual Storage Extended. It is a popular operating system for smaller 370 family processors used to support small transactional and/or batch environments.

VTAM — Virtual Telecommunications Access Method, the generic name for a series of program products for each of the major IBM operating systems (MVS, VM, and VSE), VTAM both manages the connectivity of a processor complex and provides an interface for applications to interface to devices and other applications in a teleprocessing environment.

Warmstart — During a warmstart, after a shutdown of the VM system, all spool files are saved. A warmstart is quicker than a Checkpoint Start.

XEDIT — An editor used in the creation and modification of CMS files, provided with CMS. Also a CMS command which invokes the use of XEDIT.

ZAP — A fix to object code. It acts as a patch and is applied "over" existing object code.

Index